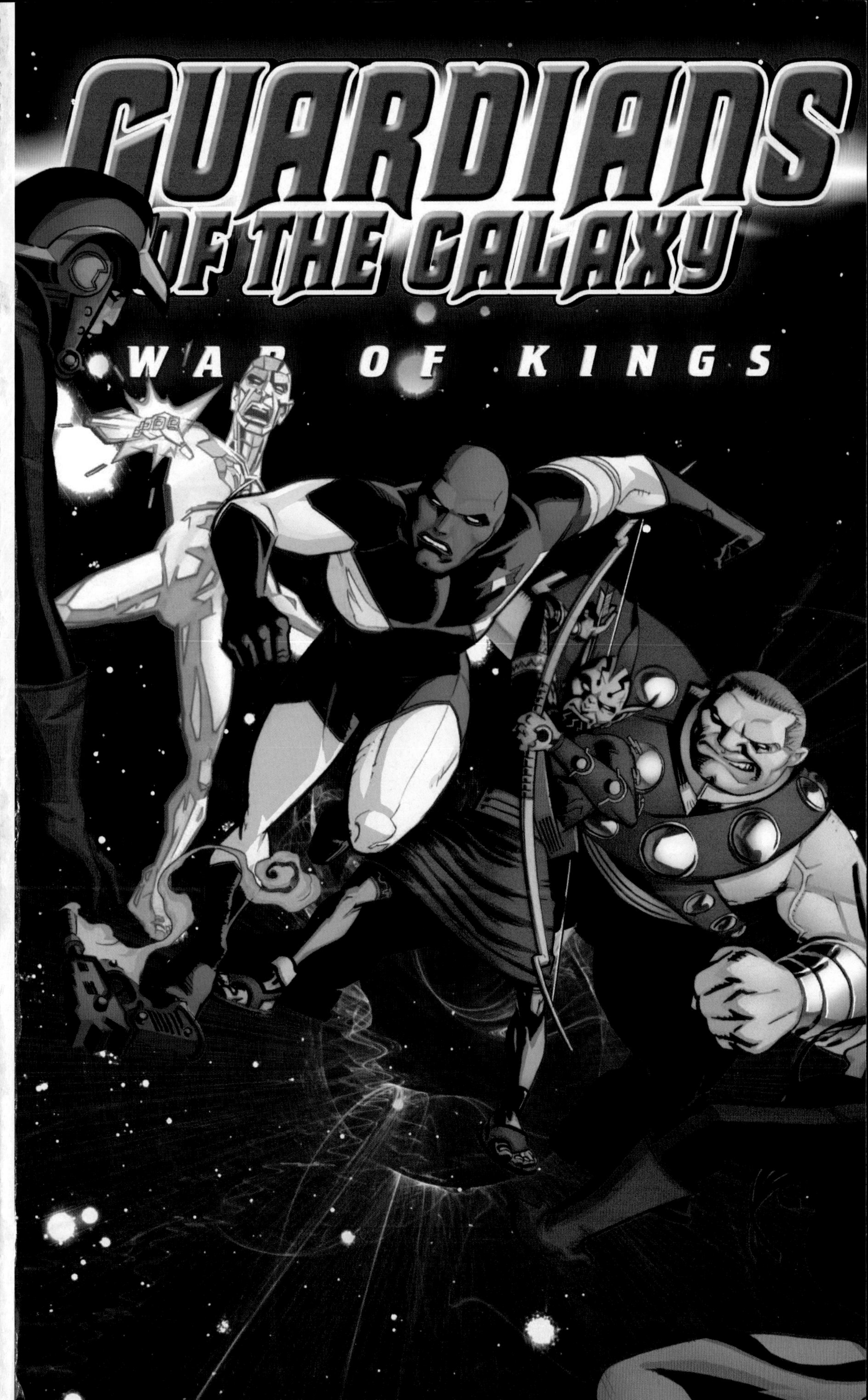
GUARDIANS OF THE GALAXY
WAR OF KINGS

GUARDIANS OF THE GALAXY

OF THE GALAXY

WAR OF KINGS

WRITERS: **DAN ABNETT & ANDY LANNING**

PENCILERS: **BRAD WALKER & WESLEY CRAIG**

INKERS: **VICTOR OLAZABA, LIVESAY, SCOTT HANNA & WESLEY CRAIG**

COLORISTS: **WIL QUINTANA, JAY DAVID RAMOS & NATHAN FAIRBAIRN**

LETTERERS: **VC'S JOE CARAMAGNA & CHRIS ELIOPOULOS**

COVER ARTISTS: **SALVADOR LARROCA, PASQUAL FERRY,**
DANIEL ACUÑA & ALEX GARNER

ASSISTANT EDITORS: **MICHAEL HORWITZ & RACHEL PINNELAS**

EDITOR: **BILL ROSEMANN**

COLLECTION EDITOR: **CORY LEVINE**

ASSISTANT EDITORS: **ALEX STARBUCK & JOHN DENNING**

EDITORS, SPECIAL PROJECTS: **JENNIFER GRÜNWALD & MARK D. BEAZLEY**

SENIOR EDITOR, SPECIAL PROJECTS: **JEFF YOUNGQUIST**

SENIOR VICE PRESIDENT OF SALES: **DAVID GABRIEL**

BOOK DESIGN: **RODOLFO MURAGUCHI**

EDITOR IN CHIEF: **JOE QUESADA**

PUBLISHER: **DAN BUCKLEY**

EXECUTIVE PRODUCER: **ALAN FINE**

GUARDIANS OF THE GALAXY VOL. 3: WAR OF KINGS BOOK 2. Contains material originally published in magazine form as GUARDIANS OF THE GALAXY #13-19. First printing 2009. Hardcover ISBN# 978-0-7851-4127-3. Softcover ISBN# 978-0-7851-4048-1. Published by MARVEL PUBLISHING, INC., a subsidiary of MARVEL ENTERTAINMENT, INC. OFFICE OF PUBLICATION: 417 5th Avenue, New York, NY 10016. Copyright © 2009 and 2010 Marvel Characters, Inc. All rights reserved. Hardcover: $24.99 per copy in the U.S. (GST #R127032852). Softcover: $19.99 per copy in the U.S. (GST #R127032852). Canadian Agreement #40668537. All characters featured in this issue and the distinctive names and likenesses thereof, and all related indicia are trademarks of Marvel Characters, Inc. No similarity between any of the names, characters, persons, and/or institutions in this magazine with those of any living or dead person or institution is intended, and any such similarity which may exist is purely coincidental. **Printed in the U.S.A.** ALAN FINE, EVP - Office Of The Chief Executive Marvel Entertainment, Inc. & CMO Marvel Characters B.V.; DAN BUCKLEY, Chief Executive Officer and Publisher - Print, Animation & Digital Media; JIM SOKOLOWSKI, Chief Operating Officer; DAVID GABRIEL, SVP of Publishing Sales & Circulation; DAVID BOGART, SVP of Business Affairs & Talent Management; MICHAEL PASCIULLO, VP Merchandising & Communications; JIM O'KEEFE, VP of Operations & Logistics; DAN CARR, Executive Director of Publishing Technology; JUSTIN F. GABRIE, Director of Publishing & Editorial Operations; SUSAN CRESPI, Editorial Operations Manager; ALEX MORALES, Publishing Operations Manager; STAN LEE, Chairman Emeritus. For information regarding advertising in Marvel Comics or on Marvel.com, please contact Mitch Dane, Advertising Director, at mdane@marvel.com. For Marvel subscription inquiries, please call 800-217-9158. **Manufactured between 11/9/09 and 12/9/09 (hardcover), and 11/9/09 and 3/17/10 (softcover), by R.R. DONNELLEY, INC., SALEM, VA, USA.**

10 9 8 7 6 5 4 3 2 1

In the wake of two catastrophic Annihilation events, the Universe is in a fragile and weakened state. With the fabric of space itself damaged, anomalous fissures are beginning to appear, fissures that could crack and spread, collapsing reality and letting in things that should not exist in our dimension.

Guided by the mystical insight of the newly returned Adam Warlock, the gun-slinging Star-Lord has forged a proactive team of proven cosmic champions ready to protect the vulnerable universe and prevent any large-scale disasters from ever happening again. Together, Star-Lord, Warlock, Gamora, Drax, Mantis and Rocket Raccoon are the Guardians of the Galaxy!

With portents warning of an approaching calamity, Star-Lord re-formed his recently fractured team in time to face it. New additions include Earthman and former vigilante Jack Flag, the resurrected Moondragon, and Martyr, Phyla-Vell's new morbid alter ego. The team appears to be back at full strength.

However, the opening shots of the War of Kings — a massive conflict between the Shi'ar Imperium and the Kree Stellar Empire — have already been fired, and the Guardians of the Galaxy may find themselves in deep trouble sooner than they imagine...

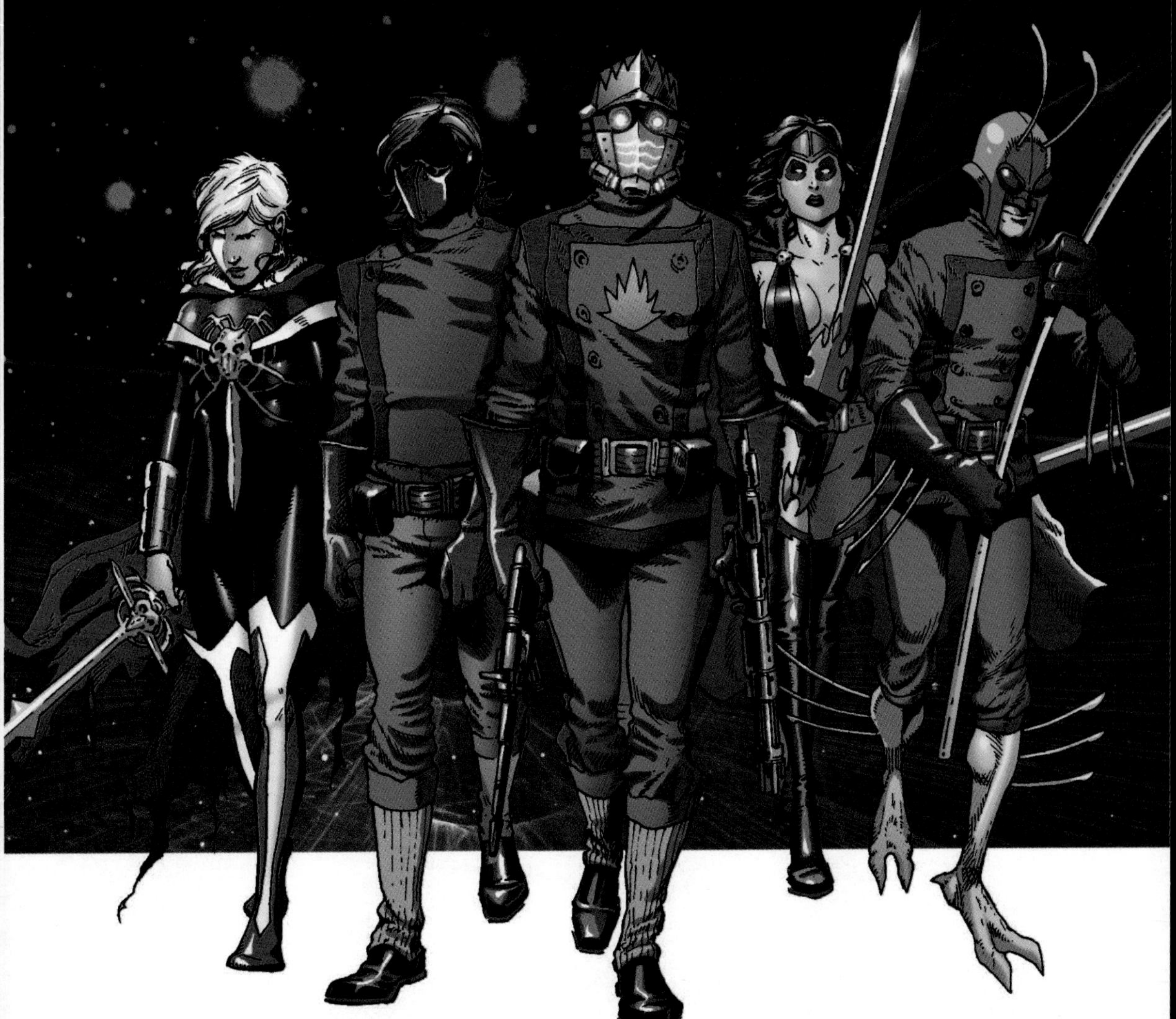

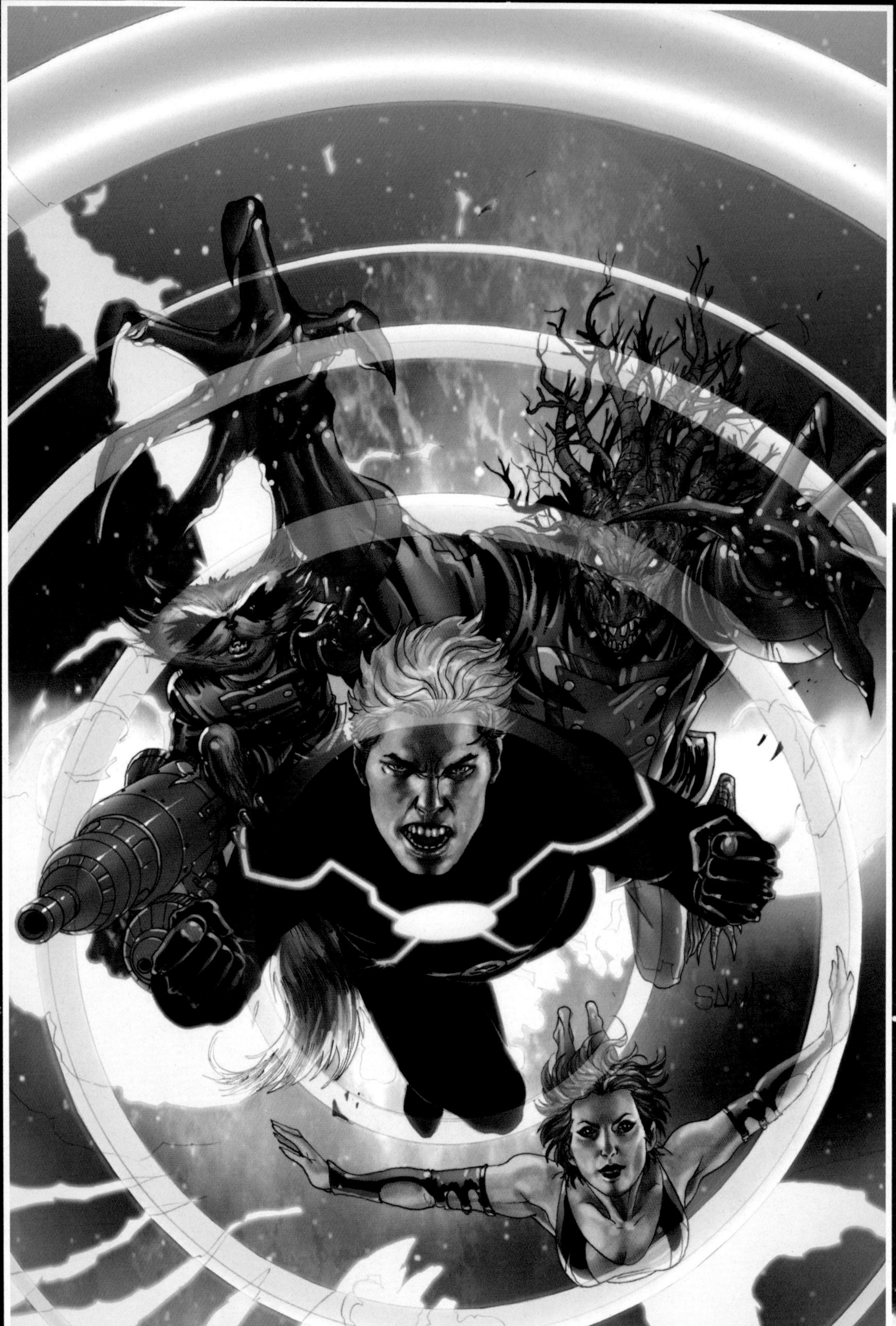

13

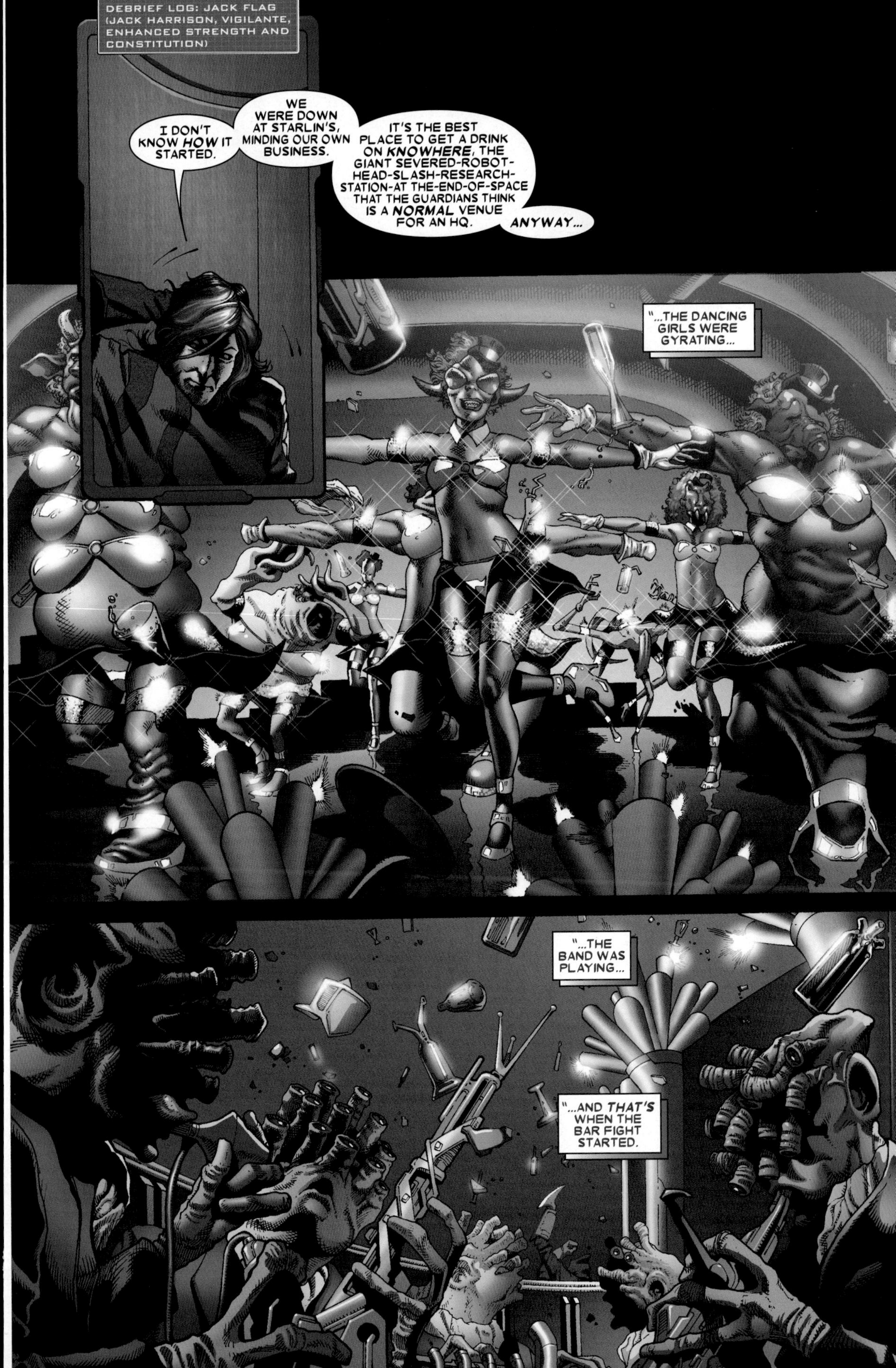

DEBRIEF LOG: JACK FLAG (JACK HARRISON, VIGILANTE, ENHANCED STRENGTH AND CONSTITUTION)
I DON'T KNOW HOW IT STARTED.
WE WERE DOWN AT STARLIN'S, MINDING OUR OWN BUSINESS.
IT'S THE BEST PLACE TO GET A DRINK ON KNOWHERE, THE GIANT SEVERED-ROBOT-HEAD-SLASH-RESEARCH-STATION-AT-THE-END-OF-SPACE THAT THE GUARDIANS THINK IS A NORMAL VENUE FOR AN HQ.
ANYWAY...
"...THE DANCING GIRLS WERE GYRATING...
"...THE BAND WAS PLAYING...
"...AND THAT'S WHEN THE BAR FIGHT STARTED.

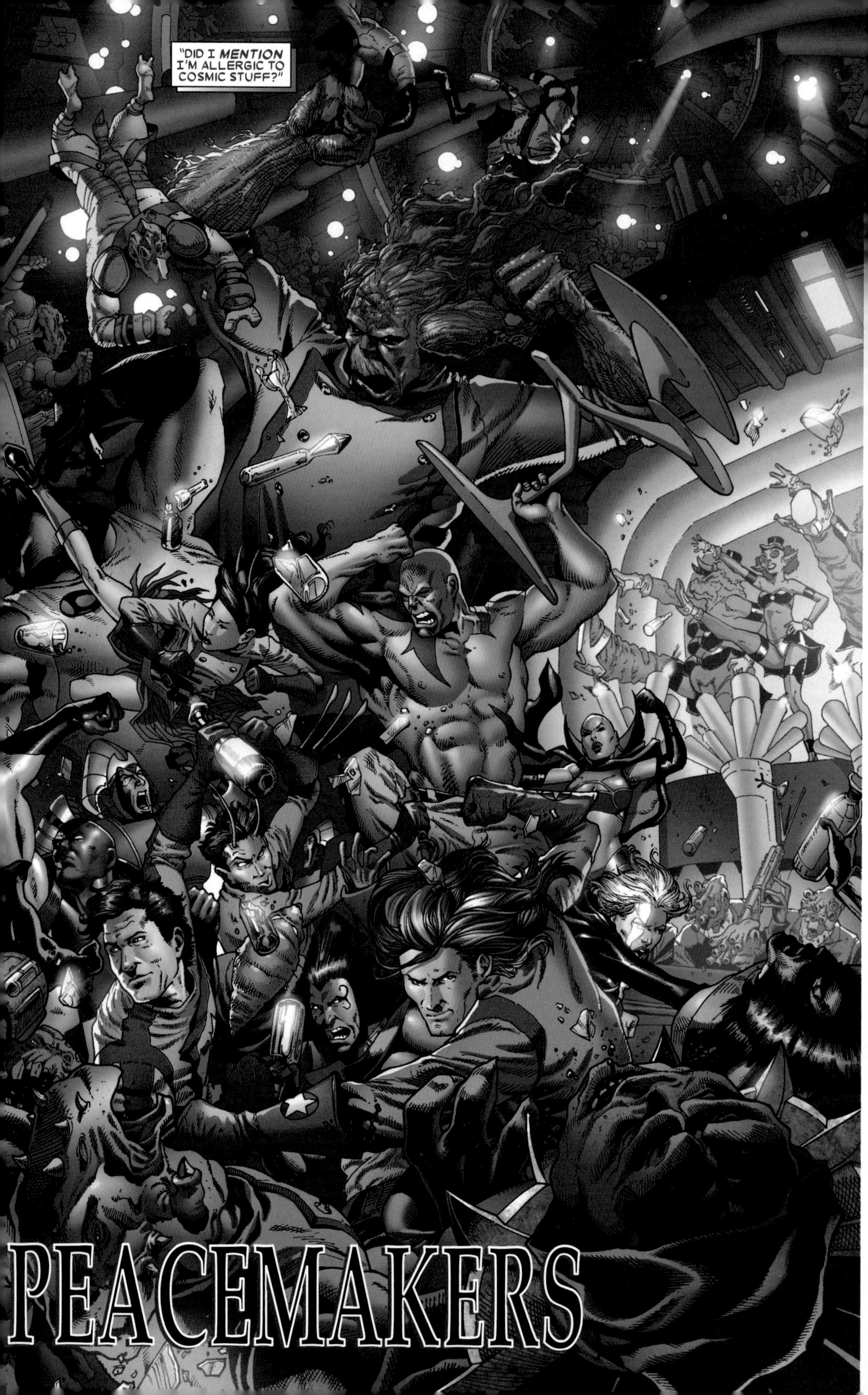
"DID I *MENTION* I'M ALLERGIC TO COSMIC STUFF?"
PEACEMAKERS

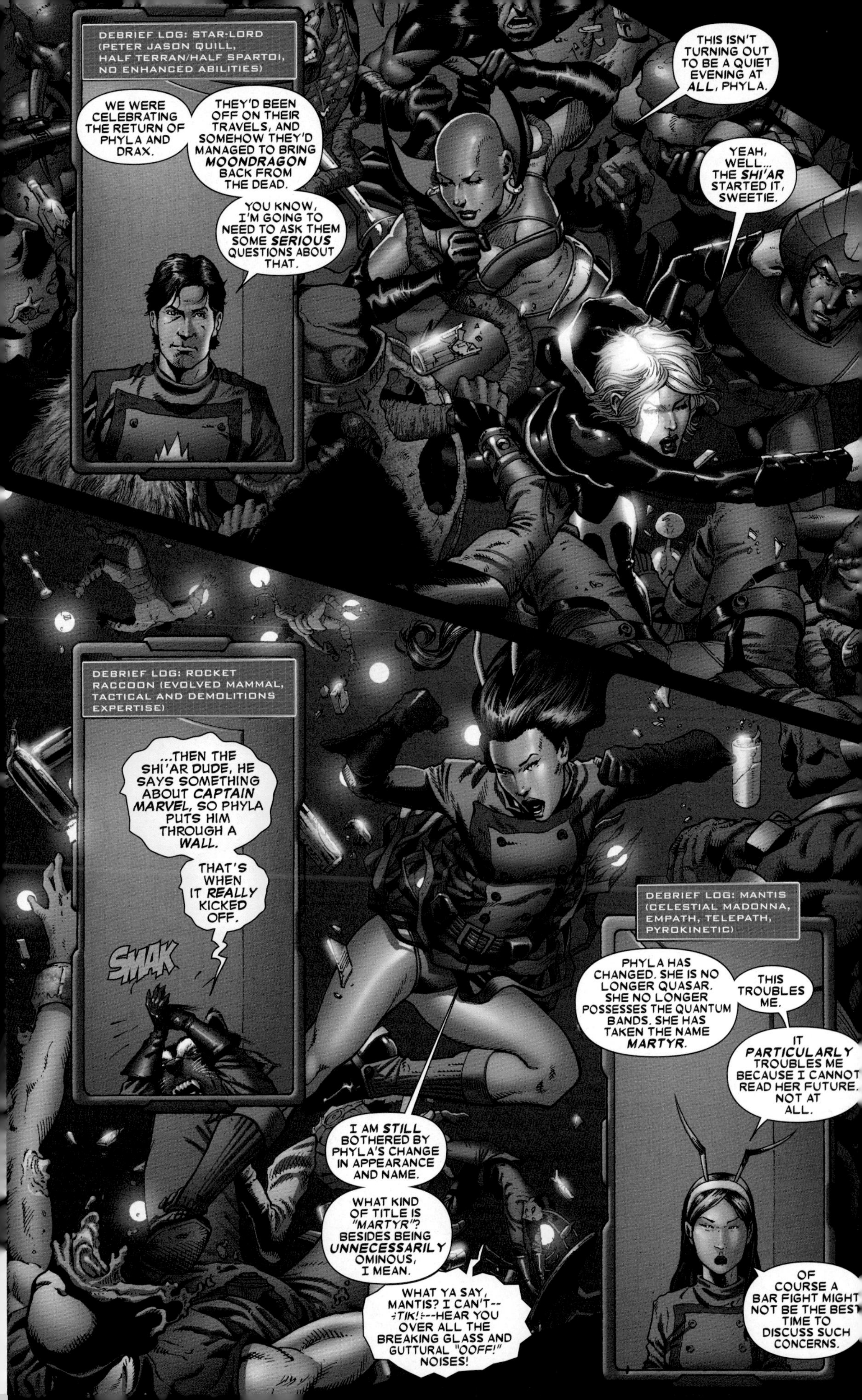
DEBRIEF LOG: STAR-LORD (PETER JASON QUILL, HALF TERRAN/HALF SPARTOI, NO ENHANCED ABILITIES)
WE WERE CELEBRATING THE RETURN OF PHYLA AND DRAX.
THEY'D BEEN OFF ON THEIR TRAVELS, AND SOMEHOW THEY'D MANAGED TO BRING MOONDRAGON BACK FROM THE DEAD.
YOU KNOW, I'M GOING TO NEED TO ASK THEM SOME SERIOUS QUESTIONS ABOUT THAT.
THIS ISN'T TURNING OUT TO BE A QUIET EVENING AT ALL, PHYLA.
YEAH, WELL... THE SHI'AR STARTED IT, SWEETIE.
DEBRIEF LOG: ROCKET RACCOON (EVOLVED MAMMAL, TACTICAL AND DEMOLITIONS EXPERTISE)
...THEN THE SHI'AR DUDE, HE SAYS SOMETHING ABOUT CAPTAIN MARVEL, SO PHYLA PUTS HIM THROUGH A WALL.
THAT'S WHEN IT REALLY KICKED OFF.
SMAK
DEBRIEF LOG: MANTIS (CELESTIAL MADONNA, EMPATH, TELEPATH, PYROKINETIC)
PHYLA HAS CHANGED. SHE IS NO LONGER QUASAR. SHE NO LONGER POSSESSES THE QUANTUM BANDS. SHE HAS TAKEN THE NAME MARTYR.
THIS TROUBLES ME.
IT PARTICULARLY TROUBLES ME BECAUSE I CANNOT READ HER FUTURE. NOT AT ALL.
I AM STILL BOTHERED BY PHYLA'S CHANGE IN APPEARANCE AND NAME.
WHAT KIND OF TITLE IS "MARTYR"? BESIDES BEING UNNECESSARILY OMINOUS, I MEAN.
OF COURSE A BAR FIGHT MIGHT NOT BE THE BEST TIME TO DISCUSS SUCH CONCERNS.
WHAT YA SAY, MANTIS? I CAN'T-- TIK! --HEAR YOU OVER ALL THE BREAKING GLASS AND GUTTURAL "OOFF!" NOISES!

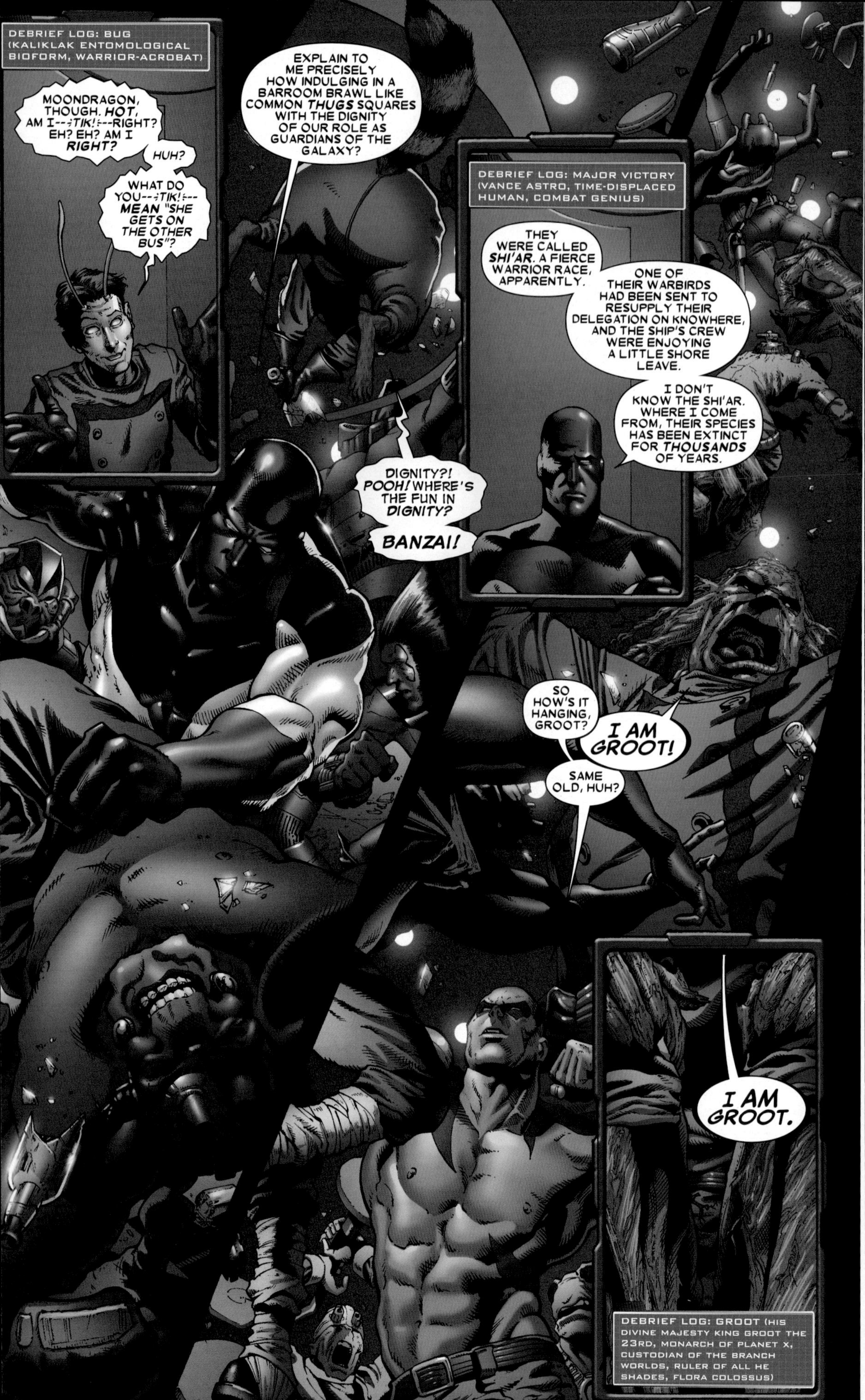

DEBRIEF LOG: BUG (KALIKLAK ENTOMOLOGICAL BIOFORM, WARRIOR-ACROBAT)
MOONDRAGON, THOUGH. HOT, AM I--TIK!--RIGHT? EH? EH? AM I RIGHT?
HUH?
WHAT DO YOU--TIK!--MEAN "SHE GETS ON THE OTHER BUS"?
EXPLAIN TO ME PRECISELY HOW INDULGING IN A BARROOM BRAWL LIKE COMMON THUGS SQUARES WITH THE DIGNITY OF OUR ROLE AS GUARDIANS OF THE GALAXY?
DIGNITY?! POOH! WHERE'S THE FUN IN DIGNITY?
BANZAI!
DEBRIEF LOG: MAJOR VICTORY (VANCE ASTRO, TIME-DISPLACED HUMAN, COMBAT GENIUS)
THEY WERE CALLED SHI'AR. A FIERCE WARRIOR RACE, APPARENTLY.
ONE OF THEIR WARBIRDS HAD BEEN SENT TO RESUPPLY THEIR DELEGATION ON KNOWHERE, AND THE SHIP'S CREW WERE ENJOYING A LITTLE SHORE LEAVE.
I DON'T KNOW THE SHI'AR. WHERE I COME FROM, THEIR SPECIES HAS BEEN EXTINCT FOR THOUSANDS OF YEARS.
SO HOW'S IT HANGING, GROOT?
I AM GROOT!
SAME OLD, HUH?
I AM GROOT.
DEBRIEF LOG: GROOT (HIS DIVINE MAJESTY KING GROOT THE 23RD, MONARCH OF PLANET X, CUSTODIAN OF THE BRANCH WORLDS, RULER OF ALL HE SHADES, FLORA COLOSSUS)

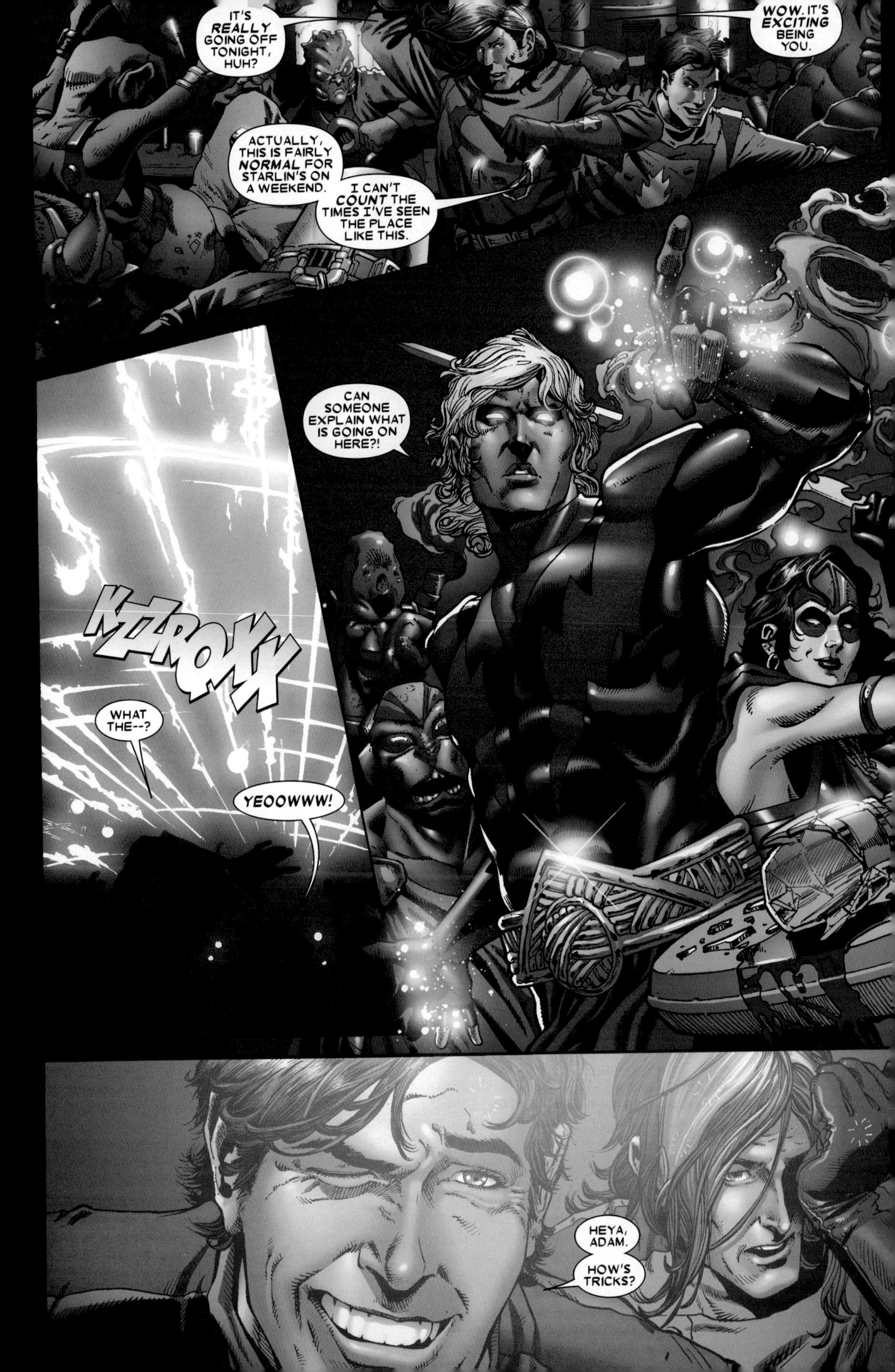

IT'S REALLY GOING OFF TONIGHT, HUH?
WOW. IT'S EXCITING BEING YOU.
ACTUALLY, THIS IS FAIRLY NORMAL FOR STARLIN'S ON A WEEKEND.
I CAN'T COUNT THE TIMES I'VE SEEN THE PLACE LIKE THIS.
CAN SOMEONE EXPLAIN WHAT IS GOING ON HERE?!
KZZROWK
WHAT THE--?
YEOOWWW!
HEYA, ADAM.
HOW'S TRICKS?

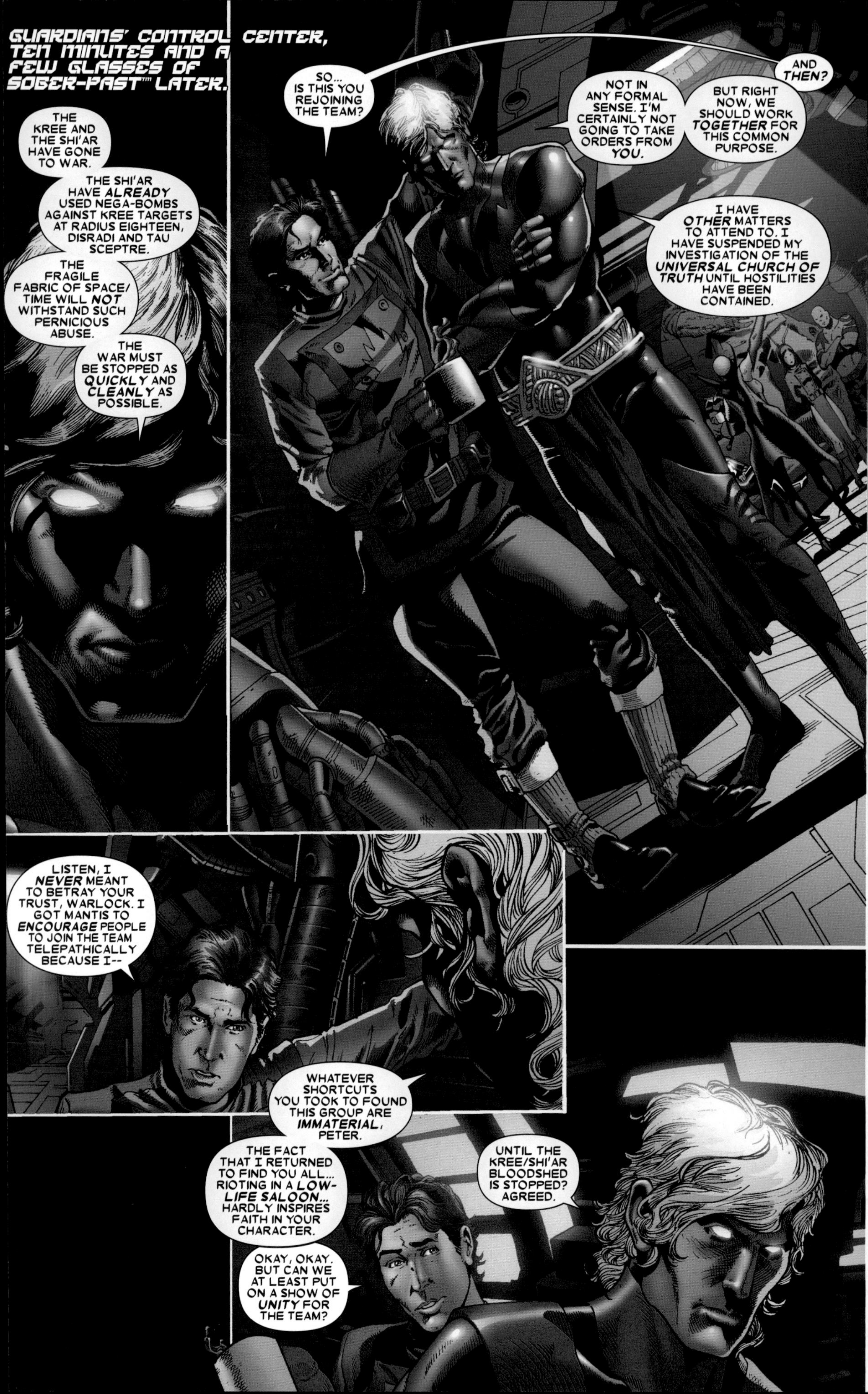
GUARDIANS' CONTROL CENTER, TEN MINUTES AND A FEW GLASSES OF SOBER-PAST™ LATER.
THE KREE AND THE SHI'AR HAVE GONE TO WAR.
THE SHI'AR HAVE ALREADY USED NEGA-BOMBS AGAINST KREE TARGETS AT RADIUS EIGHTEEN, DISRADI AND TAU SCEPTRE.
THE FRAGILE FABRIC OF SPACE/TIME WILL NOT WITHSTAND SUCH PERNICIOUS ABUSE.
THE WAR MUST BE STOPPED AS QUICKLY AND CLEANLY AS POSSIBLE.
SO... IS THIS YOU REJOINING THE TEAM?
NOT IN ANY FORMAL SENSE. I'M CERTAINLY NOT GOING TO TAKE ORDERS FROM YOU.
AND THEN?
BUT RIGHT NOW, WE SHOULD WORK TOGETHER FOR THIS COMMON PURPOSE.
I HAVE OTHER MATTERS TO ATTEND TO. I HAVE SUSPENDED MY INVESTIGATION OF THE UNIVERSAL CHURCH OF TRUTH UNTIL HOSTILITIES HAVE BEEN CONTAINED.
LISTEN, I NEVER MEANT TO BETRAY YOUR TRUST, WARLOCK. I GOT MANTIS TO ENCOURAGE PEOPLE TO JOIN THE TEAM TELEPATHICALLY BECAUSE I--
WHATEVER SHORTCUTS YOU TOOK TO FOUND THIS GROUP ARE IMMATERIAL, PETER.
THE FACT THAT I RETURNED TO FIND YOU ALL... RIOTING IN A LOW-LIFE SALOON... HARDLY INSPIRES FAITH IN YOUR CHARACTER.
OKAY, OKAY. BUT CAN WE AT LEAST PUT ON A SHOW OF UNITY FOR THE TEAM?
UNTIL THE KREE/SHI'AR BLOODSHED IS STOPPED? AGREED.

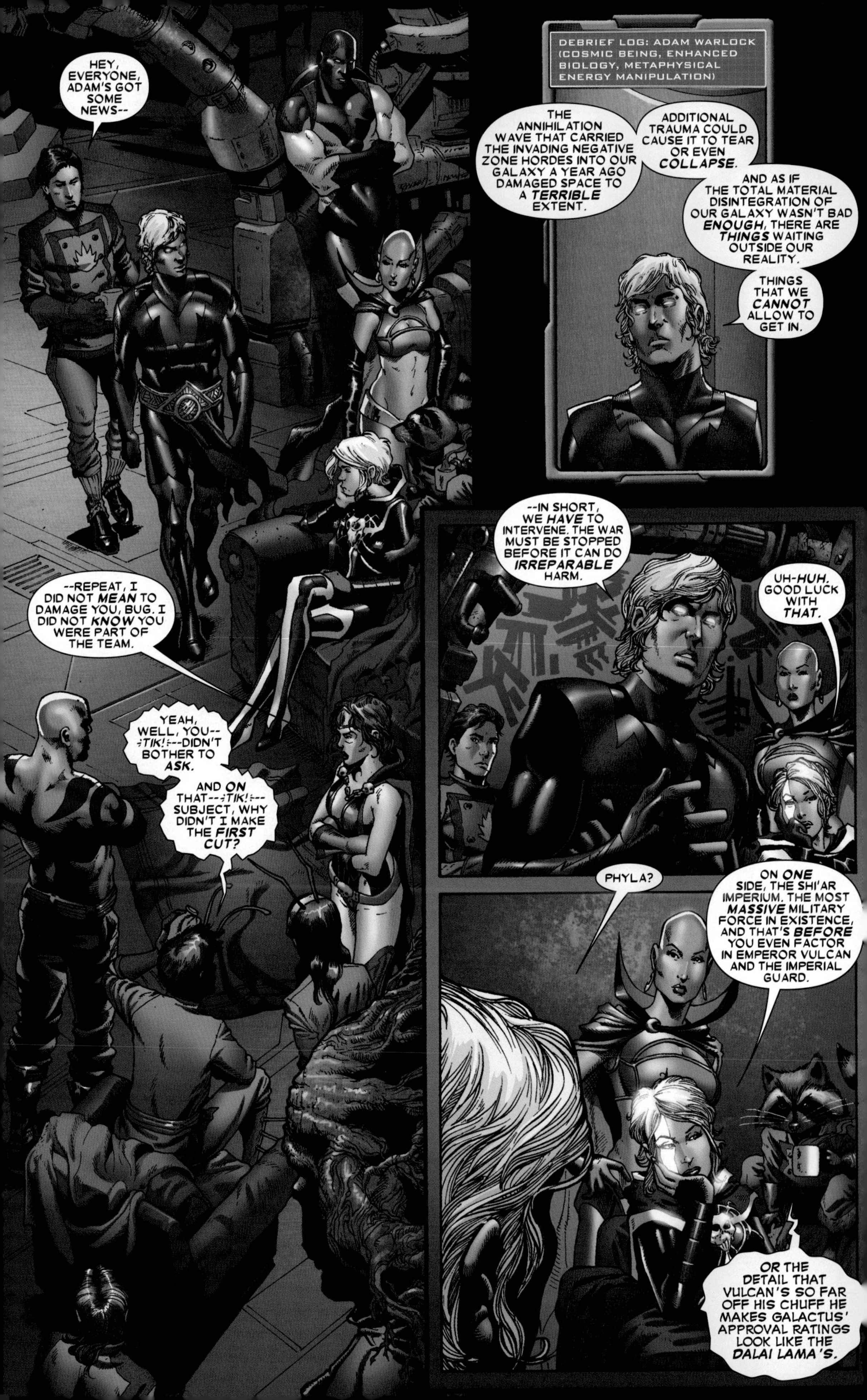
HEY, EVERYONE, ADAM'S GOT SOME NEWS--
DEBRIEF LOG: ADAM WARLOCK (COSMIC BEING, ENHANCED BIOLOGY, METAPHYSICAL ENERGY MANIPULATION)
THE ANNIHILATION WAVE THAT CARRIED THE INVADING NEGATIVE ZONE HORDES INTO OUR GALAXY A YEAR AGO DAMAGED SPACE TO A TERRIBLE EXTENT.
ADDITIONAL TRAUMA COULD CAUSE IT TO TEAR OR EVEN COLLAPSE.
AND AS IF THE TOTAL MATERIAL DISINTEGRATION OF OUR GALAXY WASN'T BAD ENOUGH, THERE ARE THINGS WAITING OUTSIDE OUR REALITY.
THINGS THAT WE CANNOT ALLOW TO GET IN.
--REPEAT, I DID NOT MEAN TO DAMAGE YOU, BUG. I DID NOT KNOW YOU WERE PART OF THE TEAM.
YEAH, WELL, YOU-- ;TIK!;--DIDN'T BOTHER TO ASK.
AND ON THAT--;TIK!;-- SUBJECT, WHY DIDN'T I MAKE THE FIRST CUT?
--IN SHORT, WE HAVE TO INTERVENE. THE WAR MUST BE STOPPED BEFORE IT CAN DO IRREPARABLE HARM.
UH-HUH. GOOD LUCK WITH THAT.
PHYLA?
ON ONE SIDE, THE SHI'AR IMPERIUM. THE MOST MASSIVE MILITARY FORCE IN EXISTENCE, AND THAT'S BEFORE YOU EVEN FACTOR IN EMPEROR VULCAN AND THE IMPERIAL GUARD.
OR THE DETAIL THAT VULCAN'S SO FAR OFF HIS CHUFF HE MAKES GALACTUS' APPROVAL RATINGS LOOK LIKE THE DALAI LAMA'S.

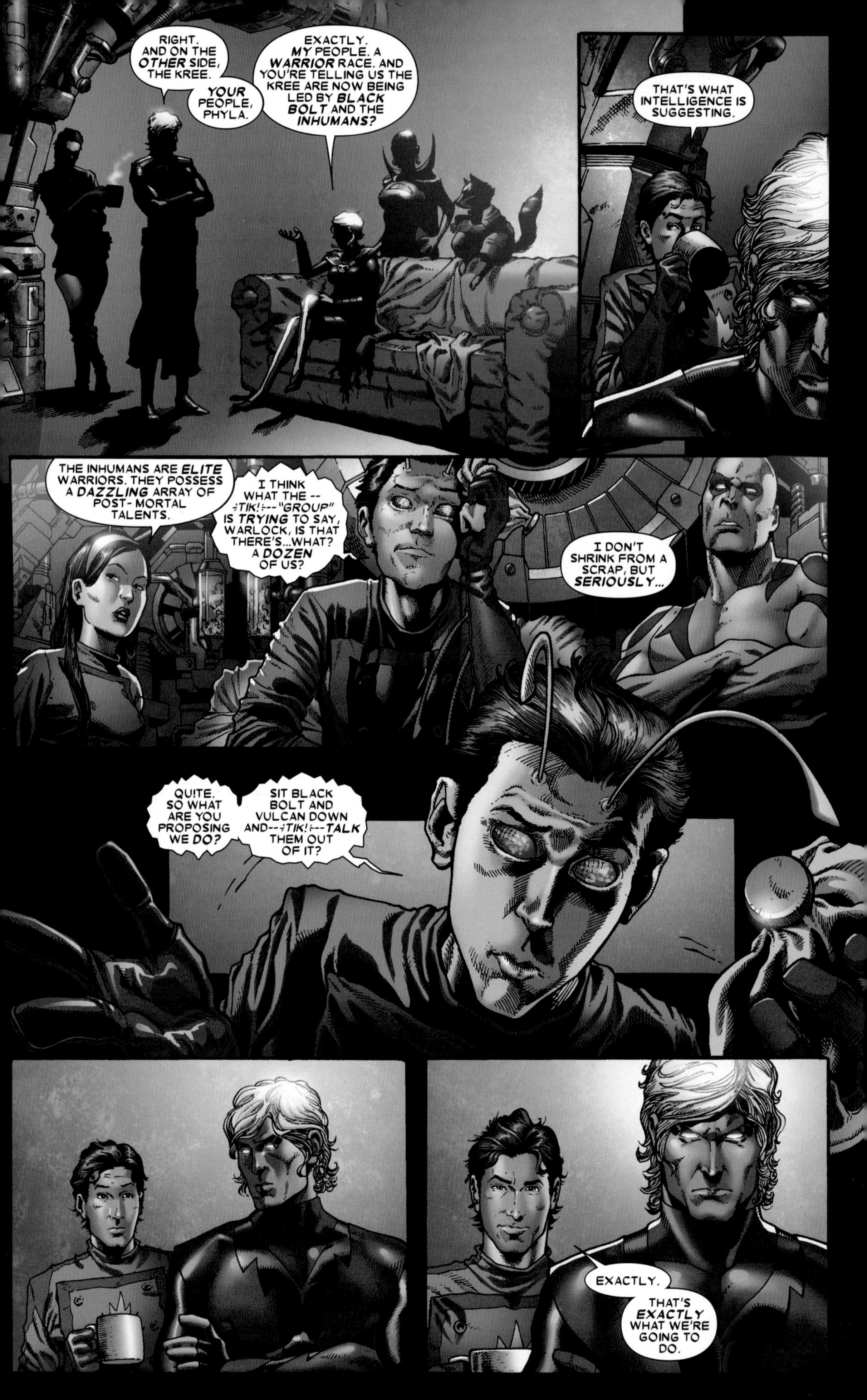
RIGHT. AND ON THE OTHER SIDE, THE KREE.
YOUR PEOPLE, PHYLA.
EXACTLY. MY PEOPLE. A WARRIOR RACE. AND YOU'RE TELLING US THE KREE ARE NOW BEING LED BY BLACK BOLT AND THE INHUMANS?
THAT'S WHAT INTELLIGENCE IS SUGGESTING.
THE INHUMANS ARE ELITE WARRIORS. THEY POSSESS A DAZZLING ARRAY OF POST-MORTAL TALENTS.
I THINK WHAT THE -- ‡TIK!‡-- "GROUP" IS TRYING TO SAY, WARLOCK, IS THAT THERE'S...WHAT? A DOZEN OF US?
I DON'T SHRINK FROM A SCRAP, BUT SERIOUSLY...
QUITE. SO WHAT ARE YOU PROPOSING WE DO?
SIT BLACK BOLT AND VULCAN DOWN AND--‡TIK!‡--TALK THEM OUT OF IT?
EXACTLY.
THAT'S EXACTLY WHAT WE'RE GOING TO DO.

TACTICS.

TWO TEAMS.

AGREED.

ONE GOES TO BLACK BOLT, ONE GOES TO VULCAN.

YOU'VE GOT MUCHO HISTORY WITH THE KREE, PETE. YOU TAKE HALA.

I'LL TACKLE THE SHI'AR END.

YOU *SURE*, ROCKY? THAT'S GONNA BE THE *TOUGH* SELL.

YEAH, WELL *THAT'S* WHY I CALL WARLOCK ON MY TEAM. *AND* GROOT *AND* MAJOR VICTORY *AND* DRAX.

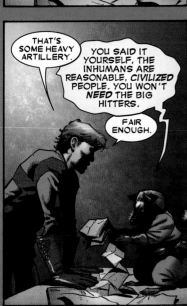

THAT'S SOME HEAVY ARTILLERY.

YOU SAID IT YOURSELF, THE INHUMANS ARE REASONABLE, *CIVILIZED* PEOPLE. YOU WON'T *NEED* THE BIG HITTERS.

FAIR ENOUGH.

BLACK BOLT WILL *LISTEN* TO YOU.

WELL, IT'S NOT LIKE HE'S GOING TO *INTERRUPT* ME.

A LITTLE SMOOTH, *STRAIGHT-TALKING* AND YOUR JOB'S AS GOOD AS DONE.

AND IF I HAVE TO GET WARLOCK AND DRAX TO GIVE VULCAN NOOGIES UNTIL HE *FOLDS*, SO BE IT.

DON'T FORGET YOU'VE GOT TO CONTAIN THE *NEGA-BOMB* DAMAGE AT DISRADI *BEFORE* YOU CONFRONT VULCAN.

CONSIDER IT DONE.

OKAY. OKAY, *GOOD*. WE CAN *DO* THIS. WE'RE THE *GUARDIANS OF THE GALAXY*.

YES, WE *ARE*.

THIS IS *EXACTLY* WHAT WE WERE FORMED TO STOP.

YES, IT *IS*.

WE *CAN* DO THIS, RIGHT?

DON'T SPOIL THE MOMENT.

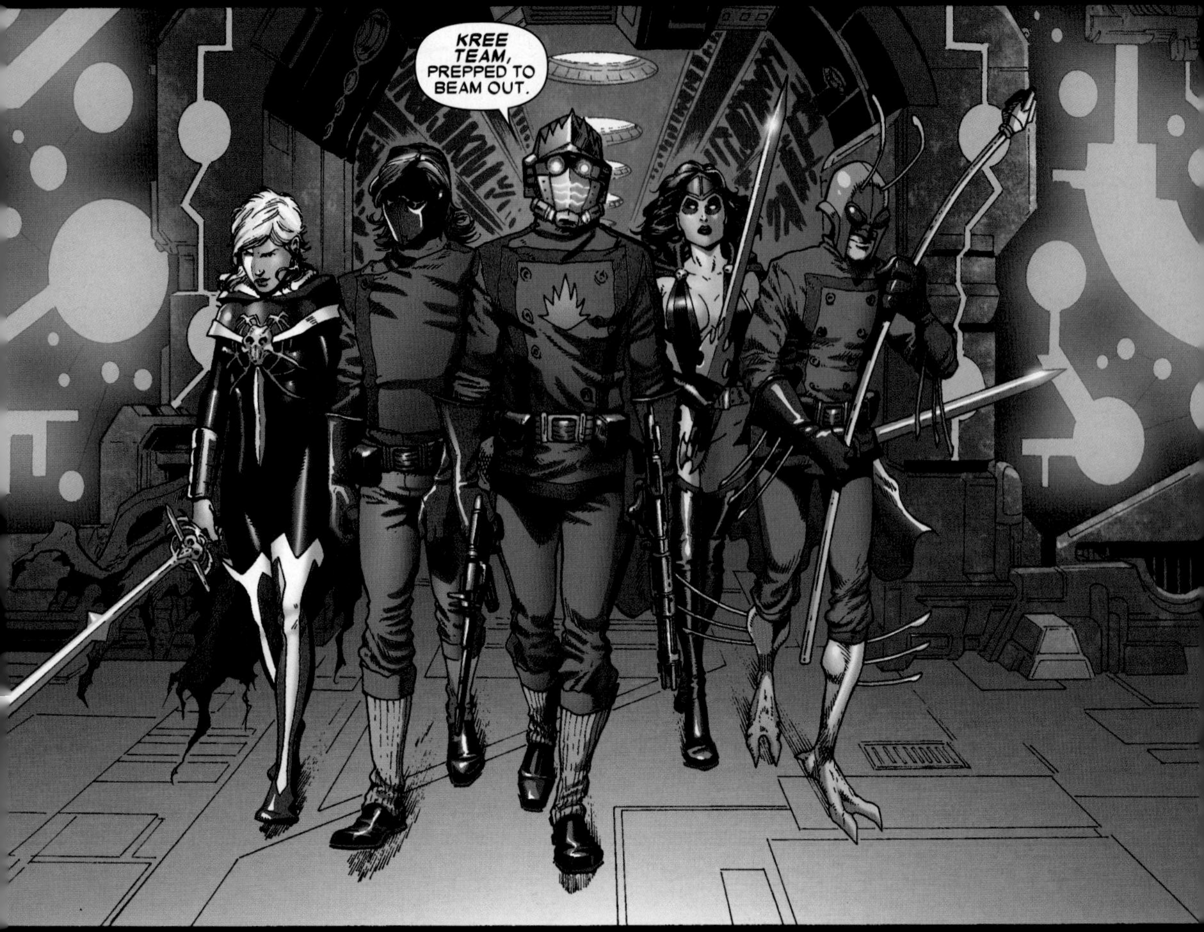
KREE TEAM, PREPPED TO BEAM OUT.

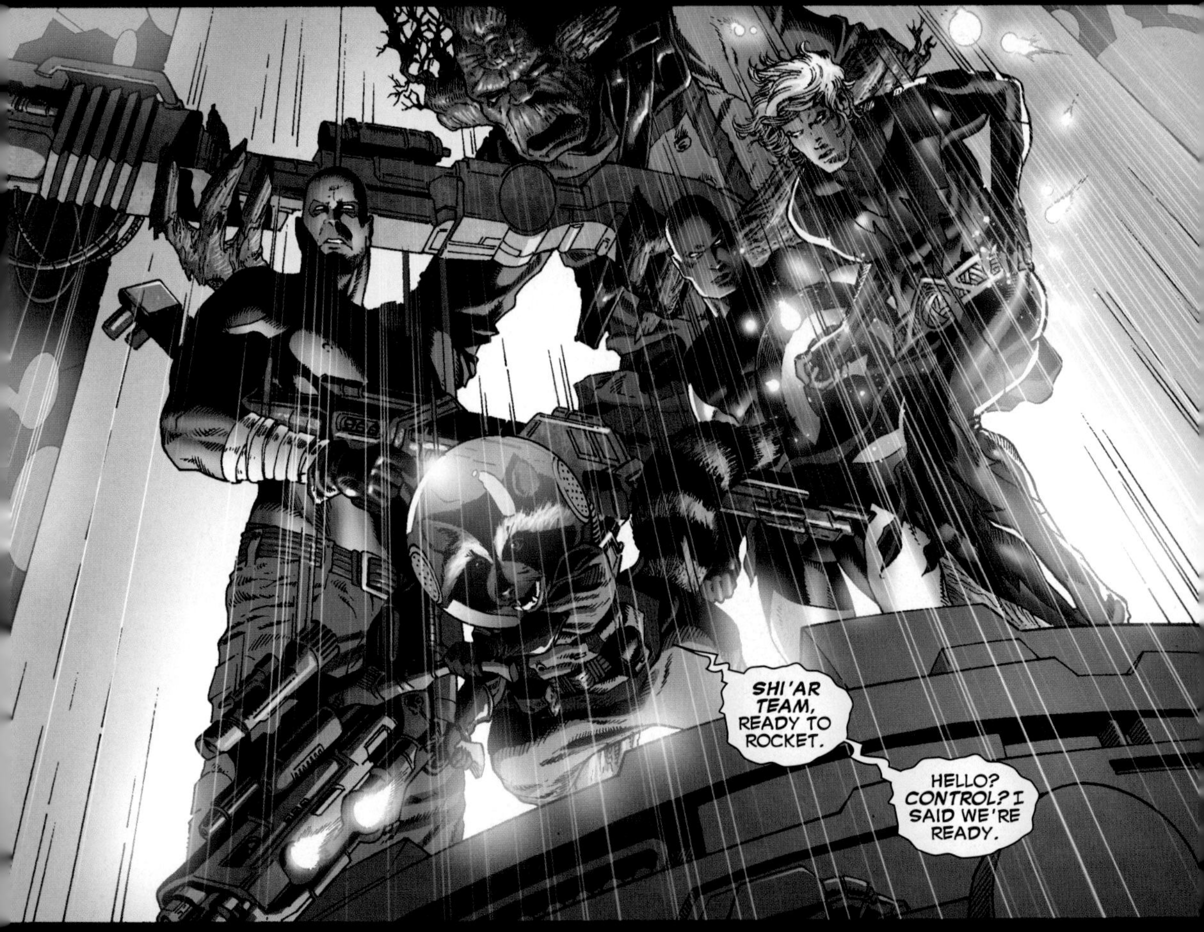
SHI'AR TEAM, READY TO ROCKET.
HELLO? CONTROL? I SAID WE'RE READY.

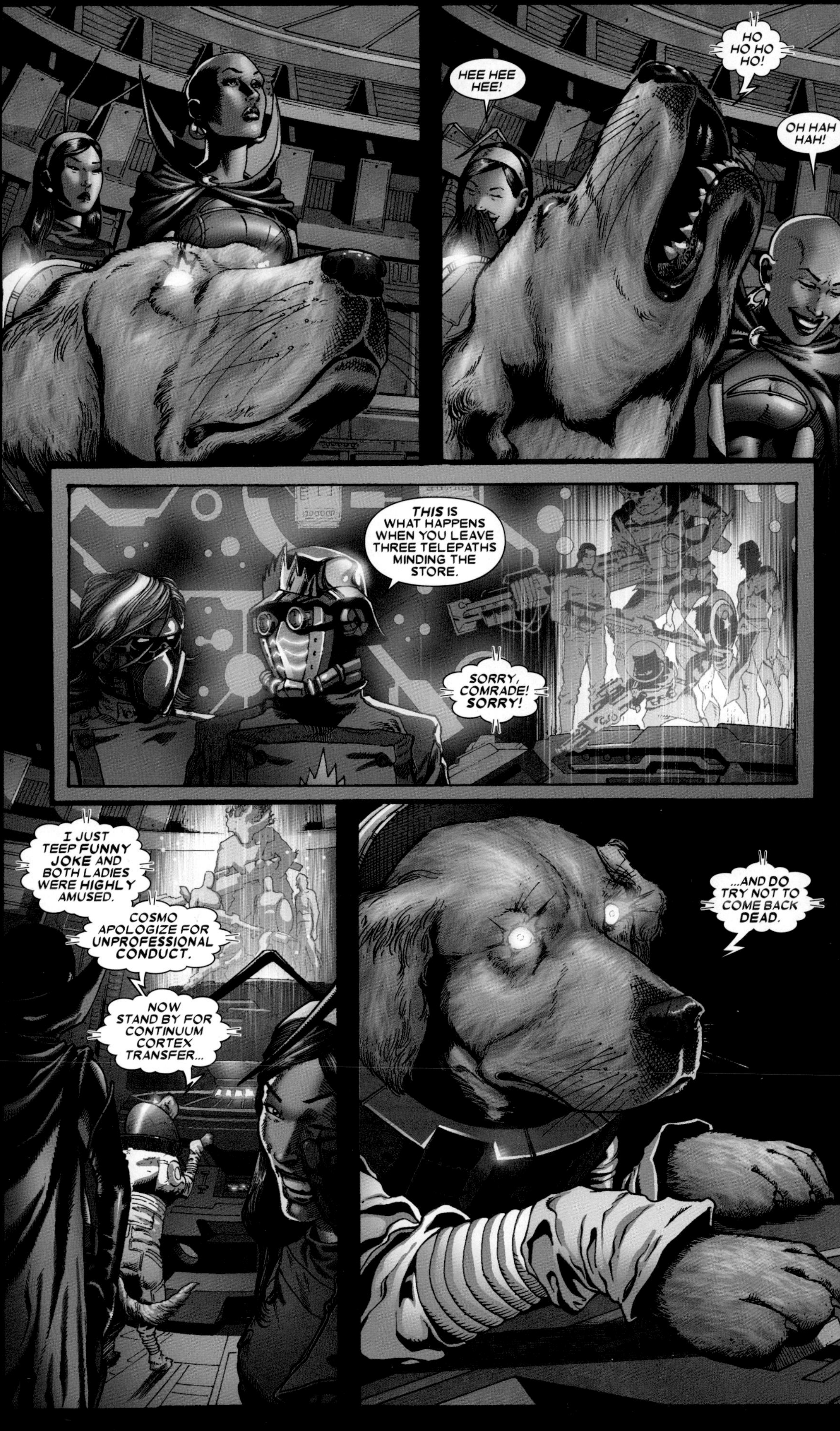
HEE HEE HEE!
HO HO HO HO!
OH HAH HAH!
THIS IS WHAT HAPPENS WHEN YOU LEAVE THREE TELEPATHS MINDING THE STORE.
SORRY, COMRADE! SORRY!
I JUST TEEP FUNNY JOKE AND BOTH LADIES WERE HIGHLY AMUSED.
COSMO APOLOGIZE FOR UNPROFESSIONAL CONDUCT.
NOW STAND BY FOR CONTINUUM CORTEX TRANSFER...
...AND DO TRY NOT TO COME BACK DEAD.

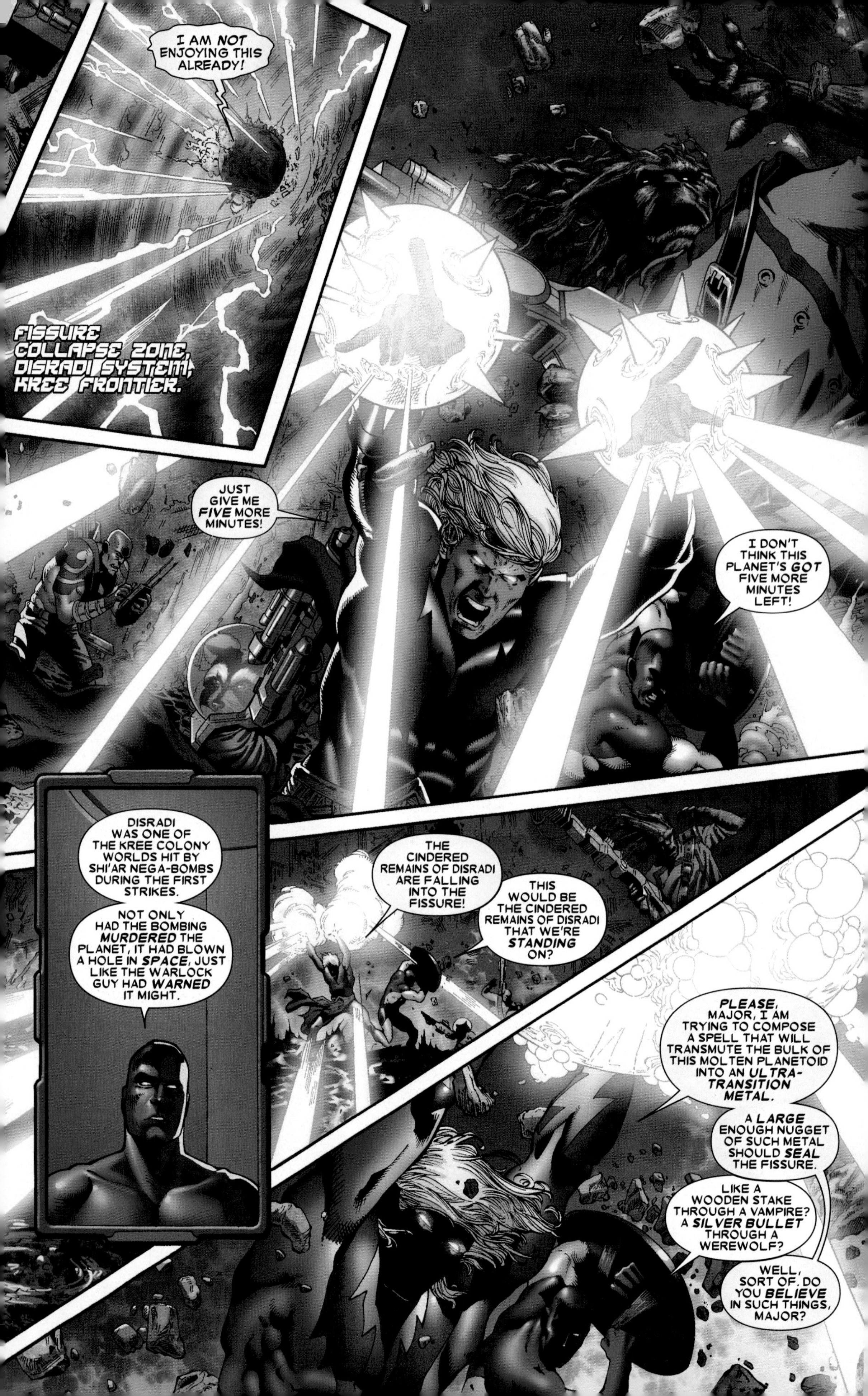

I AM NOT ENJOYING THIS ALREADY!
FISSURE COLLAPSE ZONE, DISRADI SYSTEM, KREE FRONTIER.
JUST GIVE ME FIVE MORE MINUTES!
I DON'T THINK THIS PLANET'S GOT FIVE MORE MINUTES LEFT!
DISRADI WAS ONE OF THE KREE COLONY WORLDS HIT BY SHI'AR NEGA-BOMBS DURING THE FIRST STRIKES.
NOT ONLY HAD THE BOMBING MURDERED THE PLANET, IT HAD BLOWN A HOLE IN SPACE, JUST LIKE THE WARLOCK GUY HAD WARNED IT MIGHT.
THE CINDERED REMAINS OF DISRADI ARE FALLING INTO THE FISSURE!
THIS WOULD BE THE CINDERED REMAINS OF DISRADI THAT WE'RE STANDING ON?
PLEASE, MAJOR, I AM TRYING TO COMPOSE A SPELL THAT WILL TRANSMUTE THE BULK OF THIS MOLTEN PLANETOID INTO AN ULTRA-TRANSITION METAL.
A LARGE ENOUGH NUGGET OF SUCH METAL SHOULD SEAL THE FISSURE.
LIKE A WOODEN STAKE THROUGH A VAMPIRE? A SILVER BULLET THROUGH A WEREWOLF?
WELL, SORT OF. DO YOU BELIEVE IN SUCH THINGS, MAJOR?

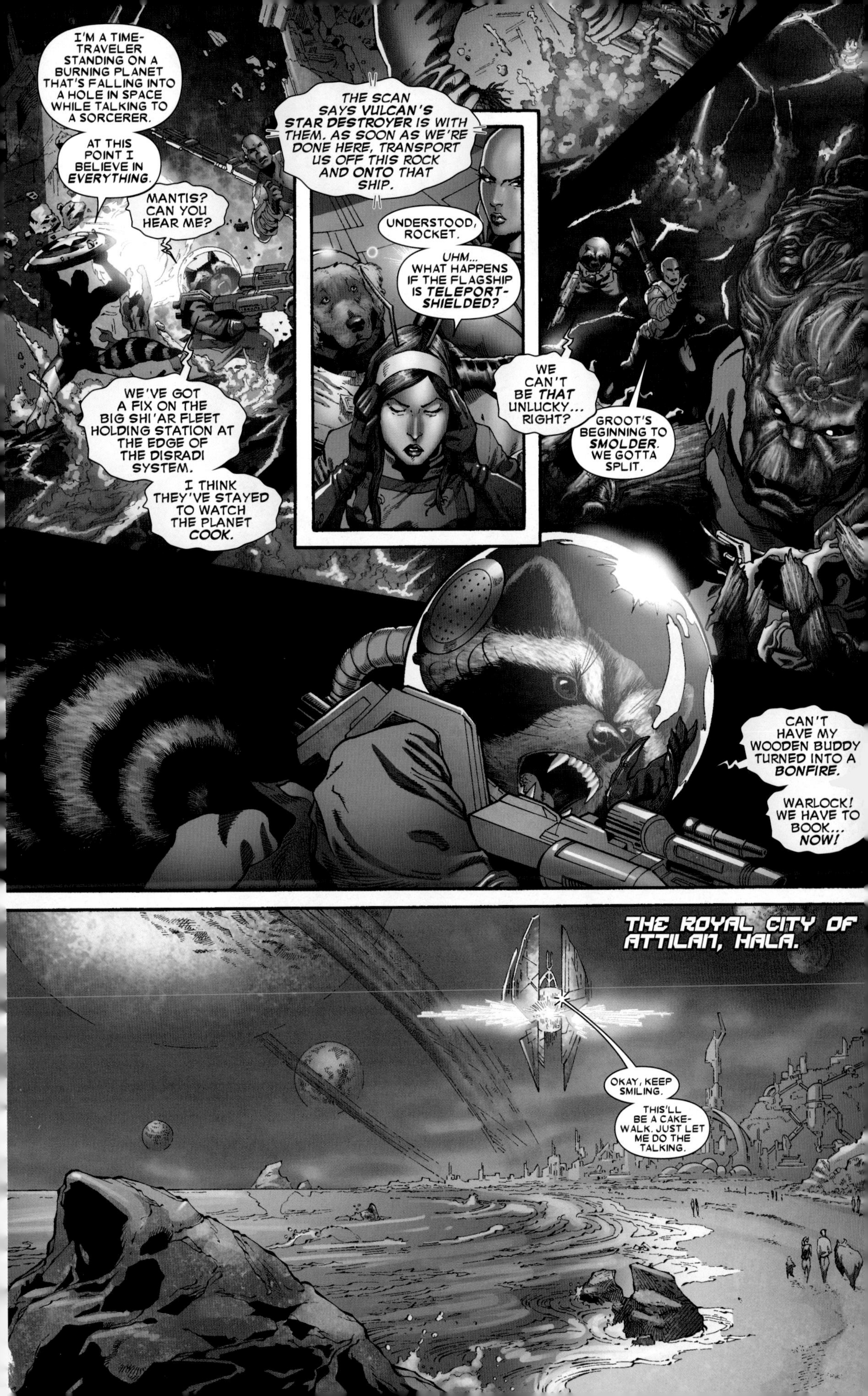
I'M A TIME-TRAVELER STANDING ON A BURNING PLANET THAT'S FALLING INTO A HOLE IN SPACE WHILE TALKING TO A SORCERER.
AT THIS POINT I BELIEVE IN EVERYTHING.
MANTIS? CAN YOU HEAR ME?
WE'VE GOT A FIX ON THE BIG SHI'AR FLEET HOLDING STATION AT THE EDGE OF THE DISRADI SYSTEM.
I THINK THEY'VE STAYED TO WATCH THE PLANET COOK.
THE SCAN SAYS VULCAN'S STAR DESTROYER IS WITH THEM. AS SOON AS WE'RE DONE HERE, TRANSPORT US OFF THIS ROCK AND ONTO THAT SHIP.
UNDERSTOOD, ROCKET.
UHM... WHAT HAPPENS IF THE FLAGSHIP IS TELEPORT-SHIELDED?
WE CAN'T BE THAT UNLUCKY... RIGHT?
GROOT'S BEGINNING TO SMOLDER. WE GOTTA SPLIT.
CAN'T HAVE MY WOODEN BUDDY TURNED INTO A BONFIRE.
WARLOCK! WE HAVE TO BOOK... NOW!
THE ROYAL CITY OF ATTILAN, HALA.
OKAY, KEEP SMILING.
THIS'LL BE A CAKE-WALK. JUST LET ME DO THE TALKING.

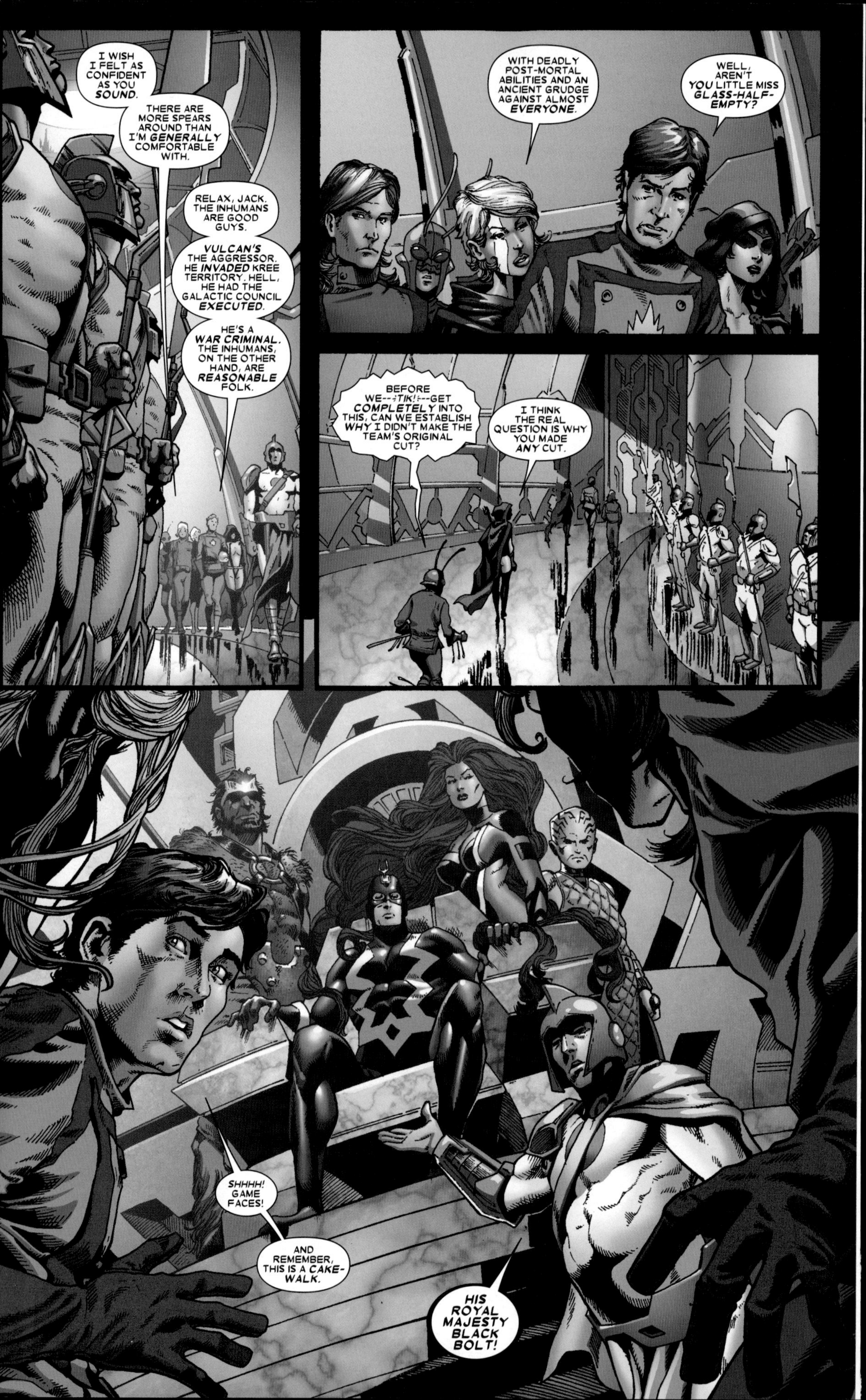
I WISH I FELT AS CONFIDENT AS YOU SOUND.
THERE ARE MORE SPEARS AROUND THAN I'M GENERALLY COMFORTABLE WITH.
RELAX, JACK. THE INHUMANS ARE GOOD GUYS.
VULCAN'S THE AGGRESSOR. HE INVADED KREE TERRITORY. HELL, HE HAD THE GALACTIC COUNCIL EXECUTED.
HE'S A WAR CRIMINAL. THE INHUMANS, ON THE OTHER HAND, ARE REASONABLE FOLK.
WITH DEADLY POST-MORTAL ABILITIES AND AN ANCIENT GRUDGE AGAINST ALMOST EVERYONE.
WELL, AREN'T YOU LITTLE MISS GLASS-HALF-EMPTY?
BEFORE WE--TIK!--GET COMPLETELY INTO THIS, CAN WE ESTABLISH WHY I DIDN'T MAKE THE TEAM'S ORIGINAL CUT?
I THINK THE REAL QUESTION IS WHY YOU MADE ANY CUT.
SHHHH! GAME FACES!
AND REMEMBER, THIS IS A CAKE-WALK.
HIS ROYAL MAJESTY BLACK BOLT!

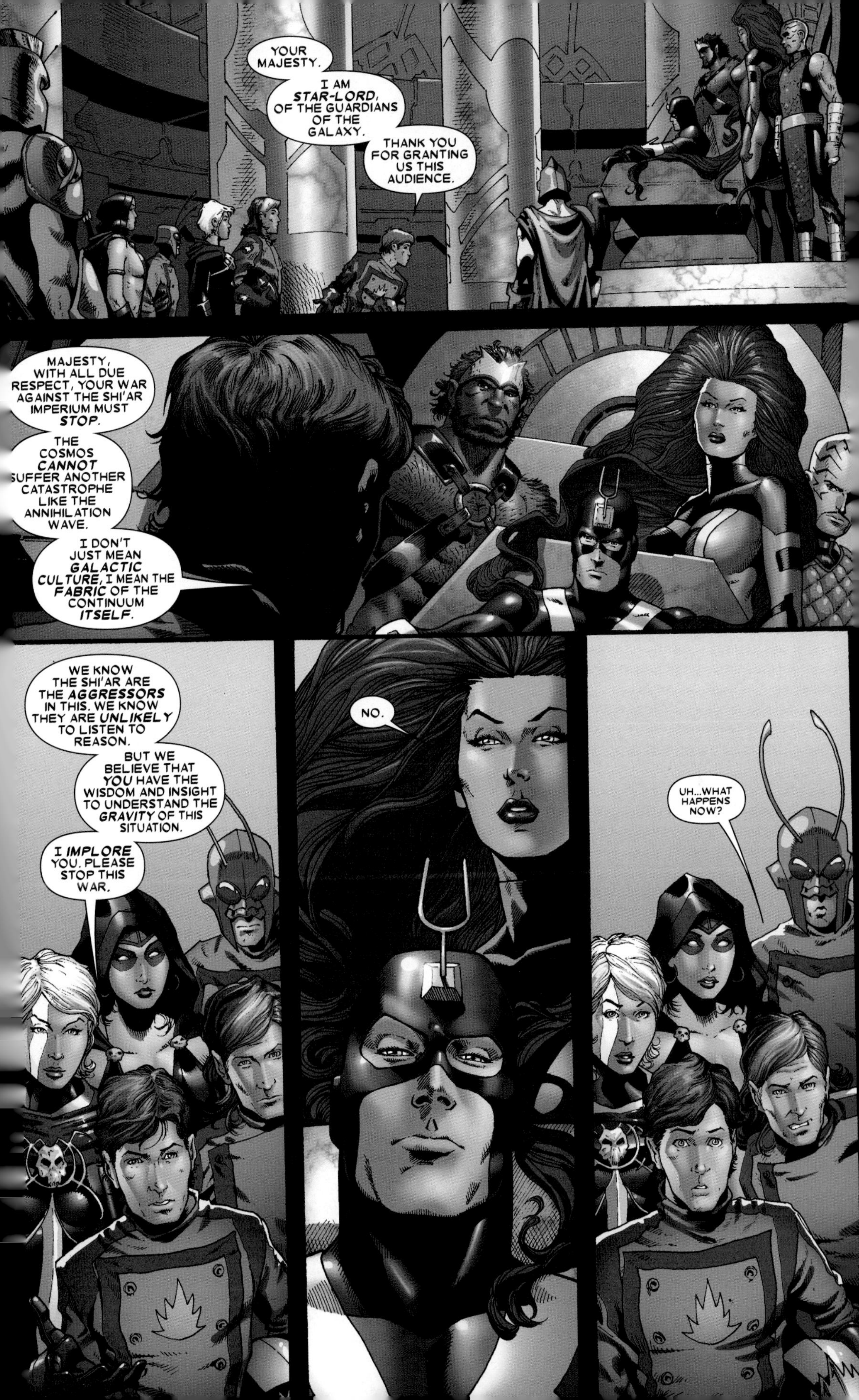
YOUR MAJESTY.
I AM STAR-LORD, OF THE GUARDIANS OF THE GALAXY.
THANK YOU FOR GRANTING US THIS AUDIENCE.
MAJESTY, WITH ALL DUE RESPECT, YOUR WAR AGAINST THE SHI'AR IMPERIUM MUST STOP.
THE COSMOS CANNOT SUFFER ANOTHER CATASTROPHE LIKE THE ANNIHILATION WAVE.
I DON'T JUST MEAN GALACTIC CULTURE, I MEAN THE FABRIC OF THE CONTINUUM ITSELF.
WE KNOW THE SHI'AR ARE THE AGGRESSORS IN THIS. WE KNOW THEY ARE UNLIKELY TO LISTEN TO REASON.
BUT WE BELIEVE THAT YOU HAVE THE WISDOM AND INSIGHT TO UNDERSTAND THE GRAVITY OF THIS SITUATION.
I IMPLORE YOU. PLEASE STOP THIS WAR.
NO.
UH...WHAT HAPPENS NOW?

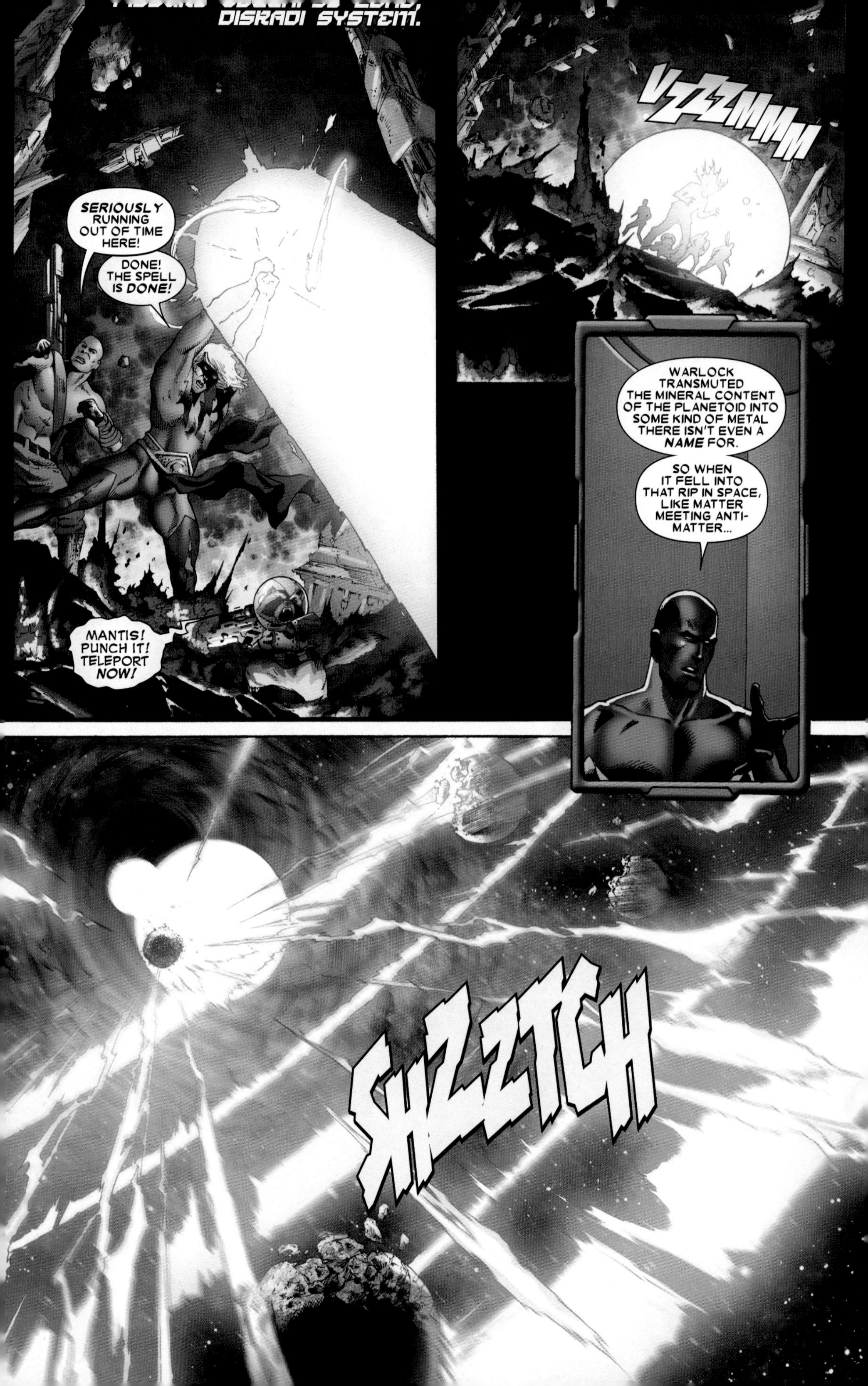
DISRADI SYSTEM.
SERIOUSLY RUNNING OUT OF TIME HERE!
DONE! THE SPELL IS DONE!
MANTIS! PUNCH IT! TELEPORT NOW!
VZZMMMM
WARLOCK TRANSMUTED THE MINERAL CONTENT OF THE PLANETOID INTO SOME KIND OF METAL THERE ISN'T EVEN A NAME FOR.
SO WHEN IT FELL INTO THAT RIP IN SPACE, LIKE MATTER MEETING ANTI-MATTER...
SHZZTCH

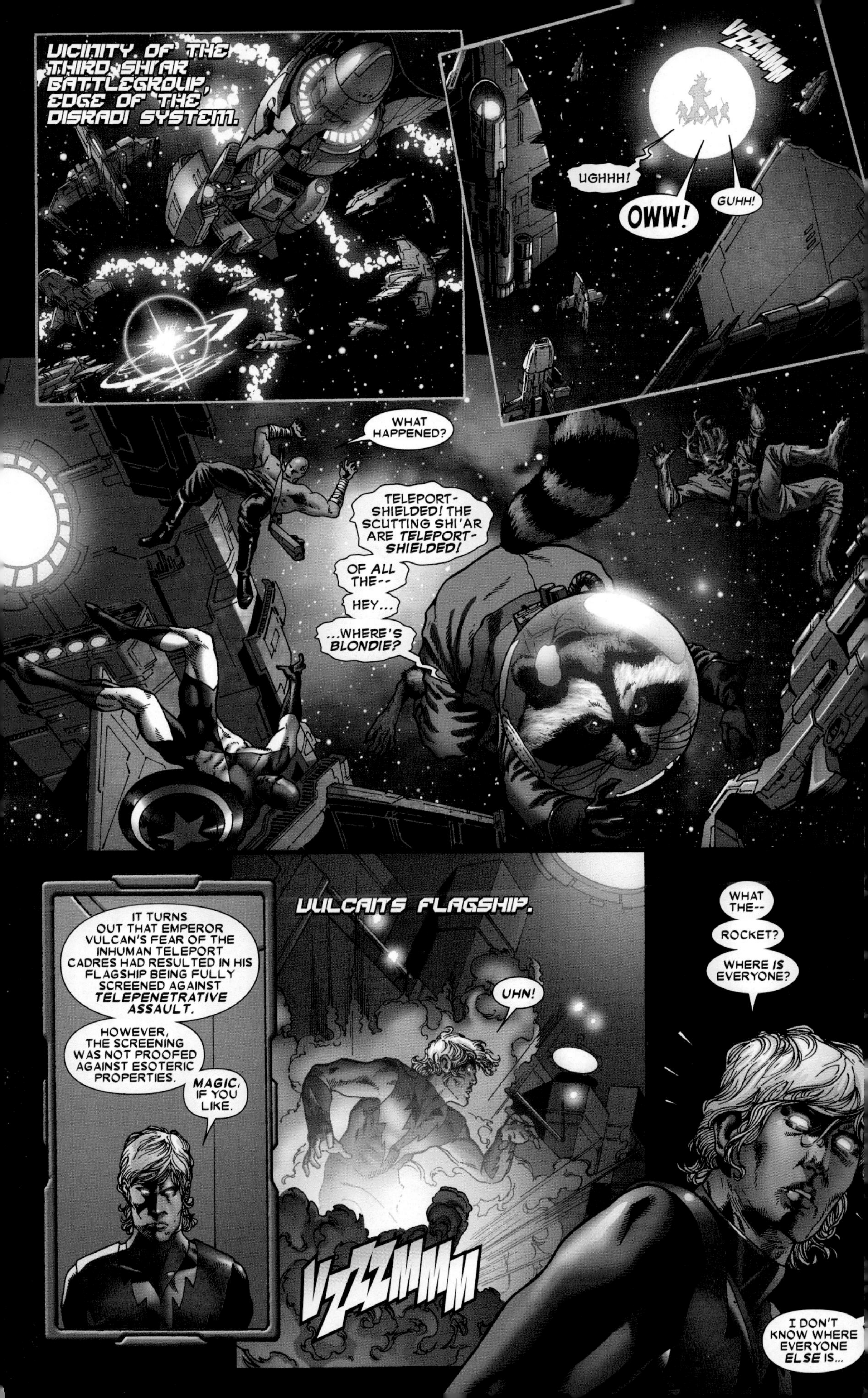
VICINITY OF THE THIRD SHI'AR BATTLEGROUP, EDGE OF THE DISRADI SYSTEM.
VZZMMM
UGHHH!
OWW!
GUHH!
WHAT HAPPENED?
TELEPORT-SHIELDED! THE SCUTTING SHI'AR ARE TELEPORT-SHIELDED!
OF ALL THE--
HEY...
...WHERE'S BLONDIE?
VULCAN'S FLAGSHIP.
IT TURNS OUT THAT EMPEROR VULCAN'S FEAR OF THE INHUMAN TELEPORT CADRES HAD RESULTED IN HIS FLAGSHIP BEING FULLY SCREENED AGAINST TELEPENETRATIVE ASSAULT.
HOWEVER, THE SCREENING WAS NOT PROOFED AGAINST ESOTERIC PROPERTIES.
MAGIC, IF YOU LIKE.
UHN!
VZZZMMM
WHAT THE--
ROCKET?
WHERE IS EVERYONE?
I DON'T KNOW WHERE EVERYONE ELSE IS...

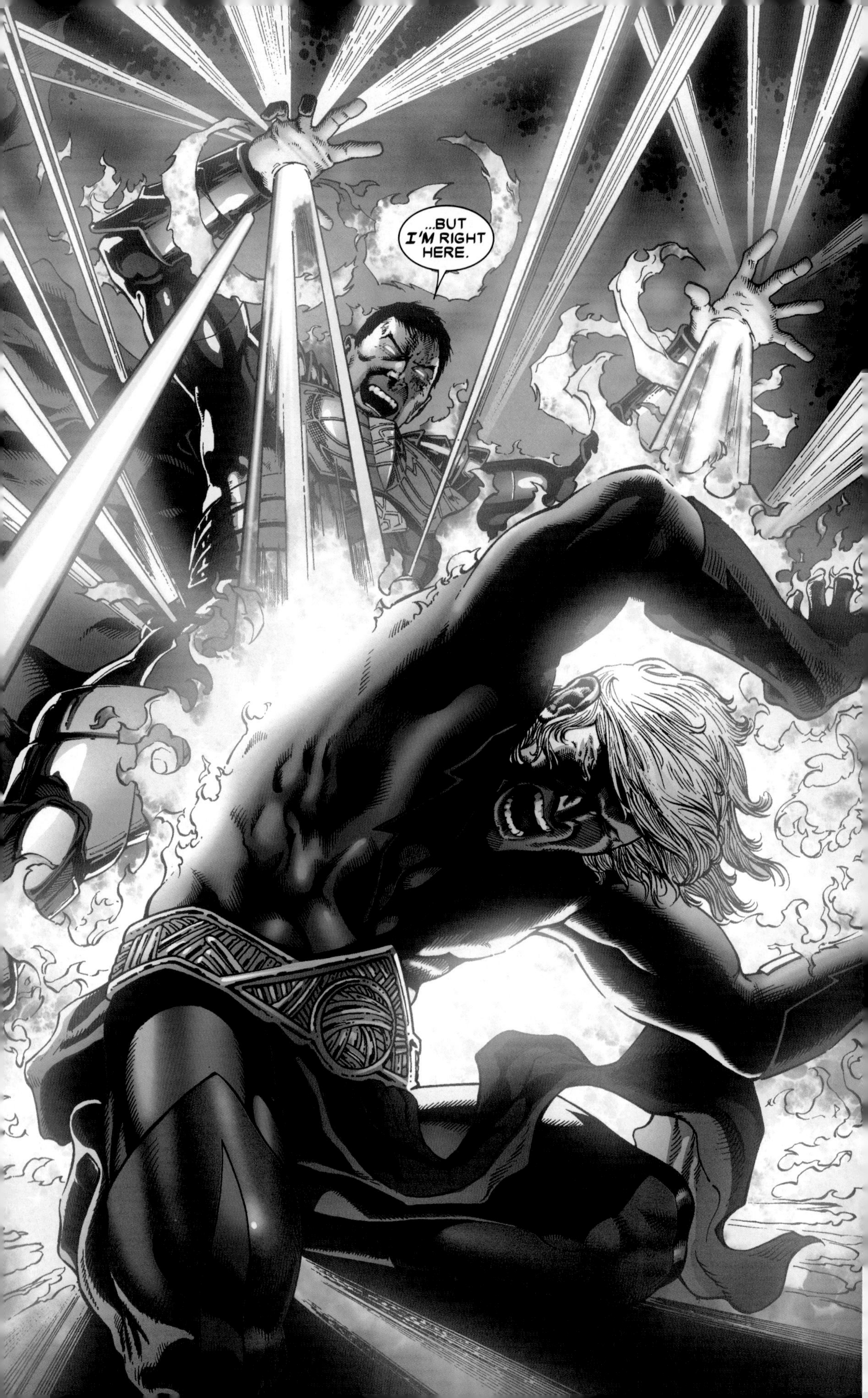
...BUT I'M RIGHT HERE.

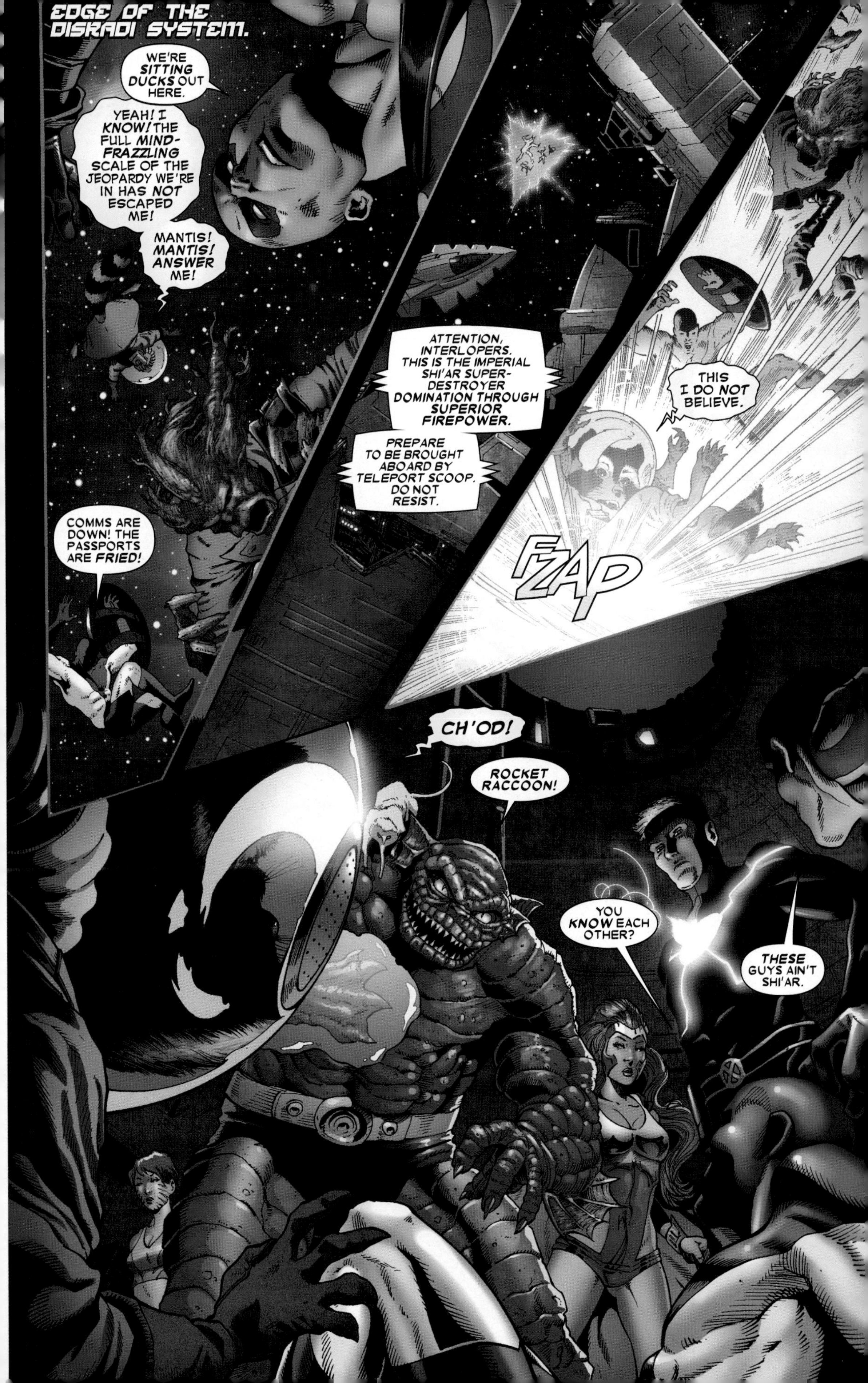
EDGE OF THE DISRADI SYSTEM.
WE'RE SITTING DUCKS OUT HERE.
YEAH! I KNOW! THE FULL MIND-FRAZZLING SCALE OF THE JEOPARDY WE'RE IN HAS NOT ESCAPED ME!
MANTIS! MANTIS! ANSWER ME!
COMMS ARE DOWN! THE PASSPORTS ARE FRIED!
ATTENTION, INTERLOPERS. THIS IS THE IMPERIAL SHI'AR SUPER-DESTROYER DOMINATION THROUGH SUPERIOR FIREPOWER.
PREPARE TO BE BROUGHT ABOARD BY TELEPORT SCOOP. DO NOT RESIST.
THIS I DO NOT BELIEVE.
FZZAP
CH'OD!
ROCKET RACCOON!
YOU KNOW EACH OTHER?
THESE GUYS AIN'T SHI'AR.

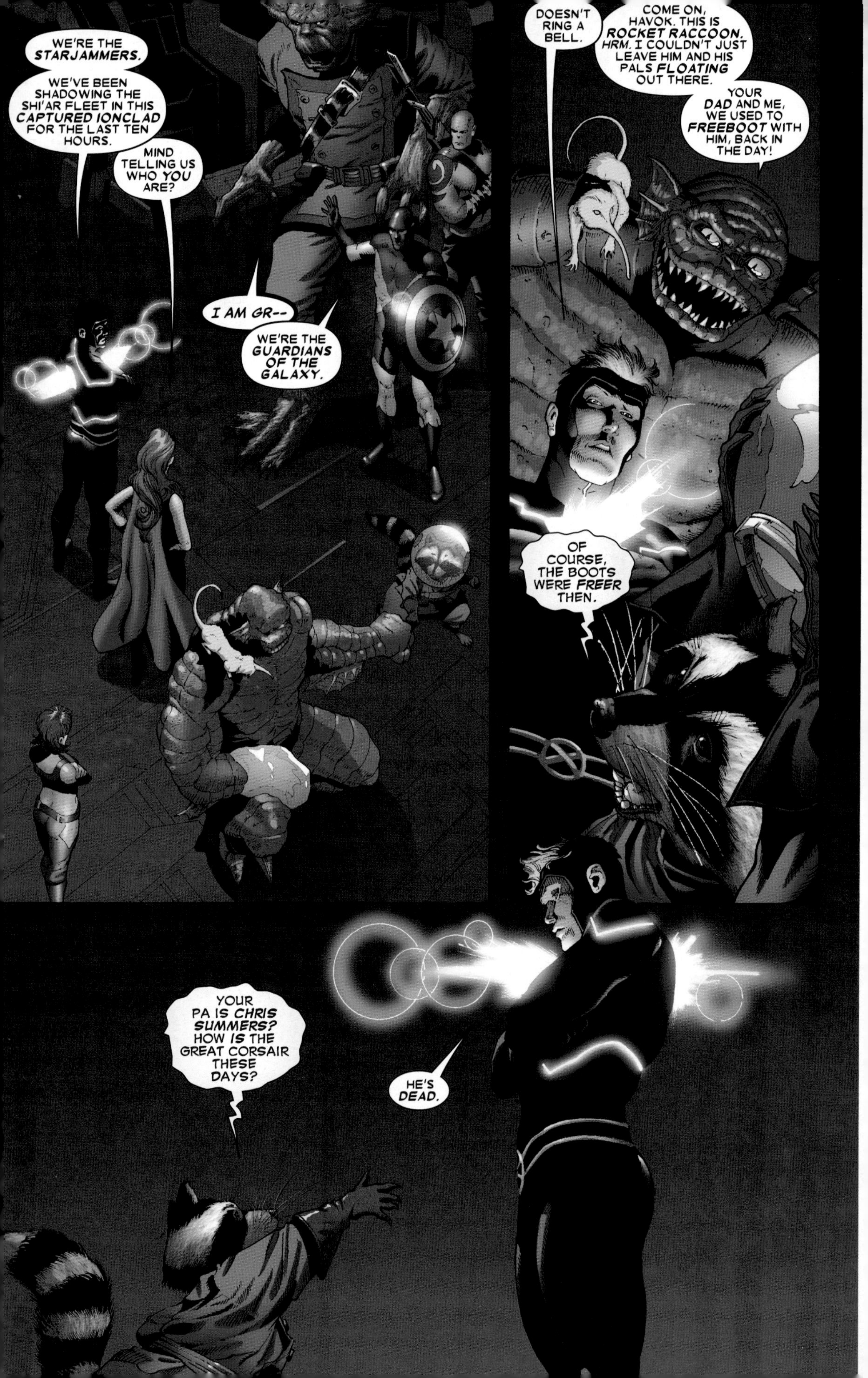
WE'RE THE STARJAMMERS.
WE'VE BEEN SHADOWING THE SHI'AR FLEET IN THIS CAPTURED IONCLAD FOR THE LAST TEN HOURS.
MIND TELLING US WHO YOU ARE?
I AM GR--
WE'RE THE GUARDIANS OF THE GALAXY.
DOESN'T RING A BELL.
COME ON, HAVOK. THIS IS ROCKET RACCOON. HRM. I COULDN'T JUST LEAVE HIM AND HIS PALS FLOATING OUT THERE.
YOUR DAD AND ME, WE USED TO FREEBOOT WITH HIM, BACK IN THE DAY!
OF COURSE, THE BOOTS WERE FREER THEN.
YOUR PA IS CHRIS SUMMERS? HOW IS THE GREAT CORSAIR THESE DAYS?
HE'S DEAD.

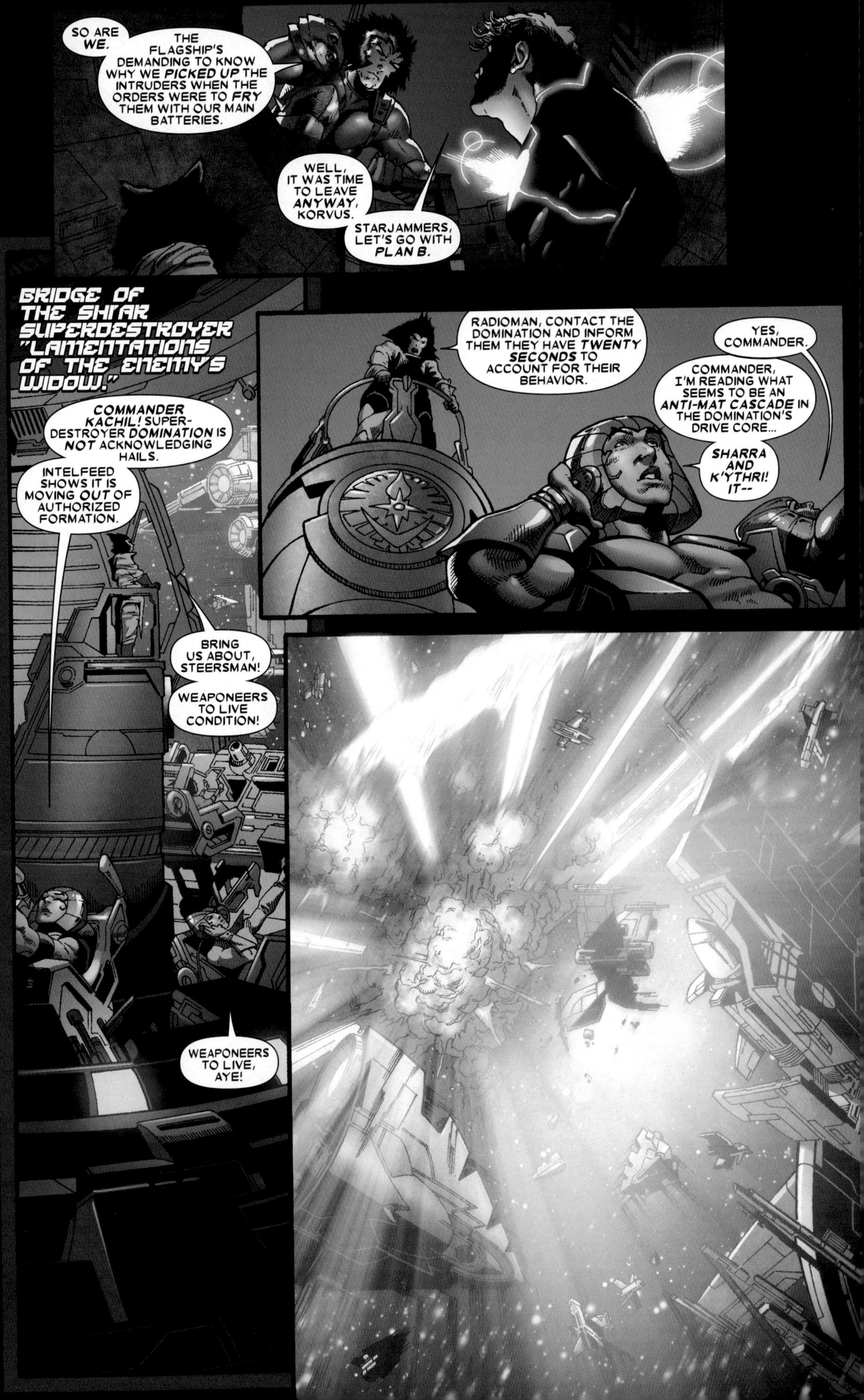
SO ARE WE.
THE FLAGSHIP'S DEMANDING TO KNOW WHY WE PICKED UP THE INTRUDERS WHEN THE ORDERS WERE TO FRY THEM WITH OUR MAIN BATTERIES.
WELL, IT WAS TIME TO LEAVE ANYWAY, KORVUS.
STARJAMMERS, LET'S GO WITH PLAN B.
BRIDGE OF THE SHI'AR SUPERDESTROYER "LAMENTATIONS OF THE ENEMY'S WIDOW."
COMMANDER KACHIL! SUPER-DESTROYER DOMINATION IS NOT ACKNOWLEDGING HAILS.
INTELFEED SHOWS IT IS MOVING OUT OF AUTHORIZED FORMATION.
RADIOMAN, CONTACT THE DOMINATION AND INFORM THEM THEY HAVE TWENTY SECONDS TO ACCOUNT FOR THEIR BEHAVIOR.
YES, COMMANDER.
COMMANDER, I'M READING WHAT SEEMS TO BE AN ANTI-MAT CASCADE IN THE DOMINATION'S DRIVE CORE...
SHARRA AND K'YTHRI! IT--
BRING US ABOUT, STEERSMAN!
WEAPONEERS TO LIVE CONDITION!
WEAPONEERS TO LIVE, AYE!

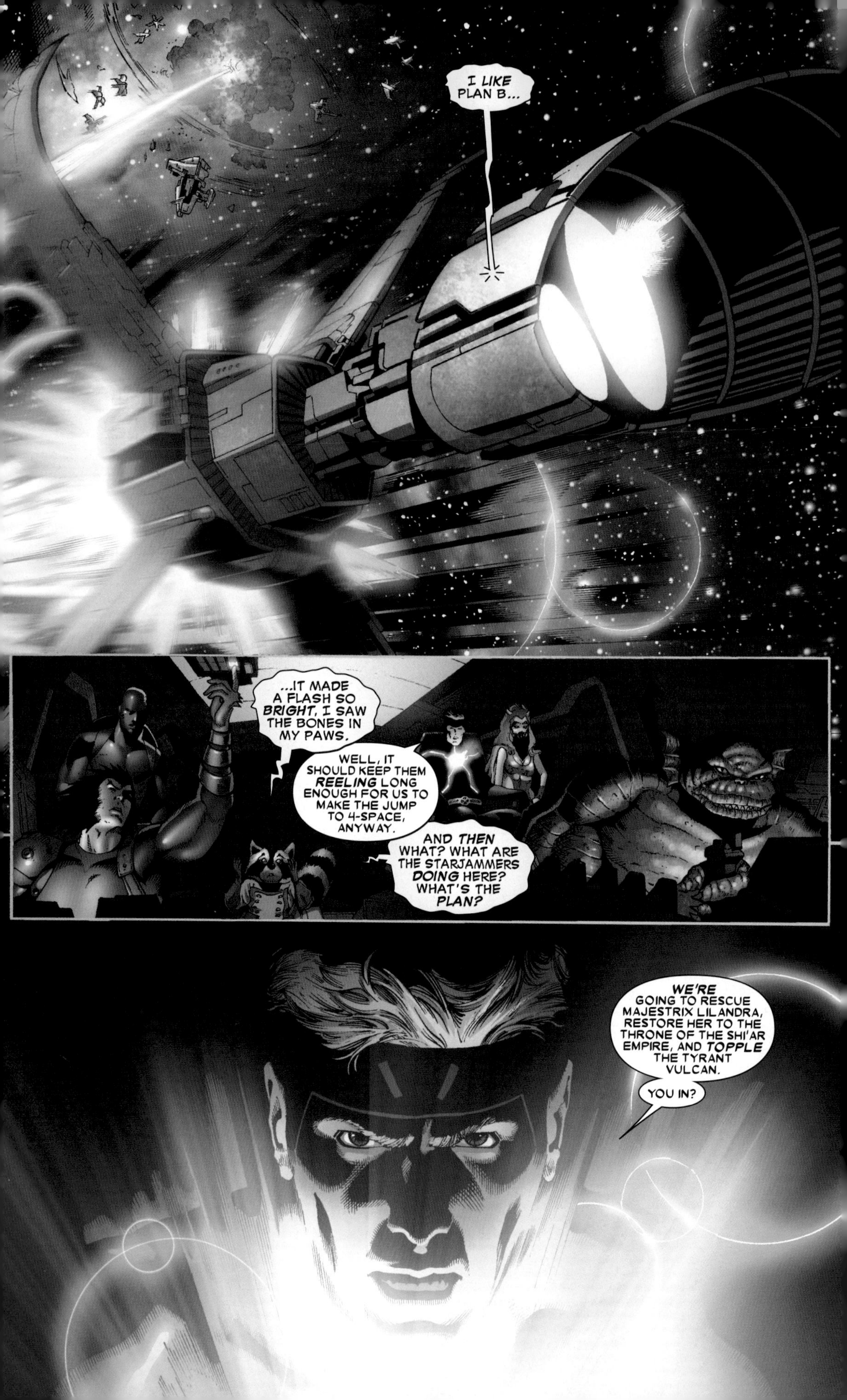
I LIKE PLAN B...
...IT MADE A FLASH SO BRIGHT, I SAW THE BONES IN MY PAWS.
WELL, IT SHOULD KEEP THEM REELING LONG ENOUGH FOR US TO MAKE THE JUMP TO 4-SPACE, ANYWAY.
AND THEN WHAT? WHAT ARE THE STARJAMMERS DOING HERE? WHAT'S THE PLAN?
WE'RE GOING TO RESCUE MAJESTRIX LILANDRA, RESTORE HER TO THE THRONE OF THE SHI'AR EMPIRE, AND TOPPLE THE TYRANT VULCAN.
YOU IN?

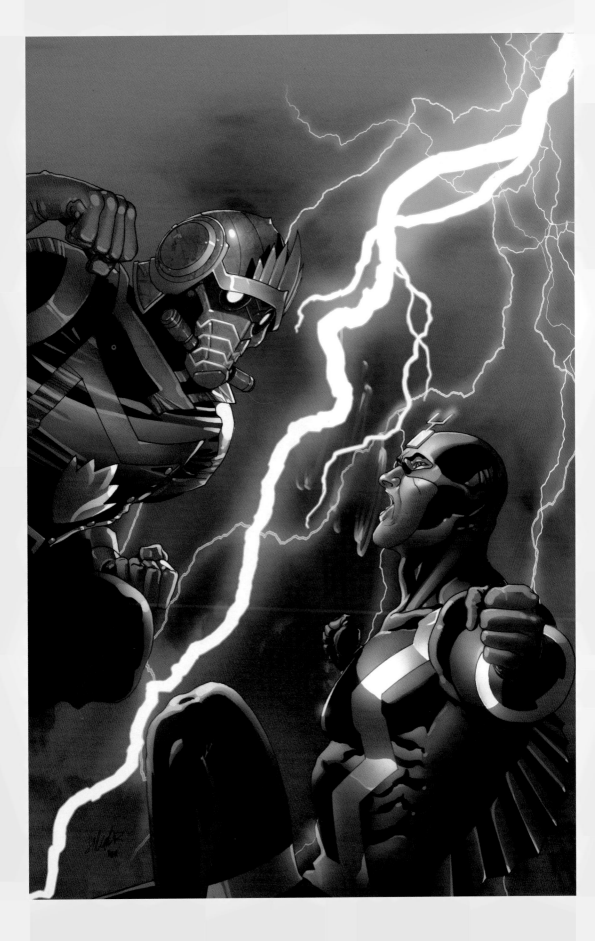

ADAM WARLOCK, BATTLE MAGE OF THE GUARDIANS OF THE GALAXY.

I WILL SAY THIS JUST *ONCE*.

STAND YOUR FLEETS AND LEGIONS DOWN *NOW*, AND *END* THIS WAR.

VULCAN, EMPEROR OF THE SHI'AR.

OKAY, I HAVE A *COUPLE* OF QUESTIONS...

FIRST, WHO ARE *YOU* SUPPOSED TO BE?

AND SECOND...OR YOU'LL DO *WHAT*?

KRA-KA-DOOM

HAMMER II, FLAGSHIP OF EMPEROR VULCAN, EDGE OF THE KISRANI SYSTEM.

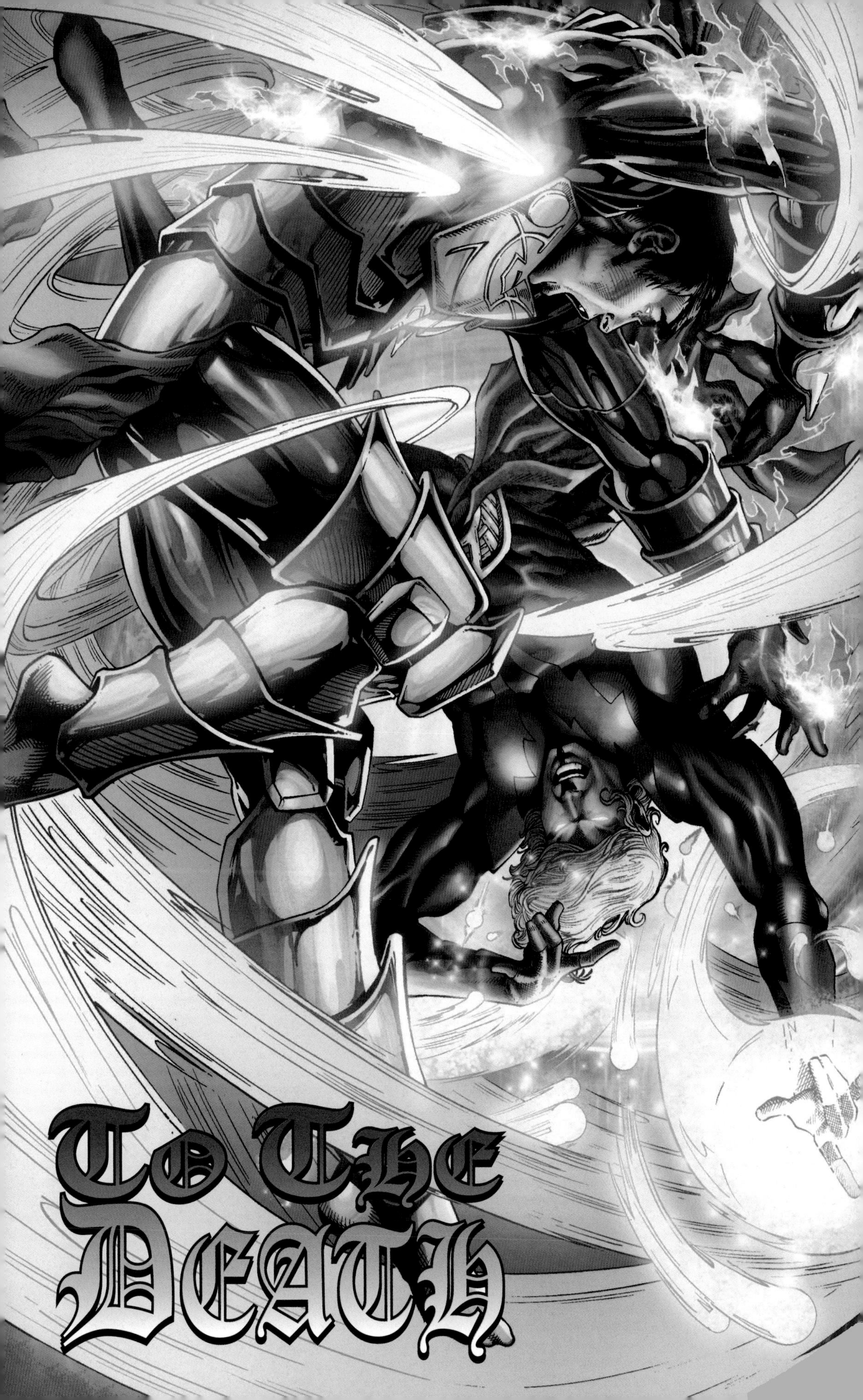
TO THE
DEATH

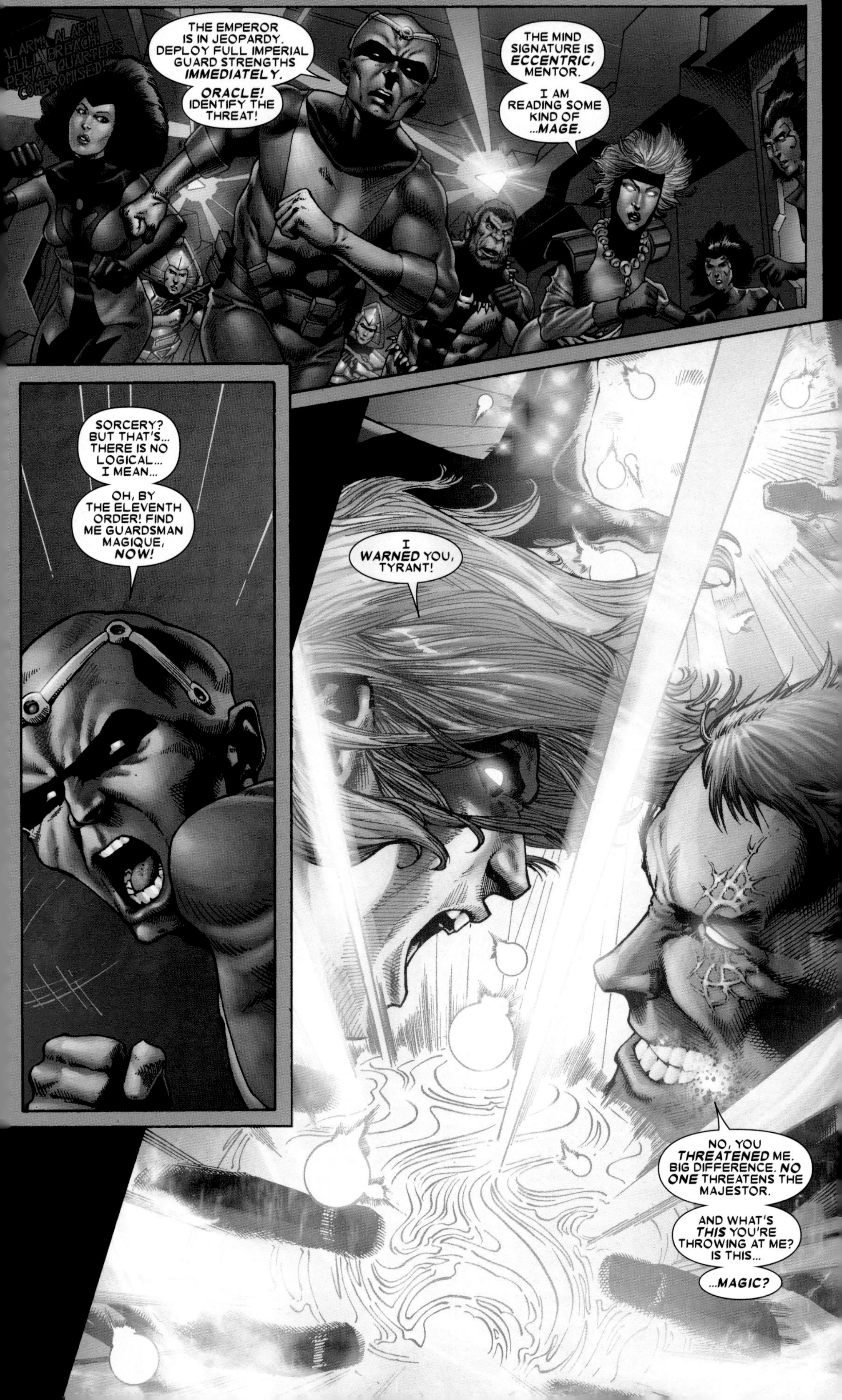
LARM! ALARM! HULL BREACH! PERIAL QUARTERS COMPROMISED!
THE EMPEROR IS IN JEOPARDY. DEPLOY FULL IMPERIAL GUARD STRENGTHS IMMEDIATELY.
ORACLE! IDENTIFY THE THREAT!
THE MIND SIGNATURE IS ECCENTRIC, MENTOR.
I AM READING SOME KIND OF ...MAGE.
SORCERY? BUT THAT'S... THERE IS NO LOGICAL... I MEAN...
OH, BY THE ELEVENTH ORDER! FIND ME GUARDSMAN MAGIQUE, NOW!
I WARNED YOU, TYRANT!
NO, YOU THREATENED ME. BIG DIFFERENCE. NO ONE THREATENS THE MAJESTOR.
AND WHAT'S THIS YOU'RE THROWING AT ME? IS THIS...
...MAGIC?

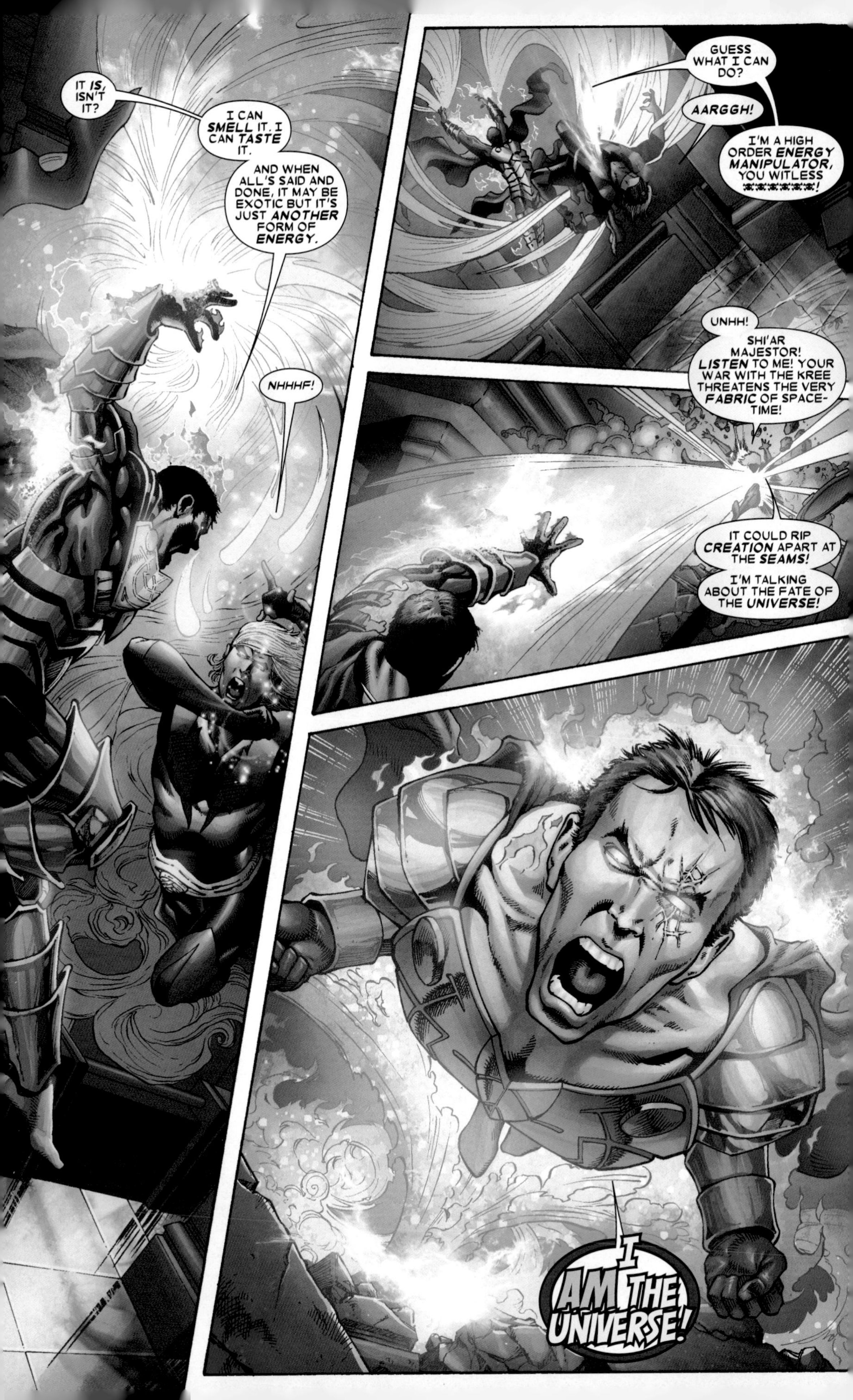

IT IS, ISN'T IT?
I CAN SMELL IT. I CAN TASTE IT.
AND WHEN ALL'S SAID AND DONE, IT MAY BE EXOTIC BUT IT'S JUST ANOTHER FORM OF ENERGY.
NHHHF!
GUESS WHAT I CAN DO?
AARGGH!
I'M A HIGH ORDER ENERGY MANIPULATOR, YOU WITLESS
UNHH!
SHI'AR MAJESTOR! LISTEN TO ME! YOUR WAR WITH THE KREE THREATENS THE VERY FABRIC OF SPACE-TIME!
IT COULD RIP CREATION APART AT THE SEAMS!
I'M TALKING ABOUT THE FATE OF THE UNIVERSE!
I AM THE UNIVERSE!

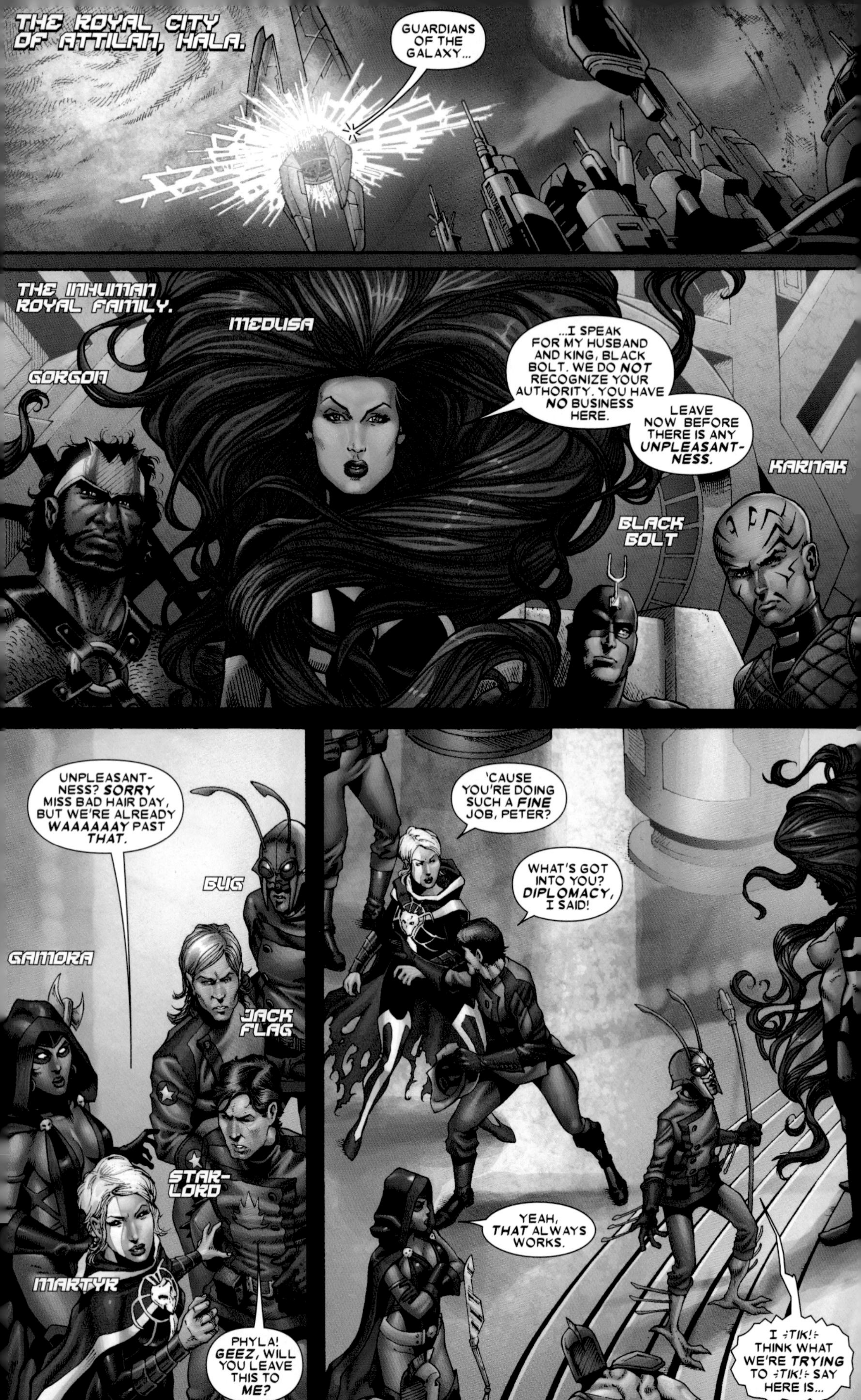

THE ROYAL CITY OF ATTILAN, HALA.
GUARDIANS OF THE GALAXY...
THE INHUMAN ROYAL FAMILY.
MEDUSA
GORGON
...I SPEAK FOR MY HUSBAND AND KING, BLACK BOLT. WE DO NOT RECOGNIZE YOUR AUTHORITY. YOU HAVE NO BUSINESS HERE.
LEAVE NOW BEFORE THERE IS ANY UNPLEASANT-NESS.
KARNAK
BLACK BOLT
UNPLEASANT-NESS? SORRY MISS BAD HAIR DAY, BUT WE'RE ALREADY WAAAAAAY PAST THAT.
BUG
GAMORA
JACK FLAG
STAR-LORD
MARTYR
PHYLA! GEEZ, WILL YOU LEAVE THIS TO ME?
'CAUSE YOU'RE DOING SUCH A FINE JOB, PETER?
WHAT'S GOT INTO YOU? DIPLOMACY, I SAID!
YEAH, THAT ALWAYS WORKS.
I ÷TIK!÷ THINK WHAT WE'RE TRYING TO ÷TIK!÷ SAY HERE IS...

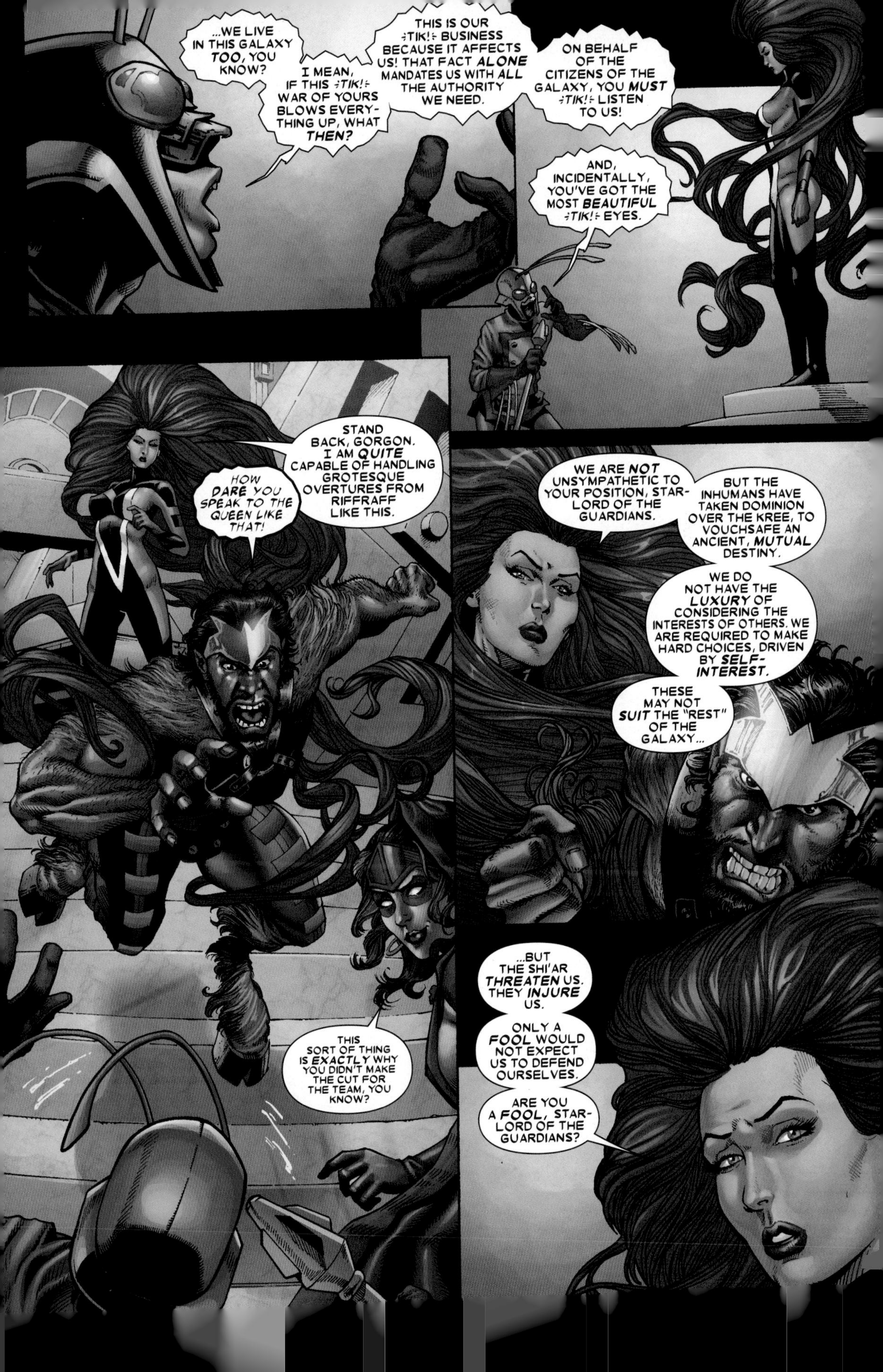

...WE LIVE IN THIS GALAXY TOO, YOU KNOW?
I MEAN, IF THIS ≑TIK!≑ WAR OF YOURS BLOWS EVERY-THING UP, WHAT THEN?
THIS IS OUR ≑TIK!≑ BUSINESS BECAUSE IT AFFECTS US! THAT FACT ALONE MANDATES US WITH ALL THE AUTHORITY WE NEED.
ON BEHALF OF THE CITIZENS OF THE GALAXY, YOU MUST ≑TIK!≑ LISTEN TO US!
AND, INCIDENTALLY, YOU'VE GOT THE MOST BEAUTIFUL ≑TIK!≑ EYES.
STAND BACK, GORGON. I AM QUITE CAPABLE OF HANDLING GROTESQUE OVERTURES FROM RIFFRAFF LIKE THIS.
HOW DARE YOU SPEAK TO THE QUEEN LIKE THAT!
THIS SORT OF THING IS EXACTLY WHY YOU DIDN'T MAKE THE CUT FOR THE TEAM, YOU KNOW?
WE ARE NOT UNSYMPATHETIC TO YOUR POSITION, STAR-LORD OF THE GUARDIANS.
BUT THE INHUMANS HAVE TAKEN DOMINION OVER THE KREE, TO VOUCHSAFE AN ANCIENT, MUTUAL DESTINY.
WE DO NOT HAVE THE LUXURY OF CONSIDERING THE INTERESTS OF OTHERS. WE ARE REQUIRED TO MAKE HARD CHOICES, DRIVEN BY SELF-INTEREST.
THESE MAY NOT SUIT THE "REST" OF THE GALAXY...
...BUT THE SHI'AR THREATEN US. THEY INJURE US.
ONLY A FOOL WOULD NOT EXPECT US TO DEFEND OURSELVES.
ARE YOU A FOOL, STAR-LORD OF THE GUARDIANS?

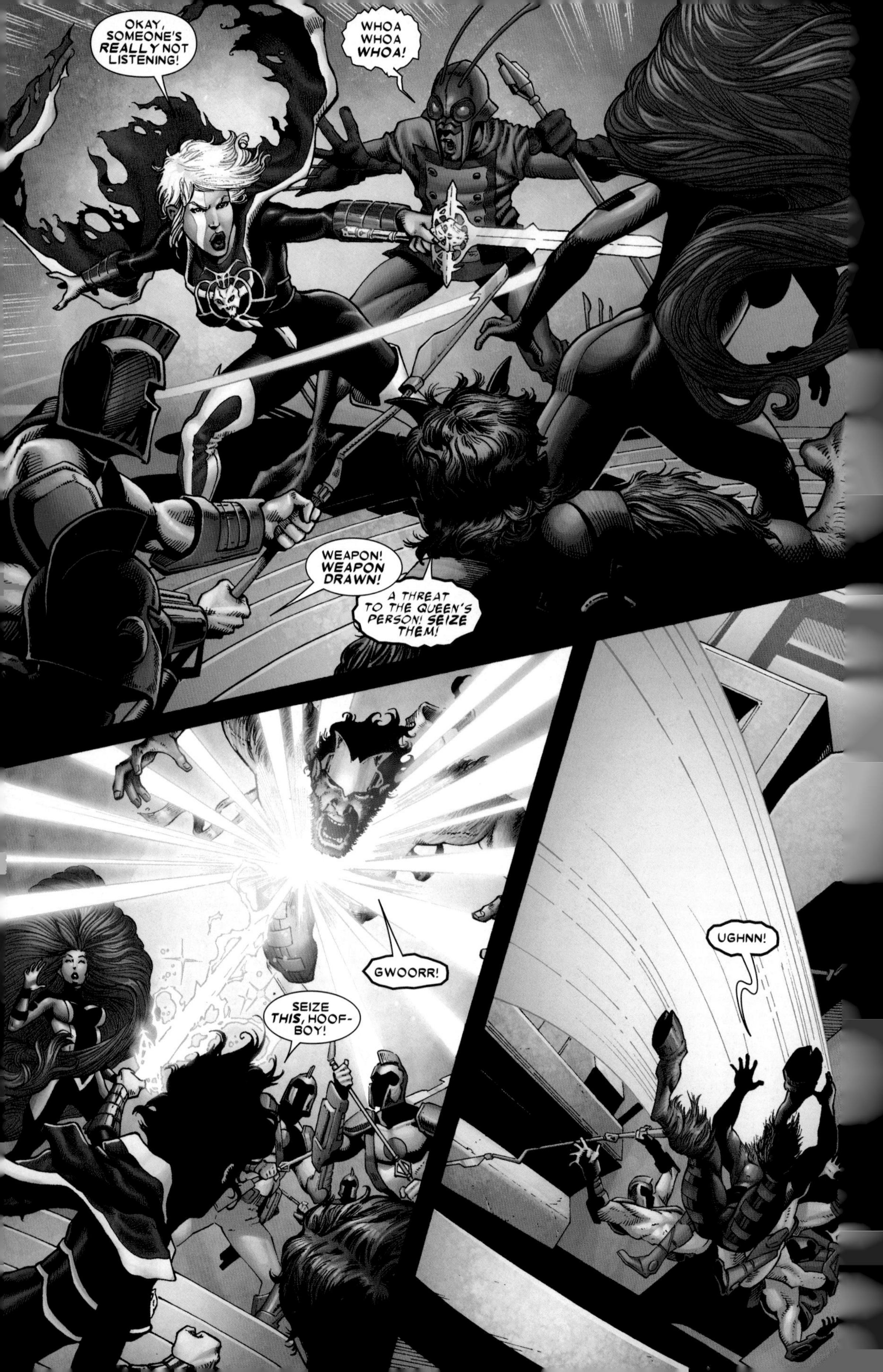
OKAY, SOMEONE'S REALLY NOT LISTENING!
WHOA WHOA WHOA!
WEAPON! WEAPON DRAWN!
A THREAT TO THE QUEEN'S PERSON! SEIZE THEM!
GWOORR!
SEIZE THIS, HOOF-BOY!
UGHNN!

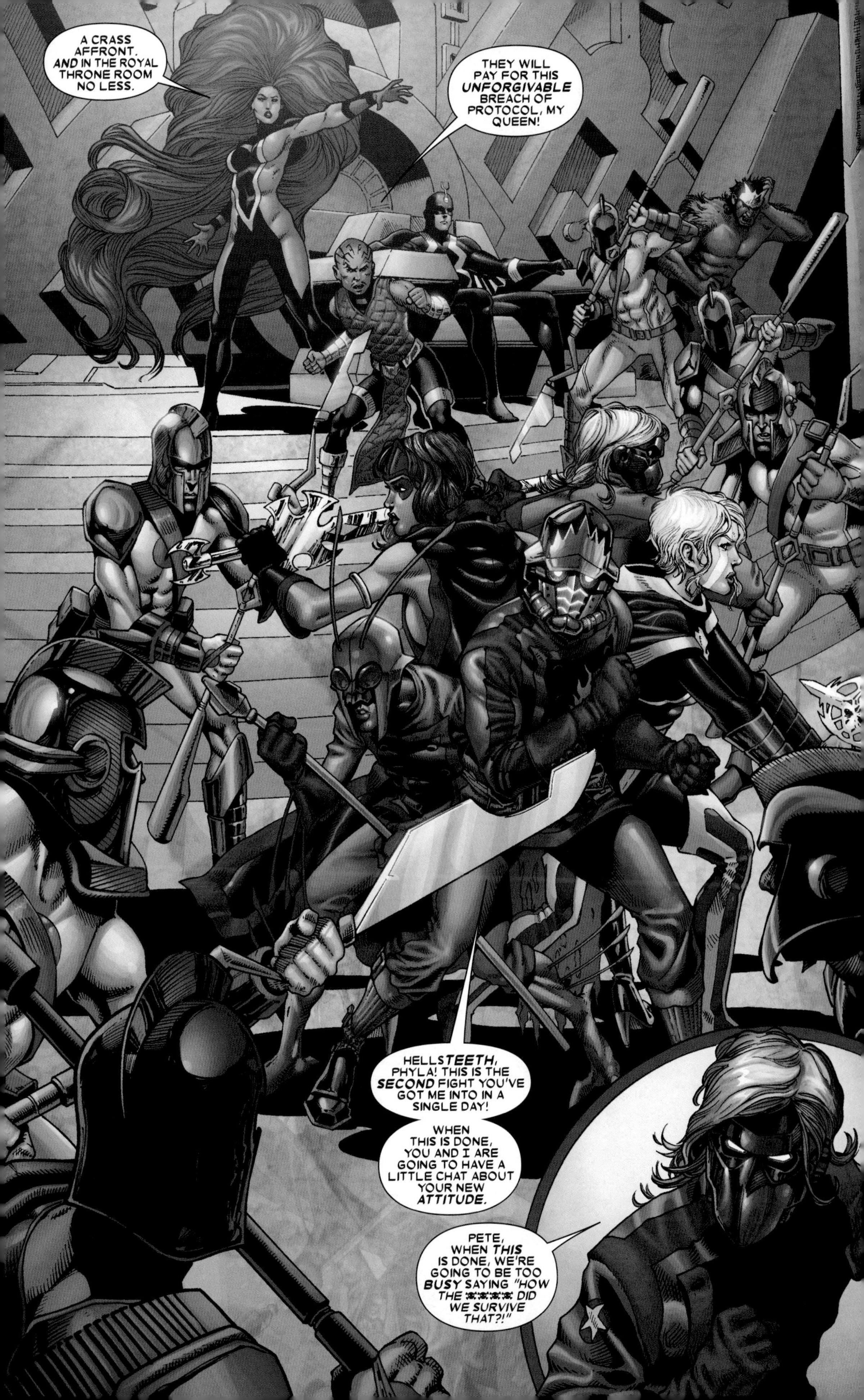
A CRASS AFFRONT. *AND* IN THE ROYAL THRONE ROOM NO LESS.
THEY WILL PAY FOR THIS *UNFORGIVABLE* BREACH OF PROTOCOL, MY QUEEN!
HELLS*TEETH*, PHYLA! THIS IS THE *SECOND* FIGHT YOU'VE GOT ME INTO IN A SINGLE DAY!
WHEN THIS IS DONE, YOU AND I ARE GOING TO HAVE A LITTLE CHAT ABOUT YOUR NEW *ATTITUDE*.
PETE, WHEN *THIS* IS DONE, WE'RE GOING TO BE TOO *BUSY* SAYING *"HOW THE ✱✱✱✱ DID WE SURVIVE THAT?!"*

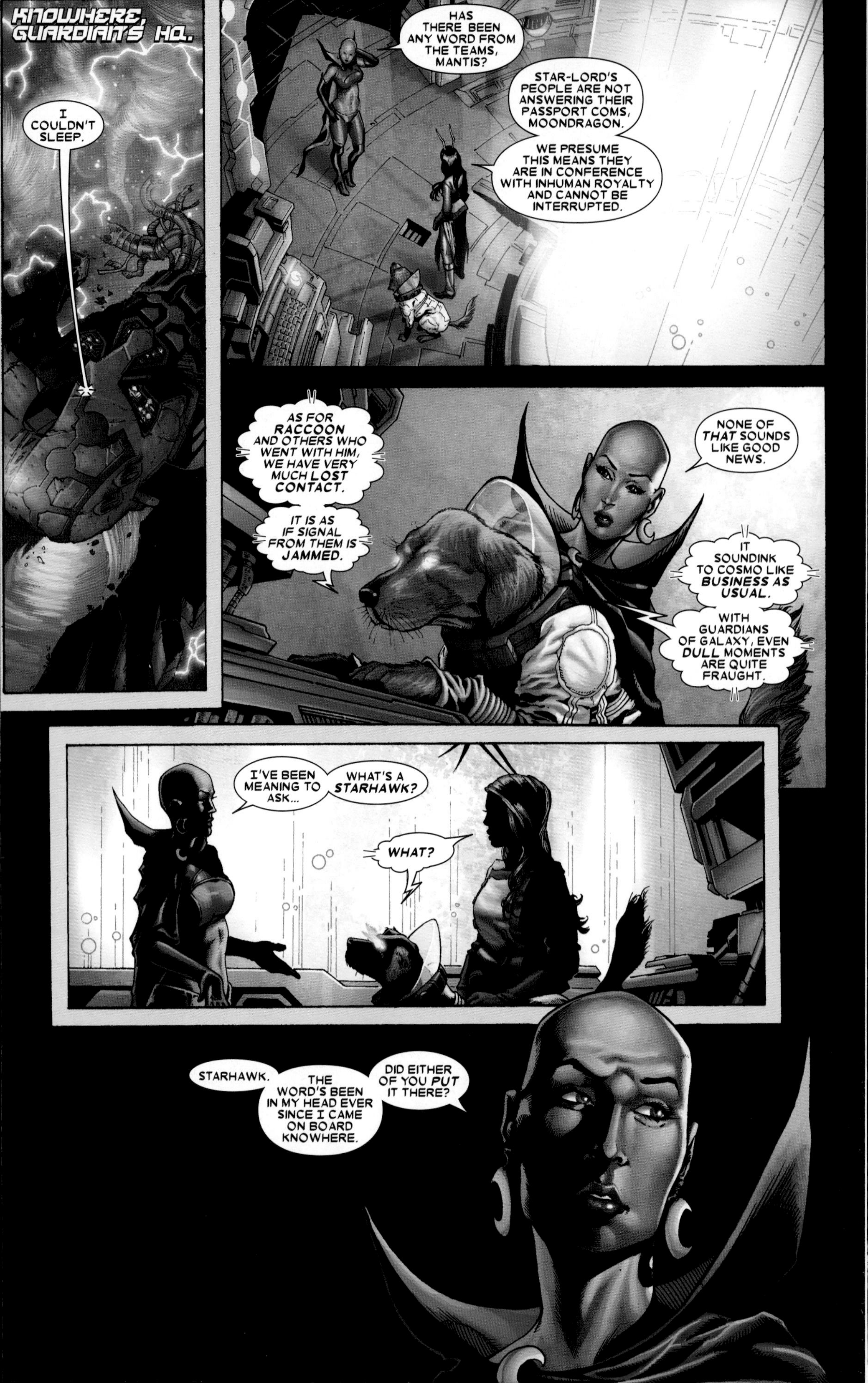
KNOWHERE, GUARDIANS HQ.
I COULDN'T SLEEP.
HAS THERE BEEN ANY WORD FROM THE TEAMS, MANTIS?
STAR-LORD'S PEOPLE ARE NOT ANSWERING THEIR PASSPORT COMS, MOONDRAGON.
WE PRESUME THIS MEANS THEY ARE IN CONFERENCE WITH INHUMAN ROYALTY AND CANNOT BE INTERRUPTED.
AS FOR RACCOON AND OTHERS WHO WENT WITH HIM, WE HAVE VERY MUCH LOST CONTACT.
IT IS AS IF SIGNAL FROM THEM IS JAMMED.
NONE OF THAT SOUNDS LIKE GOOD NEWS.
IT SOUNDINK TO COSMO LIKE BUSINESS AS USUAL.
WITH GUARDIANS OF GALAXY, EVEN DULL MOMENTS ARE QUITE FRAUGHT.
I'VE BEEN MEANING TO ASK...
WHAT'S A STARHAWK?
WHAT?
STARHAWK.
THE WORD'S BEEN IN MY HEAD EVER SINCE I CAME ON BOARD KNOWHERE.
DID EITHER OF YOU PUT IT THERE?

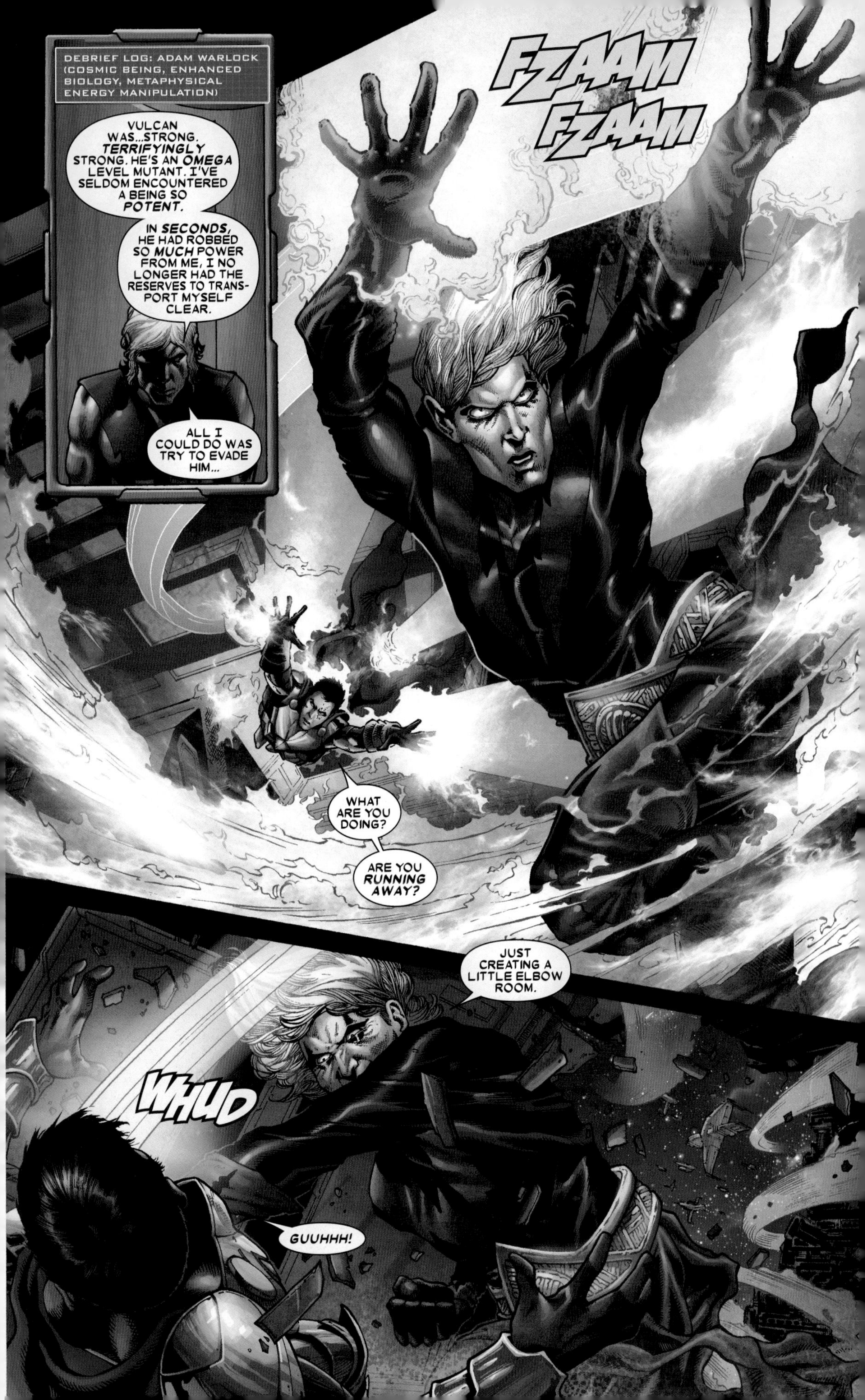
DEBRIEF LOG: ADAM WARLOCK (COSMIC BEING, ENHANCED BIOLOGY, METAPHYSICAL ENERGY MANIPULATION)
VULCAN WAS...STRONG. TERRIFYINGLY STRONG. HE'S AN OMEGA LEVEL MUTANT. I'VE SELDOM ENCOUNTERED A BEING SO POTENT.
IN SECONDS, HE HAD ROBBED SO MUCH POWER FROM ME, I NO LONGER HAD THE RESERVES TO TRANSPORT MYSELF CLEAR.
ALL I COULD DO WAS TRY TO EVADE HIM...
FZAAM FZAAM
WHAT ARE YOU DOING?
ARE YOU RUNNING AWAY?
JUST CREATING A LITTLE ELBOW ROOM.
WHUD
GUUHHH!

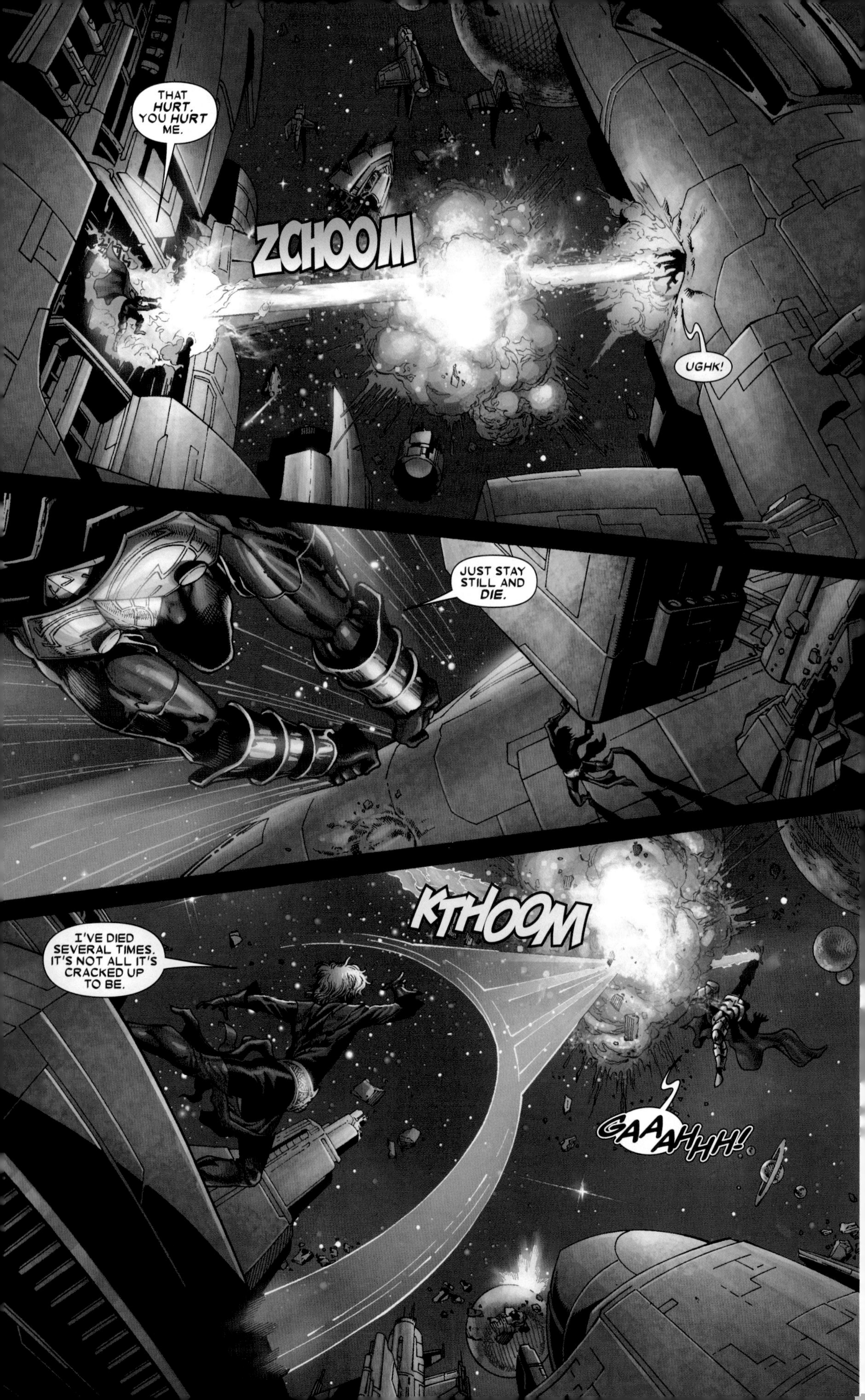
THAT HURT. YOU HURT ME.
ZCHOOM
UGHK!
JUST STAY STILL AND DIE.
KTHOOM
I'VE DIED SEVERAL TIMES. IT'S NOT ALL IT'S CRACKED UP TO BE.
GAAAHHH!

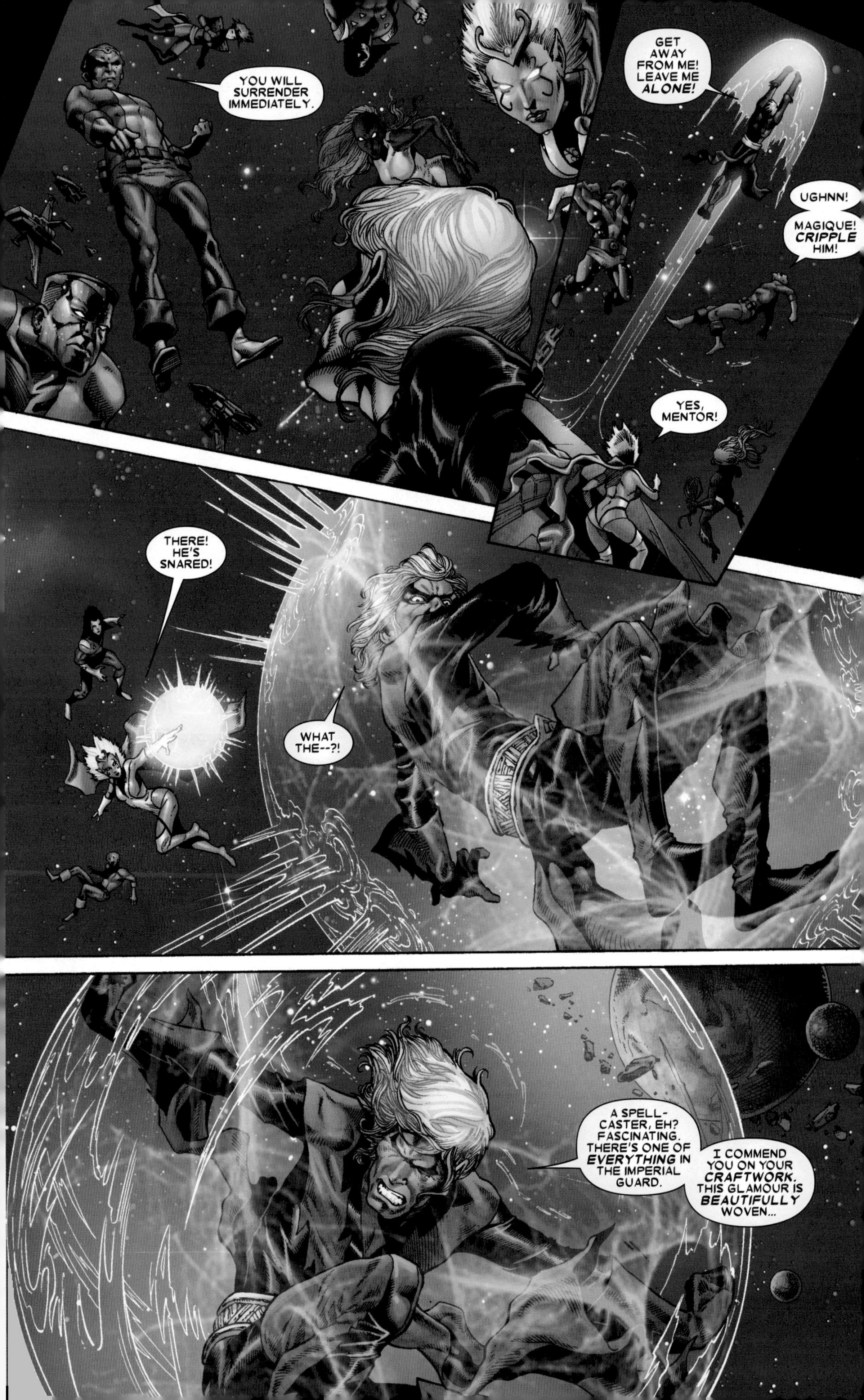
YOU WILL SURRENDER IMMEDIATELY.
GET AWAY FROM ME! LEAVE ME ALONE!
UGHNN!
MAGIQUE! CRIPPLE HIM!
YES, MENTOR!
THERE! HE'S SNARED!
WHAT THE--?!
A SPELL-CASTER, EH? FASCINATING. THERE'S ONE OF EVERYTHING IN THE IMPERIAL GUARD.
I COMMEND YOU ON YOUR CRAFTWORK. THIS GLAMOUR IS BEAUTIFULLY WOVEN...

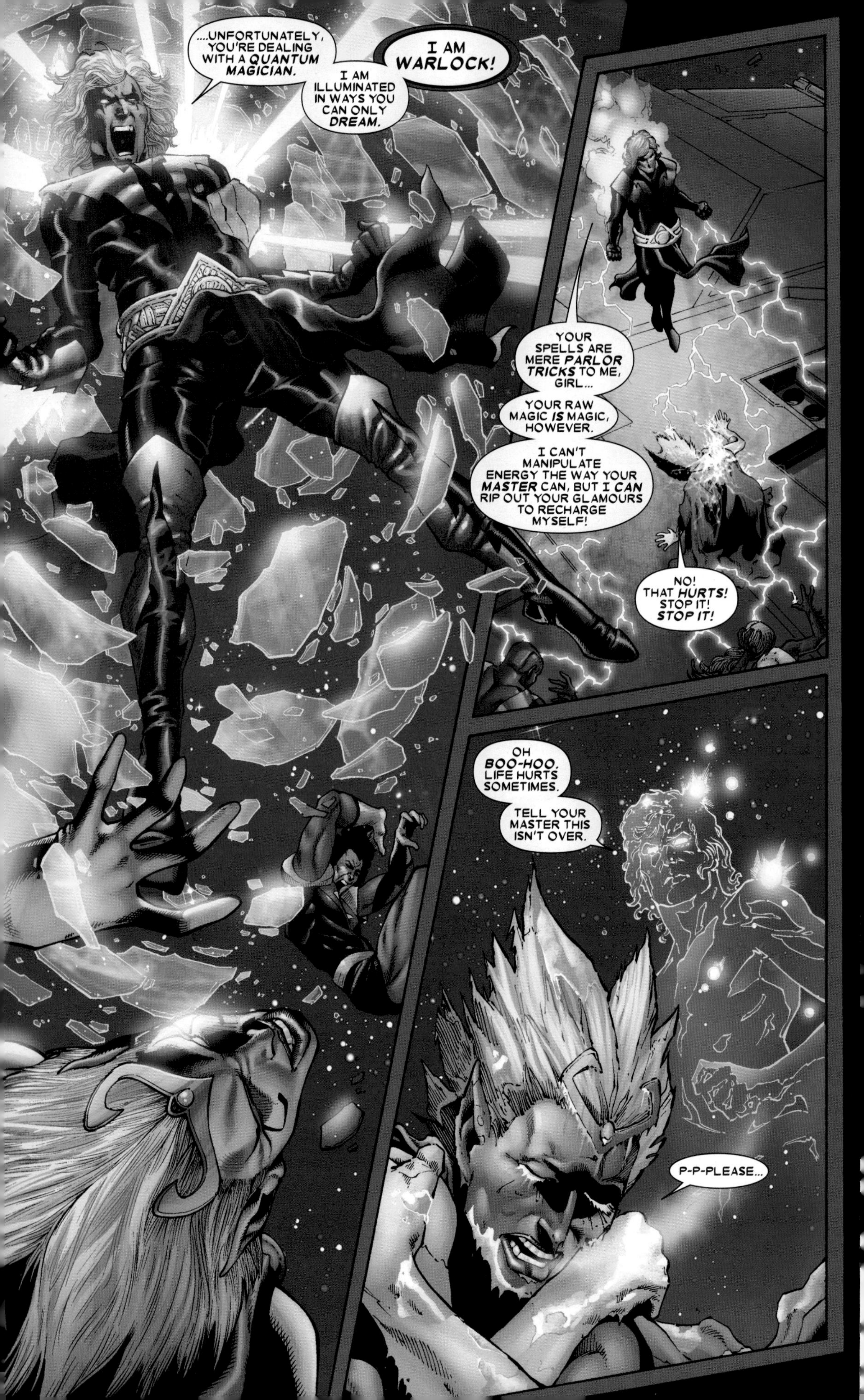
....UNFORTUNATELY, YOU'RE DEALING WITH A QUANTUM MAGICIAN.
I AM ILLUMINATED IN WAYS YOU CAN ONLY DREAM.
I AM WARLOCK!
YOUR SPELLS ARE MERE PARLOR TRICKS TO ME, GIRL...
YOUR RAW MAGIC IS MAGIC, HOWEVER.
I CAN'T MANIPULATE ENERGY THE WAY YOUR MASTER CAN, BUT I CAN RIP OUT YOUR GLAMOURS TO RECHARGE MYSELF!
NO! THAT HURTS! STOP IT! STOP IT!
OH BOO-HOO. LIFE HURTS SOMETIMES.
TELL YOUR MASTER THIS ISN'T OVER.
P-P-PLEASE...

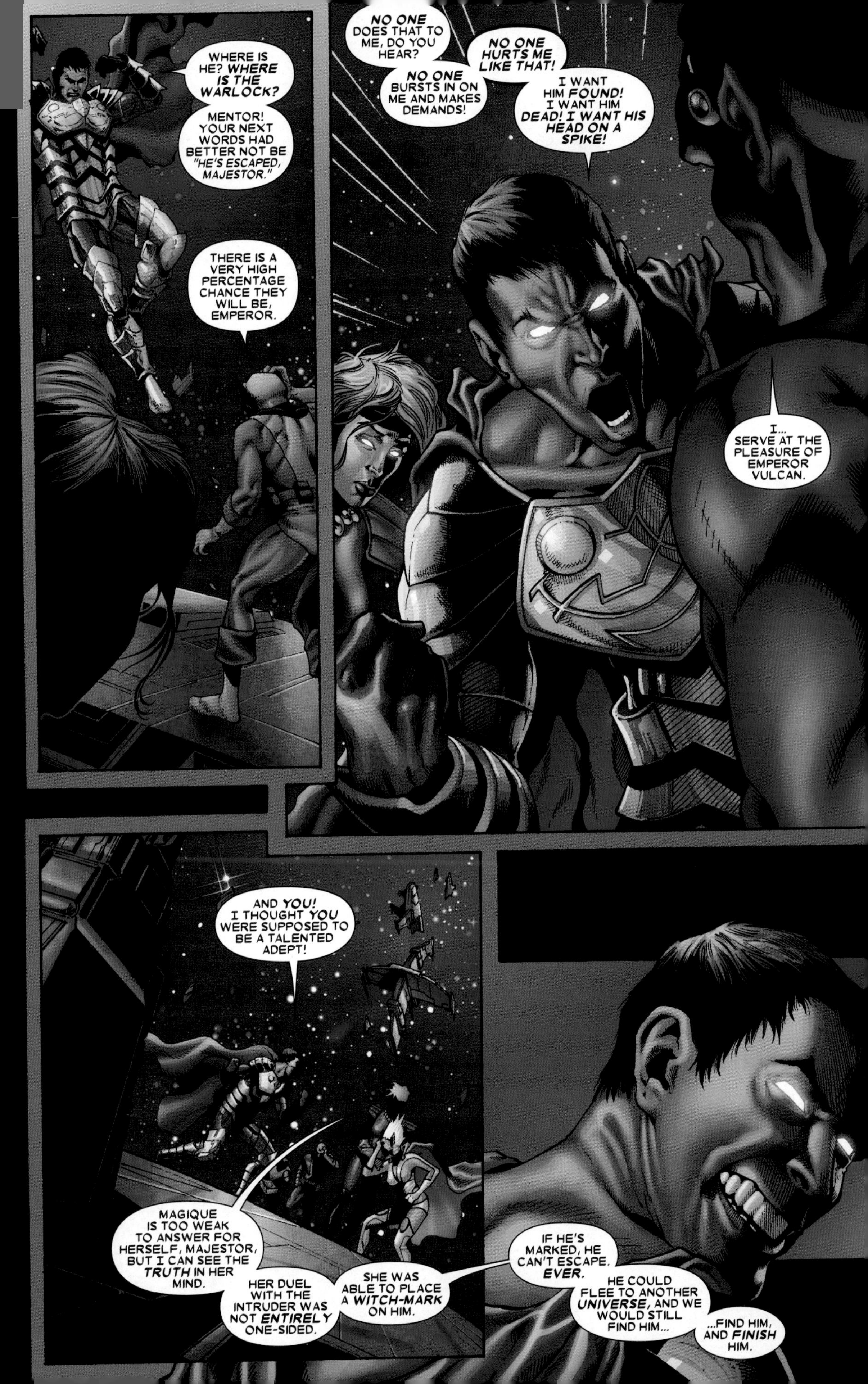
WHERE IS HE? WHERE IS THE WARLOCK?
MENTOR! YOUR NEXT WORDS HAD BETTER NOT BE "HE'S ESCAPED, MAJESTOR."
THERE IS A VERY HIGH PERCENTAGE CHANCE THEY WILL BE, EMPEROR.
NO ONE DOES THAT TO ME, DO YOU HEAR?
NO ONE BURSTS IN ON ME AND MAKES DEMANDS!
NO ONE HURTS ME LIKE THAT!
I WANT HIM FOUND! I WANT HIM DEAD! I WANT HIS HEAD ON A SPIKE!
I... SERVE AT THE PLEASURE OF EMPEROR VULCAN.
AND YOU! I THOUGHT YOU WERE SUPPOSED TO BE A TALENTED ADEPT!
MAGIQUE IS TOO WEAK TO ANSWER FOR HERSELF, MAJESTOR, BUT I CAN SEE THE TRUTH IN HER MIND.
HER DUEL WITH THE INTRUDER WAS NOT ENTIRELY ONE-SIDED.
SHE WAS ABLE TO PLACE A WITCH-MARK ON HIM.
IF HE'S MARKED, HE CAN'T ESCAPE. EVER.
HE COULD FLEE TO ANOTHER UNIVERSE, AND WE WOULD STILL FIND HIM...
...FIND HIM, AND FINISH HIM.

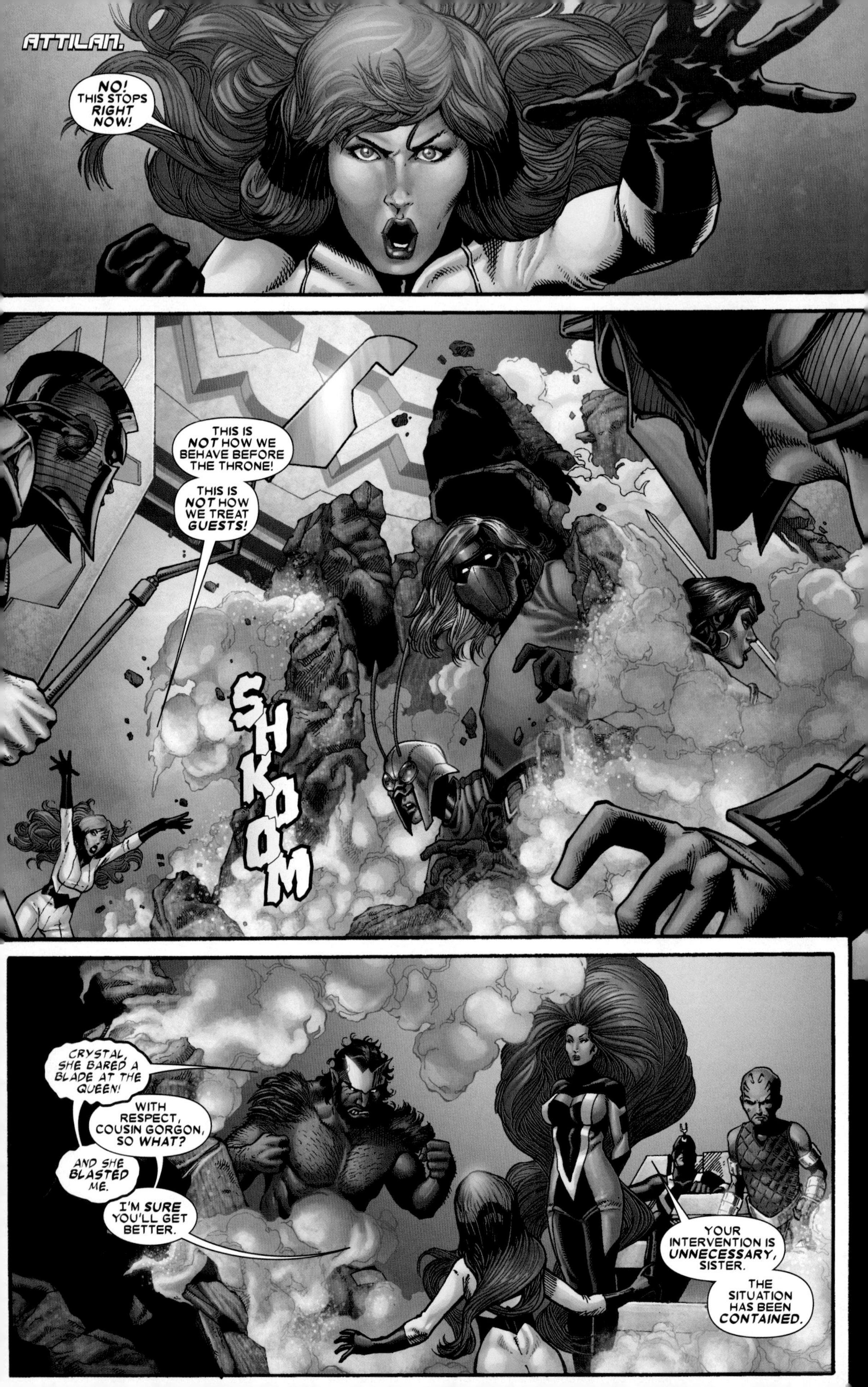

ATTILAN.
NO! THIS STOPS RIGHT NOW!
THIS IS NOT HOW WE BEHAVE BEFORE THE THRONE!
THIS IS NOT HOW WE TREAT GUESTS!
SHKOOM
CRYSTAL, SHE BARED A BLADE AT THE QUEEN!
WITH RESPECT, COUSIN GORGON, SO WHAT?
AND SHE BLASTED ME.
I'M SURE YOU'LL GET BETTER.
YOUR INTERVENTION IS UNNECESSARY, SISTER.
THE SITUATION HAS BEEN CONTAINED.

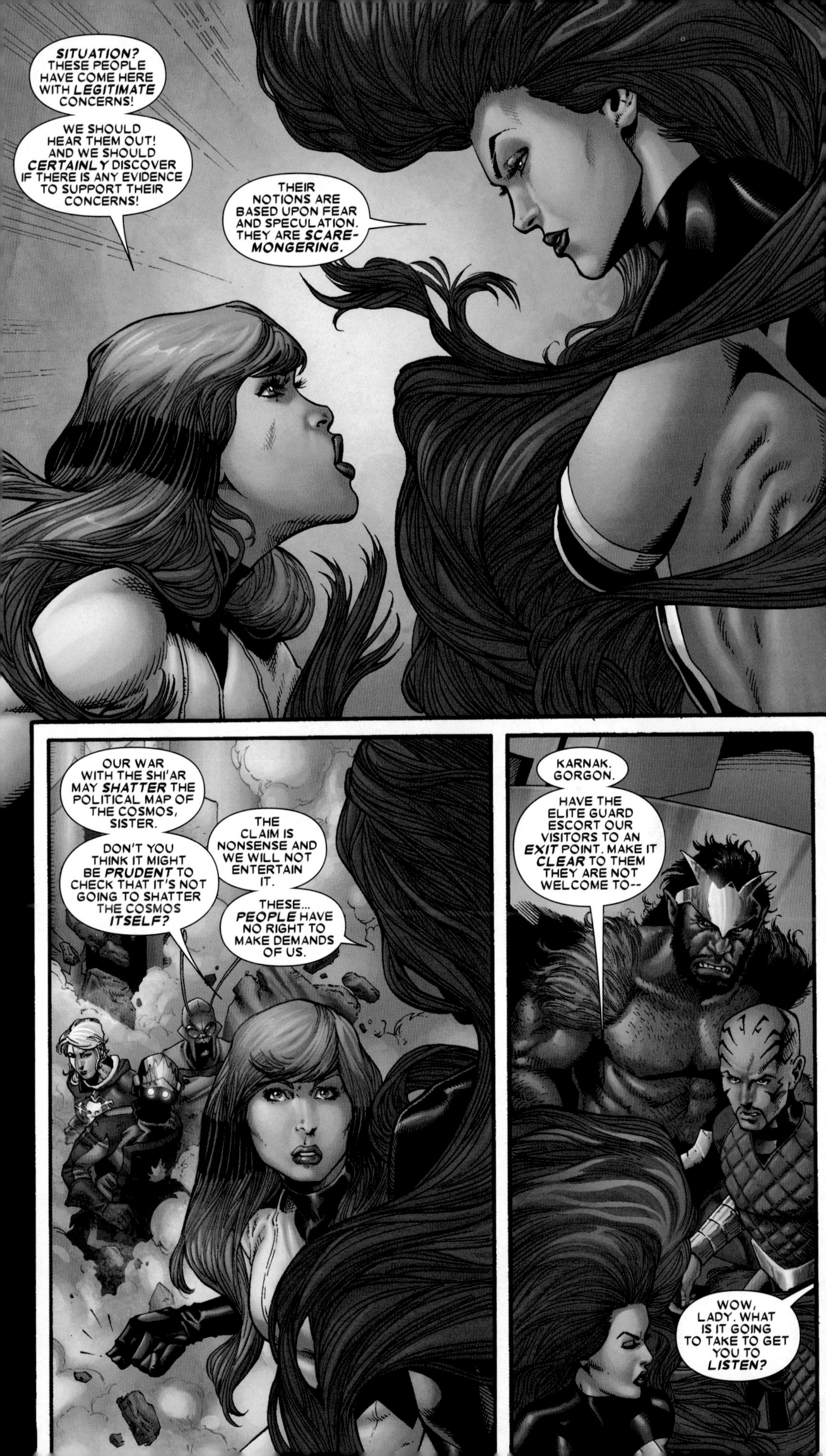
SITUATION? THESE PEOPLE HAVE COME HERE WITH LEGITIMATE CONCERNS!
WE SHOULD HEAR THEM OUT! AND WE SHOULD CERTAINLY DISCOVER IF THERE IS ANY EVIDENCE TO SUPPORT THEIR CONCERNS!
THEIR NOTIONS ARE BASED UPON FEAR AND SPECULATION. THEY ARE SCARE-MONGERING.
OUR WAR WITH THE SHI'AR MAY SHATTER THE POLITICAL MAP OF THE COSMOS, SISTER.
DON'T YOU THINK IT MIGHT BE PRUDENT TO CHECK THAT IT'S NOT GOING TO SHATTER THE COSMOS ITSELF?
THE CLAIM IS NONSENSE AND WE WILL NOT ENTERTAIN IT.
THESE... PEOPLE HAVE NO RIGHT TO MAKE DEMANDS OF US.
KARNAK. GORGON.
HAVE THE ELITE GUARD ESCORT OUR VISITORS TO AN EXIT POINT. MAKE IT CLEAR TO THEM THEY ARE NOT WELCOME TO--
WOW, LADY. WHAT IS IT GOING TO TAKE TO GET YOU TO LISTEN?

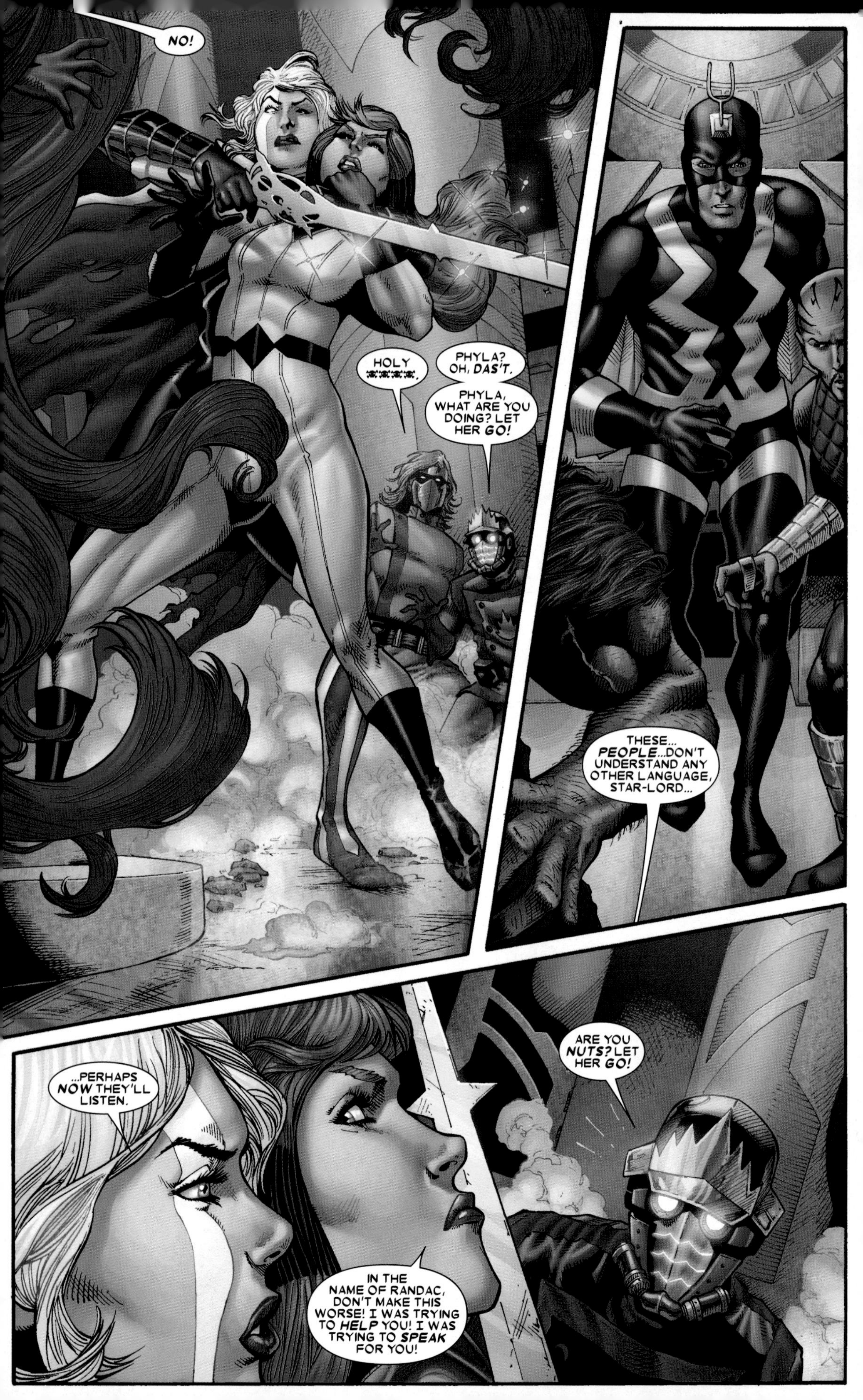
NO!
HOLY [symbols].
PHYLA? OH, DAS'T.
PHYLA, WHAT ARE YOU DOING? LET HER GO!
THESE... PEOPLE...DON'T UNDERSTAND ANY OTHER LANGUAGE, STAR-LORD...
...PERHAPS NOW THEY'LL LISTEN.
ARE YOU NUTS? LET HER GO!
IN THE NAME OF RANDAC, DON'T MAKE THIS WORSE! I WAS TRYING TO HELP YOU! I WAS TRYING TO SPEAK FOR YOU!

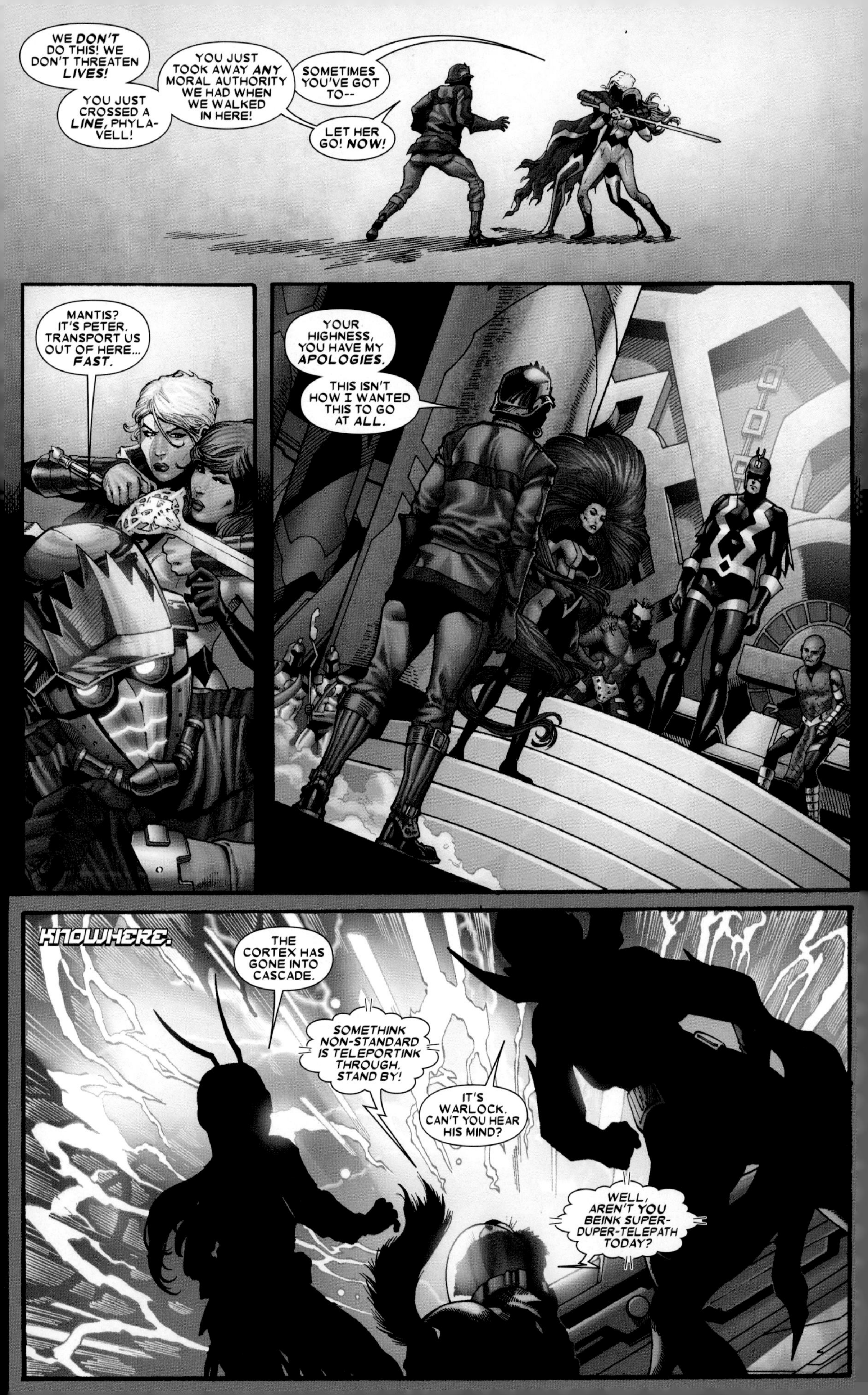
WE DON'T DO THIS! WE DON'T THREATEN LIVES!
YOU JUST CROSSED A LINE, PHYLA-VELL!
YOU JUST TOOK AWAY ANY MORAL AUTHORITY WE HAD WHEN WE WALKED IN HERE!
SOMETIMES YOU'VE GOT TO--
LET HER GO! NOW!
MANTIS? IT'S PETER. TRANSPORT US OUT OF HERE... FAST.
YOUR HIGHNESS, YOU HAVE MY APOLOGIES.
THIS ISN'T HOW I WANTED THIS TO GO AT ALL.
KNOWHERE.
THE CORTEX HAS GONE INTO CASCADE.
SOMETHINK NON-STANDARD IS TELEPORTINK THROUGH. STAND BY!
IT'S WARLOCK. CAN'T YOU HEAR HIS MIND?
WELL, AREN'T YOU BEINK SUPER-DUPER-TELEPATH TODAY?

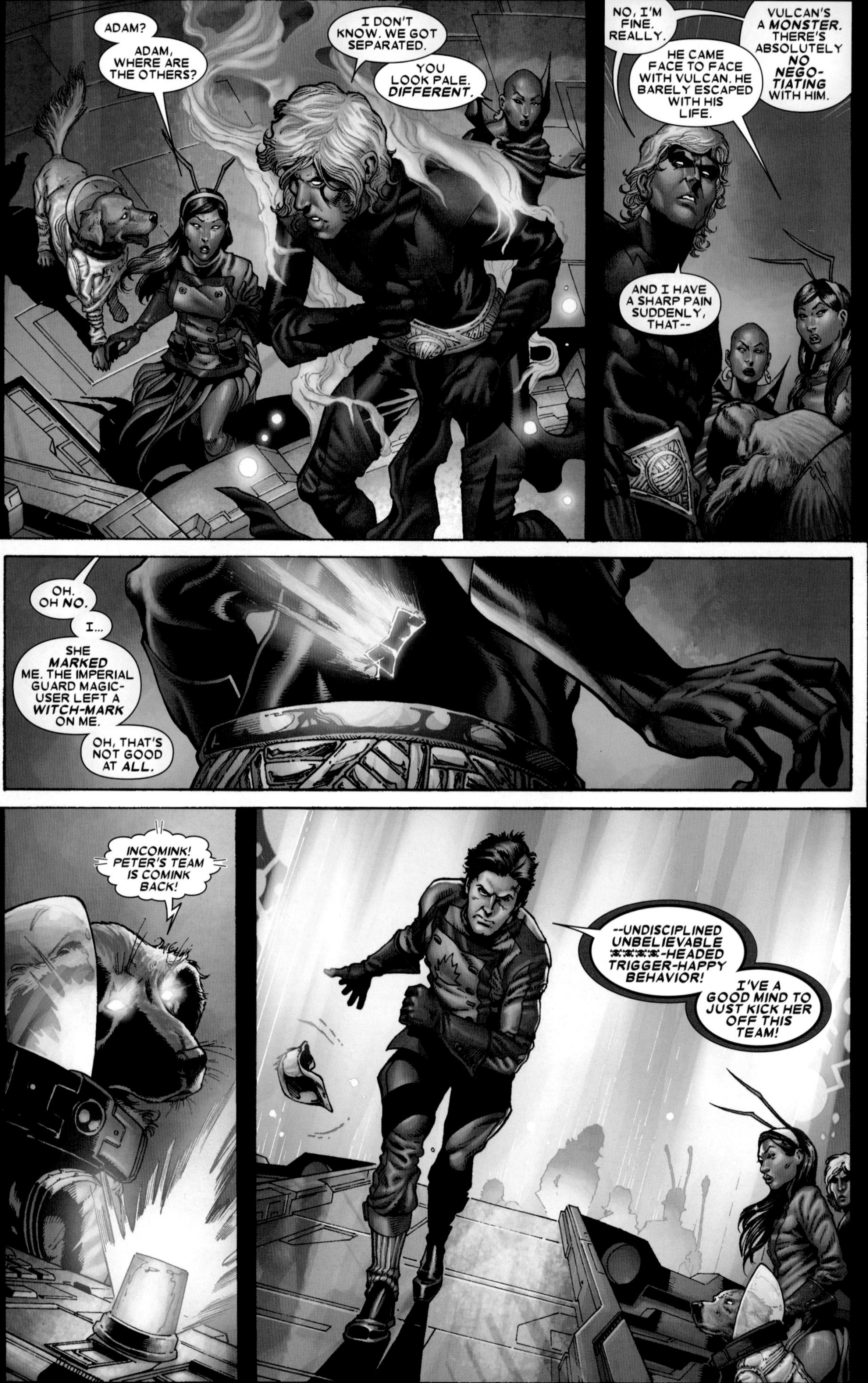
ADAM?
ADAM, WHERE ARE THE OTHERS?
I DON'T KNOW. WE GOT SEPARATED.
YOU LOOK PALE. *DIFFERENT.*
NO, I'M FINE. REALLY.
HE CAME FACE TO FACE WITH VULCAN. HE BARELY ESCAPED WITH HIS LIFE.
VULCAN'S A *MONSTER.* THERE'S ABSOLUTELY *NO NEGO-TIATING* WITH HIM.
AND I HAVE A SHARP PAIN SUDDENLY, THAT--
OH. OH *NO.*
I...
SHE *MARKED* ME. THE IMPERIAL GUARD MAGIC-USER LEFT A *WITCH-MARK* ON ME.
OH, THAT'S NOT GOOD AT *ALL.*
INCOMINK! PETER'S TEAM IS COMINK BACK!
--UNDISCIPLINED UNBELIEVABLE ☠☠☠☠-HEADED TRIGGER-HAPPY BEHAVIOR!
I'VE A GOOD MIND TO JUST KICK HER OFF THIS TEAM!

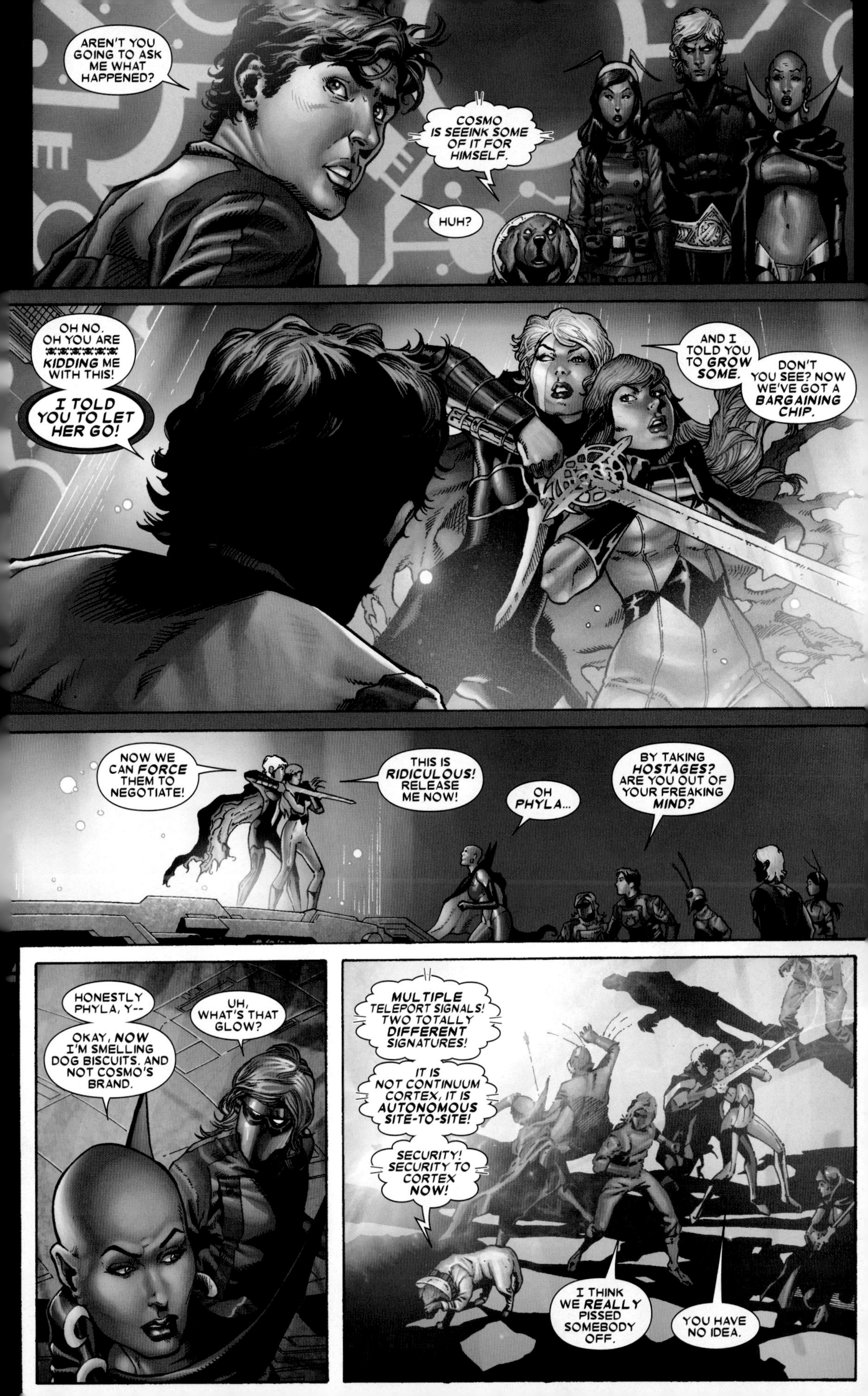
AREN'T YOU GOING TO ASK ME WHAT HAPPENED?
COSMO IS SEEINK SOME OF IT FOR HIMSELF.
HUH?
OH NO. OH YOU ARE KIDDING ME WITH THIS!
I TOLD YOU TO LET HER GO!
AND I TOLD YOU TO GROW SOME.
DON'T YOU SEE? NOW WE'VE GOT A BARGAINING CHIP.
NOW WE CAN FORCE THEM TO NEGOTIATE!
THIS IS RIDICULOUS! RELEASE ME NOW!
OH PHYLA...
BY TAKING HOSTAGES? ARE YOU OUT OF YOUR FREAKING MIND?
HONESTLY PHYLA, Y--
OKAY, NOW I'M SMELLING DOG BISCUITS. AND NOT COSMO'S BRAND.
UH, WHAT'S THAT GLOW?
MULTIPLE TELEPORT SIGNALS! TWO TOTALLY DIFFERENT SIGNATURES!
IT IS NOT CONTINUUM CORTEX, IT IS AUTONOMOUS SITE-TO-SITE!
SECURITY! SECURITY TO CORTEX NOW!
I THINK WE REALLY PISSED SOMEBODY OFF.
YOU HAVE NO IDEA.

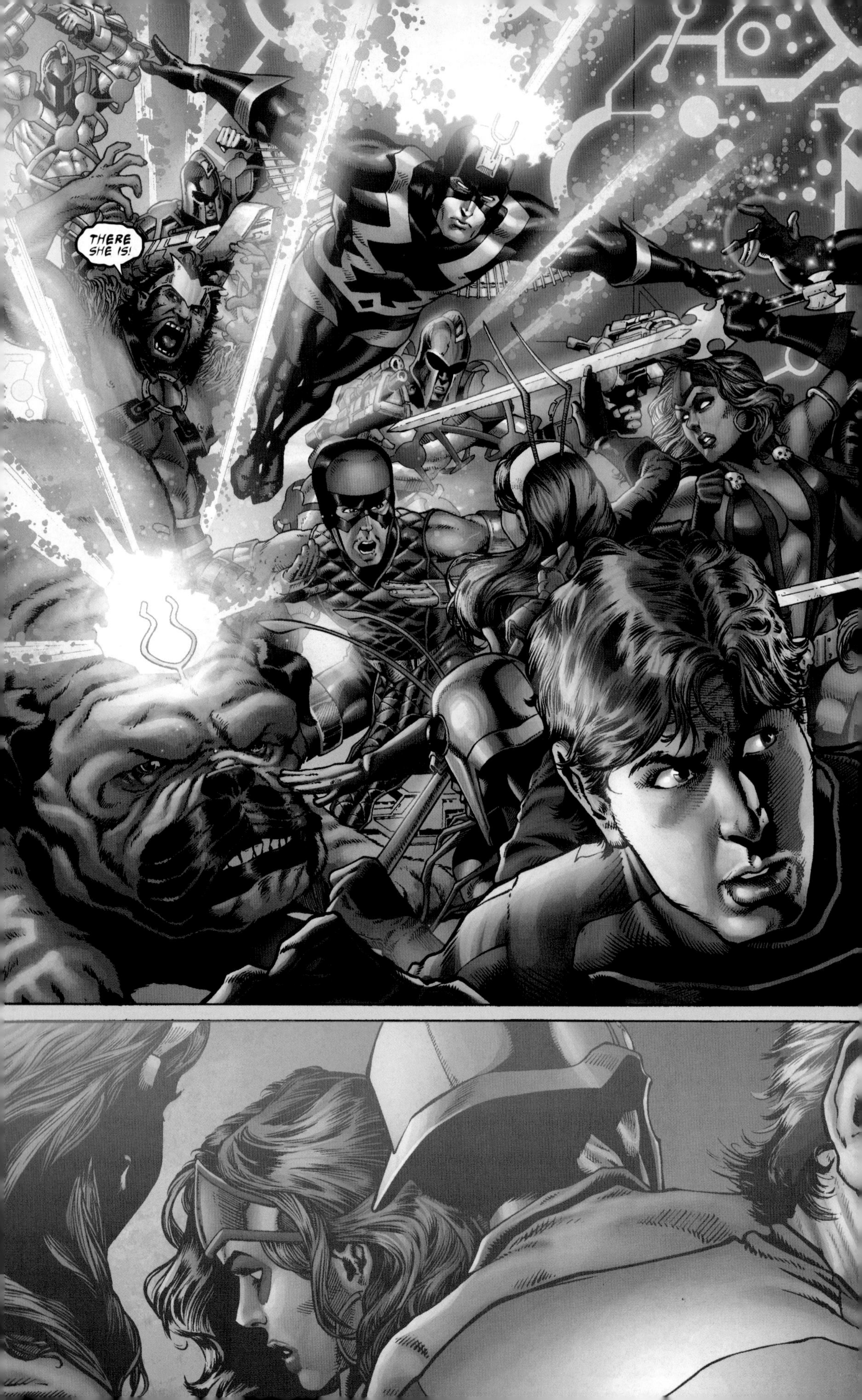
THERE SHE IS!

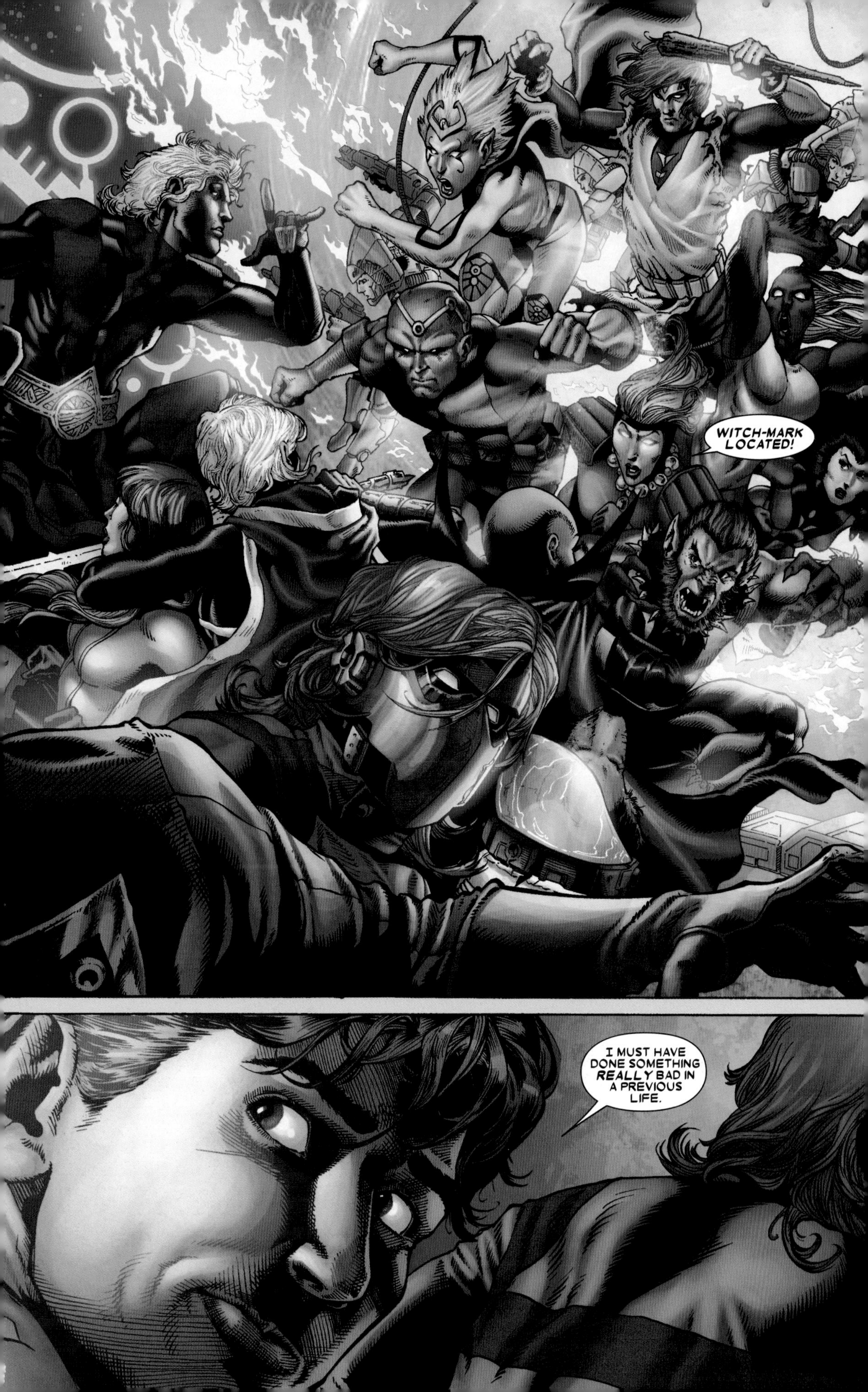
WITCH-MARK LOCATED!
I MUST HAVE DONE SOMETHING REALLY BAD IN A PREVIOUS LIFE.

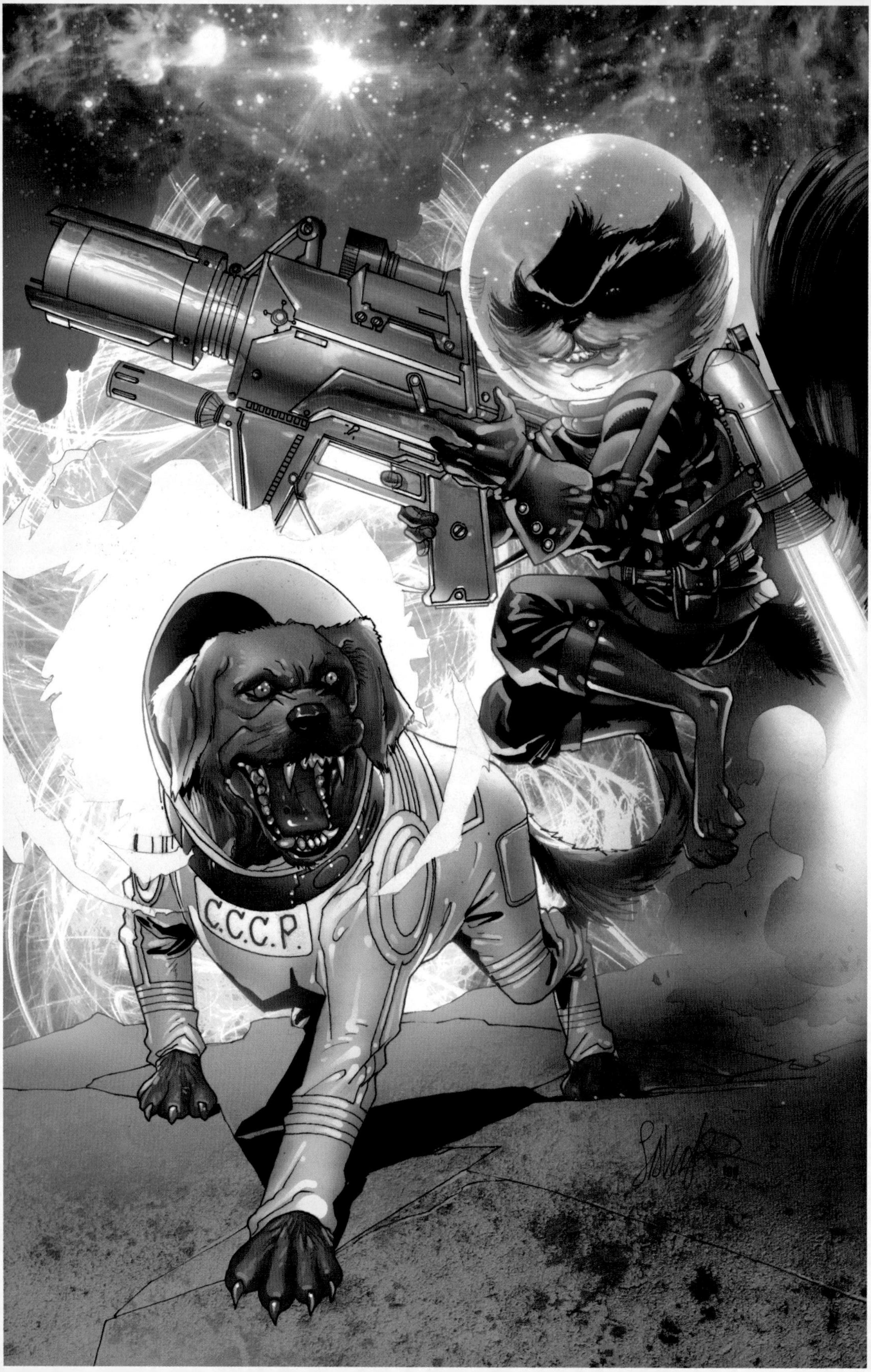
C.C.C.P

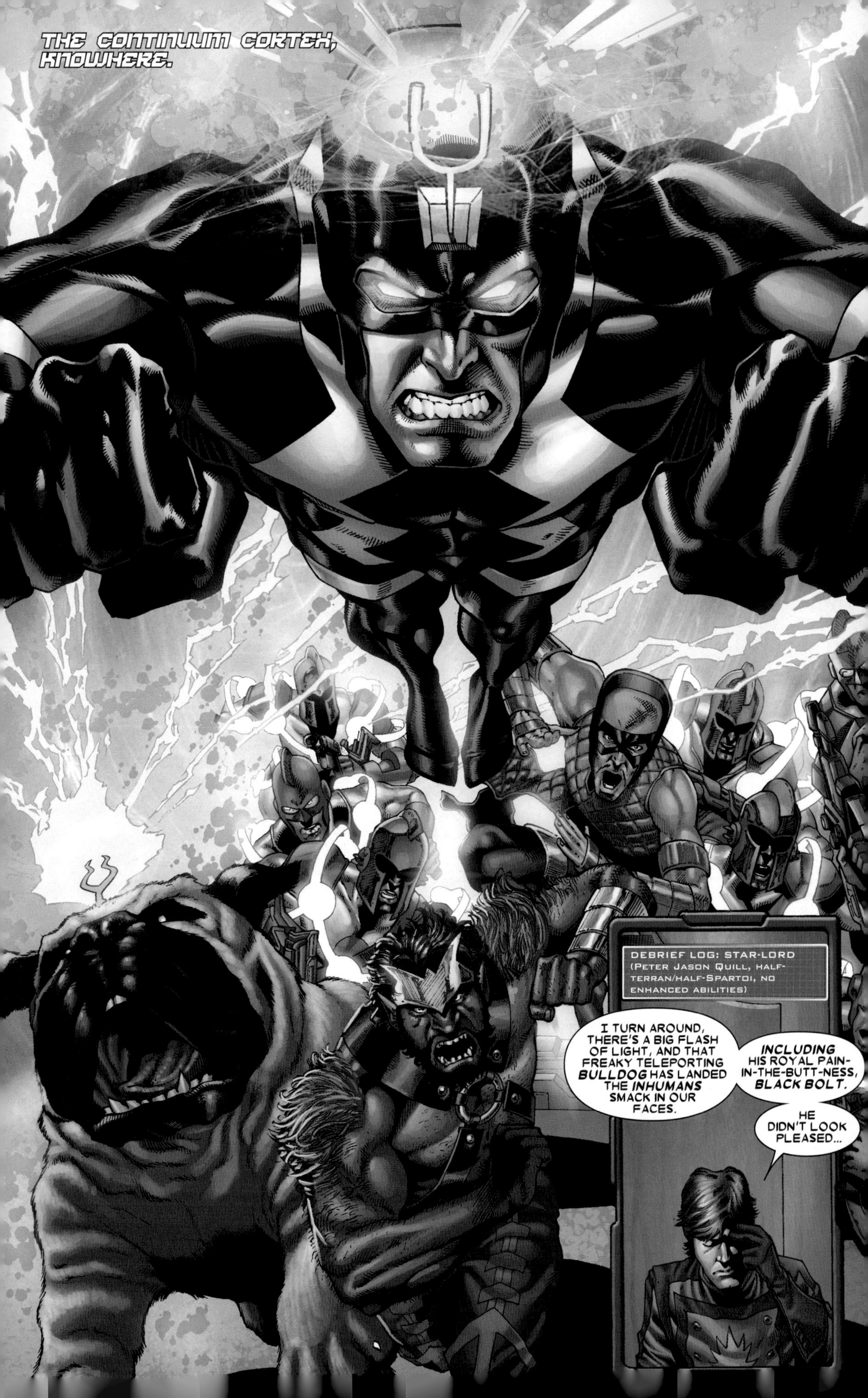
THE CONTINUUM CORTEX, KNOWHERE.
DEBRIEF LOG: STAR-LORD (PETER JASON QUILL, HALF-TERRAN/HALF-SPARTOI, NO ENHANCED ABILITIES)
I TURN AROUND, THERE'S A BIG FLASH OF LIGHT, AND THAT FREAKY TELEPORTING BULLDOG HAS LANDED THE INHUMANS SMACK IN OUR FACES.
INCLUDING HIS ROYAL PAIN-IN-THE-BUTT-NESS, BLACK BOLT.
HE DIDN'T LOOK PLEASED...

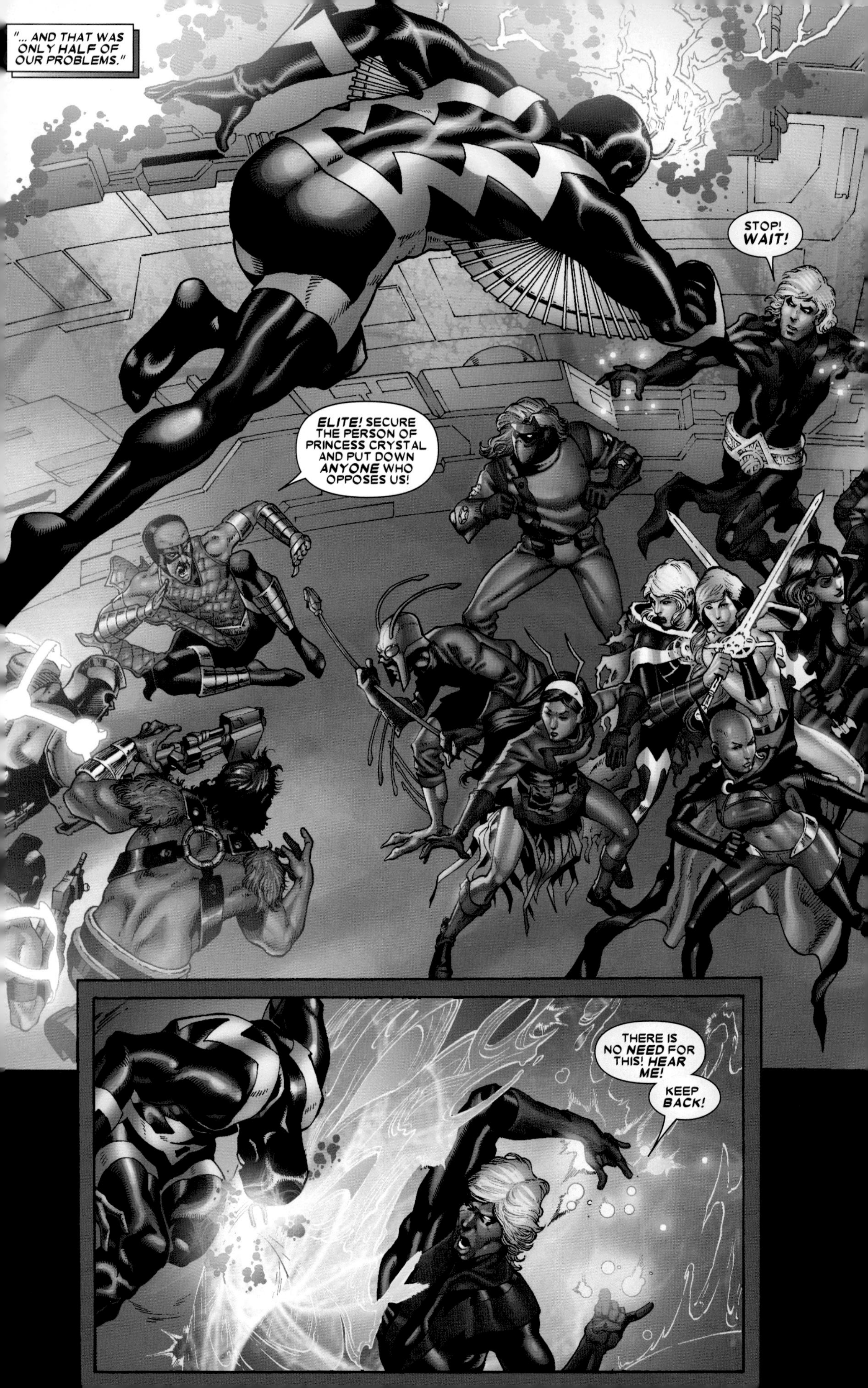
"... AND THAT WAS ONLY HALF OF OUR PROBLEMS."
STOP! WAIT!
ELITE! SECURE THE PERSON OF PRINCESS CRYSTAL AND PUT DOWN ANYONE WHO OPPOSES US!
THERE IS NO NEED FOR THIS! HEAR ME!
KEEP BACK!

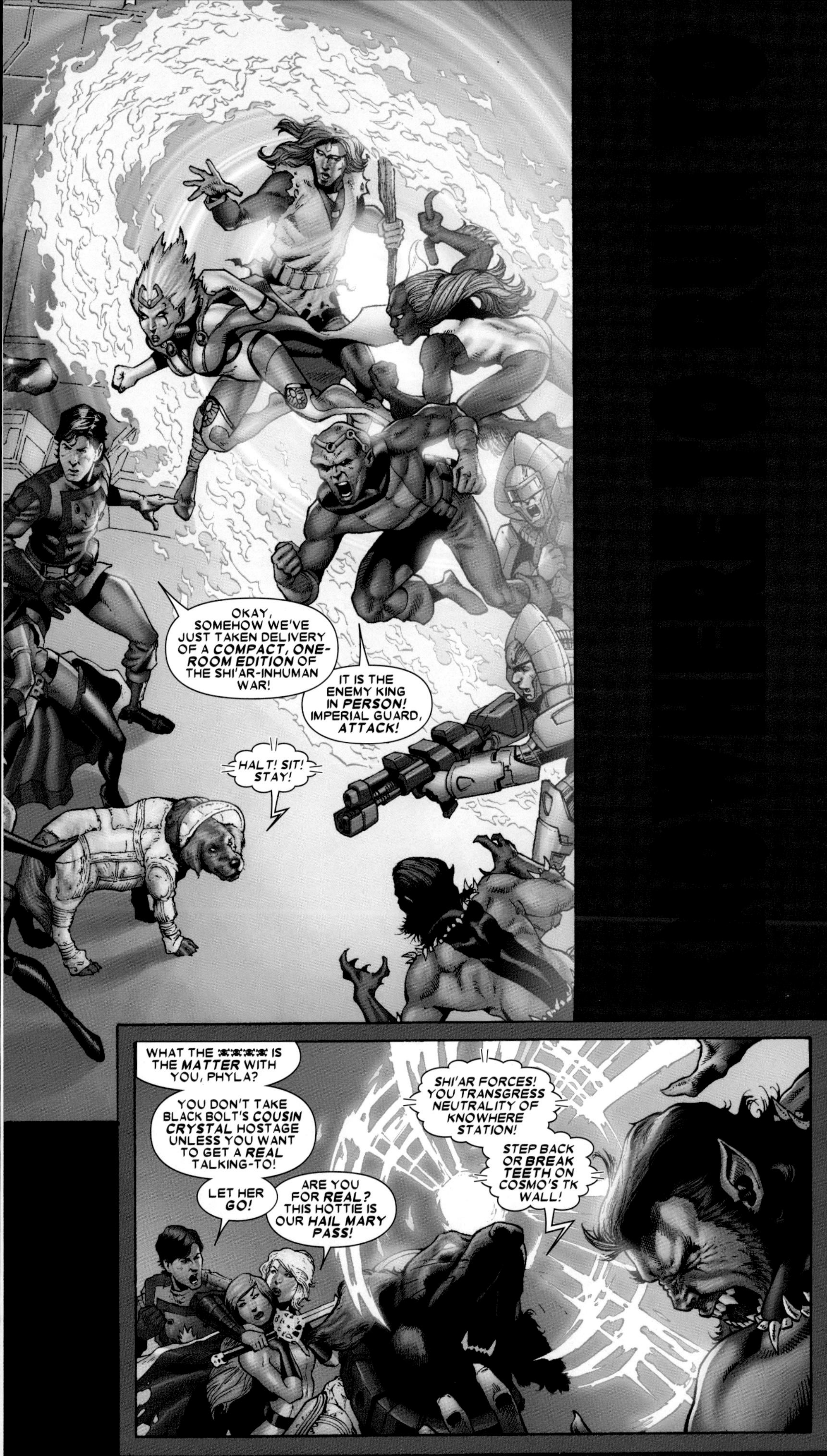
OKAY, SOMEHOW WE'VE JUST TAKEN DELIVERY OF A COMPACT, ONE-ROOM EDITION OF THE SHI'AR-INHUMAN WAR!
IT IS THE ENEMY KING IN PERSON! IMPERIAL GUARD, ATTACK!
HALT! SIT! STAY!
WHAT THE ✱✱✱✱ IS THE MATTER WITH YOU, PHYLA?
YOU DON'T TAKE BLACK BOLT'S COUSIN CRYSTAL HOSTAGE UNLESS YOU WANT TO GET A REAL TALKING-TO!
LET HER GO!
ARE YOU FOR REAL? THIS HOTTIE IS OUR HAIL MARY PASS!
SHI'AR FORCES! YOU TRANSGRESS NEUTRALITY OF KNOWHERE STATION!
STEP BACK OR BREAK TEETH ON COSMO'S TK WALL!

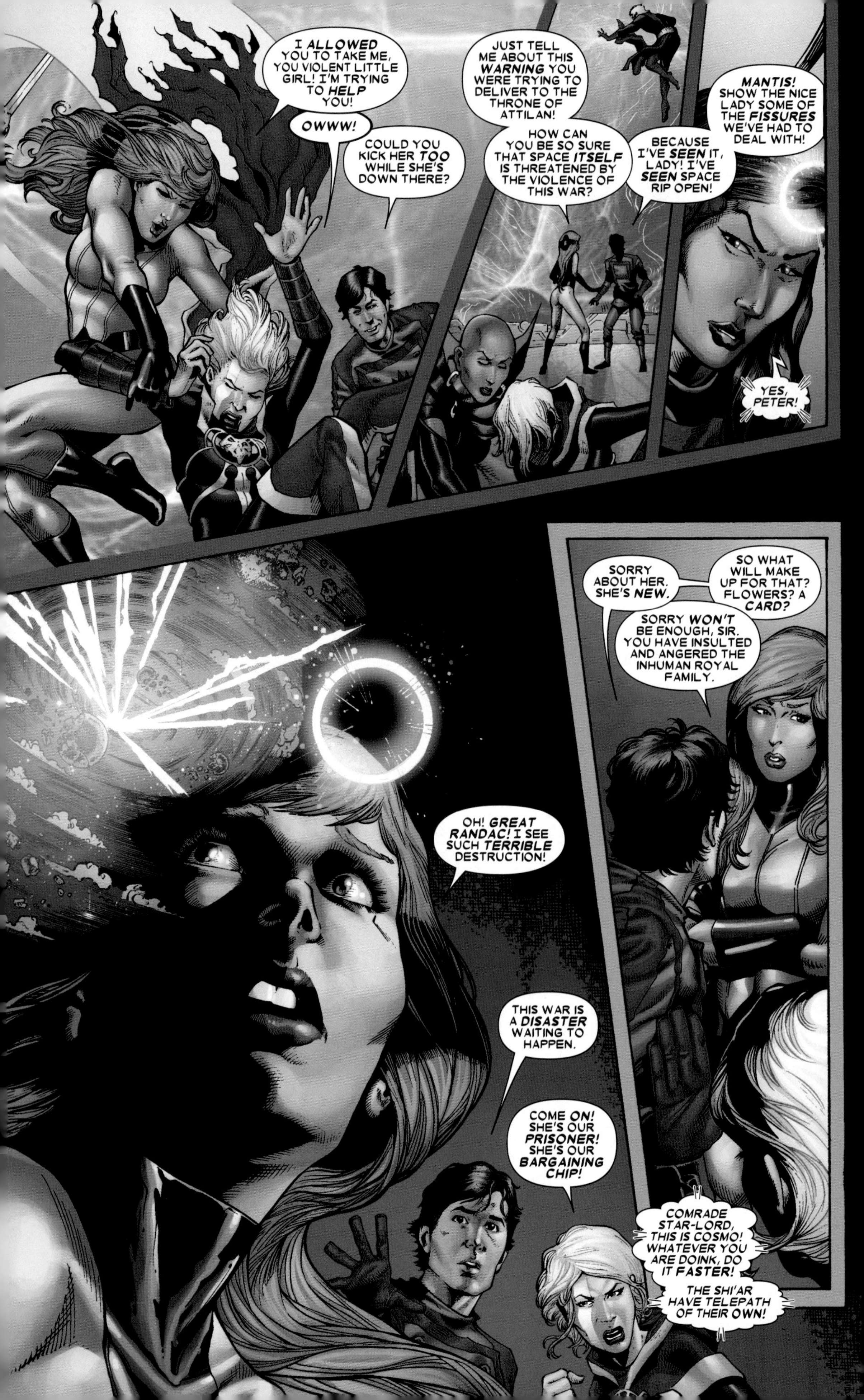
I ALLOWED YOU TO TAKE ME, YOU VIOLENT LITTLE GIRL! I'M TRYING TO HELP YOU!
OWWW!
COULD YOU KICK HER TOO WHILE SHE'S DOWN THERE?
JUST TELL ME ABOUT THIS WARNING YOU WERE TRYING TO DELIVER TO THE THRONE OF ATTILAN!
HOW CAN YOU BE SO SURE THAT SPACE ITSELF IS THREATENED BY THE VIOLENCE OF THIS WAR?
BECAUSE I'VE SEEN IT, LADY! I'VE SEEN SPACE RIP OPEN!
MANTIS! SHOW THE NICE LADY SOME OF THE FISSURES WE'VE HAD TO DEAL WITH!
YES, PETER!
OH! GREAT RANDAC! I SEE SUCH TERRIBLE DESTRUCTION!
THIS WAR IS A DISASTER WAITING TO HAPPEN.
COME ON! SHE'S OUR PRISONER! SHE'S OUR BARGAINING CHIP!
SORRY ABOUT HER. SHE'S NEW.
SO WHAT WILL MAKE UP FOR THAT? FLOWERS? A CARD?
SORRY WON'T BE ENOUGH, SIR. YOU HAVE INSULTED AND ANGERED THE INHUMAN ROYAL FAMILY.
COMRADE STAR-LORD, THIS IS COSMO! WHATEVER YOU ARE DOINK, DO IT FASTER!
THE SHI'AR HAVE TELEPATH OF THEIR OWN!

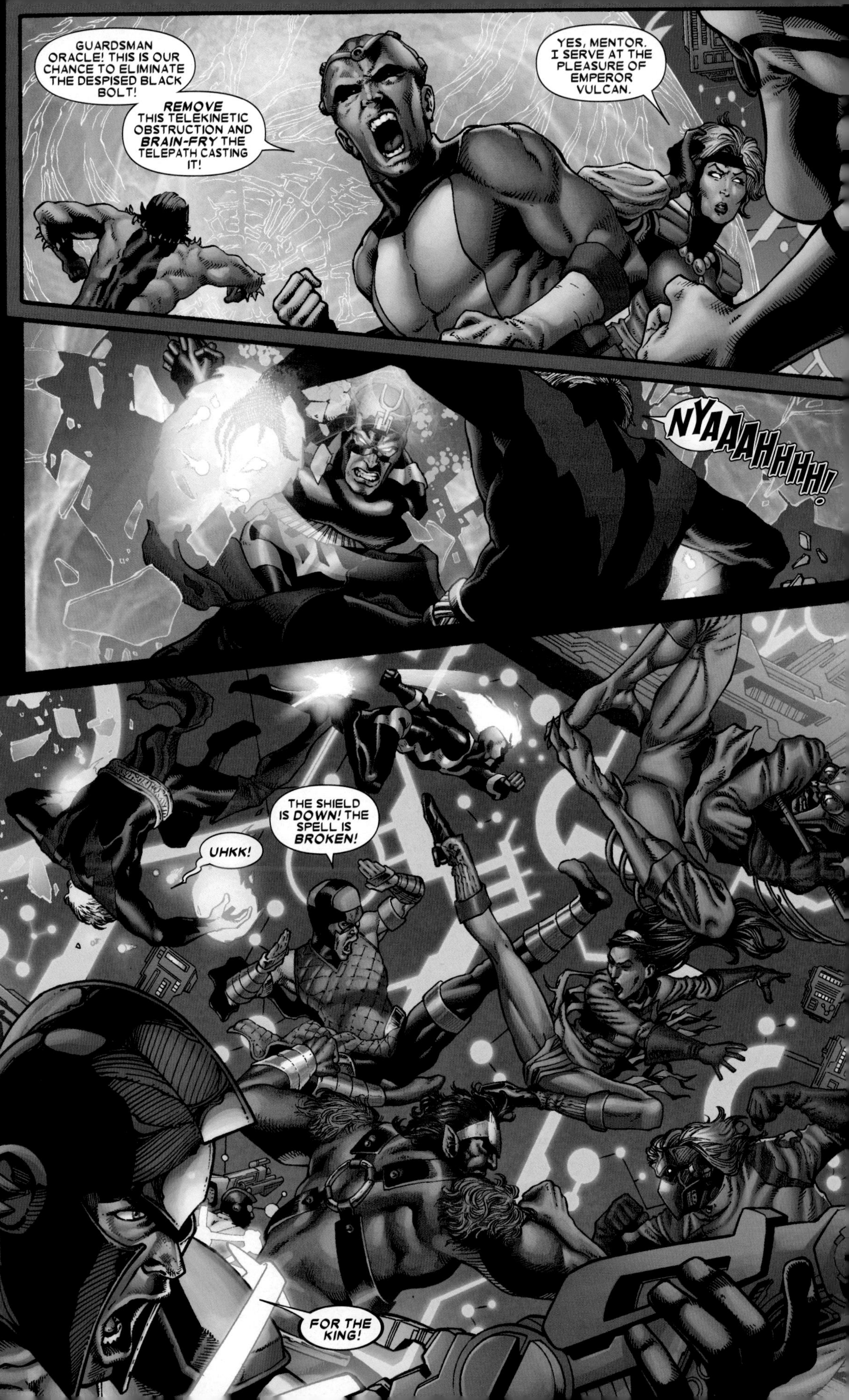
GUARDSMAN ORACLE! THIS IS OUR CHANCE TO ELIMINATE THE DESPISED BLACK BOLT!
REMOVE THIS TELEKINETIC OBSTRUCTION AND BRAIN-FRY THE TELEPATH CASTING IT!
YES, MENTOR. I SERVE AT THE PLEASURE OF EMPEROR VULCAN.
NYAAAAHHHH!
THE SHIELD IS DOWN! THE SPELL IS BROKEN!
UHKK!
FOR THE KING!

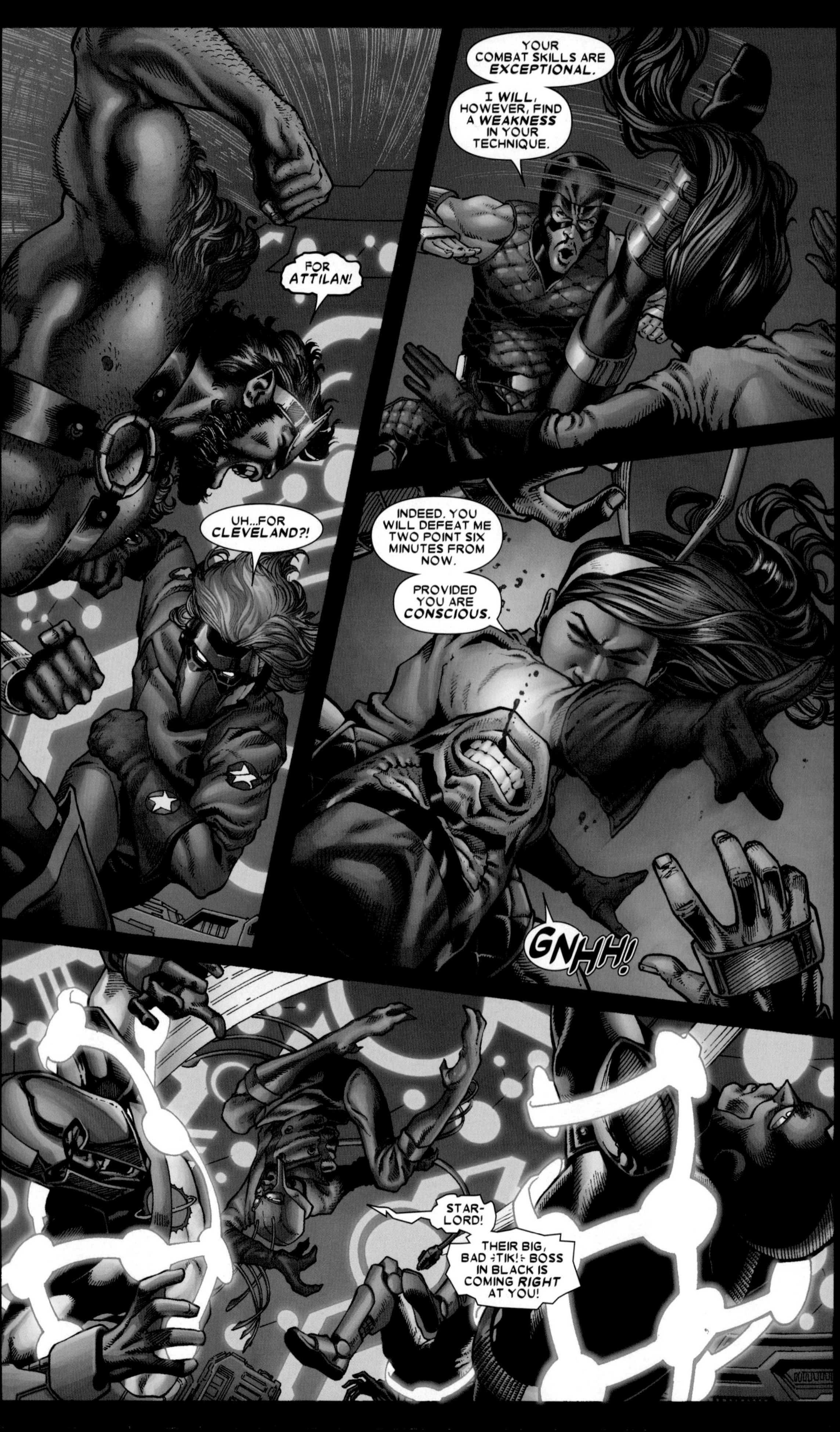

YOUR COMBAT SKILLS ARE EXCEPTIONAL.
I WILL, HOWEVER, FIND A WEAKNESS IN YOUR TECHNIQUE.
FOR ATTILAN!
UH...FOR CLEVELAND?!
INDEED. YOU WILL DEFEAT ME TWO POINT SIX MINUTES FROM NOW.
PROVIDED YOU ARE CONSCIOUS.
GNHH!
STAR-LORD!
THEIR BIG, BAD ÷TIK!÷ BOSS IN BLACK IS COMING RIGHT AT YOU!

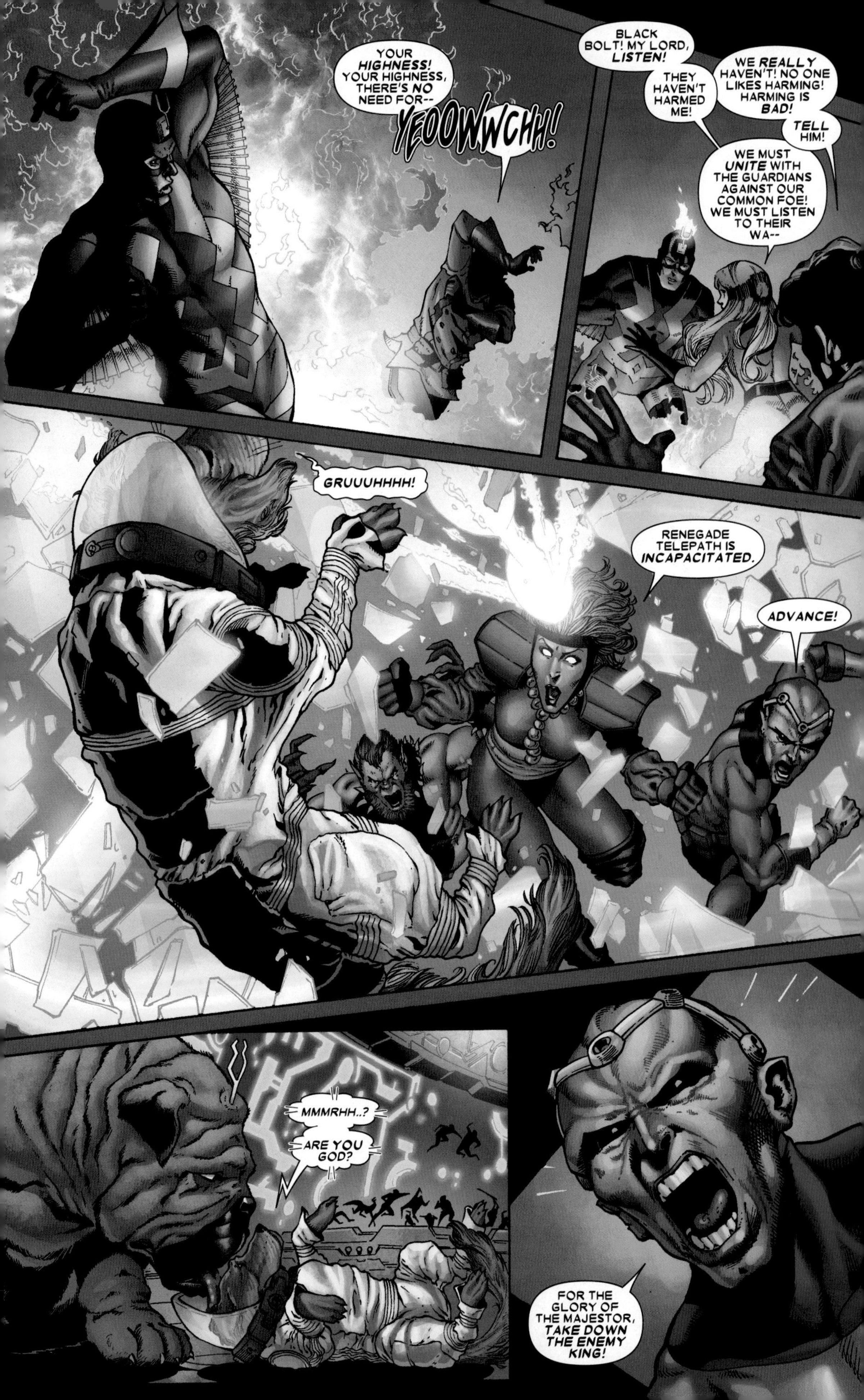

YOUR HIGHNESS! YOUR HIGHNESS, THERE'S NO NEED FOR--
YEOOWWCHH!
BLACK BOLT! MY LORD, LISTEN!
THEY HAVEN'T HARMED ME!
WE REALLY HAVEN'T! NO ONE LIKES HARMING! HARMING IS BAD!
TELL HIM!
WE MUST UNITE WITH THE GUARDIANS AGAINST OUR COMMON FOE! WE MUST LISTEN TO THEIR WA--
GRUUUHHHH!
RENEGADE TELEPATH IS INCAPACITATED.
ADVANCE!
MMMRHH..?
ARE YOU GOD?
FOR THE GLORY OF THE MAJESTOR, TAKE DOWN THE ENEMY KING!

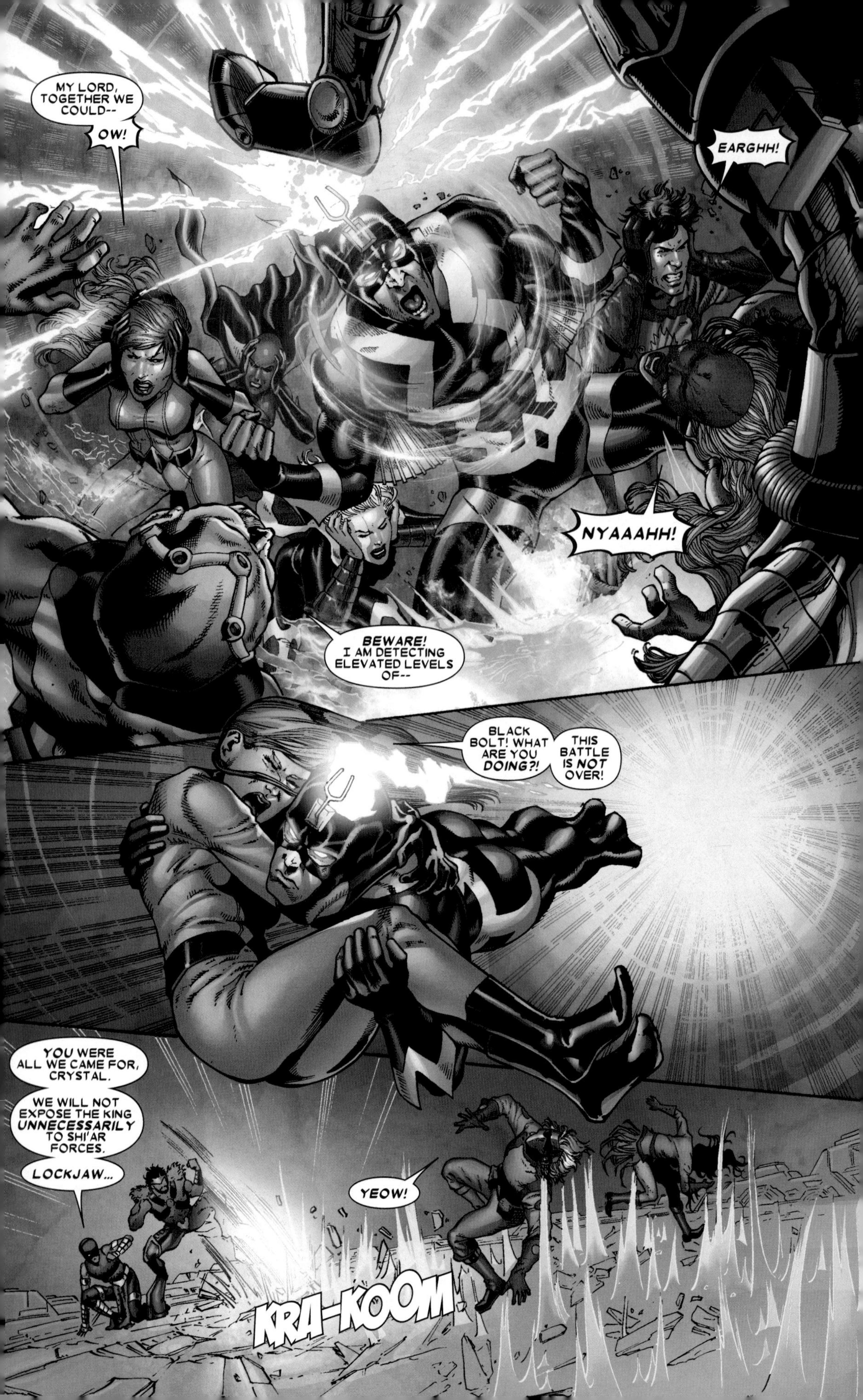
MY LORD, TOGETHER WE COULD--
OW!
EARGHH!
NYAAAHH!
BEWARE! I AM DETECTING ELEVATED LEVELS OF--
BLACK BOLT! WHAT ARE YOU DOING?!
THIS BATTLE IS NOT OVER!
YOU WERE ALL WE CAME FOR, CRYSTAL.
WE WILL NOT EXPOSE THE KING UNNECESSARILY TO SHI'AR FORCES.
LOCKJAW...
YEOW!
KRA-KOOM

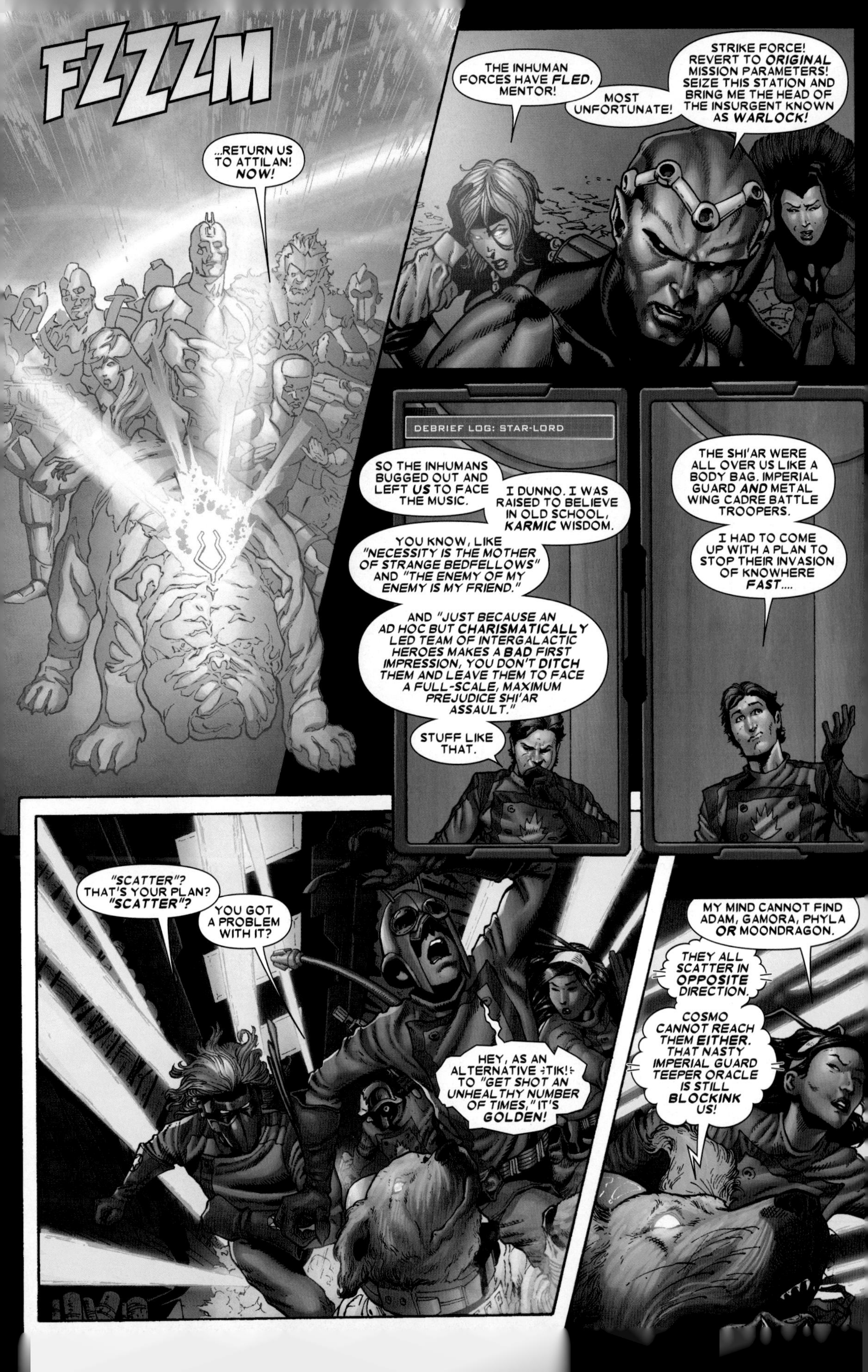
FZZZM
...RETURN US TO ATTILAN! NOW!
THE INHUMAN FORCES HAVE FLED, MENTOR!
MOST UNFORTUNATE!
STRIKE FORCE! REVERT TO ORIGINAL MISSION PARAMETERS! SEIZE THIS STATION AND BRING ME THE HEAD OF THE INSURGENT KNOWN AS WARLOCK!
DEBRIEF LOG: STAR-LORD
SO THE INHUMANS BUGGED OUT AND LEFT US TO FACE THE MUSIC.
I DUNNO. I WAS RAISED TO BELIEVE IN OLD SCHOOL, KARMIC WISDOM.
YOU KNOW, LIKE "NECESSITY IS THE MOTHER OF STRANGE BEDFELLOWS" AND "THE ENEMY OF MY ENEMY IS MY FRIEND."
AND "JUST BECAUSE AN AD HOC BUT CHARISMATICALLY LED TEAM OF INTERGALACTIC HEROES MAKES A BAD FIRST IMPRESSION, YOU DON'T DITCH THEM AND LEAVE THEM TO FACE A FULL-SCALE, MAXIMUM PREJUDICE SHI'AR ASSAULT."
STUFF LIKE THAT.
THE SHI'AR WERE ALL OVER US LIKE A BODY BAG. IMPERIAL GUARD AND METAL WING CADRE BATTLE TROOPERS.
I HAD TO COME UP WITH A PLAN TO STOP THEIR INVASION OF KNOWHERE FAST....
"SCATTER"? THAT'S YOUR PLAN? "SCATTER"?
YOU GOT A PROBLEM WITH IT?
HEY, AS AN ALTERNATIVE -TIK!- TO "GET SHOT AN UNHEALTHY NUMBER OF TIMES," IT'S GOLDEN!
MY MIND CANNOT FIND ADAM, GAMORA, PHYLA OR MOONDRAGON.
THEY ALL SCATTER IN OPPOSITE DIRECTION.
COSMO CANNOT REACH THEM EITHER. THAT NASTY IMPERIAL GUARD TEEPER ORACLE IS STILL BLOCKINK US!

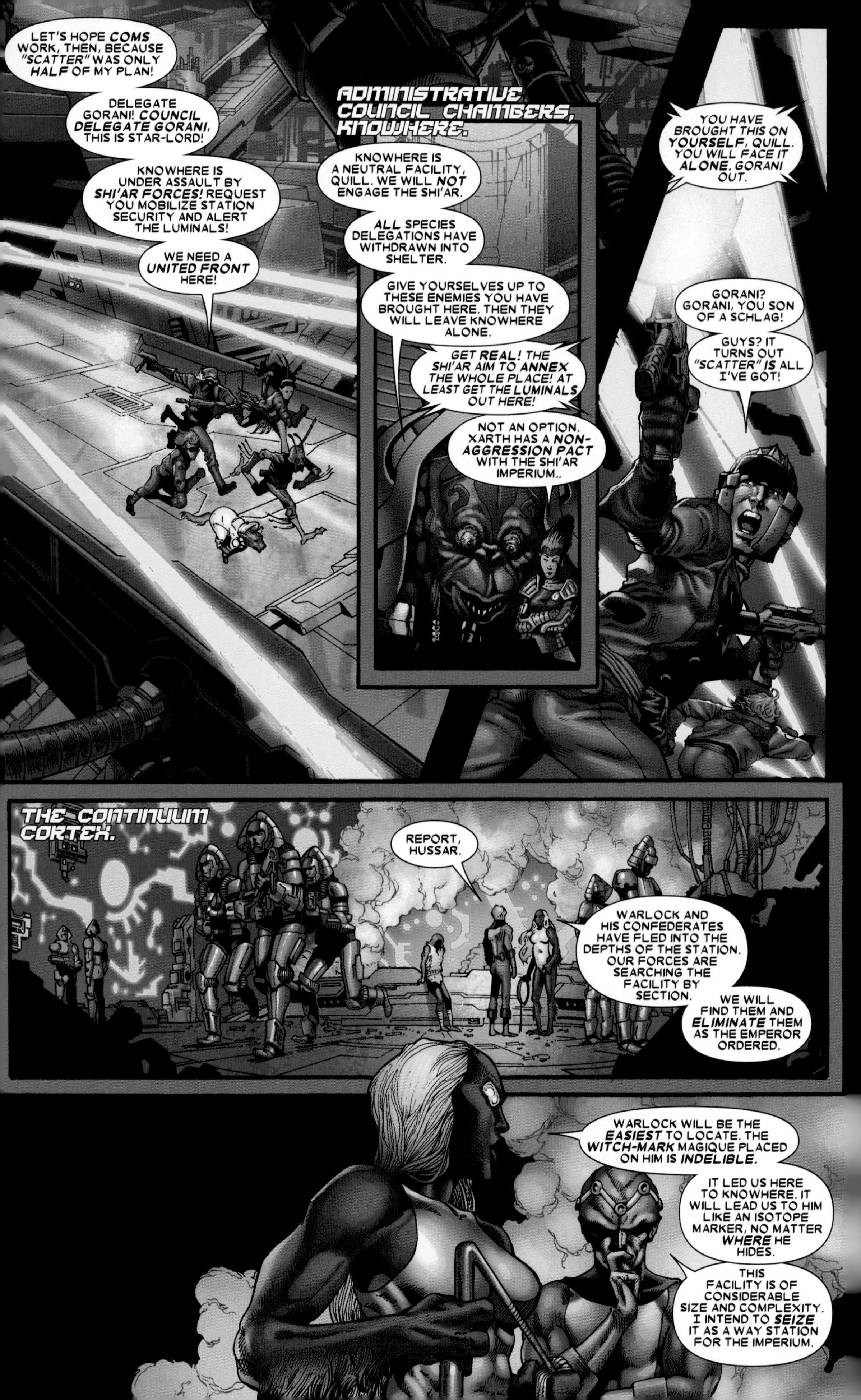
LET'S HOPE COMS WORK, THEN, BECAUSE "SCATTER" WAS ONLY HALF OF MY PLAN!
DELEGATE GORANI! COUNCIL DELEGATE GORANI, THIS IS STAR-LORD!
KNOWHERE IS UNDER ASSAULT BY SHI'AR FORCES! REQUEST YOU MOBILIZE STATION SECURITY AND ALERT THE LUMINALS!
WE NEED A UNITED FRONT HERE!
ADMINISTRATIVE COUNCIL CHAMBERS, KNOWHERE.
KNOWHERE IS A NEUTRAL FACILITY, QUILL. WE WILL NOT ENGAGE THE SHI'AR.
ALL SPECIES DELEGATIONS HAVE WITHDRAWN INTO SHELTER.
GIVE YOURSELVES UP TO THESE ENEMIES YOU HAVE BROUGHT HERE. THEN THEY WILL LEAVE KNOWHERE ALONE.
GET REAL! THE SHI'AR AIM TO ANNEX THE WHOLE PLACE! AT LEAST GET THE LUMINALS OUT HERE!
NOT AN OPTION. XARTH HAS A NON-AGGRESSION PACT WITH THE SHI'AR IMPERIUM..
YOU HAVE BROUGHT THIS ON YOURSELF, QUILL. YOU WILL FACE IT ALONE. GORANI OUT.
GORANI? GORANI, YOU SON OF A SCHLAG!
GUYS? IT TURNS OUT "SCATTER" IS ALL I'VE GOT!
THE CONTINUUM CORTEX.
REPORT, HUSSAR.
WARLOCK AND HIS CONFEDERATES HAVE FLED INTO THE DEPTHS OF THE STATION. OUR FORCES ARE SEARCHING THE FACILITY BY SECTION.
WE WILL FIND THEM AND ELIMINATE THEM AS THE EMPEROR ORDERED.
WARLOCK WILL BE THE EASIEST TO LOCATE. THE WITCH-MARK MAGIQUE PLACED ON HIM IS INDELIBLE.
IT LED US HERE TO KNOWHERE. IT WILL LEAD US TO HIM LIKE AN ISOTOPE MARKER, NO MATTER WHERE HE HIDES.
THIS FACILITY IS OF CONSIDERABLE SIZE AND COMPLEXITY. I INTEND TO SEIZE IT AS A WAY STATION FOR THE IMPERIUM.

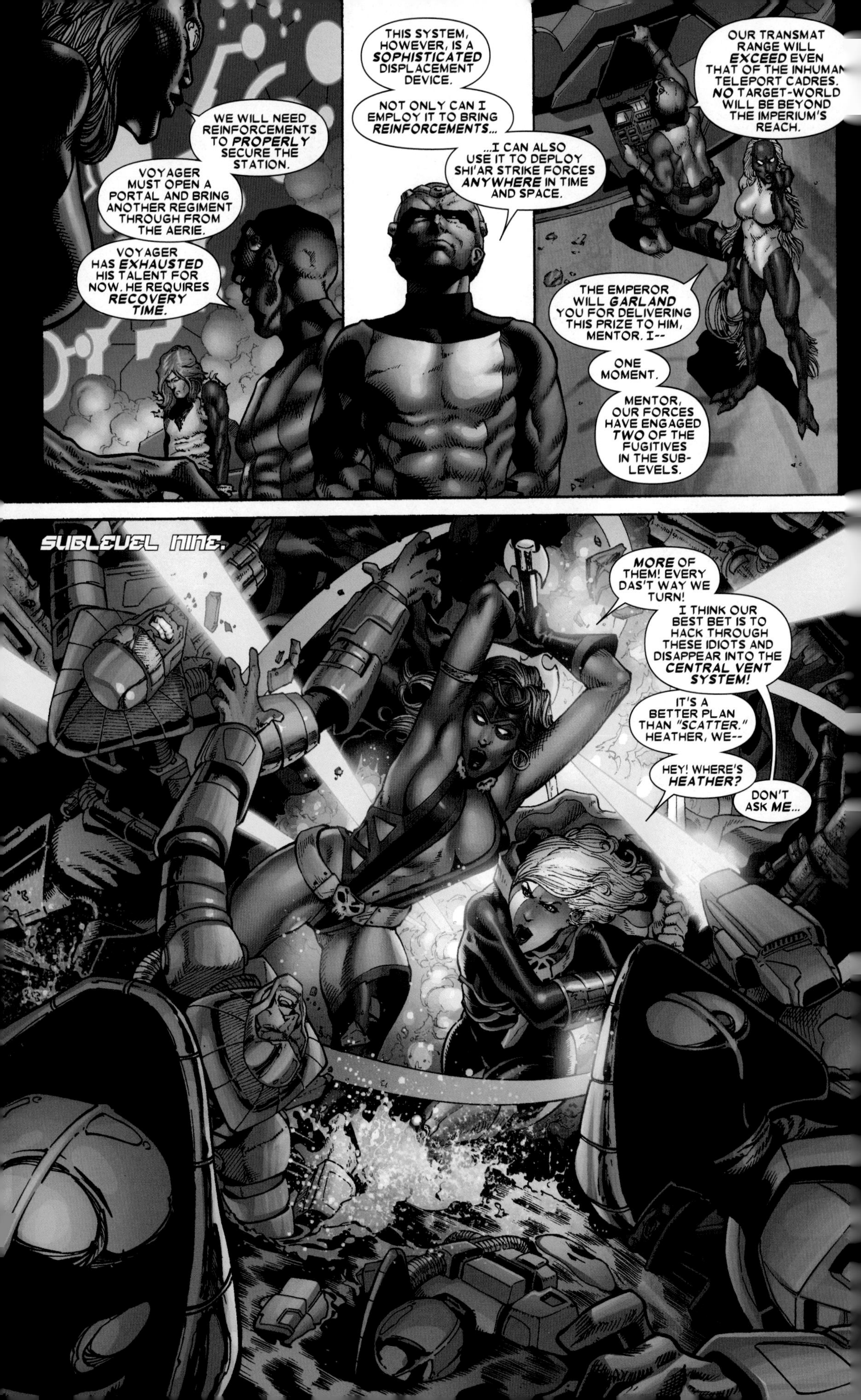
WE WILL NEED REINFORCEMENTS TO PROPERLY SECURE THE STATION.
VOYAGER MUST OPEN A PORTAL AND BRING ANOTHER REGIMENT THROUGH FROM THE AERIE.
VOYAGER HAS EXHAUSTED HIS TALENT FOR NOW. HE REQUIRES RECOVERY TIME.
THIS SYSTEM, HOWEVER, IS A SOPHISTICATED DISPLACEMENT DEVICE.
NOT ONLY CAN I EMPLOY IT TO BRING REINFORCEMENTS...
...I CAN ALSO USE IT TO DEPLOY SHI'AR STRIKE FORCES ANYWHERE IN TIME AND SPACE.
OUR TRANSMAT RANGE WILL EXCEED EVEN THAT OF THE INHUMAN TELEPORT CADRES. NO TARGET-WORLD WILL BE BEYOND THE IMPERIUM'S REACH.
THE EMPEROR WILL GARLAND YOU FOR DELIVERING THIS PRIZE TO HIM, MENTOR. I--
ONE MOMENT.
MENTOR, OUR FORCES HAVE ENGAGED TWO OF THE FUGITIVES IN THE SUB-LEVELS.
SUBLEVEL NINE.
MORE OF THEM! EVERY DAS'T WAY WE TURN!
I THINK OUR BEST BET IS TO HACK THROUGH THESE IDIOTS AND DISAPPEAR INTO THE CENTRAL VENT SYSTEM!
IT'S A BETTER PLAN THAN "SCATTER." HEATHER, WE--
HEY! WHERE'S HEATHER?
DON'T ASK ME...

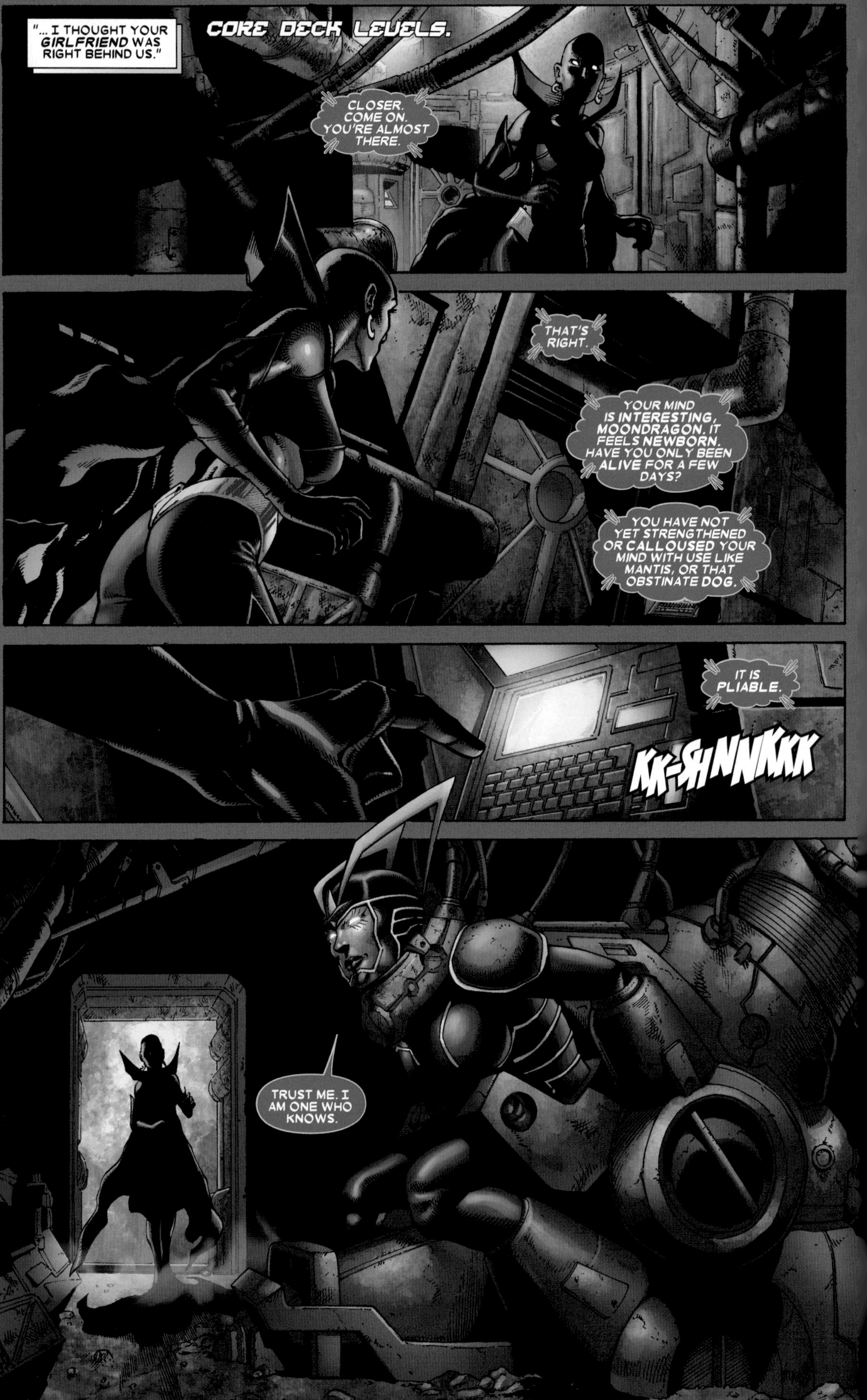
"... I THOUGHT YOUR GIRLFRIEND WAS RIGHT BEHIND US."
CORE DECK LEVELS.
CLOSER. COME ON. YOU'RE ALMOST THERE.
THAT'S RIGHT.
YOUR MIND IS INTERESTING, MOONDRAGON. IT FEELS NEWBORN. HAVE YOU ONLY BEEN ALIVE FOR A FEW DAYS?
YOU HAVE NOT YET STRENGTHENED OR CALLOUSED YOUR MIND WITH USE LIKE MANTIS, OR THAT OBSTINATE DOG.
IT IS PLIABLE.
KK-SHNNKKK
TRUST ME. I AM ONE WHO KNOWS.

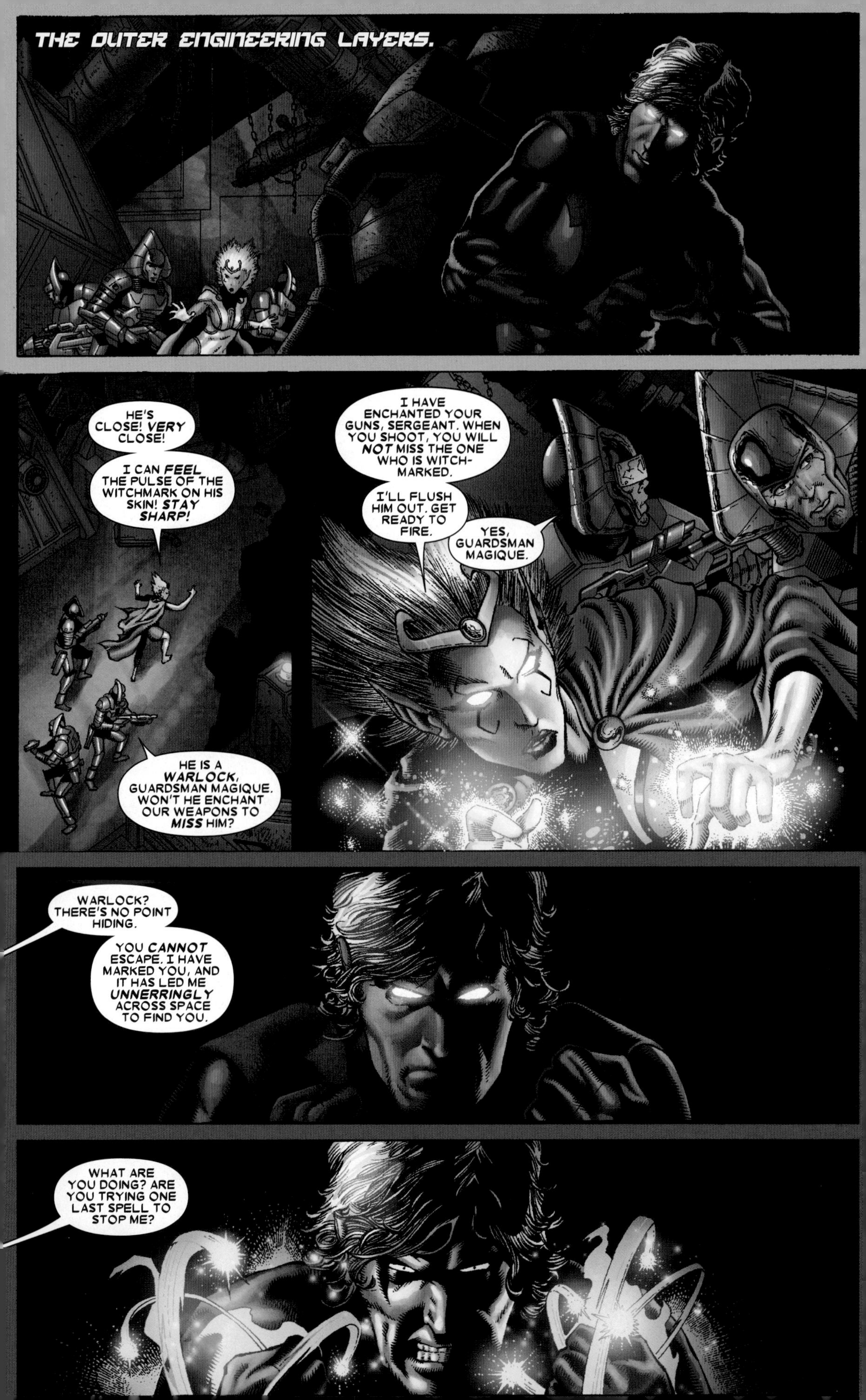
THE OUTER ENGINEERING LAYERS.
HE'S CLOSE! VERY CLOSE!
I CAN FEEL THE PULSE OF THE WITCHMARK ON HIS SKIN! STAY SHARP!
HE IS A WARLOCK, GUARDSMAN MAGIQUE. WON'T HE ENCHANT OUR WEAPONS TO MISS HIM?
I HAVE ENCHANTED YOUR GUNS, SERGEANT. WHEN YOU SHOOT, YOU WILL NOT MISS THE ONE WHO IS WITCH-MARKED.
I'LL FLUSH HIM OUT. GET READY TO FIRE.
YES, GUARDSMAN MAGIQUE.
WARLOCK? THERE'S NO POINT HIDING.
YOU CANNOT ESCAPE. I HAVE MARKED YOU, AND IT HAS LED ME UNNERRINGLY ACROSS SPACE TO FIND YOU.
WHAT ARE YOU DOING? ARE YOU TRYING ONE LAST SPELL TO STOP ME?

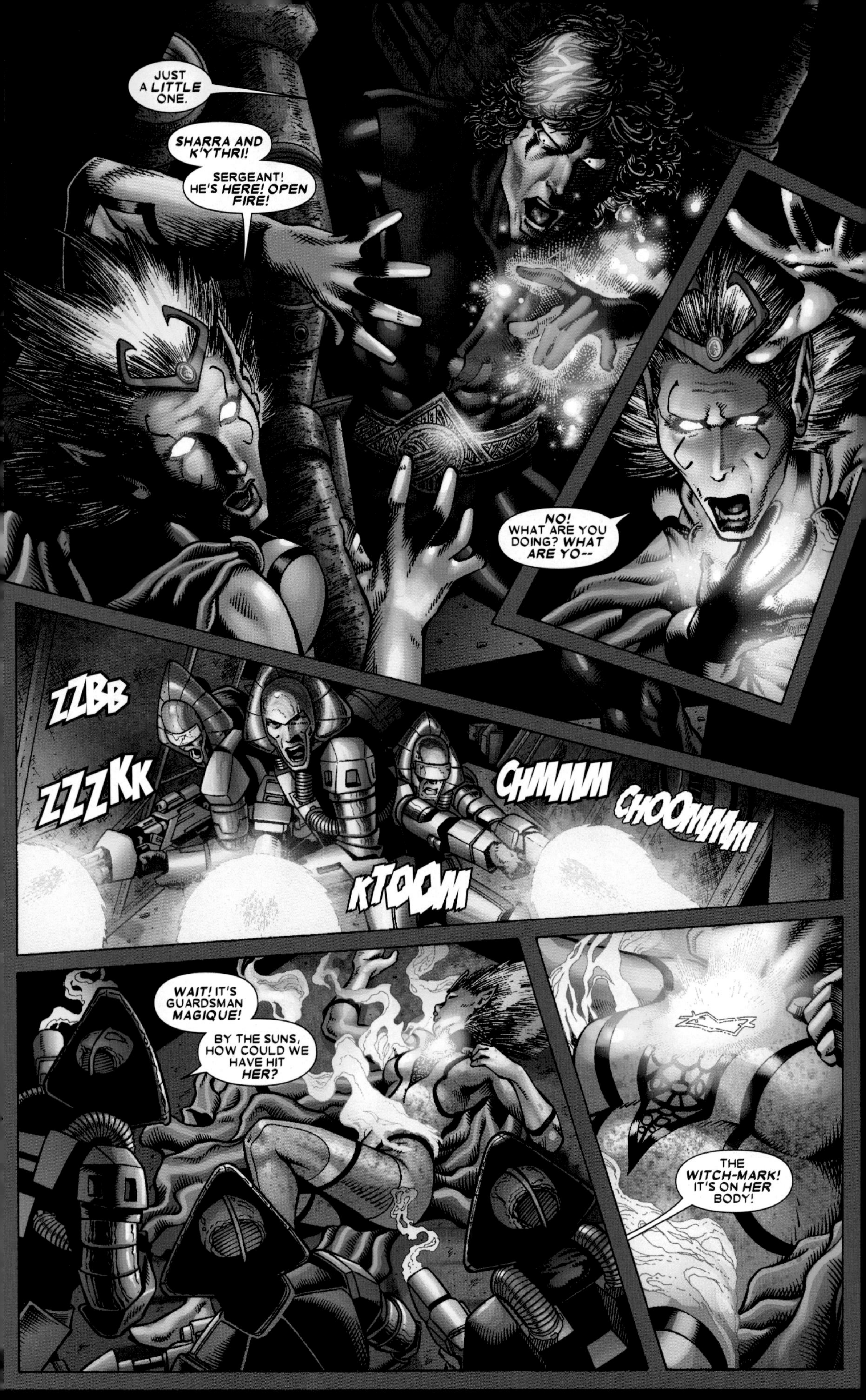
JUST A LITTLE ONE.
SHARRA AND K'YTHRI!
SERGEANT! HE'S HERE! OPEN FIRE!
NO! WHAT ARE YOU DOING? WHAT ARE YO--
ZZBB
ZZZKK
CHMMM
CHOOMMM
KTOOM
WAIT! IT'S GUARDSMAN MAGIQUE!
BY THE SUNS, HOW COULD WE HAVE HIT HER?
THE WITCH-MARK! IT'S ON HER BODY!

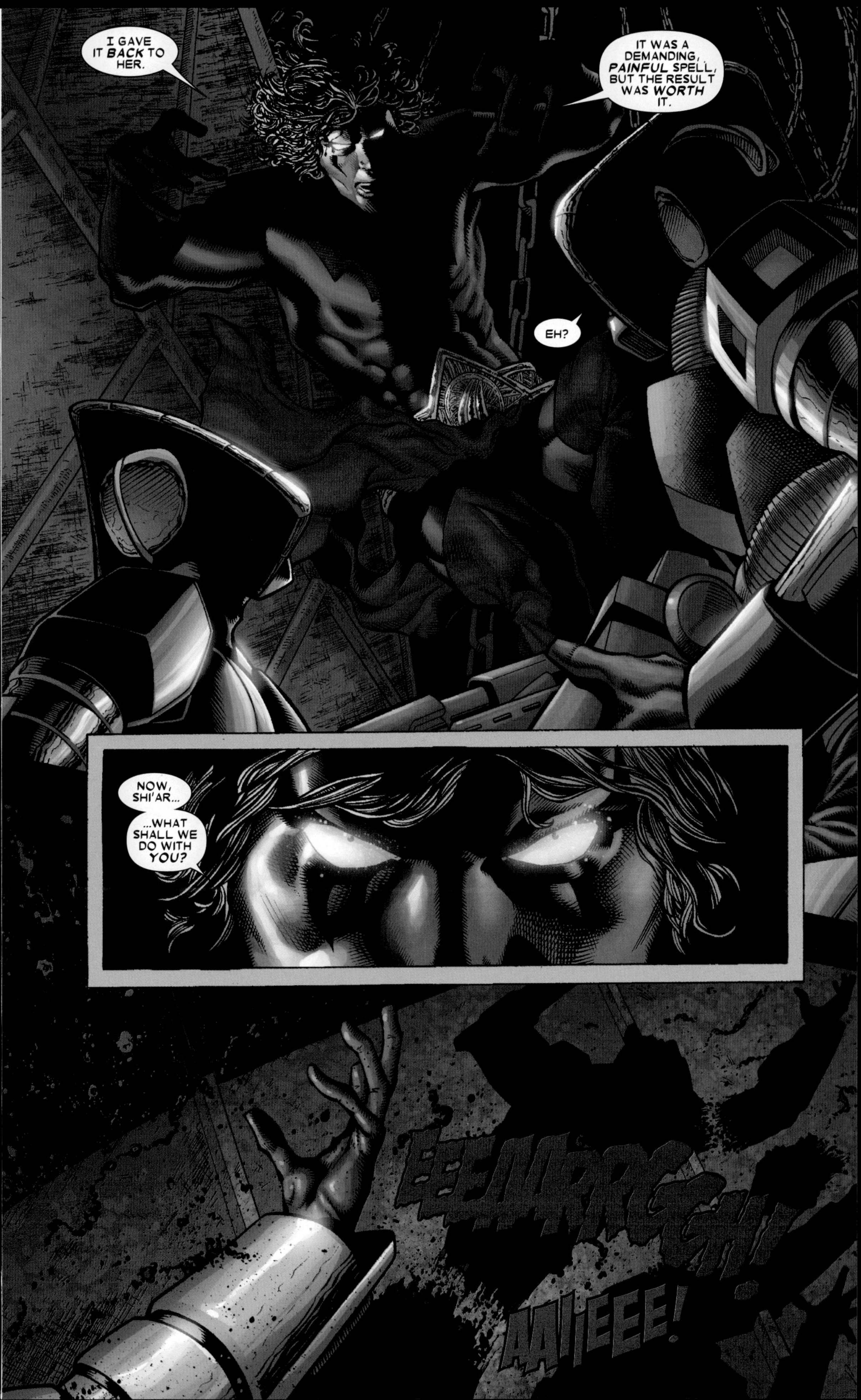
I GAVE IT BACK TO HER.
IT WAS A DEMANDING, PAINFUL SPELL, BUT THE RESULT WAS WORTH IT.
EH?
NOW, SHI'AR...
...WHAT SHALL WE DO WITH YOU?
AAIIEEE!

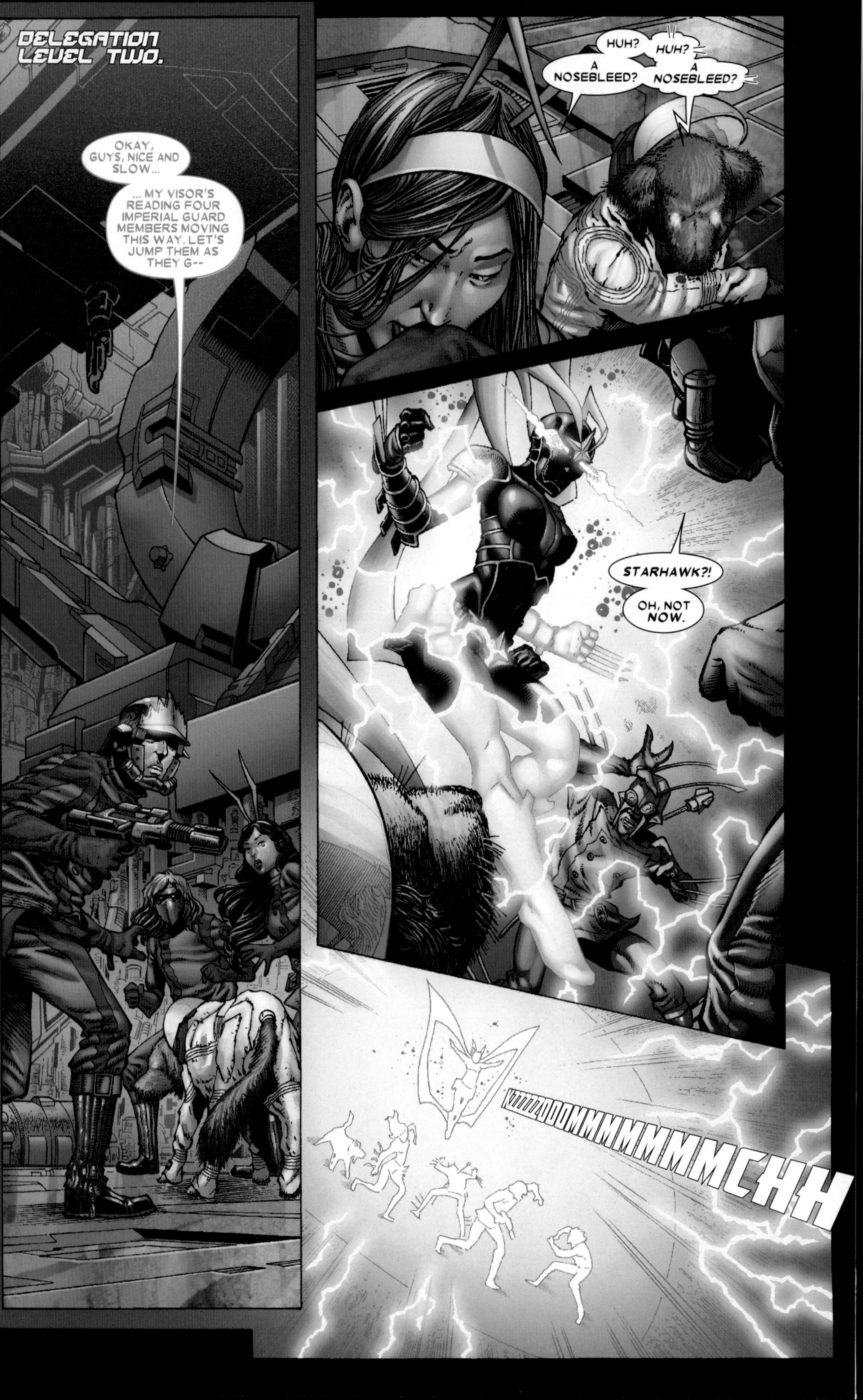
DELEGATION LEVEL TWO.
OKAY, GUYS, NICE AND SLOW...
... MY VISOR'S READING FOUR IMPERIAL GUARD MEMBERS MOVING THIS WAY. LET'S JUMP THEM AS THEY G--
HUH?
A NOSEBLEED?
HUH?
A NOSEBLEED?
STARHAWK?!
OH, NOT NOW.
VZZZZZDOOMMMMMMMMMMCHH

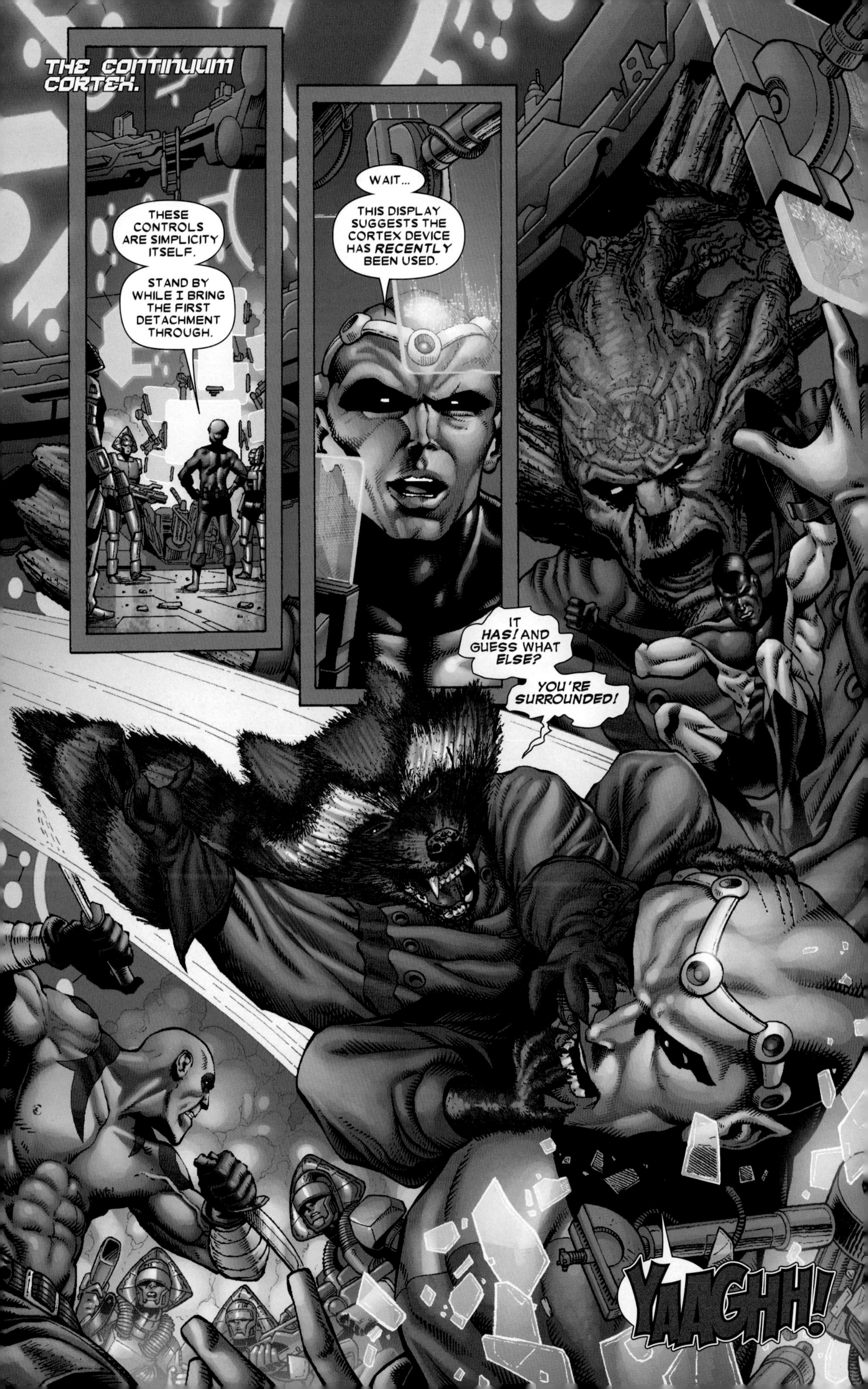
THE CONTINUUM CORTEX.
THESE CONTROLS ARE SIMPLICITY ITSELF.
STAND BY WHILE I BRING THE FIRST DETACHMENT THROUGH.
WAIT...
THIS DISPLAY SUGGESTS THE CORTEX DEVICE HAS *RECENTLY* BEEN USED.
IT *HAS!* AND GUESS WHAT *ELSE?*
YOU'RE SURROUNDED!
YAAGHH!

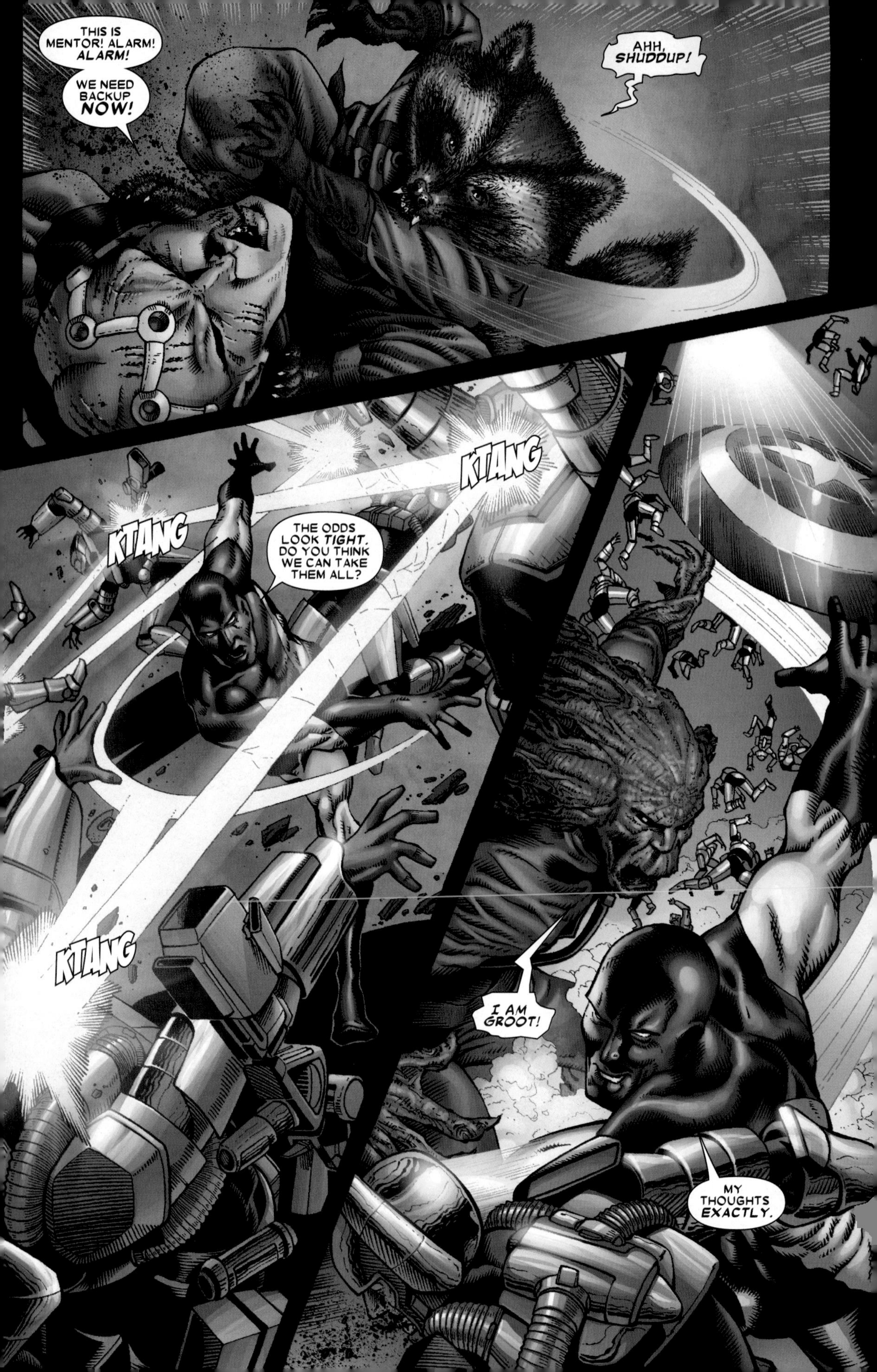
THIS IS MENTOR! ALARM! ALARM!
WE NEED BACKUP NOW!
AHH, SHUDDUP!
KTANG
KTANG
THE ODDS LOOK TIGHT. DO YOU THINK WE CAN TAKE THEM ALL?
KTANG
I AM GROOT!
MY THOUGHTS EXACTLY.

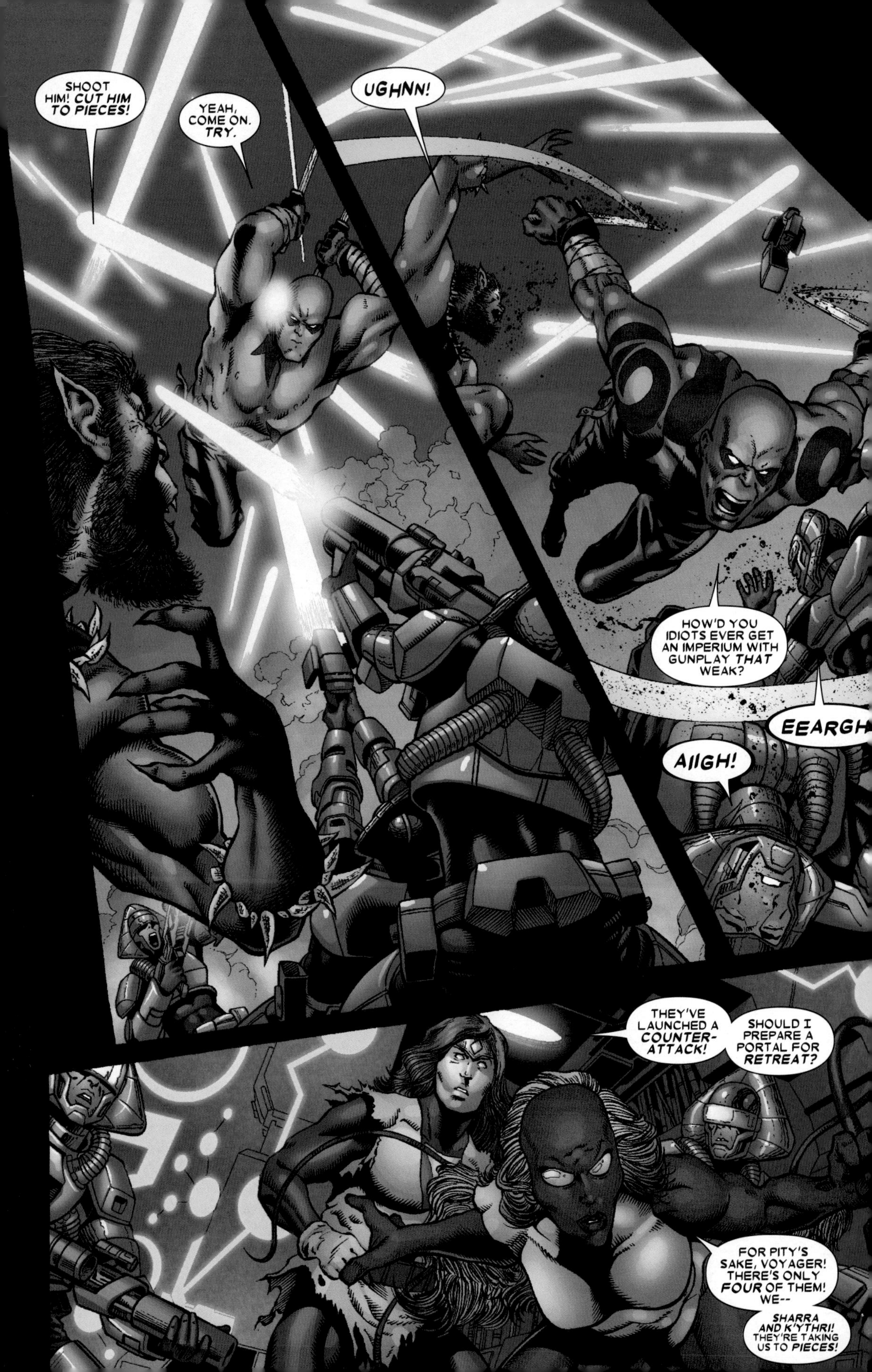
SHOOT HIM! CUT HIM TO PIECES!
YEAH, COME ON. TRY.
UGHNN!
HOW'D YOU IDIOTS EVER GET AN IMPERIUM WITH GUNPLAY THAT WEAK?
EEARGH
AIIGH!
THEY'VE LAUNCHED A COUNTER-ATTACK!
SHOULD I PREPARE A PORTAL FOR RETREAT?
FOR PITY'S SAKE, VOYAGER! THERE'S ONLY FOUR OF THEM! WE--
SHARRA AND K'YTHRI! THEY'RE TAKING US TO PIECES!

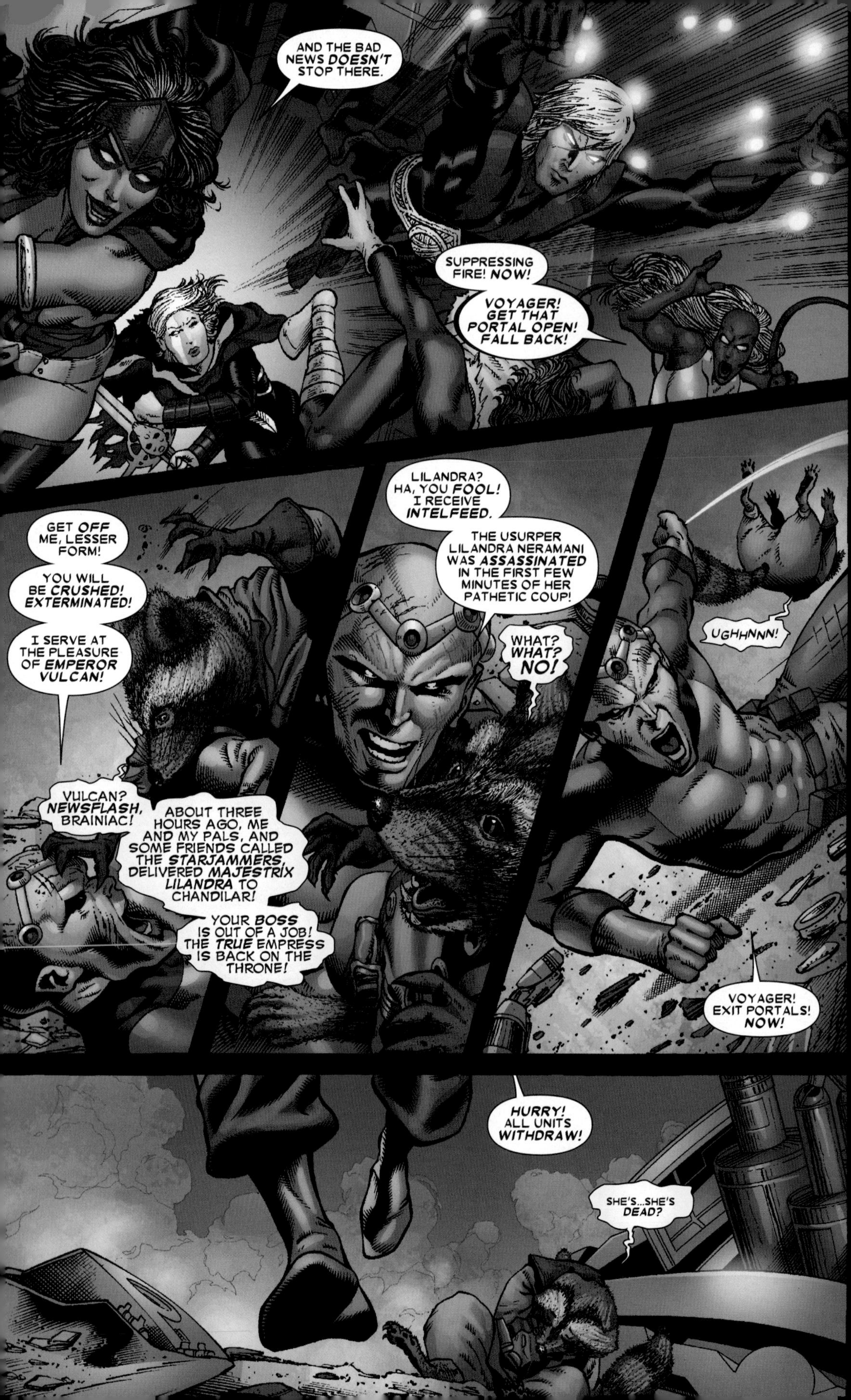
AND THE BAD NEWS DOESN'T STOP THERE.
SUPPRESSING FIRE! NOW!
VOYAGER! GET THAT PORTAL OPEN! FALL BACK!
GET OFF ME, LESSER FORM!
YOU WILL BE CRUSHED! EXTERMINATED!
I SERVE AT THE PLEASURE OF EMPEROR VULCAN!
VULCAN? NEWSFLASH, BRAINIAC!
ABOUT THREE HOURS AGO, ME AND MY PALS, AND SOME FRIENDS CALLED THE STARJAMMERS, DELIVERED MAJESTRIX LILANDRA TO CHANDILAR!
YOUR BOSS IS OUT OF A JOB! THE TRUE EMPRESS IS BACK ON THE THRONE!
LILANDRA? HA, YOU FOOL! I RECEIVE INTELFEED.
THE USURPER LILANDRA NERAMANI WAS ASSASSINATED IN THE FIRST FEW MINUTES OF HER PATHETIC COUP!
WHAT? WHAT? NO!
UGHHNNN!
VOYAGER! EXIT PORTALS! NOW!
HURRY! ALL UNITS WITHDRAW!
SHE'S...SHE'S DEAD?

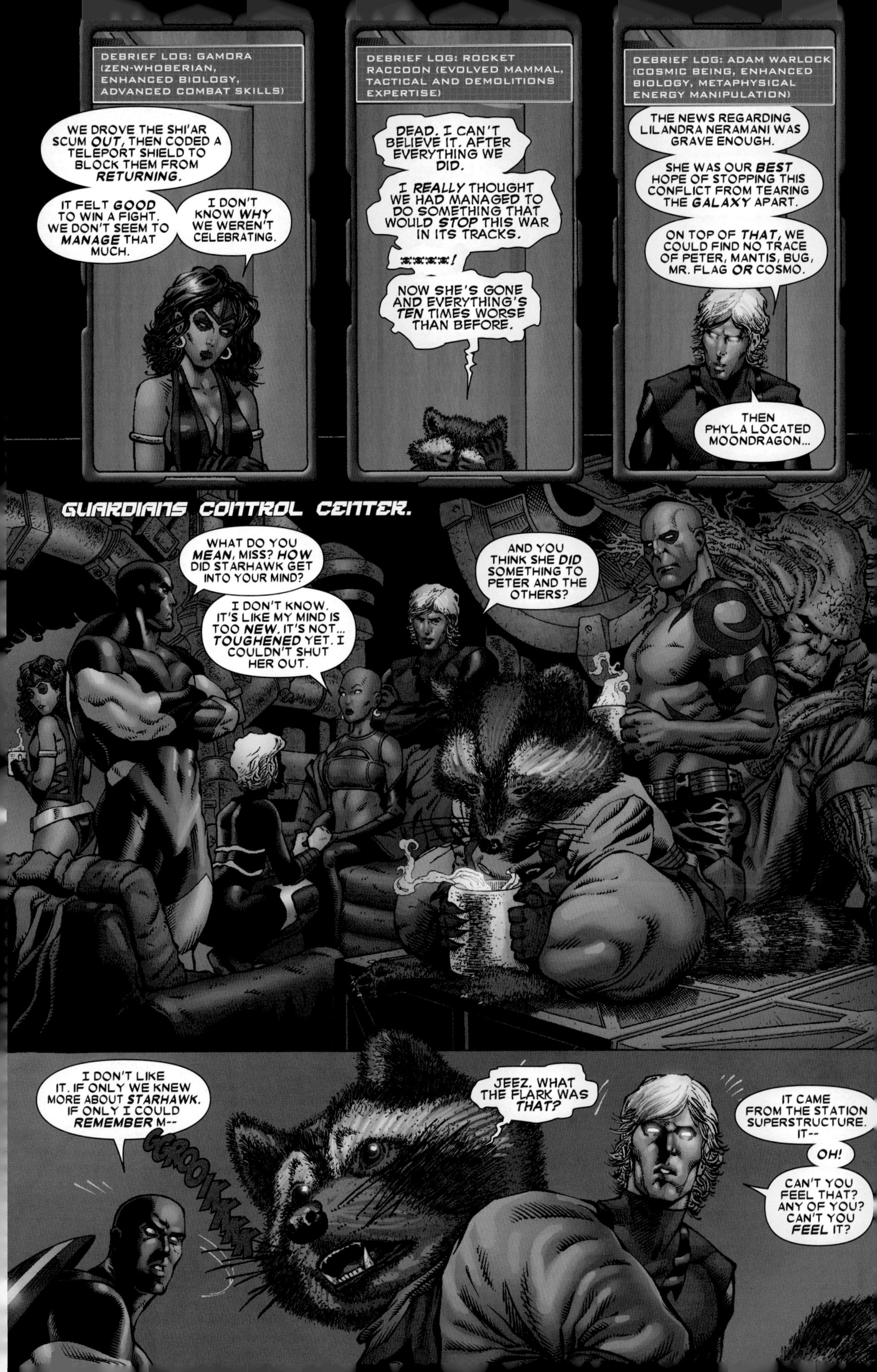
DEBRIEF LOG: GAMORA (ZEN-WHOBERIAN, ENHANCED BIOLOGY, ADVANCED COMBAT SKILLS)
WE DROVE THE SHI'AR SCUM OUT, THEN CODED A TELEPORT SHIELD TO BLOCK THEM FROM RETURNING.
IT FELT GOOD TO WIN A FIGHT. WE DON'T SEEM TO MANAGE THAT MUCH.
I DON'T KNOW WHY WE WEREN'T CELEBRATING.
DEBRIEF LOG: ROCKET RACCOON (EVOLVED MAMMAL, TACTICAL AND DEMOLITIONS EXPERTISE)
DEAD. I CAN'T BELIEVE IT. AFTER EVERYTHING WE DID.
I REALLY THOUGHT WE HAD MANAGED TO DO SOMETHING THAT WOULD STOP THIS WAR IN ITS TRACKS.
NOW SHE'S GONE AND EVERYTHING'S TEN TIMES WORSE THAN BEFORE.
DEBRIEF LOG: ADAM WARLOCK (COSMIC BEING, ENHANCED BIOLOGY, METAPHYSICAL ENERGY MANIPULATION)
THE NEWS REGARDING LILANDRA NERAMANI WAS GRAVE ENOUGH.
SHE WAS OUR BEST HOPE OF STOPPING THIS CONFLICT FROM TEARING THE GALAXY APART.
ON TOP OF THAT, WE COULD FIND NO TRACE OF PETER, MANTIS, BUG, MR. FLAG OR COSMO.
THEN PHYLA LOCATED MOONDRAGON...
GUARDIANS CONTROL CENTER.
WHAT DO YOU MEAN, MISS? HOW DID STARHAWK GET INTO YOUR MIND?
I DON'T KNOW. IT'S LIKE MY MIND IS TOO NEW. IT'S NOT... TOUGHENED YET. I COULDN'T SHUT HER OUT.
AND YOU THINK SHE DID SOMETHING TO PETER AND THE OTHERS?
I DON'T LIKE IT. IF ONLY WE KNEW MORE ABOUT STARHAWK. IF ONLY I COULD REMEMBER M--
GGROOIKKKK
JEEZ. WHAT THE FLARK WAS THAT?
IT CAME FROM THE STATION SUPERSTRUCTURE. IT--
OH!
CAN'T YOU FEEL THAT? ANY OF YOU? CAN'T YOU FEEL IT?

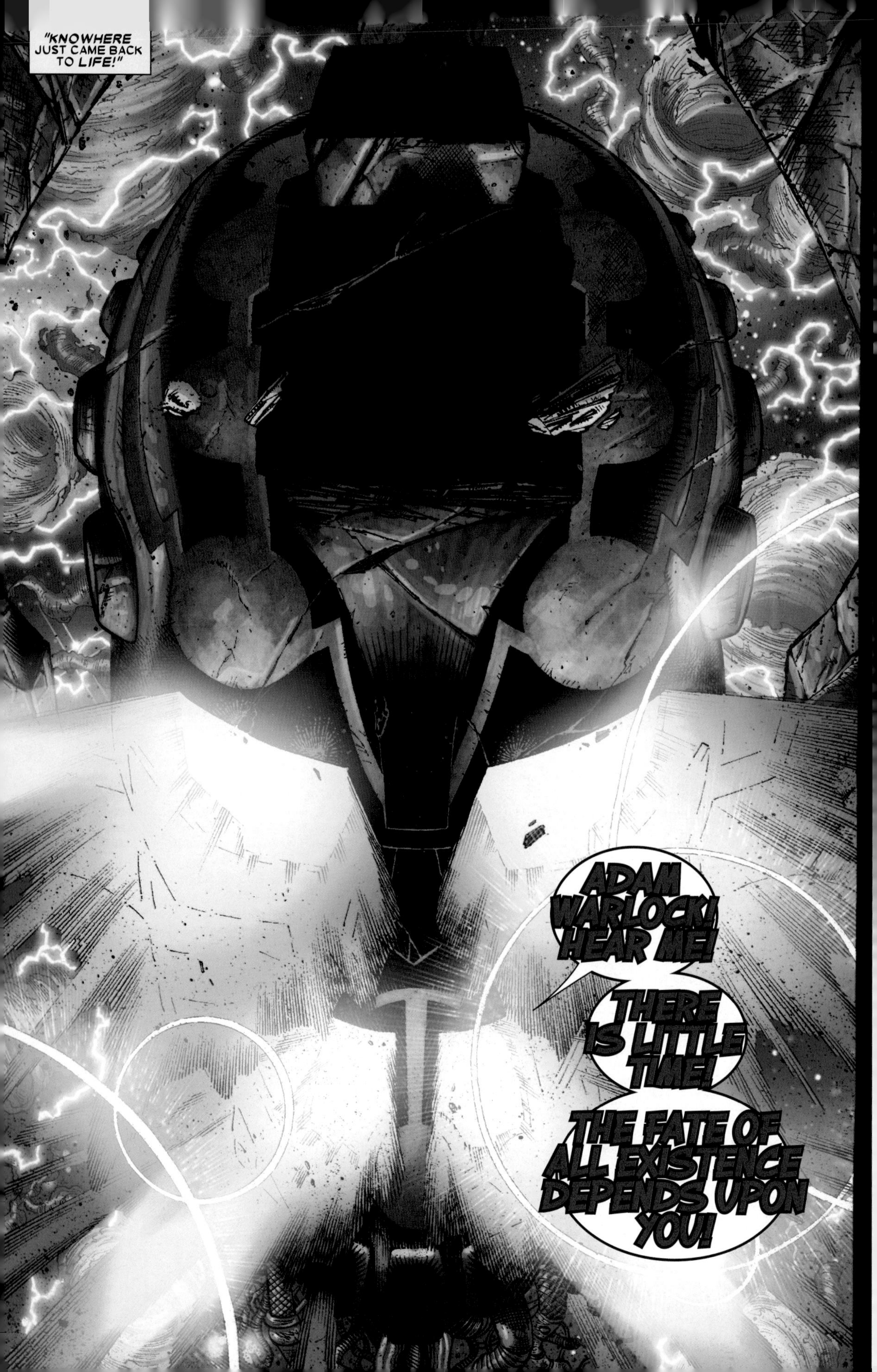
"KNOWHERE JUST CAME BACK TO LIFE!"
ADAM WARLOCK! HEAR ME!
THERE IS LITTLE TIME!
THE FATE OF ALL EXISTENCE DEPENDS UPON YOU!

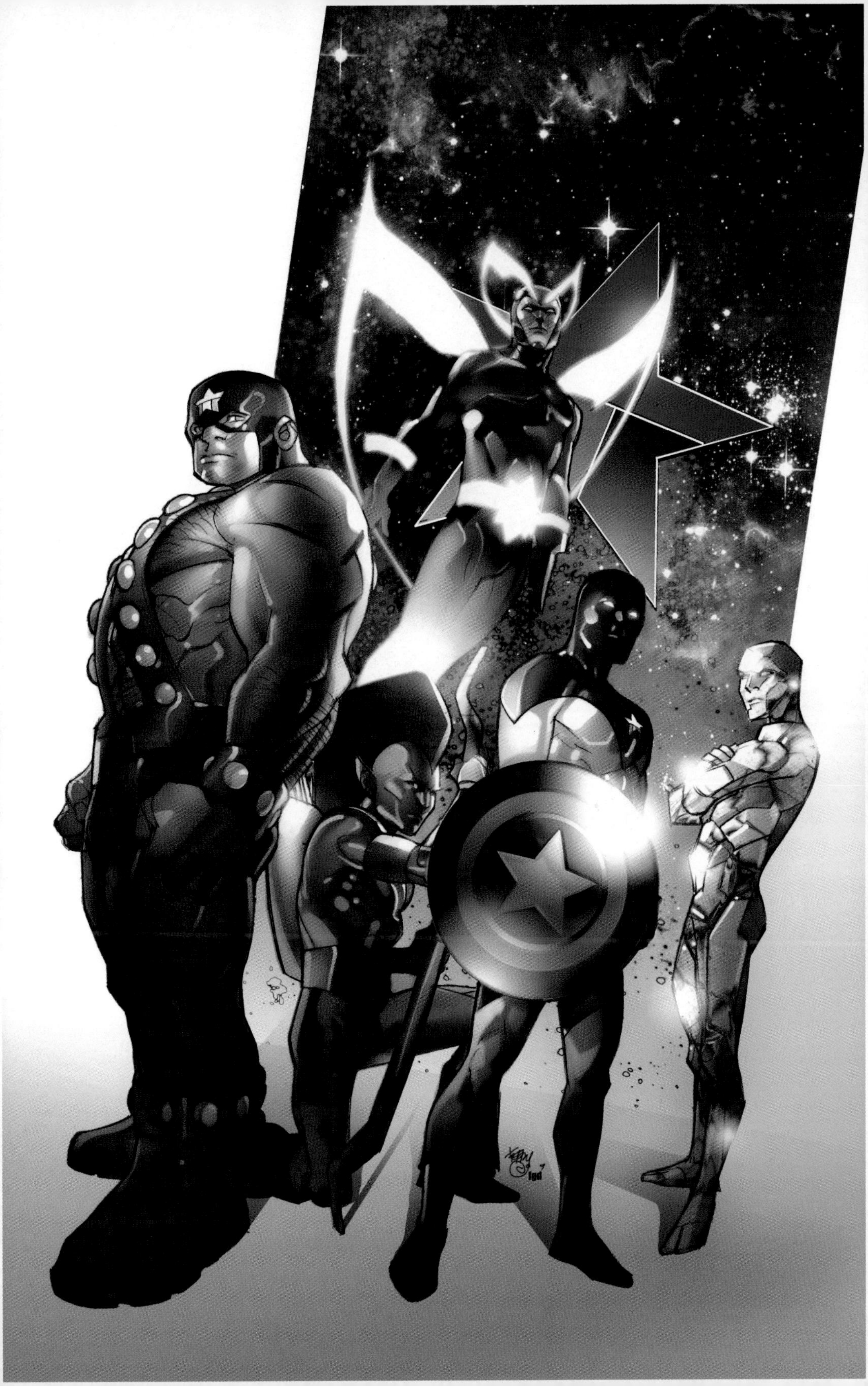

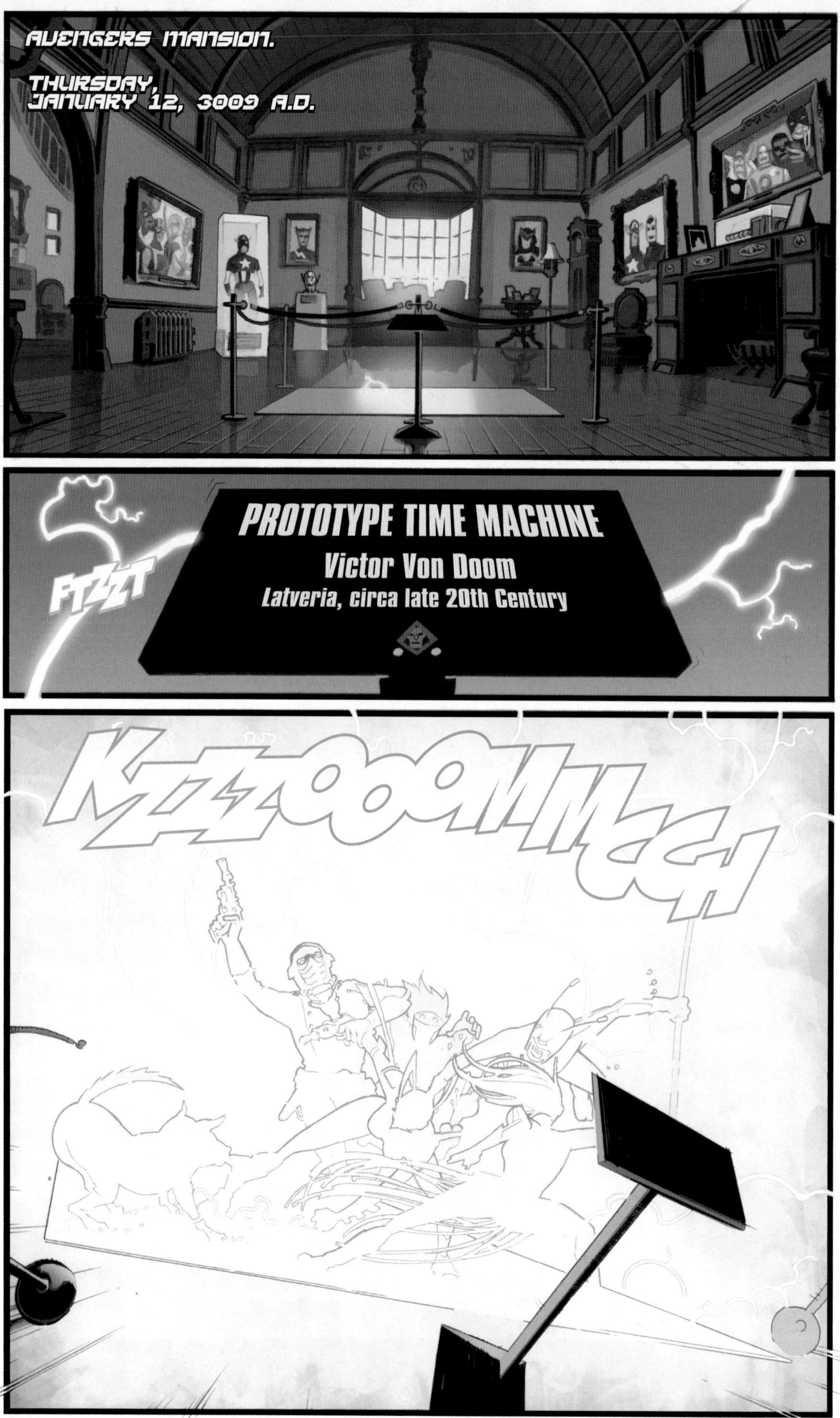

AVENGERS MANSION.
THURSDAY, JANUARY 12, 3009 A.D.
FTZZT
PROTOTYPE TIME MACHINE
Victor Von Doom
Latveria, circa late 20th Century
KZZOOOMMCCH

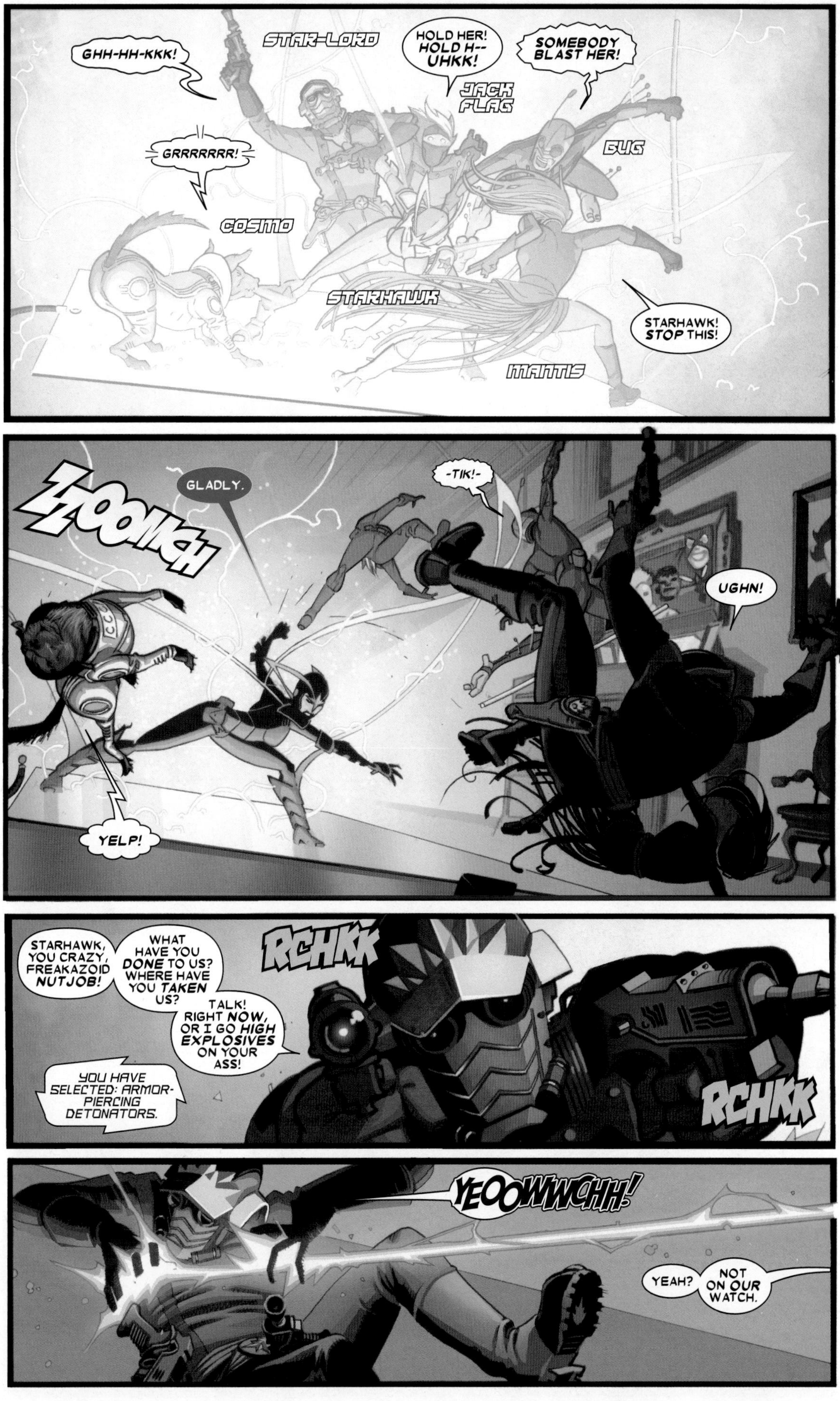
GHH-HH-KKK!
STAR-LORD
HOLD HER! HOLD H-- UHKK!
JACK FLAG
SOMEBODY BLAST HER!
GRRRRRRR!
BUG
COSMO
STARHAWK
STARHAWK! STOP THIS!
MANTIS
ZZOOMCH
GLADLY.
-TIK!-
UGHN!
YELP!
STARHAWK, YOU CRAZY, FREAKAZOID NUTJOB!
WHAT HAVE YOU DONE TO US? WHERE HAVE YOU TAKEN US?
RCHKK
TALK! RIGHT NOW, OR I GO HIGH EXPLOSIVES ON YOUR ASS!
YOU HAVE SELECTED: ARMOR-PIERCING DETONATORS.
RCHKK
YEOOWWCHH!
YEAH?
NOT ON OUR WATCH.

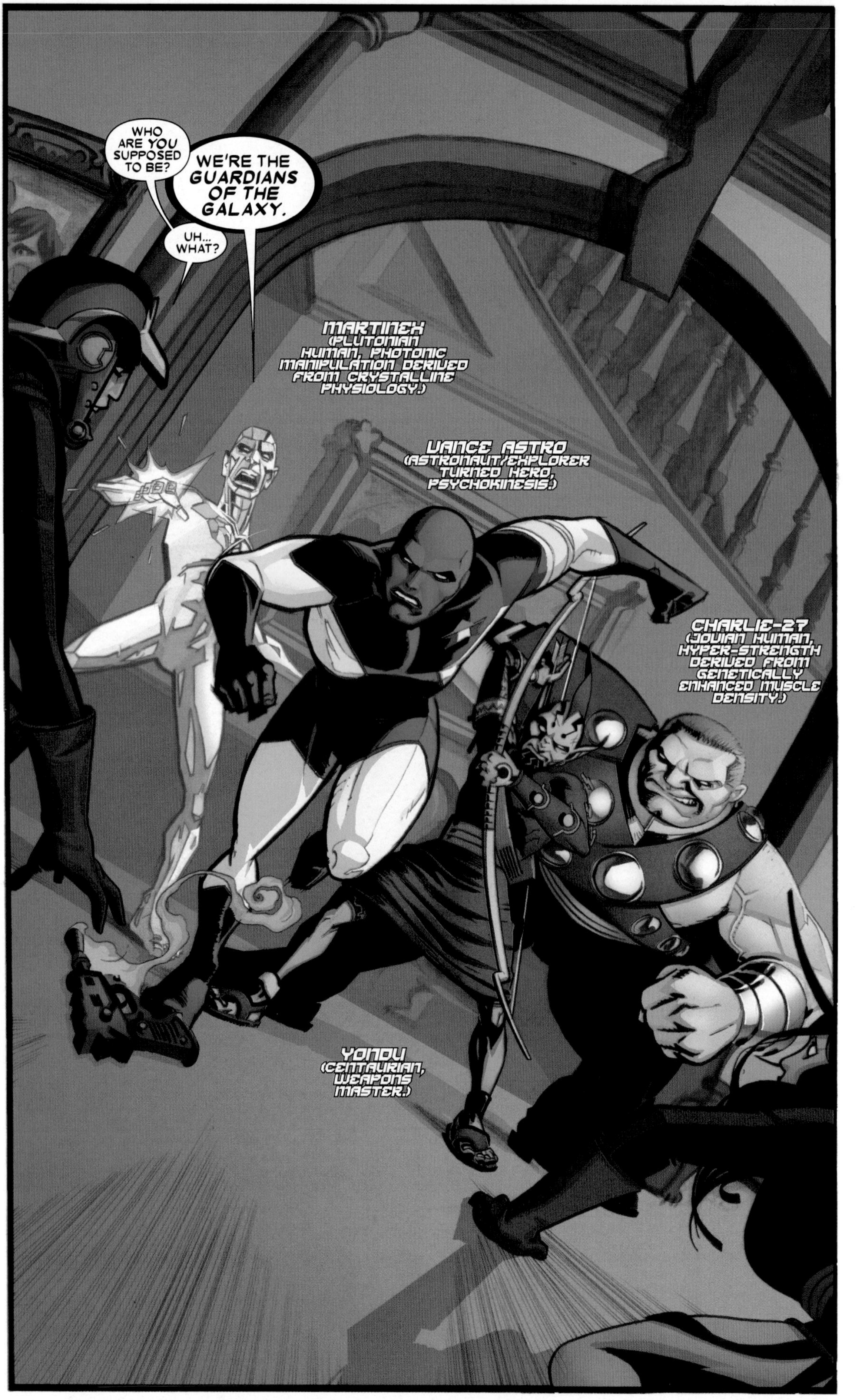
WHO ARE YOU SUPPOSED TO BE?
WE'RE THE GUARDIANS OF THE GALAXY.
UH... WHAT?
MARTINEX (PLUTONIAN HUMAN, PHOTONIC MANIPULATION DERIVED FROM CRYSTALLINE PHYSIOLOGY.)
VANCE ASTRO (ASTRONAUT/EXPLORER TURNED HERO, PSYCHOKINESIS.)
CHARLIE-27 (JOVIAN HUMAN, HYPER-STRENGTH DERIVED FROM GENETICALLY ENHANCED MUSCLE DENSITY.)
YONDU (CENTAURIAN, WEAPONS MASTER.)

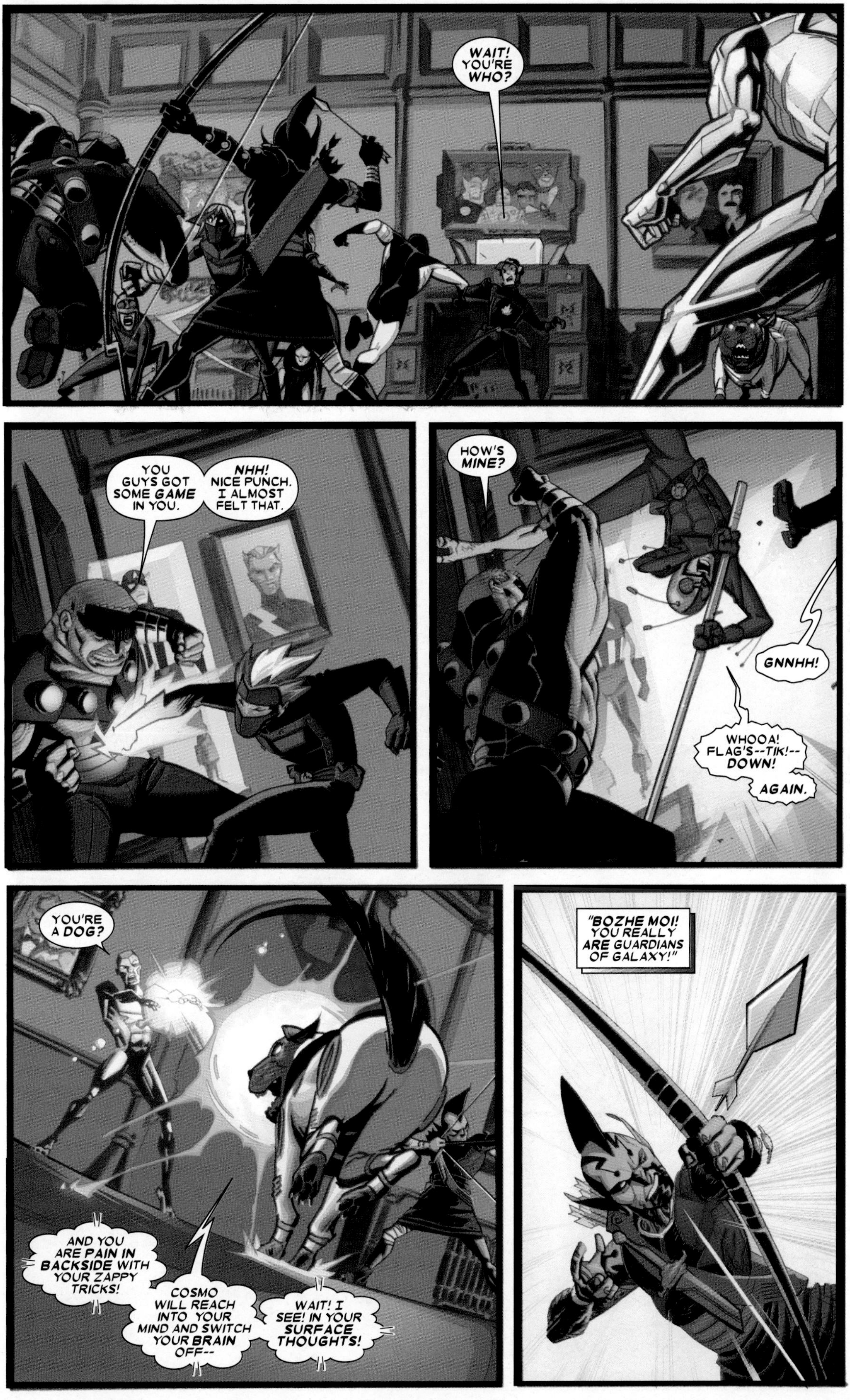
WAIT! YOU'RE WHO?
YOU GUYS GOT SOME GAME IN YOU.
NHH! NICE PUNCH. I ALMOST FELT THAT.
HOW'S MINE?
GNNHH!
WHOOA! FLAG'S--TIK!--DOWN!
AGAIN.
YOU'RE A DOG?
AND YOU ARE PAIN IN BACKSIDE WITH YOUR ZAPPY TRICKS!
COSMO WILL REACH INTO YOUR MIND AND SWITCH YOUR BRAIN OFF--
WAIT! I SEE! IN YOUR SURFACE THOUGHTS!
"BOZHE MOI! YOU REALLY ARE GUARDIANS OF GALAXY!"

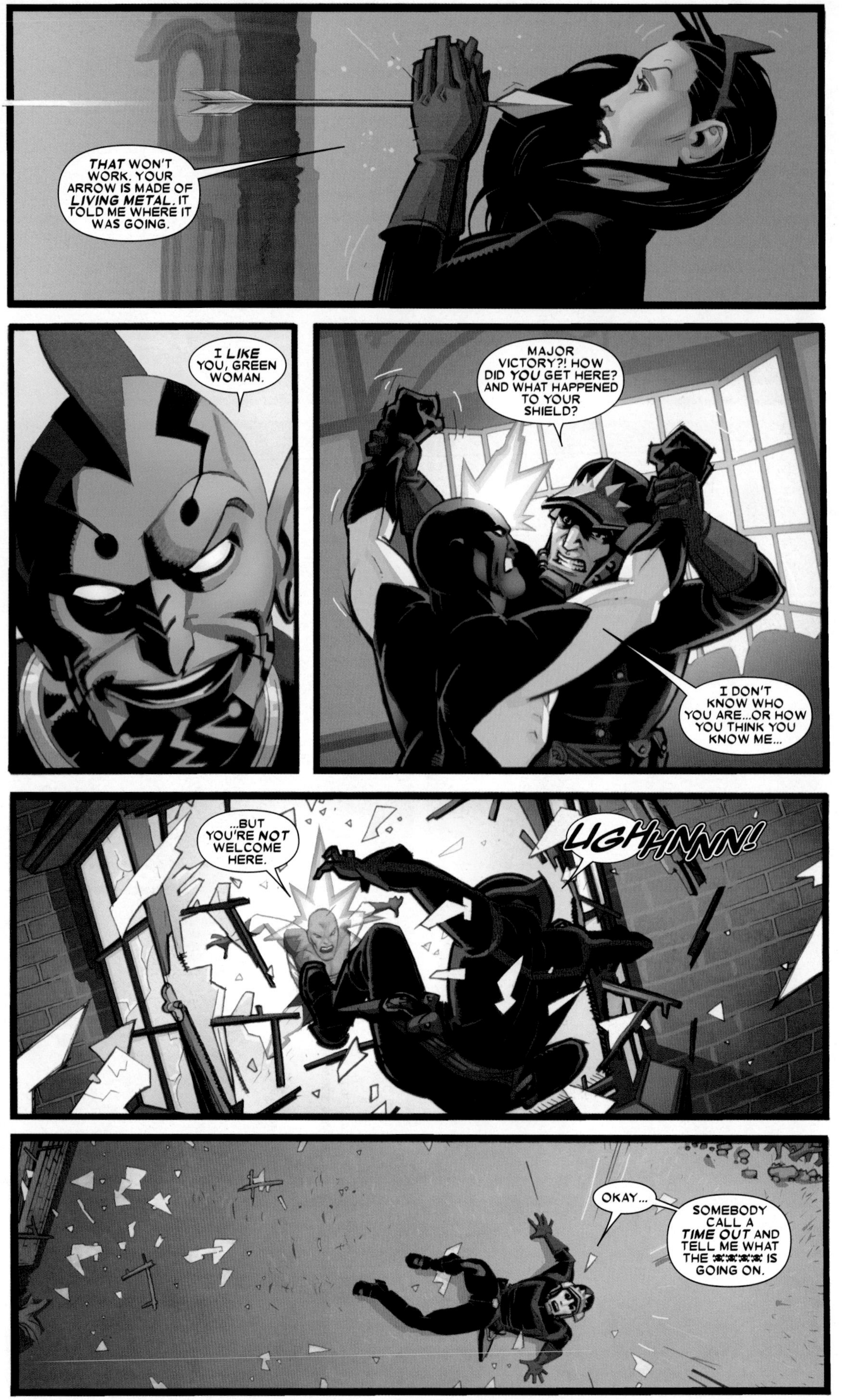
THAT WON'T WORK. YOUR ARROW IS MADE OF LIVING METAL. IT TOLD ME WHERE IT WAS GOING.
I LIKE YOU, GREEN WOMAN.
MAJOR VICTORY?! HOW DID YOU GET HERE? AND WHAT HAPPENED TO YOUR SHIELD?
I DON'T KNOW WHO YOU ARE...OR HOW YOU THINK YOU KNOW ME...
...BUT YOU'RE NOT WELCOME HERE.
UGHHNNN!
OKAY...
SOMEBODY CALL A TIME OUT AND TELL ME WHAT THE ☠☠☠☠ IS GOING ON.

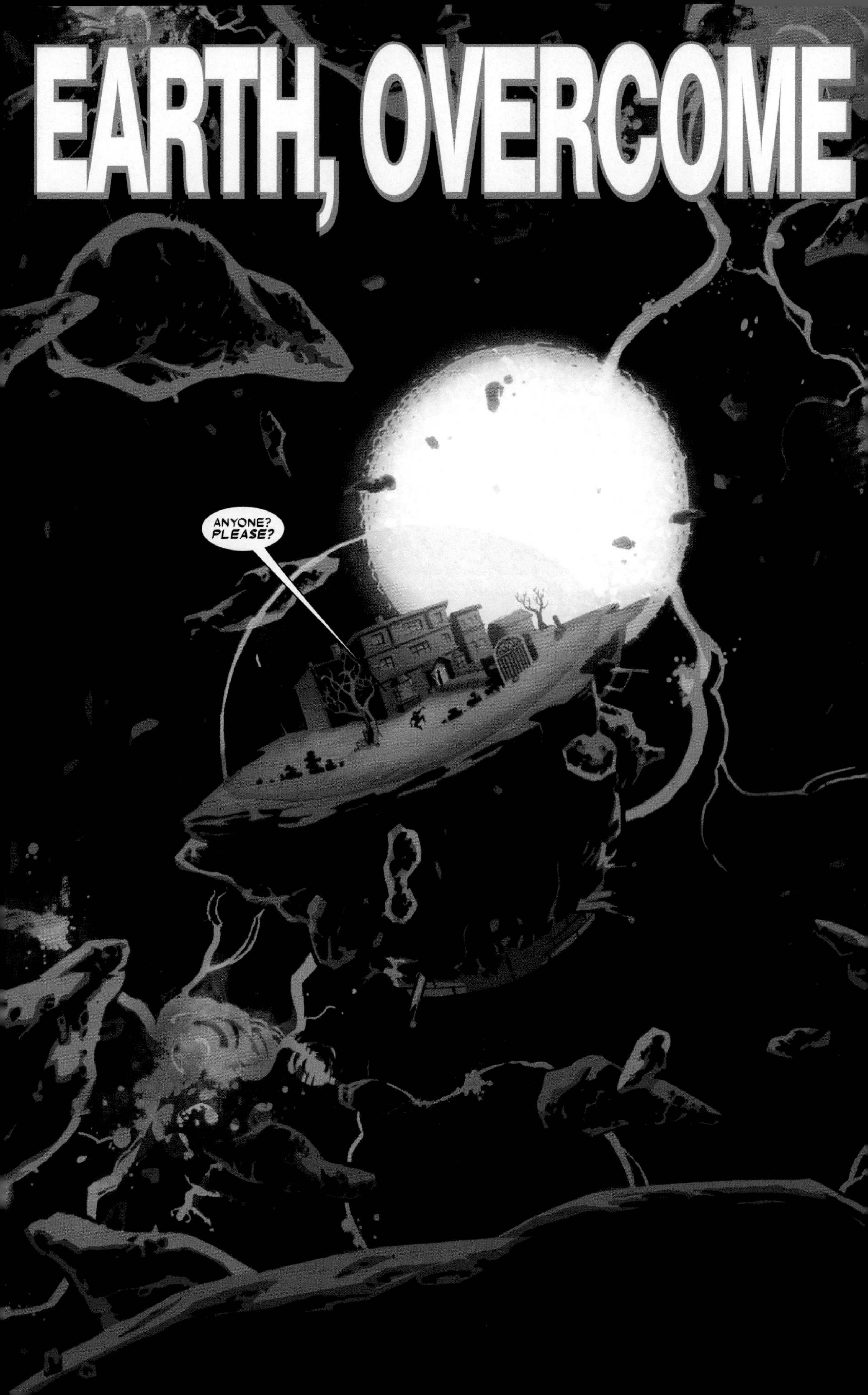
EARTH, OVERCOME
ANYONE? PLEASE?

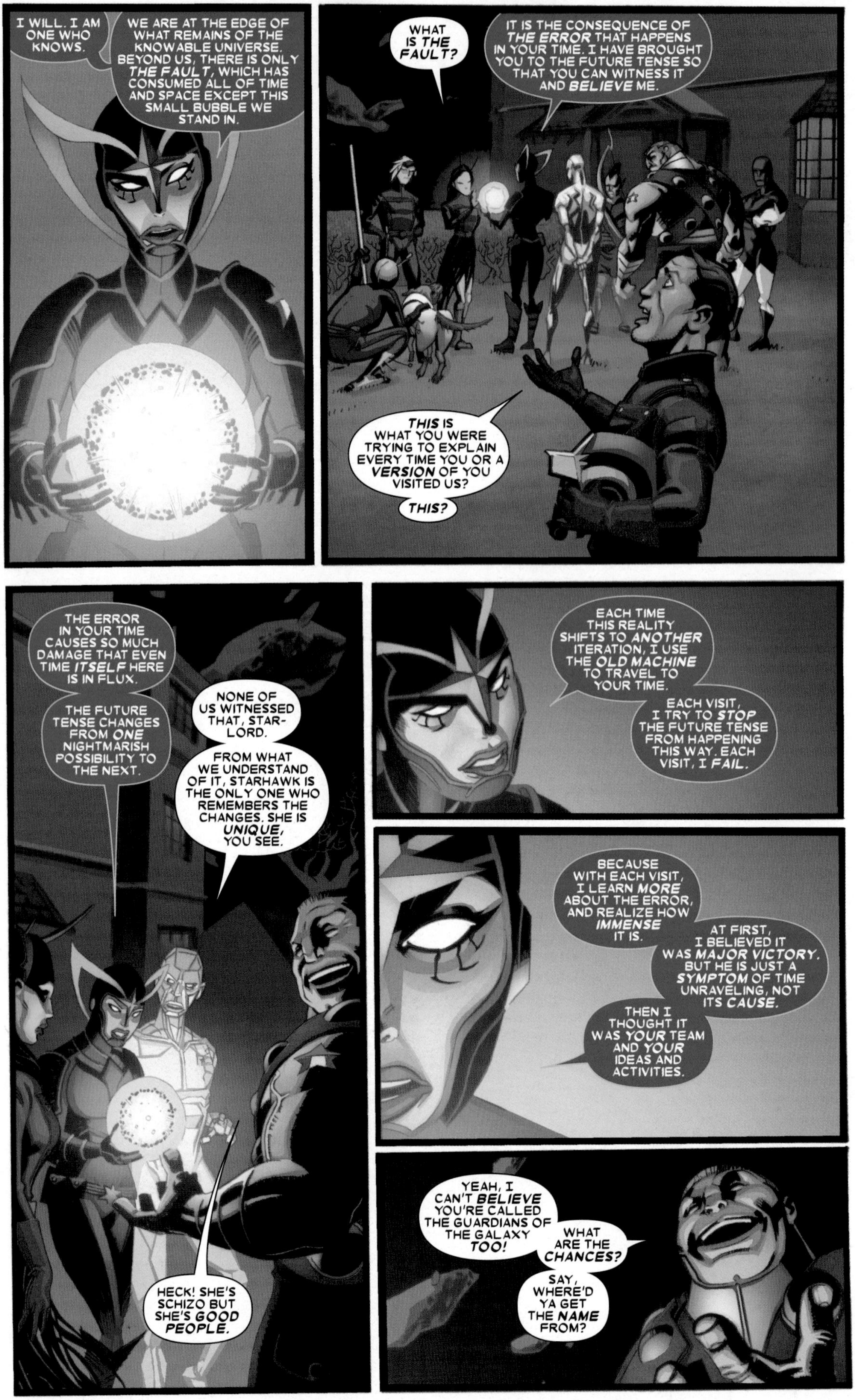

I WILL. I AM ONE WHO KNOWS.
WE ARE AT THE EDGE OF WHAT REMAINS OF THE KNOWABLE UNIVERSE. BEYOND US, THERE IS ONLY THE FAULT, WHICH HAS CONSUMED ALL OF TIME AND SPACE EXCEPT THIS SMALL BUBBLE WE STAND IN.
WHAT IS THE FAULT?
IT IS THE CONSEQUENCE OF THE ERROR THAT HAPPENS IN YOUR TIME. I HAVE BROUGHT YOU TO THE FUTURE TENSE SO THAT YOU CAN WITNESS IT AND BELIEVE ME.
THIS IS WHAT YOU WERE TRYING TO EXPLAIN EVERY TIME YOU OR A VERSION OF YOU VISITED US?
THIS?
THE ERROR IN YOUR TIME CAUSES SO MUCH DAMAGE THAT EVEN TIME ITSELF HERE IS IN FLUX.
THE FUTURE TENSE CHANGES FROM ONE NIGHTMARISH POSSIBILITY TO THE NEXT.
NONE OF US WITNESSED THAT, STAR-LORD.
FROM WHAT WE UNDERSTAND OF IT, STARHAWK IS THE ONLY ONE WHO REMEMBERS THE CHANGES. SHE IS UNIQUE, YOU SEE.
HECK! SHE'S SCHIZO BUT SHE'S GOOD PEOPLE.
EACH TIME THIS REALITY SHIFTS TO ANOTHER ITERATION, I USE THE OLD MACHINE TO TRAVEL TO YOUR TIME.
EACH VISIT, I TRY TO STOP THE FUTURE TENSE FROM HAPPENING THIS WAY. EACH VISIT, I FAIL.
BECAUSE WITH EACH VISIT, I LEARN MORE ABOUT THE ERROR, AND REALIZE HOW IMMENSE IT IS.
AT FIRST, I BELIEVED IT WAS MAJOR VICTORY. BUT HE IS JUST A SYMPTOM OF TIME UNRAVELING, NOT ITS CAUSE.
THEN I THOUGHT IT WAS YOUR TEAM AND YOUR IDEAS AND ACTIVITIES.
YEAH, I CAN'T BELIEVE YOU'RE CALLED THE GUARDIANS OF THE GALAXY TOO!
WHAT ARE THE CHANCES?
SAY, WHERE'D YA GET THE NAME FROM?

OH, *RIGHT.* I GET IT. *"NOT THE TIME FOR CHIT-CHAT, CHARLIE."* IT'S JUST THAT WE HAVEN'T HAD VISITORS IN THE *LONGEST* TIME.

ON MY *LAST* VISIT, YOU *DETAINED* ME.

THIS GAVE ME TIME TO STUDY, TO *PROBE.*

THEN THE FORCES OF THE *SHI'AR* AND THE *INHUMANS* ARRIVED ON YOUR STATION, AND MY MIND WAS BROUGHT INTO *CLOSE* PROXIMITY TO THE THOUGHTS OF THE INHUMAN KING.

AND AT LAST I SAW THE *TRUTH.*

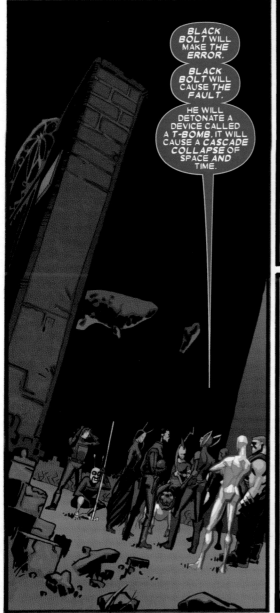

BLACK BOLT WILL MAKE *THE ERROR.*

BLACK BOLT WILL CAUSE *THE FAULT.*

HE WILL DETONATE A DEVICE CALLED A *T-BOMB.* IT WILL CAUSE A *CASCADE COLLAPSE* OF SPACE *AND* TIME.

THOSE STUPID ✖✖✖✖✖✖*!*

THIS IS *EXACTLY* WHAT ADAM WARLOCK HAS BEEN WARNING US OF ALL ALONG. THE UNIVERSE IS TOO *FRAGILE* TO WITHSTAND THE PUNISHMENT OF A STELLAR WAR.

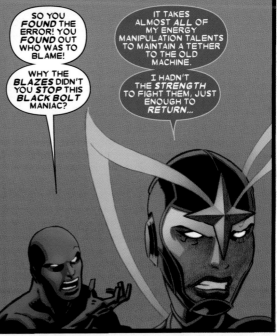

SO YOU *FOUND* THE ERROR! YOU *FOUND* OUT WHO WAS TO BLAME!

WHY THE *BLAZES* DIDN'T YOU *STOP* THIS *BLACK BOLT* MANIAC?

IT TAKES ALMOST *ALL* OF MY ENERGY MANIPULATION TALENTS TO MAINTAIN A TETHER TO THE OLD MACHINE.

I HADN'T THE *STRENGTH* TO FIGHT THEM, JUST ENOUGH TO *RETURN...*

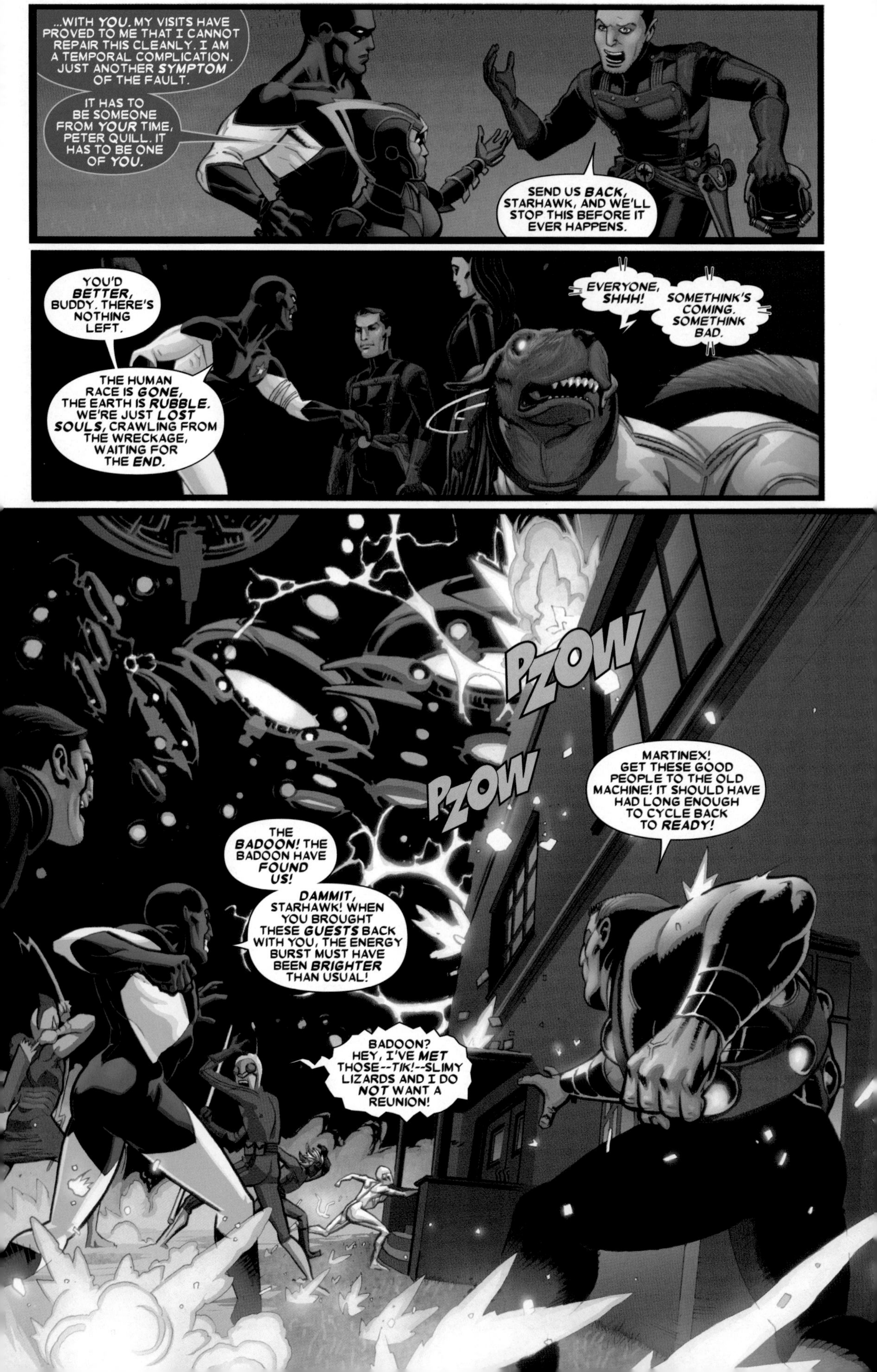
...WITH YOU. MY VISITS HAVE PROVED TO ME THAT I CANNOT REPAIR THIS CLEANLY. I AM A TEMPORAL COMPLICATION. JUST ANOTHER SYMPTOM OF THE FAULT.
IT HAS TO BE SOMEONE FROM YOUR TIME, PETER QUILL. IT HAS TO BE ONE OF YOU.
SEND US BACK, STARHAWK, AND WE'LL STOP THIS BEFORE IT EVER HAPPENS.
YOU'D BETTER, BUDDY. THERE'S NOTHING LEFT.
THE HUMAN RACE IS GONE, THE EARTH IS RUBBLE. WE'RE JUST LOST SOULS, CRAWLING FROM THE WRECKAGE, WAITING FOR THE END.
EVERYONE, SHHH!
SOMETHINK'S COMING. SOMETHINK BAD.
PZOW
PZOW
MARTINEX! GET THESE GOOD PEOPLE TO THE OLD MACHINE! IT SHOULD HAVE HAD LONG ENOUGH TO CYCLE BACK TO READY!
THE BADOON! THE BADOON HAVE FOUND US!
DAMMIT, STARHAWK! WHEN YOU BROUGHT THESE GUESTS BACK WITH YOU, THE ENERGY BURST MUST HAVE BEEN BRIGHTER THAN USUAL!
BADOON? HEY, I'VE MET THOSE--TIK!--SLIMY LIZARDS AND I DO NOT WANT A REUNION!

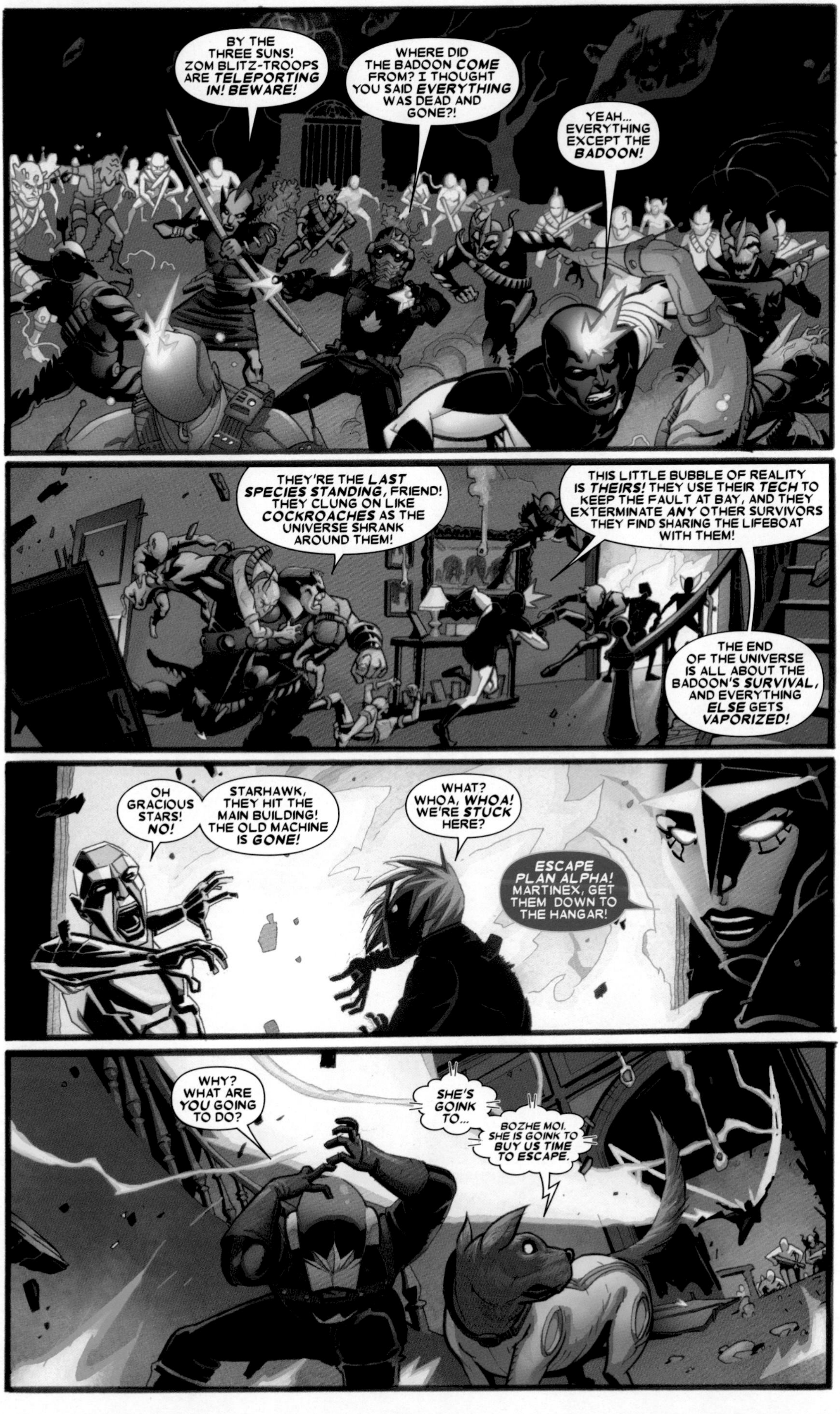
BY THE THREE SUNS! ZOM BLITZ-TROOPS ARE TELEPORTING IN! BEWARE!
WHERE DID THE BADOON COME FROM? I THOUGHT YOU SAID EVERYTHING WAS DEAD AND GONE?!
YEAH... EVERYTHING EXCEPT THE BADOON!
THEY'RE THE LAST SPECIES STANDING, FRIEND! THEY CLUNG ON LIKE COCKROACHES AS THE UNIVERSE SHRANK AROUND THEM!
THIS LITTLE BUBBLE OF REALITY IS THEIRS! THEY USE THEIR TECH TO KEEP THE FAULT AT BAY, AND THEY EXTERMINATE ANY OTHER SURVIVORS THEY FIND SHARING THE LIFEBOAT WITH THEM!
THE END OF THE UNIVERSE IS ALL ABOUT THE BADOON'S SURVIVAL, AND EVERYTHING ELSE GETS VAPORIZED!
OH GRACIOUS STARS! NO!
STARHAWK, THEY HIT THE MAIN BUILDING! THE OLD MACHINE IS GONE!
WHAT? WHOA, WHOA! WE'RE STUCK HERE?
ESCAPE PLAN ALPHA! MARTINEX, GET THEM DOWN TO THE HANGAR!
WHY? WHAT ARE YOU GOING TO DO?
SHE'S GOINK TO...
BOZHE MOI. SHE IS GOINK TO BUY US TIME TO ESCAPE.

BADOON! MOST OF YOU WILL *NOT* SURVIVE THE *NEXT THIRTY SECONDS!* TRUST ME ON THIS...

....I AM ONE WHO KNOWS.

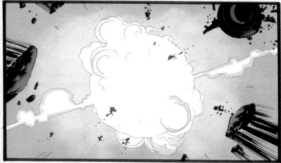

WHOOOOMMMP!

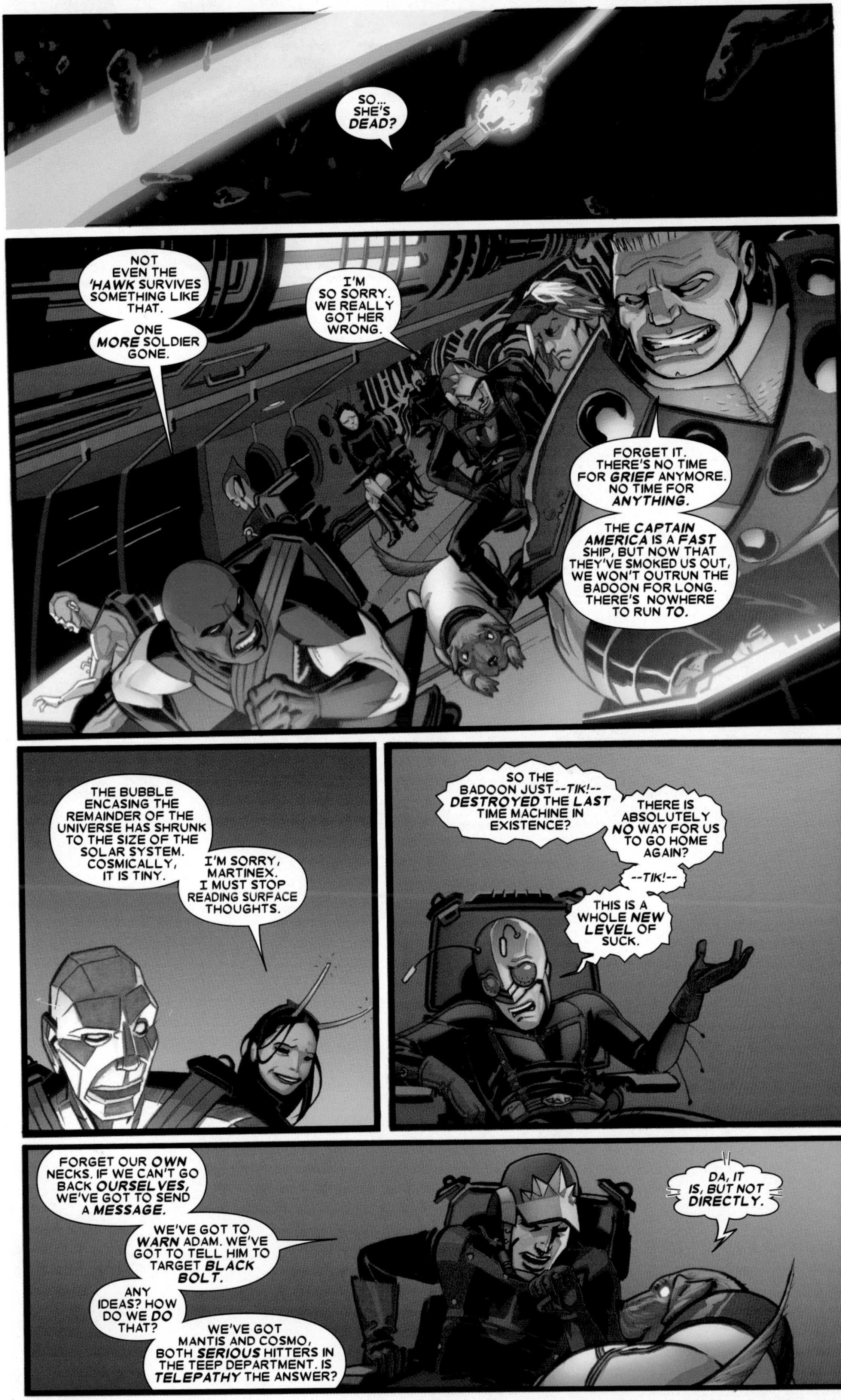
SO... SHE'S DEAD?
NOT EVEN THE 'HAWK SURVIVES SOMETHING LIKE THAT.
ONE MORE SOLDIER GONE.
I'M SO SORRY. WE REALLY GOT HER WRONG.
FORGET IT. THERE'S NO TIME FOR GRIEF ANYMORE. NO TIME FOR ANYTHING.
THE CAPTAIN AMERICA IS A FAST SHIP, BUT NOW THAT THEY'VE SMOKED US OUT, WE WON'T OUTRUN THE BADOON FOR LONG. THERE'S NOWHERE TO RUN TO.
THE BUBBLE ENCASING THE REMAINDER OF THE UNIVERSE HAS SHRUNK TO THE SIZE OF THE SOLAR SYSTEM. COSMICALLY, IT IS TINY.
I'M SORRY, MARTINEX. I MUST STOP READING SURFACE THOUGHTS.
SO THE BADOON JUST--TIK!--DESTROYED THE LAST TIME MACHINE IN EXISTENCE?
THERE IS ABSOLUTELY NO WAY FOR US TO GO HOME AGAIN?
--TIK!--
THIS IS A WHOLE NEW LEVEL OF SUCK.
FORGET OUR OWN NECKS. IF WE CAN'T GO BACK OURSELVES, WE'VE GOT TO SEND A MESSAGE.
WE'VE GOT TO WARN ADAM. WE'VE GOT TO TELL HIM TO TARGET BLACK BOLT.
ANY IDEAS? HOW DO WE DO THAT?
WE'VE GOT MANTIS AND COSMO, BOTH SERIOUS HITTERS IN THE TEEP DEPARTMENT. IS TELEPATHY THE ANSWER?
DA, IT IS, BUT NOT DIRECTLY.

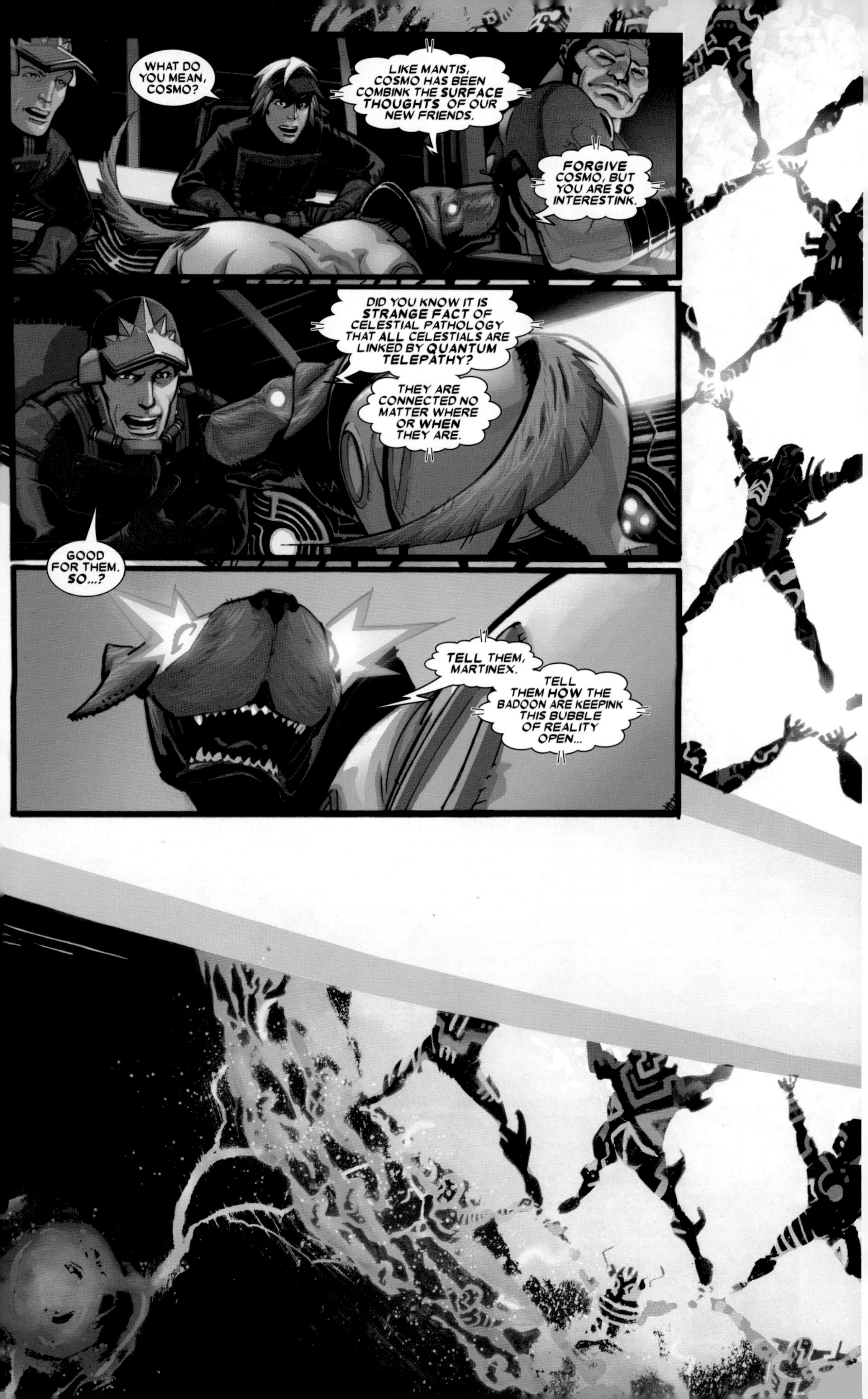
WHAT DO YOU MEAN, COSMO?
LIKE MANTIS, COSMO HAS BEEN COMBINK THE SURFACE THOUGHTS OF OUR NEW FRIENDS.
FORGIVE COSMO, BUT YOU ARE SO INTERESTINK.
DID YOU KNOW IT IS STRANGE FACT OF CELESTIAL PATHOLOGY THAT ALL CELESTIALS ARE LINKED BY QUANTUM TELEPATHY?
THEY ARE CONNECTED NO MATTER WHERE OR WHEN THEY ARE.
GOOD FOR THEM. SO...?
TELL THEM, MARTINEX.
TELL THEM HOW THE BADOON ARE KEEPINK THIS BUBBLE OF REALITY OPEN...

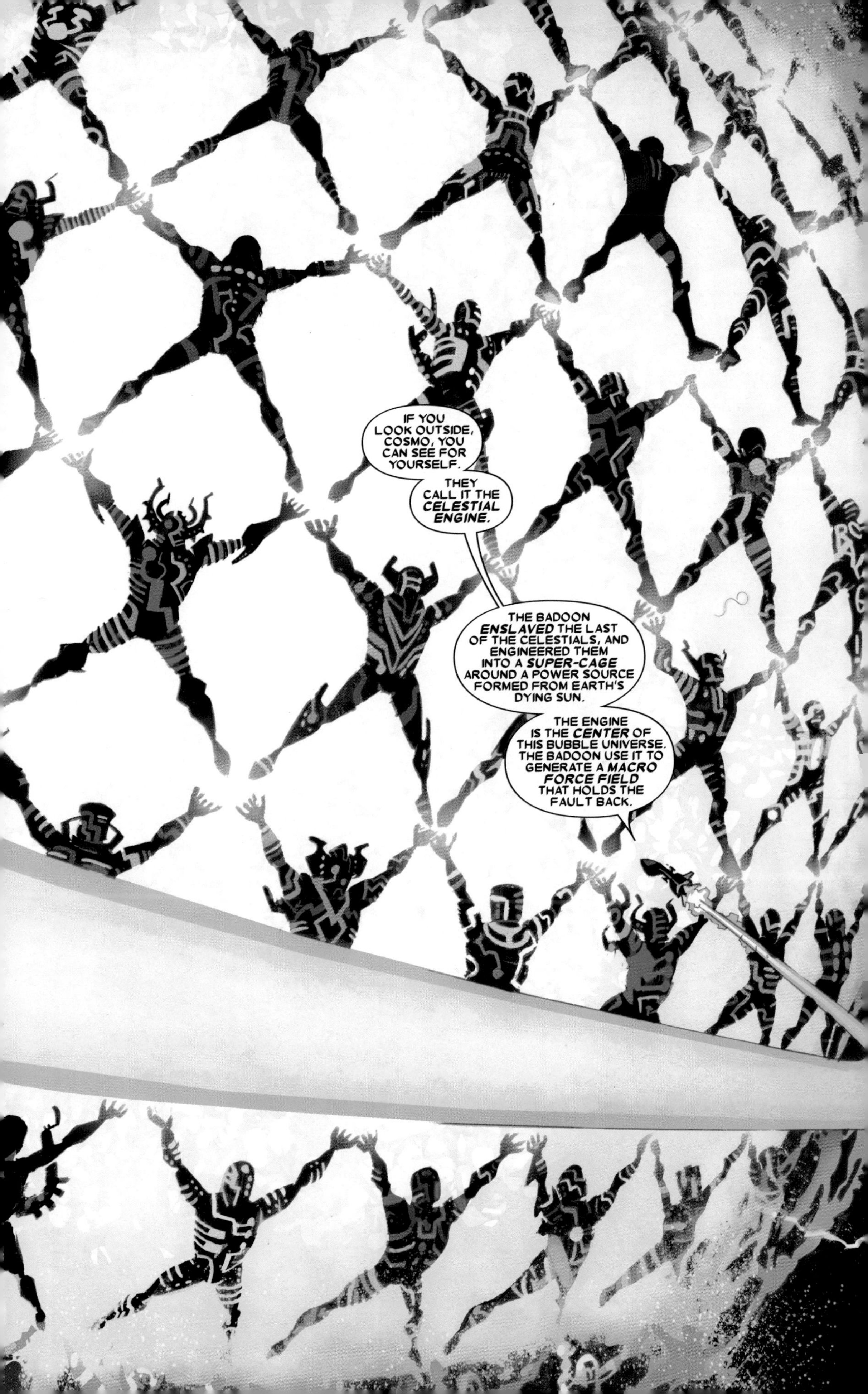
IF YOU LOOK OUTSIDE, COSMO, YOU CAN SEE FOR YOURSELF.
THEY CALL IT THE *CELESTIAL ENGINE.*
THE BADOON *ENSLAVED* THE LAST OF THE CELESTIALS, AND ENGINEERED THEM INTO A *SUPER-CAGE* AROUND A POWER SOURCE FORMED FROM EARTH'S DYING SUN.
THE ENGINE IS THE *CENTER* OF THIS BUBBLE UNIVERSE. THE BADOON USE IT TO GENERATE A *MACRO FORCE FIELD* THAT HOLDS THE FAULT BACK.

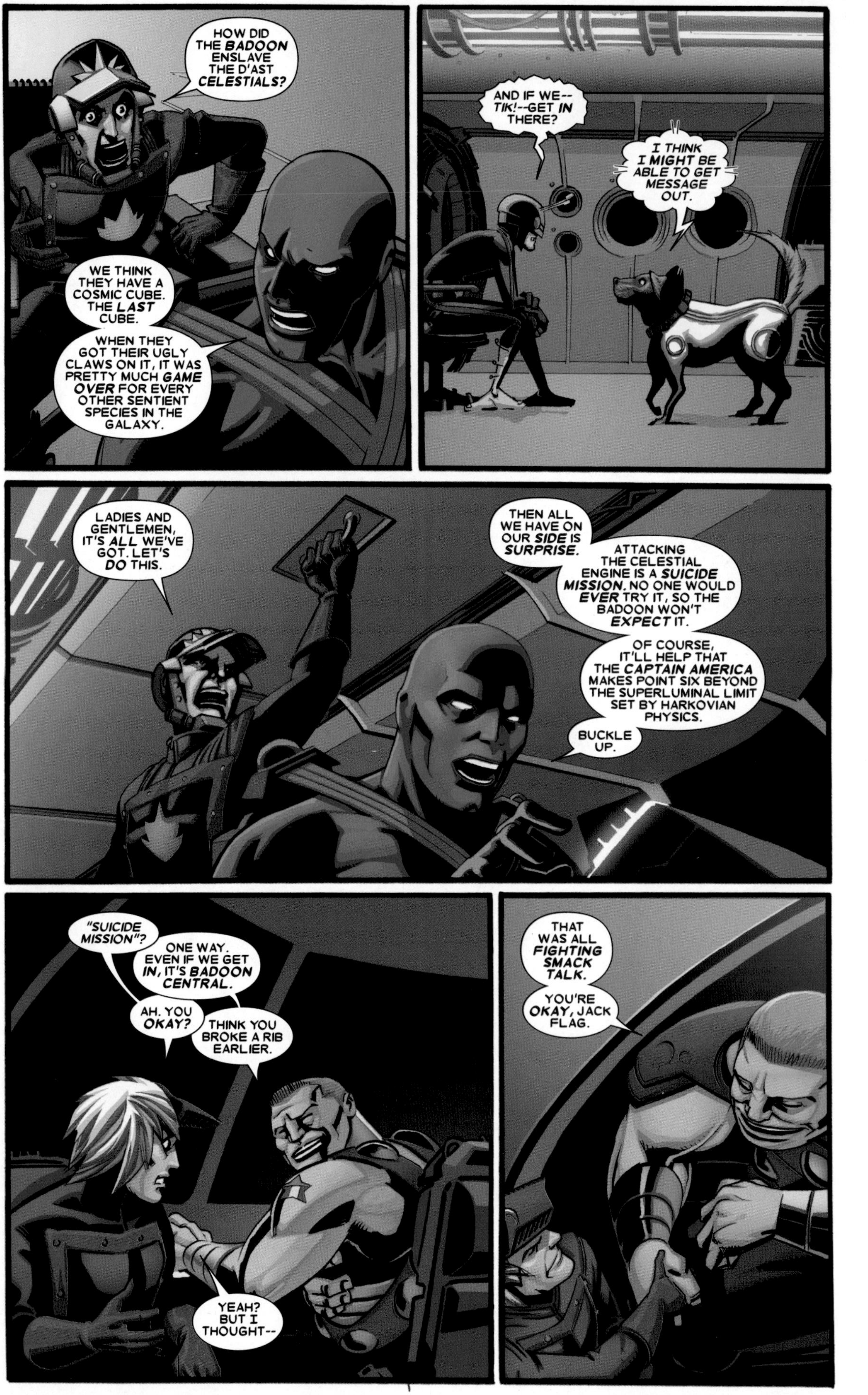
HOW DID THE BADOON ENSLAVE THE D'AST CELESTIALS?
WE THINK THEY HAVE A COSMIC CUBE. THE LAST CUBE.
WHEN THEY GOT THEIR UGLY CLAWS ON IT, IT WAS PRETTY MUCH GAME OVER FOR EVERY OTHER SENTIENT SPECIES IN THE GALAXY.
AND IF WE--TIK!--GET IN THERE?
I THINK I MIGHT BE ABLE TO GET MESSAGE OUT.
LADIES AND GENTLEMEN, IT'S ALL WE'VE GOT. LET'S DO THIS.
THEN ALL WE HAVE ON OUR SIDE IS SURPRISE.
ATTACKING THE CELESTIAL ENGINE IS A SUICIDE MISSION. NO ONE WOULD EVER TRY IT, SO THE BADOON WON'T EXPECT IT.
OF COURSE, IT'LL HELP THAT THE CAPTAIN AMERICA MAKES POINT SIX BEYOND THE SUPERLUMINAL LIMIT SET BY HARKOVIAN PHYSICS.
BUCKLE UP.
"SUICIDE MISSION"?
ONE WAY. EVEN IF WE GET IN, IT'S BADOON CENTRAL.
AH. YOU OKAY?
THINK YOU BROKE A RIB EARLIER.
YEAH? BUT I THOUGHT--
THAT WAS ALL FIGHTING SMACK TALK.
YOU'RE OKAY, JACK FLAG.

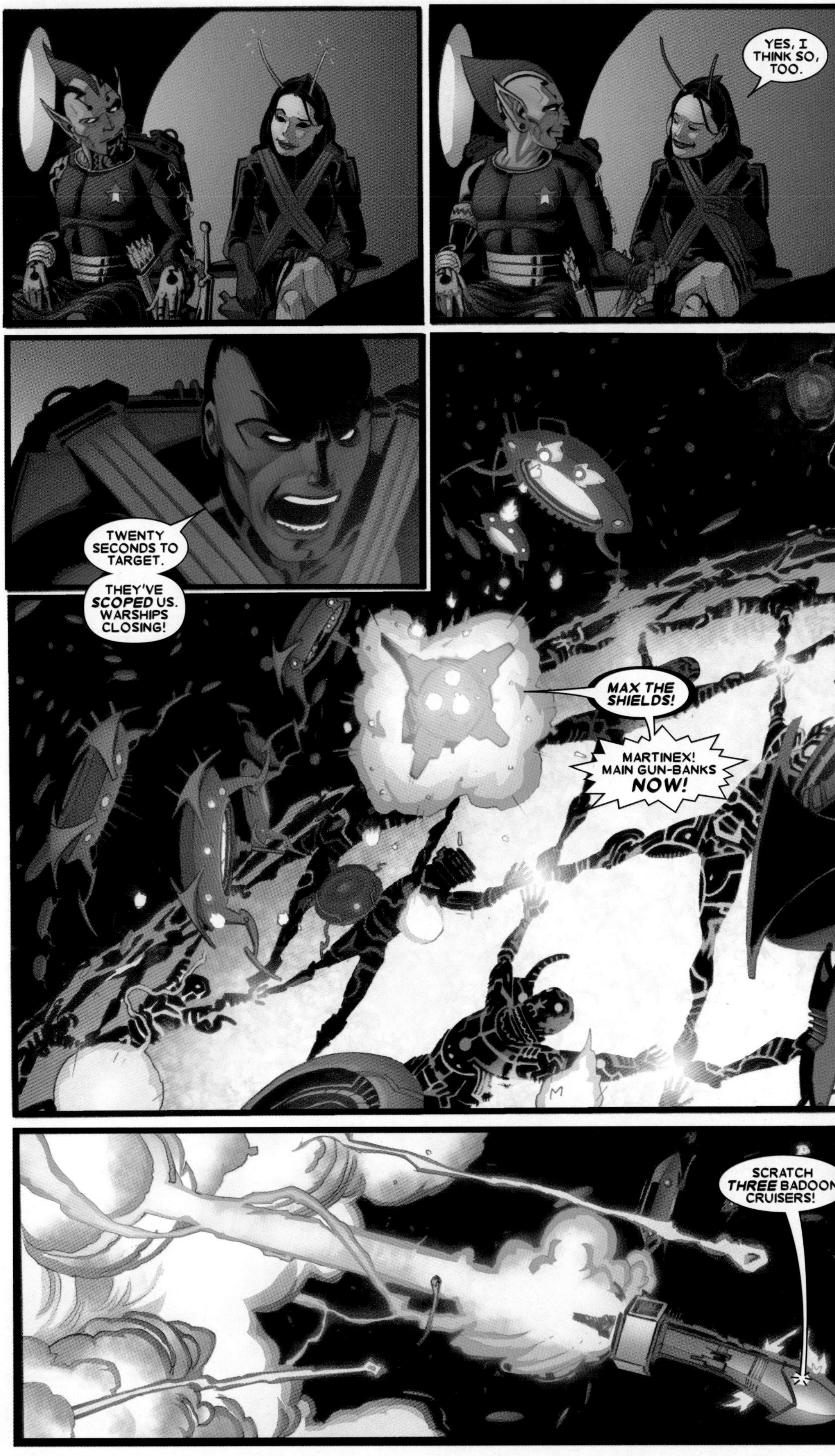
YES, I THINK SO, TOO.
TWENTY SECONDS TO TARGET.
THEY'VE SCOPED US. WARSHIPS CLOSING!
MAX THE SHIELDS!
MARTINEX! MAIN GUN-BANKS NOW!
SCRATCH THREE BADOON CRUISERS!

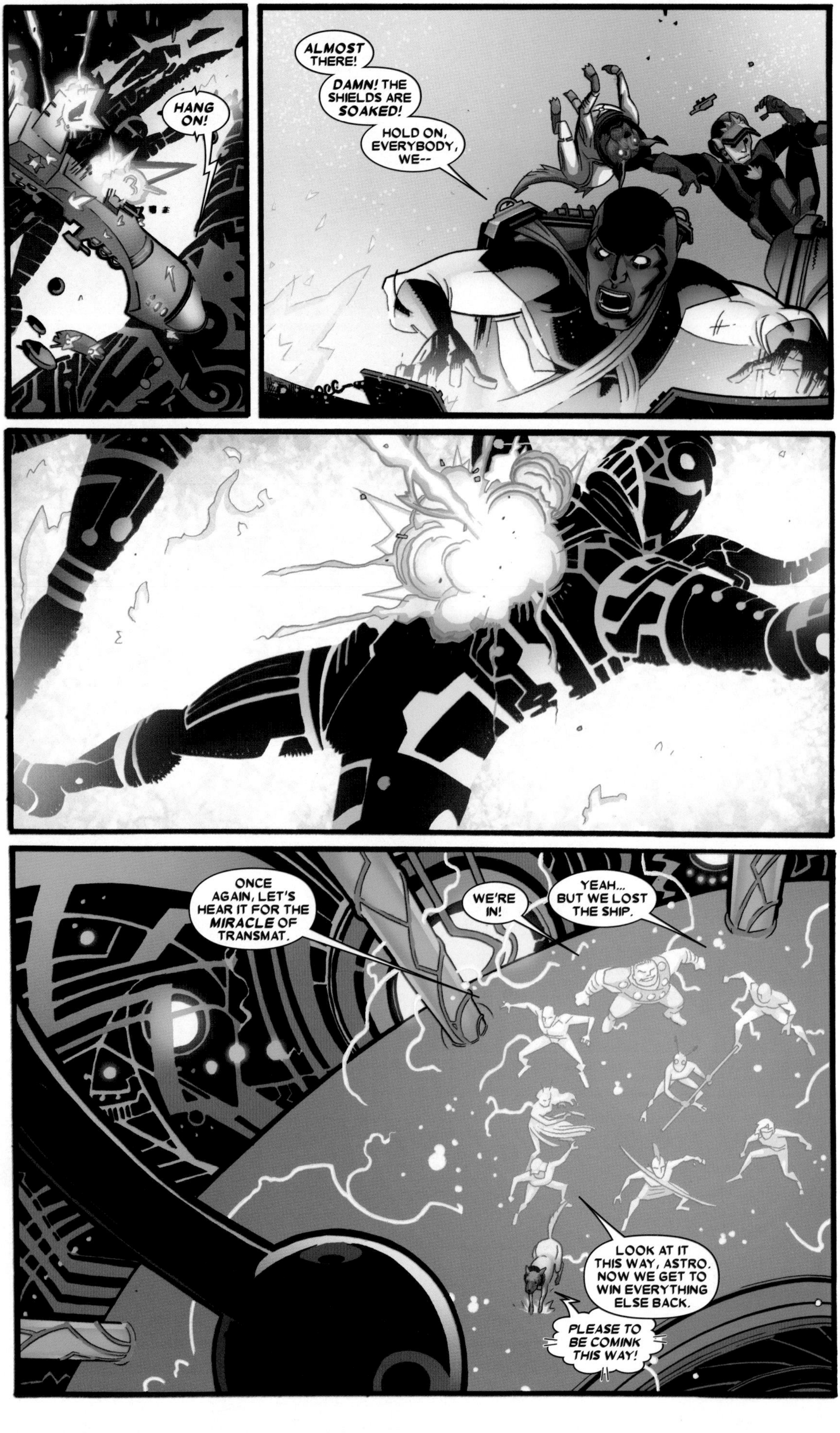
HANG ON!
ALMOST THERE!
DAMN! THE SHIELDS ARE SOAKED!
HOLD ON, EVERYBODY, WE--
ONCE AGAIN, LET'S HEAR IT FOR THE MIRACLE OF TRANSMAT.
WE'RE IN!
YEAH... BUT WE LOST THE SHIP.
LOOK AT IT THIS WAY, ASTRO. NOW WE GET TO WIN EVERYTHING ELSE BACK.
PLEASE TO BE COMINK THIS WAY!

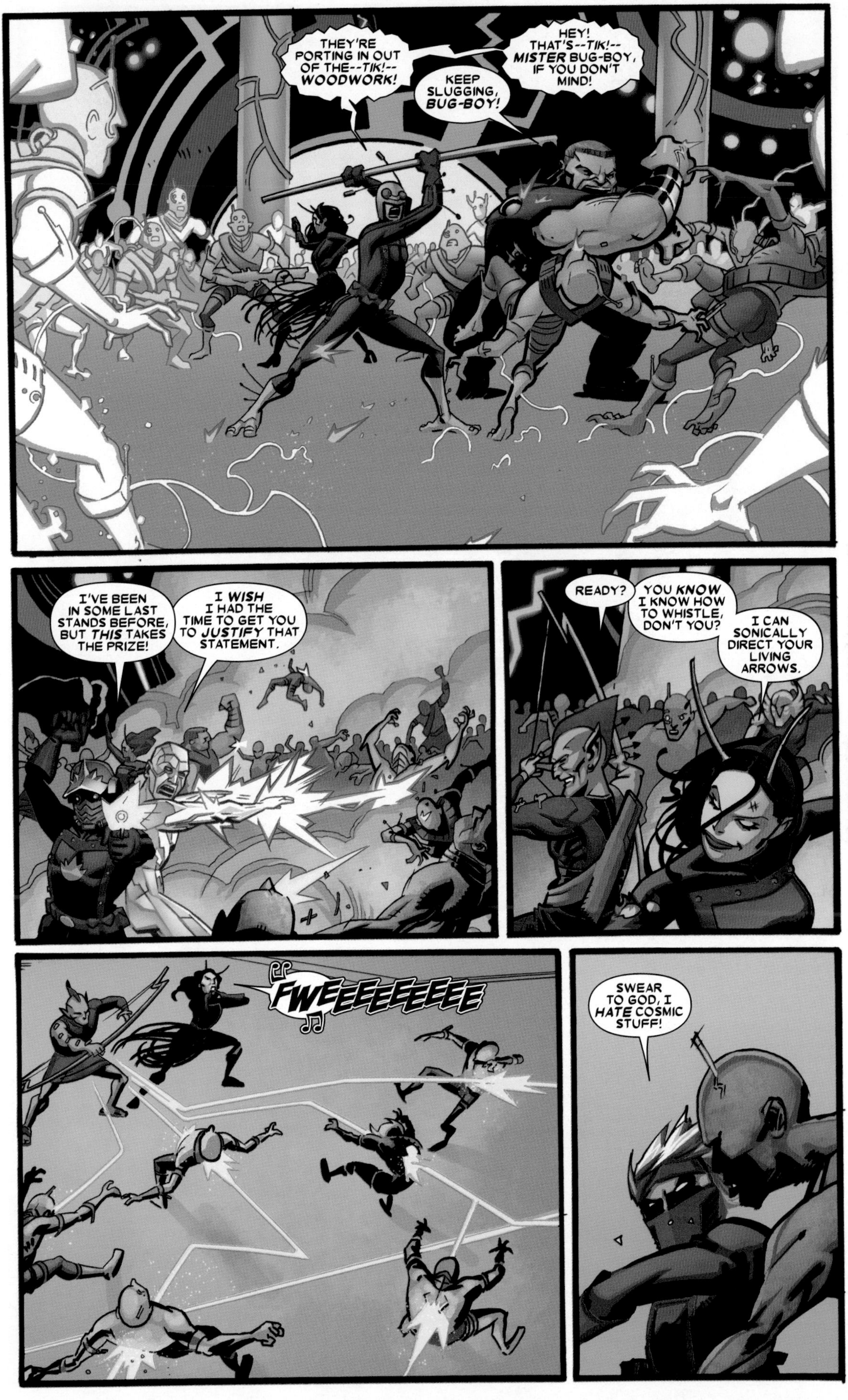
THEY'RE PORTING IN OUT OF THE--TIK!-- WOODWORK!
KEEP SLUGGING, BUG-BOY!
HEY! THAT'S--TIK!-- MISTER BUG-BOY, IF YOU DON'T MIND!
I'VE BEEN IN SOME LAST STANDS BEFORE, BUT THIS TAKES THE PRIZE!
I WISH I HAD THE TIME TO GET YOU TO JUSTIFY THAT STATEMENT.
READY?
YOU KNOW I KNOW HOW TO WHISTLE, DON'T YOU?
I CAN SONICALLY DIRECT YOUR LIVING ARROWS.
FWEEEEEEEEEE
SWEAR TO GOD, I HATE COSMIC STUFF!

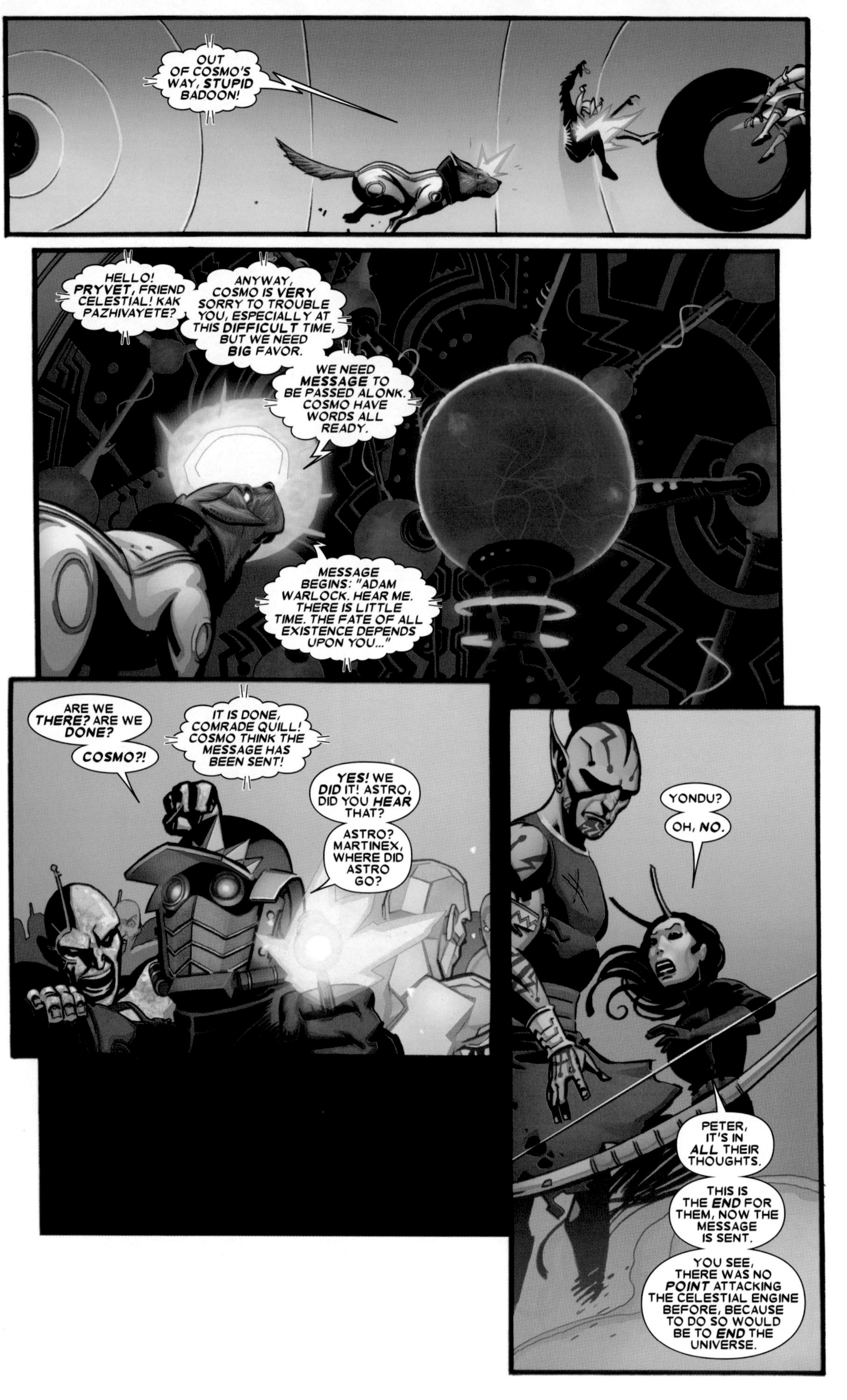
OUT OF COSMO'S WAY, **STUPID** BADOON!
HELLO! **PRYVET**, FRIEND CELESTIAL! KAK PAZHIVAYETE?
ANYWAY, COSMO IS **VERY** SORRY TO TROUBLE YOU, ESPECIALLY AT THIS **DIFFICULT** TIME, BUT WE NEED **BIG** FAVOR.
WE NEED **MESSAGE** TO BE PASSED ALONK. COSMO HAVE WORDS ALL READY.
MESSAGE BEGINS: "ADAM WARLOCK. HEAR ME. THERE IS LITTLE TIME. THE FATE OF ALL EXISTENCE DEPENDS UPON YOU..."
ARE WE **THERE?** ARE WE **DONE?**
COSMO?!
IT IS DONE, COMRADE QUILL! COSMO THINK THE MESSAGE HAS BEEN SENT!
YES! WE **DID** IT! ASTRO, DID YOU **HEAR** THAT?
ASTRO? MARTINEX, WHERE DID ASTRO GO?
YONDU?
OH, **NO.**
PETER, IT'S IN **ALL** THEIR THOUGHTS.
THIS IS THE **END** FOR THEM, NOW THE MESSAGE IS SENT.
YOU SEE, THERE WAS NO **POINT** ATTACKING THE CELESTIAL ENGINE BEFORE, BECAUSE TO DO SO WOULD BE TO **END** THE UNIVERSE.

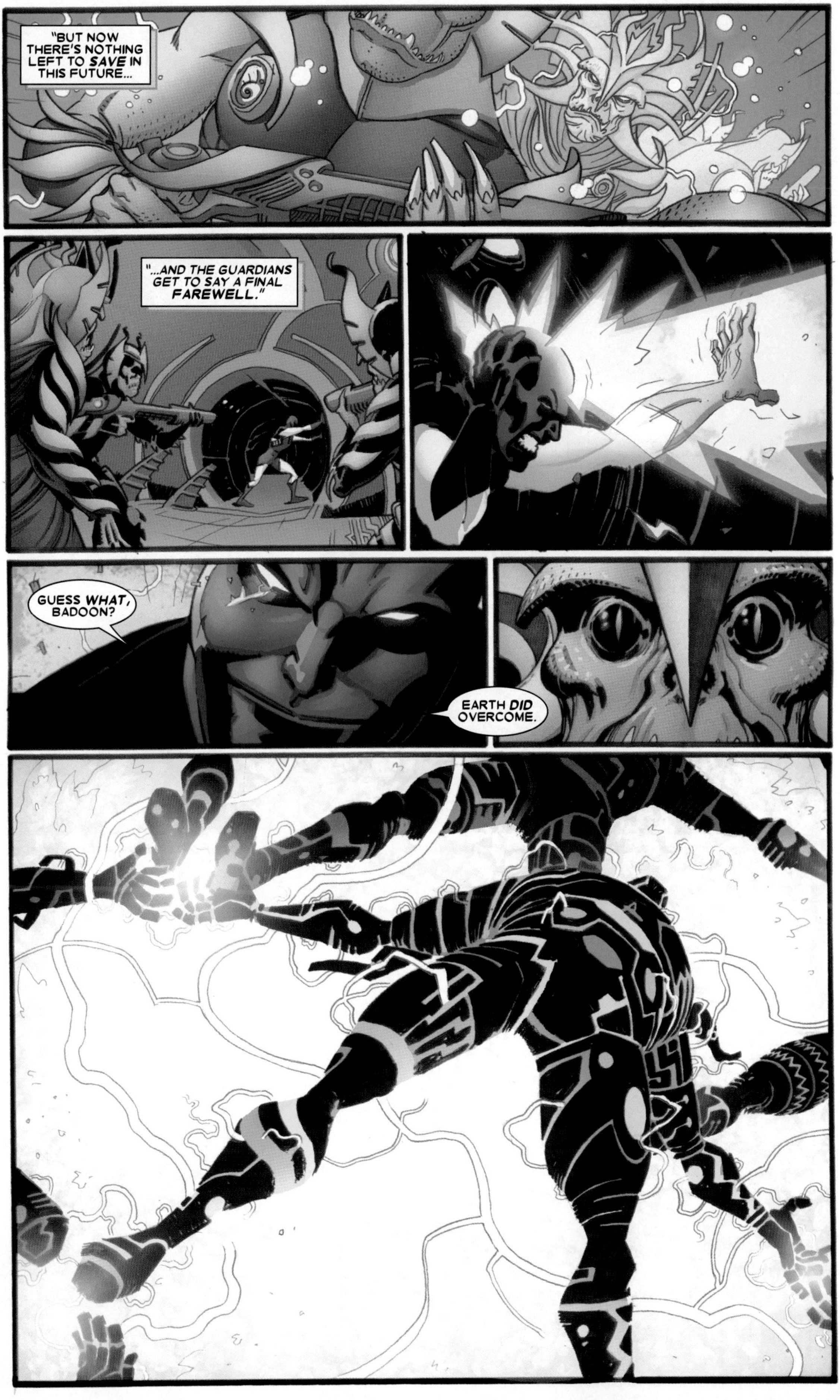
"BUT NOW THERE'S NOTHING LEFT TO SAVE IN THIS FUTURE...
"...AND THE GUARDIANS GET TO SAY A FINAL FAREWELL."
GUESS WHAT, BADOON?
EARTH DID OVERCOME.

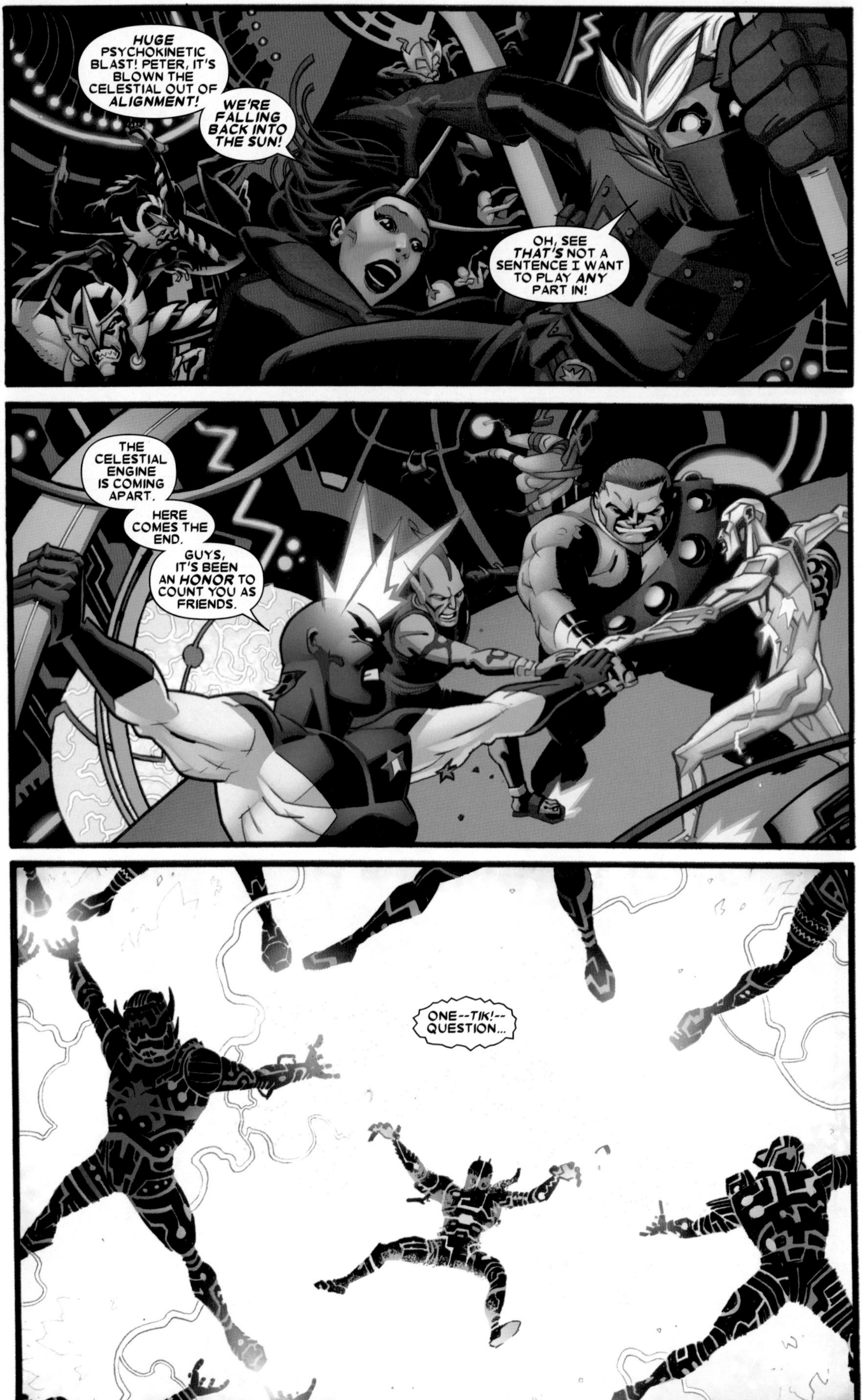
HUGE PSYCHOKINETIC BLAST! PETER, IT'S BLOWN THE CELESTIAL OUT OF ALIGNMENT!
WE'RE FALLING BACK INTO THE SUN!
OH, SEE THAT'S NOT A SENTENCE I WANT TO PLAY ANY PART IN!
THE CELESTIAL ENGINE IS COMING APART.
HERE COMES THE END.
GUYS, IT'S BEEN AN HONOR TO COUNT YOU AS FRIENDS.
ONE--TIK!-- QUESTION...

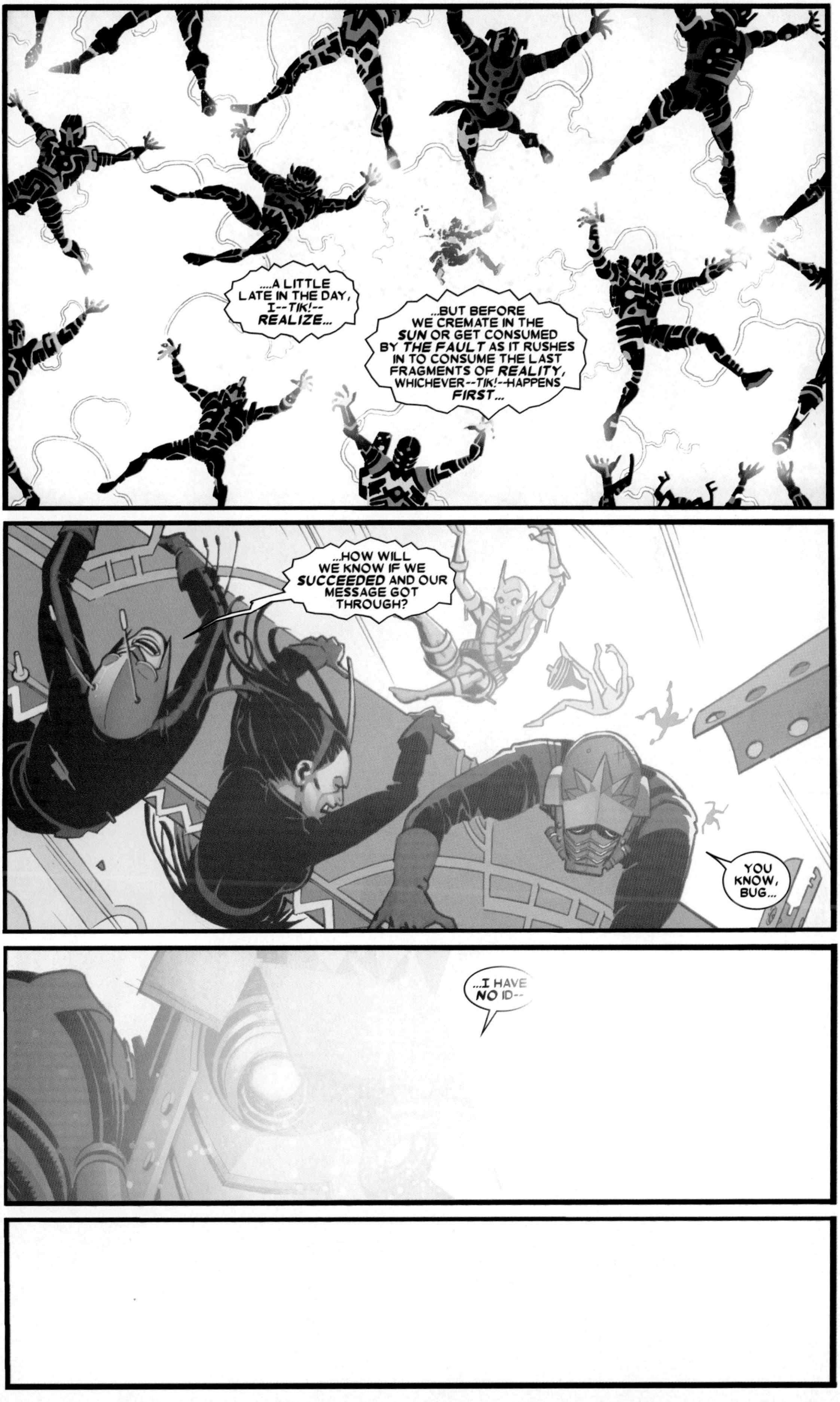
....A LITTLE LATE IN THE DAY, I--TIK!-- REALIZE...
...BUT BEFORE WE CREMATE IN THE SUN OR GET CONSUMED BY THE FAULT AS IT RUSHES IN TO CONSUME THE LAST FRAGMENTS OF REALITY, WHICHEVER--TIK!--HAPPENS FIRST...
...HOW WILL WE KNOW IF WE SUCCEEDED AND OUR MESSAGE GOT THROUGH?
YOU KNOW, BUG...
...I HAVE NO ID--

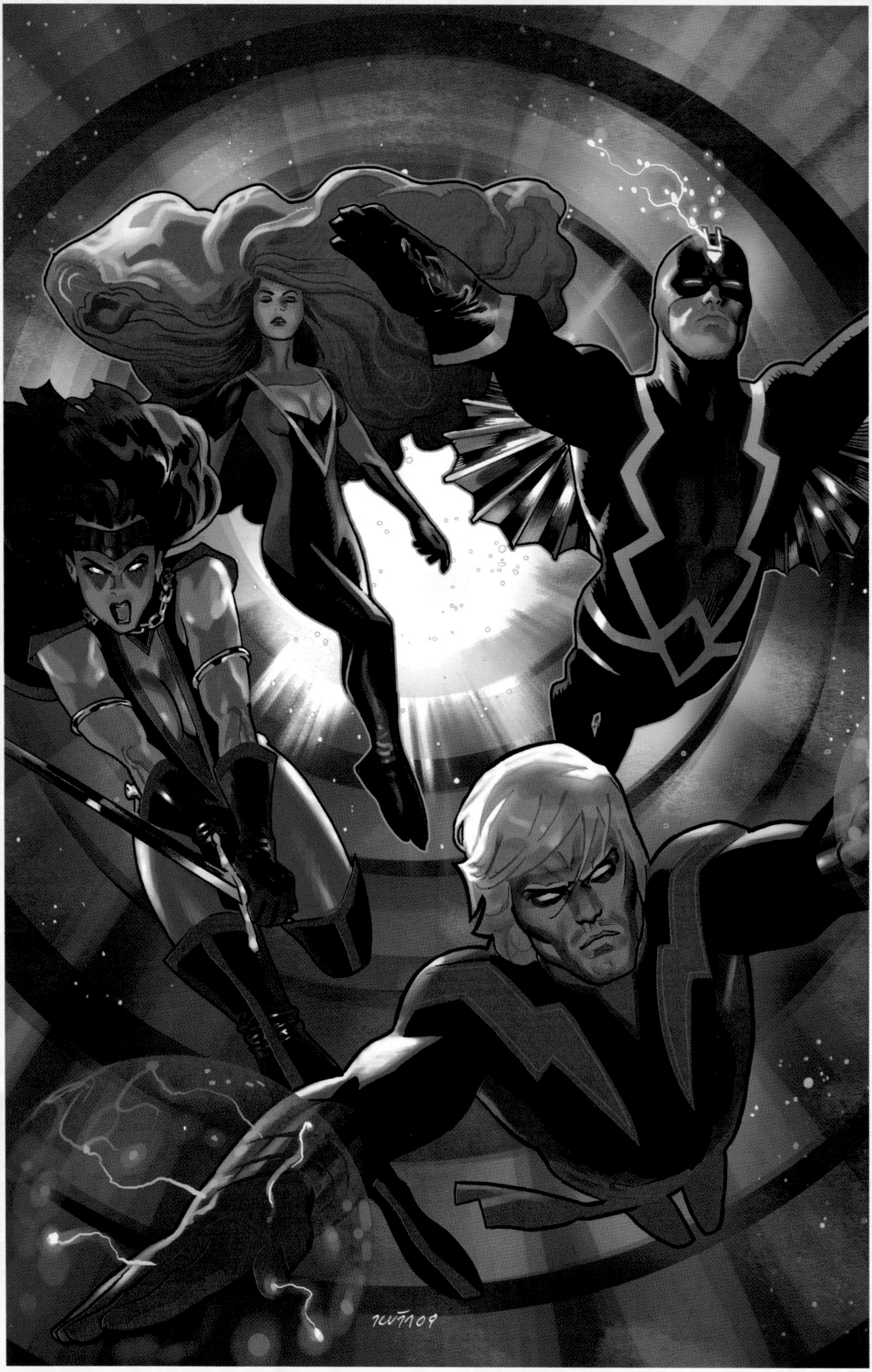

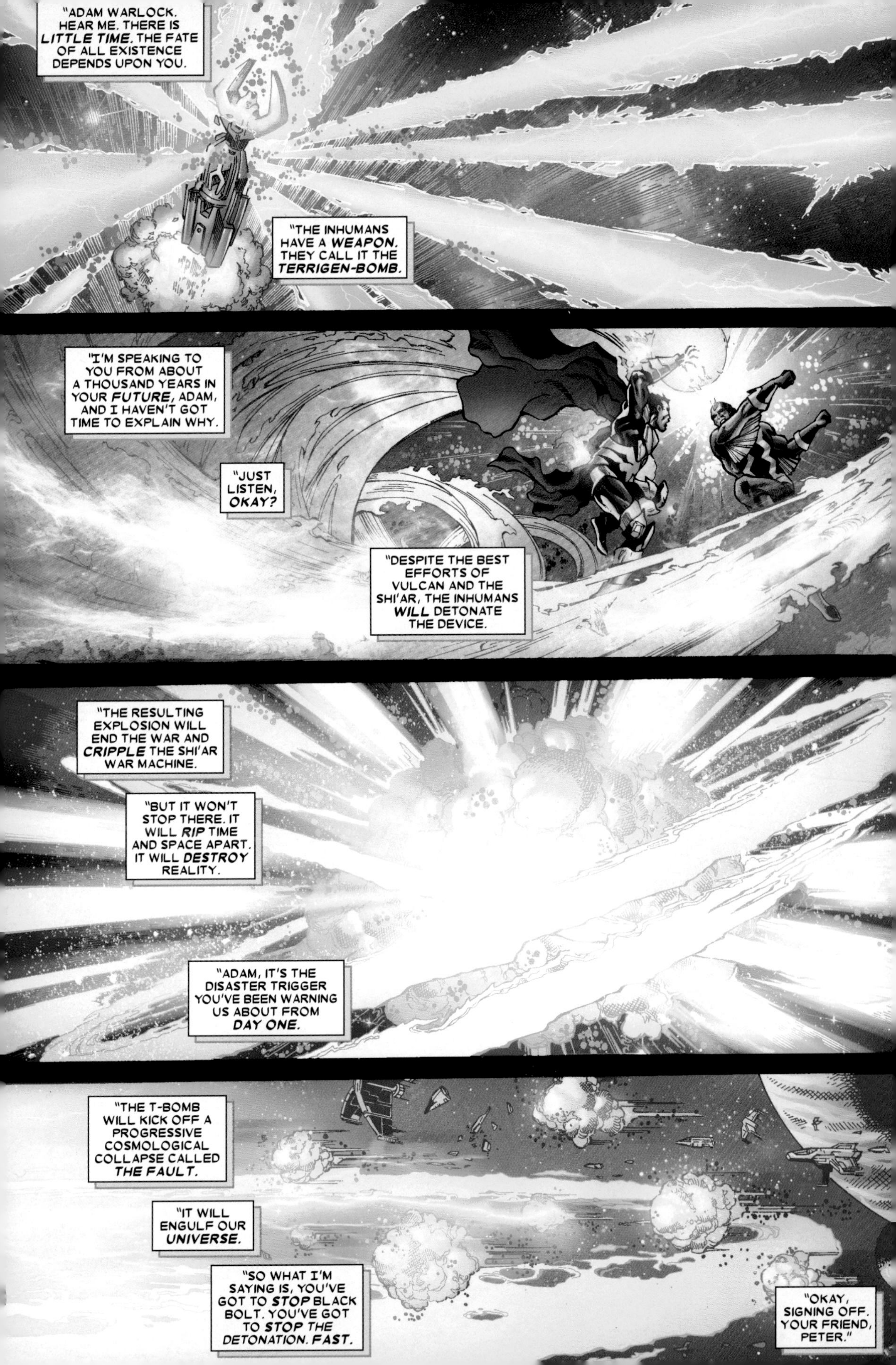
"ADAM WARLOCK. HEAR ME. THERE IS LITTLE TIME. THE FATE OF ALL EXISTENCE DEPENDS UPON YOU.
"THE INHUMANS HAVE A WEAPON. THEY CALL IT THE TERRIGEN-BOMB.
"I'M SPEAKING TO YOU FROM ABOUT A THOUSAND YEARS IN YOUR FUTURE, ADAM, AND I HAVEN'T GOT TIME TO EXPLAIN WHY.
"JUST LISTEN, OKAY?
"DESPITE THE BEST EFFORTS OF VULCAN AND THE SHI'AR, THE INHUMANS WILL DETONATE THE DEVICE.
"THE RESULTING EXPLOSION WILL END THE WAR AND CRIPPLE THE SHI'AR WAR MACHINE.
"BUT IT WON'T STOP THERE. IT WILL RIP TIME AND SPACE APART. IT WILL DESTROY REALITY.
"ADAM, IT'S THE DISASTER TRIGGER YOU'VE BEEN WARNING US ABOUT FROM DAY ONE.
"THE T-BOMB WILL KICK OFF A PROGRESSIVE COSMOLOGICAL COLLAPSE CALLED THE FAULT.
"IT WILL ENGULF OUR UNIVERSE.
"SO WHAT I'M SAYING IS, YOU'VE GOT TO STOP BLACK BOLT. YOU'VE GOT TO STOP THE DETONATION. FAST.
"OKAY, SIGNING OFF. YOUR FRIEND, PETER."

WHAT JUST HAPPENED?

GUARDIANS CONTROL CENTER.

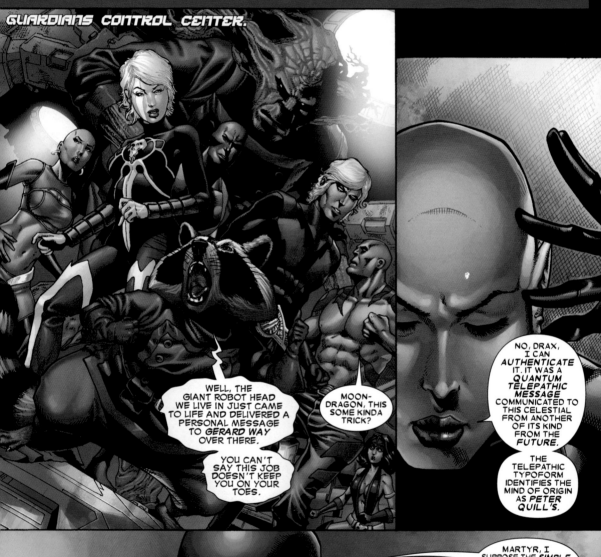

WELL, THE GIANT ROBOT HEAD WE LIVE IN JUST CAME TO LIFE AND DELIVERED A PERSONAL MESSAGE TO *GERARD WAY* OVER THERE.

YOU CAN'T SAY THIS JOB DOESN'T KEEP YOU ON YOUR TOES.

MOON-DRAGON, THIS SOME KINDA TRICK?

NO, DRAX, I CAN *AUTHENTICATE* IT. IT WAS A *QUANTUM TELEPATHIC MESSAGE* COMMUNICATED TO THIS CELESTIAL FROM ANOTHER OF ITS KIND FROM THE FUTURE.

THE TELEPATHIC TYPOFORM IDENTIFIES THE MIND OF ORIGIN AS *PETER QUILL'S.*

MARTYR, I SUPPOSE THE *SIMPLE* ANSWER TO "HOW THE HELL IS STAR-LORD TALKING TO US FROM THE FUTURE," HAS GOT TO BE *STARHAWK.*

IT CERTAINLY EXPLAINS WHY THEIR HALF OF THE TEAM HAS *VANISHED.*

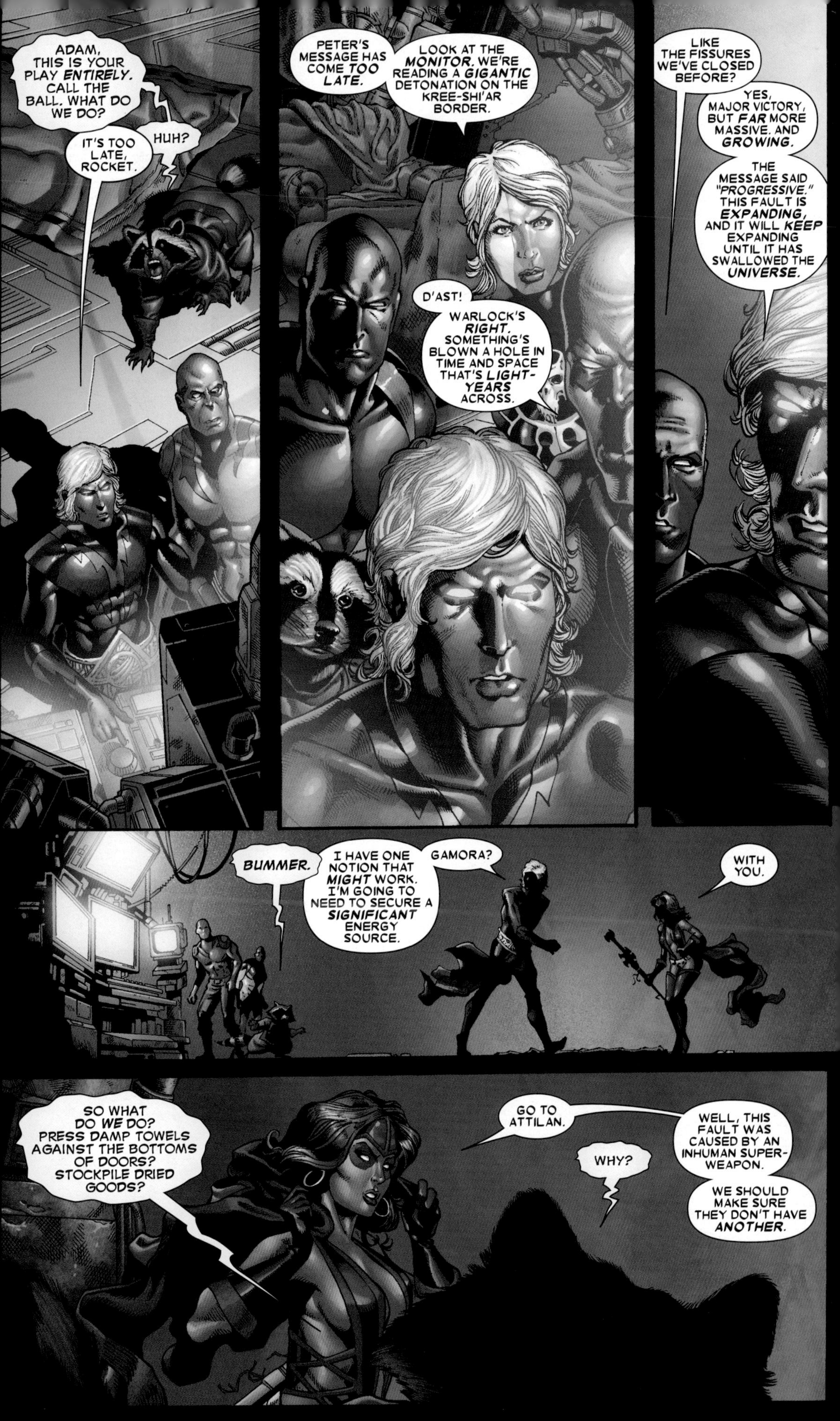
ADAM, THIS IS YOUR PLAY ENTIRELY. CALL THE BALL. WHAT DO WE DO?
IT'S TOO LATE, ROCKET.
HUH?
PETER'S MESSAGE HAS COME TOO LATE.
LOOK AT THE MONITOR. WE'RE READING A GIGANTIC DETONATION ON THE KREE-SHI'AR BORDER.
D'AST!
WARLOCK'S RIGHT. SOMETHING'S BLOWN A HOLE IN TIME AND SPACE THAT'S LIGHT-YEARS ACROSS.
LIKE THE FISSURES WE'VE CLOSED BEFORE?
YES, MAJOR VICTORY, BUT FAR MORE MASSIVE. AND GROWING.
THE MESSAGE SAID "PROGRESSIVE." THIS FAULT IS EXPANDING, AND IT WILL KEEP EXPANDING UNTIL IT HAS SWALLOWED THE UNIVERSE.
BUMMER.
I HAVE ONE NOTION THAT MIGHT WORK. I'M GOING TO NEED TO SECURE A SIGNIFICANT ENERGY SOURCE.
GAMORA?
WITH YOU.
SO WHAT DO WE DO? PRESS DAMP TOWELS AGAINST THE BOTTOMS OF DOORS? STOCKPILE DRIED GOODS?
GO TO ATTILAN.
WHY?
WELL, THIS FAULT WAS CAUSED BY AN INHUMAN SUPER-WEAPON.
WE SHOULD MAKE SURE THEY DON'T HAVE ANOTHER.

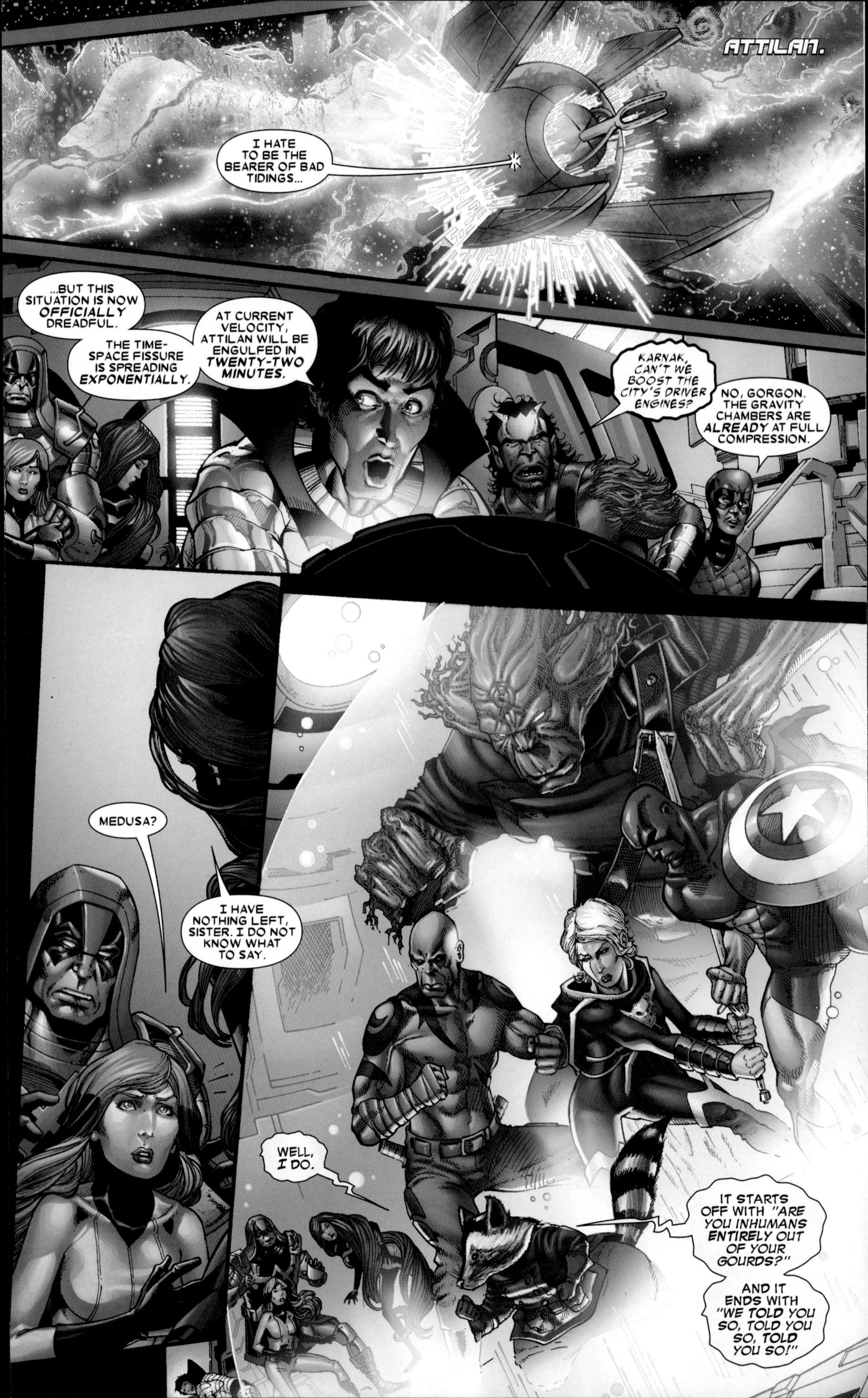

ATTILAN.
I HATE TO BE THE BEARER OF BAD TIDINGS...
...BUT THIS SITUATION IS NOW OFFICIALLY DREADFUL.
THE TIME-SPACE FISSURE IS SPREADING EXPONENTIALLY.
AT CURRENT VELOCITY, ATTILAN WILL BE ENGULFED IN TWENTY-TWO MINUTES.
KARNAK, CAN'T WE BOOST THE CITY'S DRIVER ENGINES?
NO, GORGON. THE GRAVITY CHAMBERS ARE ALREADY AT FULL COMPRESSION.
MEDUSA?
I HAVE NOTHING LEFT, SISTER. I DO NOT KNOW WHAT TO SAY.
WELL, I DO.
IT STARTS OFF WITH "ARE YOU INHUMANS ENTIRELY OUT OF YOUR GOURDS?"
AND IT ENDS WITH "WE TOLD YOU SO, TOLD YOU SO, TOLD YOU SO!"

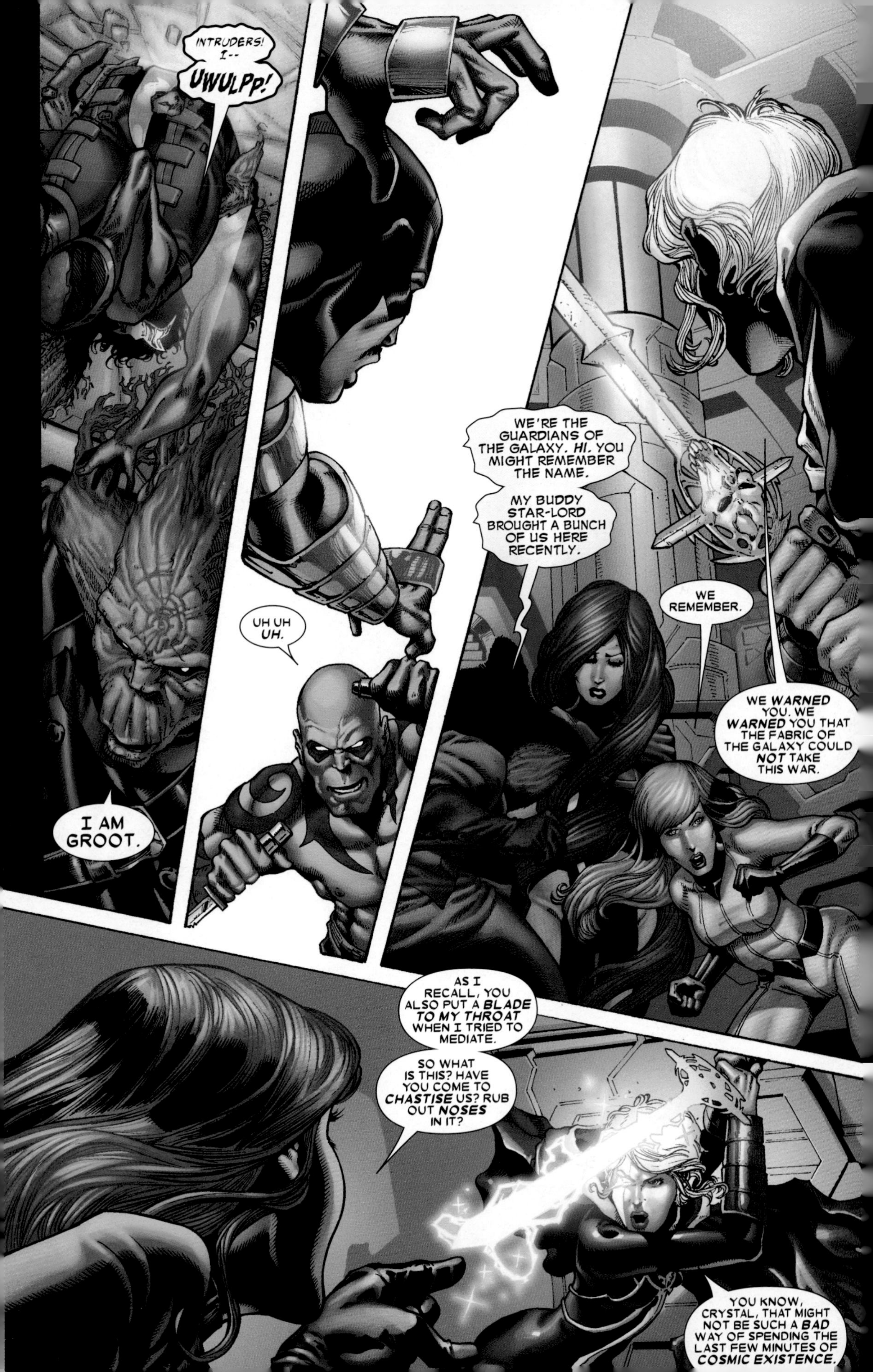

INTRUDERS! I--
UWULPP!
I AM GROOT.
UH UH UH.
WE'RE THE GUARDIANS OF THE GALAXY. HI. YOU MIGHT REMEMBER THE NAME.
MY BUDDY STAR-LORD BROUGHT A BUNCH OF US HERE RECENTLY.
WE REMEMBER.
WE WARNED YOU. WE WARNED YOU THAT THE FABRIC OF THE GALAXY COULD NOT TAKE THIS WAR.
AS I RECALL, YOU ALSO PUT A BLADE TO MY THROAT WHEN I TRIED TO MEDIATE.
SO WHAT IS THIS? HAVE YOU COME TO CHASTISE US? RUB OUT NOSES IN IT?
YOU KNOW, CRYSTAL, THAT MIGHT NOT BE SUCH A BAD WAY OF SPENDING THE LAST FEW MINUTES OF COSMIC EXISTENCE.

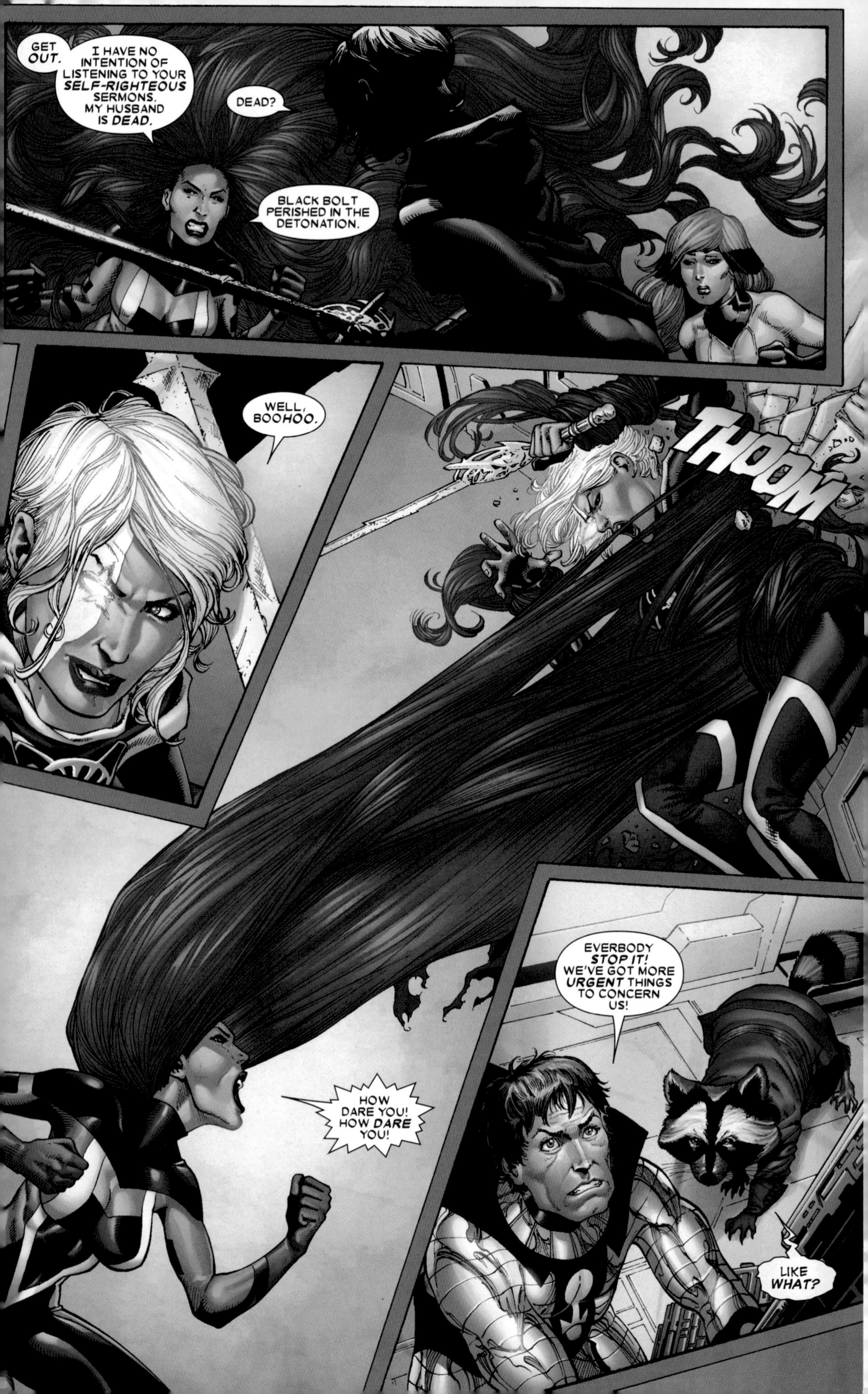
GET OUT.
I HAVE NO INTENTION OF LISTENING TO YOUR SELF-RIGHTEOUS SERMONS. MY HUSBAND IS DEAD.
DEAD?
BLACK BOLT PERISHED IN THE DETONATION.
WELL, BOOHOO.
THOOM
HOW DARE YOU! HOW DARE YOU!
EVERBODY STOP IT! WE'VE GOT MORE URGENT THINGS TO CONCERN US!
LIKE WHAT?

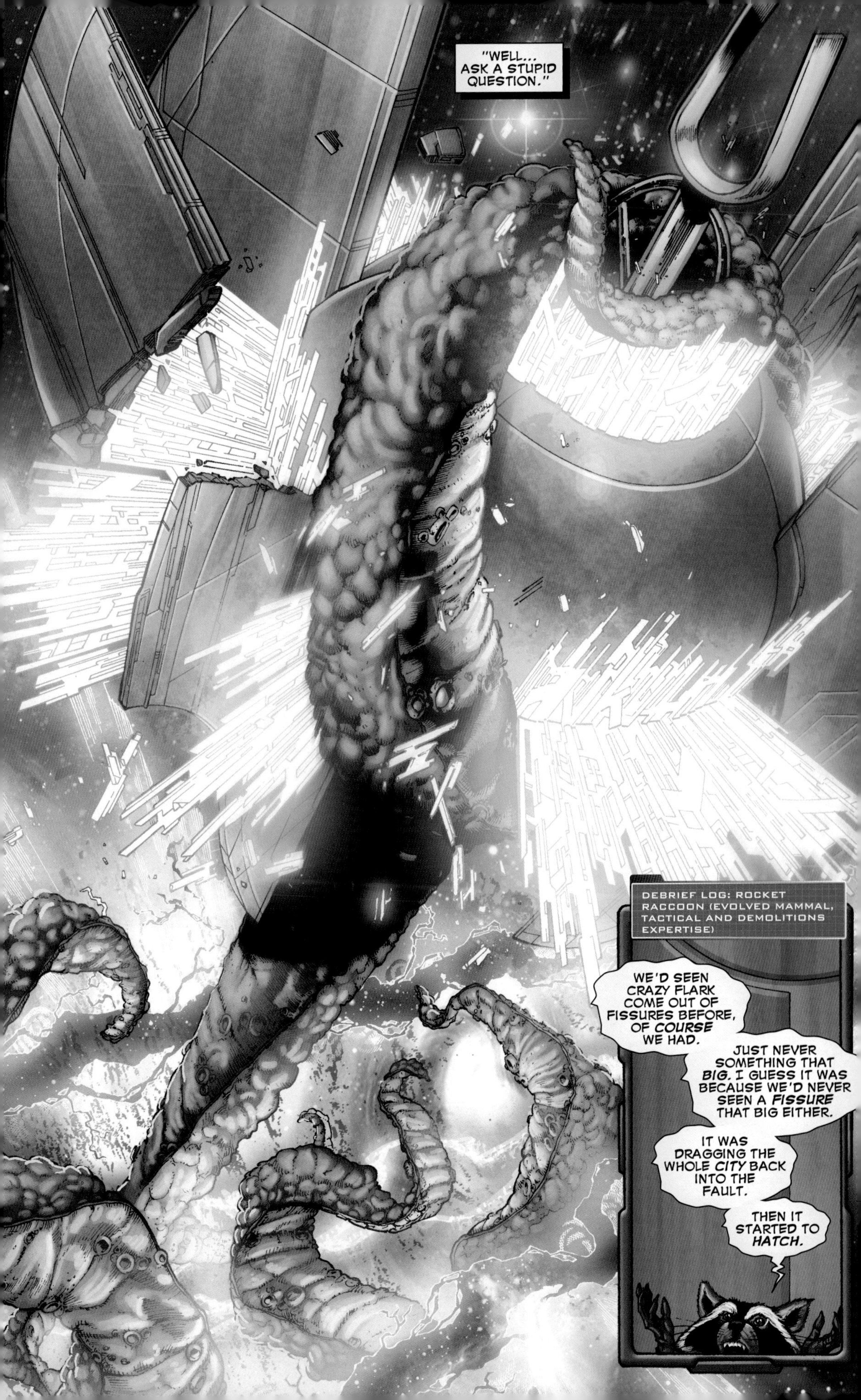
"WELL... ASK A STUPID QUESTION."
DEBRIEF LOG: ROCKET RACCOON (EVOLVED MAMMAL, TACTICAL AND DEMOLITIONS EXPERTISE)
WE'D SEEN CRAZY FLARK COME OUT OF FISSURES BEFORE, OF COURSE WE HAD.
JUST NEVER SOMETHING THAT BIG. I GUESS IT WAS BECAUSE WE'D NEVER SEEN A FISSURE THAT BIG EITHER.
IT WAS DRAGGING THE WHOLE CITY BACK INTO THE FAULT.
THEN IT STARTED TO HATCH.

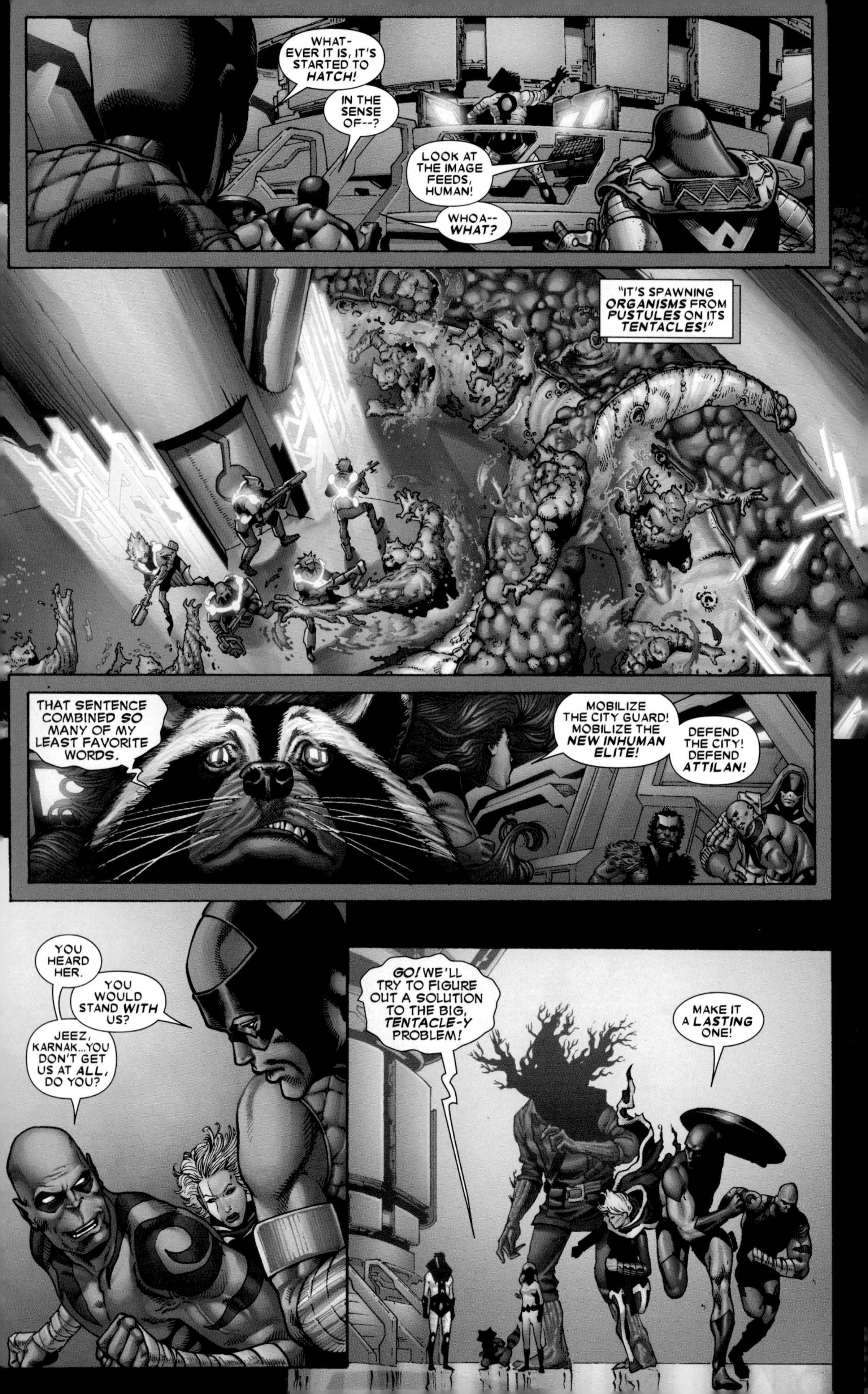
WHAT-EVER IT IS, IT'S STARTED TO HATCH!
IN THE SENSE OF--?
LOOK AT THE IMAGE FEEDS, HUMAN!
WHOA-- WHAT?
"IT'S SPAWNING ORGANISMS FROM PUSTULES ON ITS TENTACLES!"
THAT SENTENCE COMBINED SO MANY OF MY LEAST FAVORITE WORDS.
MOBILIZE THE CITY GUARD! MOBILIZE THE NEW INHUMAN ELITE!
DEFEND THE CITY! DEFEND ATTILAN!
YOU HEARD HER.
YOU WOULD STAND WITH US?
JEEZ, KARNAK...YOU DON'T GET US AT ALL, DO YOU?
GO! WE'LL TRY TO FIGURE OUT A SOLUTION TO THE BIG, TENTACLE-Y PROBLEM!
MAKE IT A LASTING ONE!

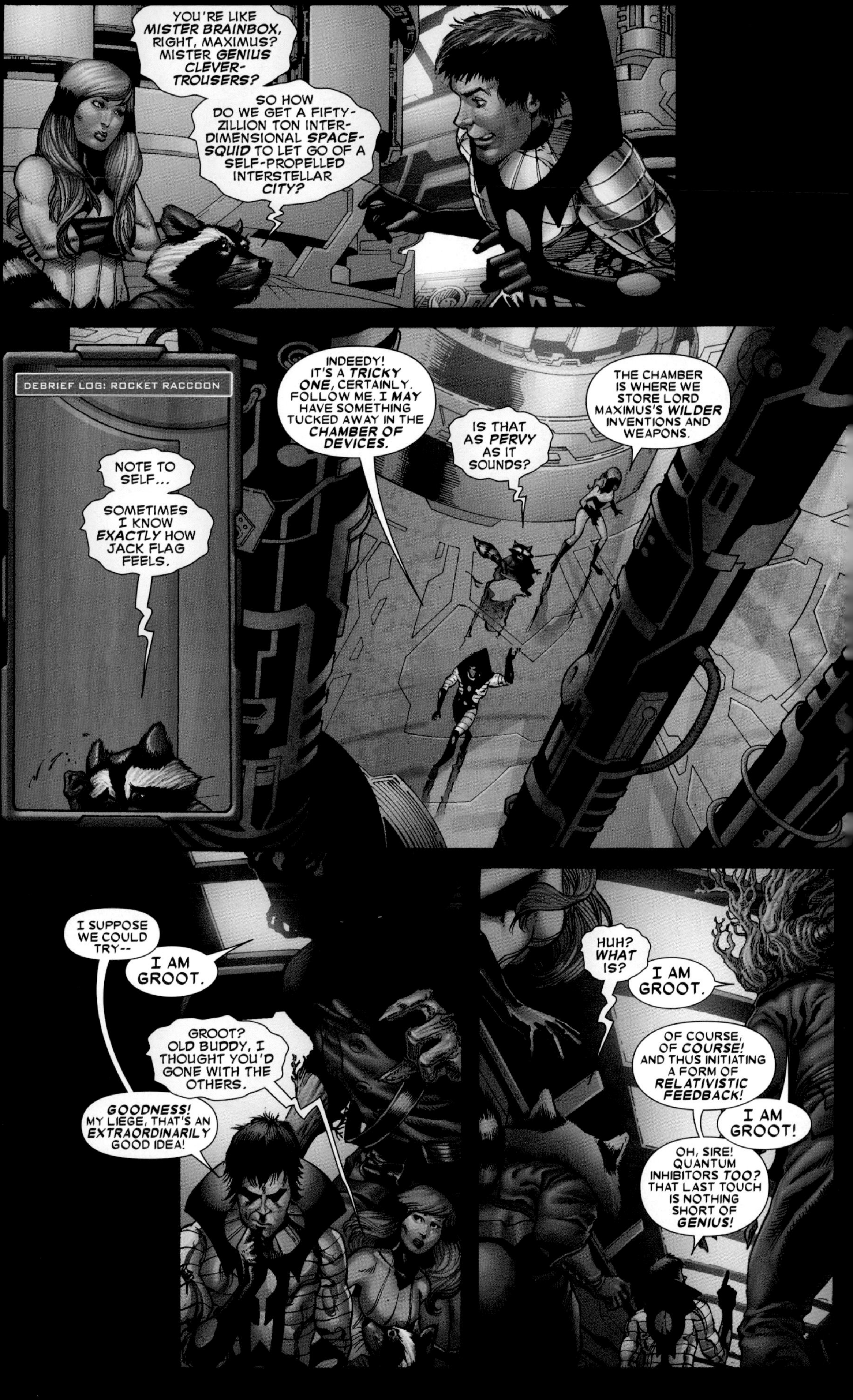

YOU'RE LIKE MISTER BRAINBOX, RIGHT, MAXIMUS? MISTER GENIUS CLEVER-TROUSERS?
SO HOW DO WE GET A FIFTY-ZILLION TON INTER-DIMENSIONAL SPACE-SQUID TO LET GO OF A SELF-PROPELLED INTERSTELLAR CITY?
DEBRIEF LOG: ROCKET RACCOON
NOTE TO SELF...
SOMETIMES I KNOW EXACTLY HOW JACK FLAG FEELS.
INDEEDY! IT'S A TRICKY ONE, CERTAINLY. FOLLOW ME. I MAY HAVE SOMETHING TUCKED AWAY IN THE CHAMBER OF DEVICES.
IS THAT AS PERVY AS IT SOUNDS?
THE CHAMBER IS WHERE WE STORE LORD MAXIMUS'S WILDER INVENTIONS AND WEAPONS.
I SUPPOSE WE COULD TRY--
I AM GROOT.
GROOT? OLD BUDDY, I THOUGHT YOU'D GONE WITH THE OTHERS.
GOODNESS! MY LIEGE, THAT'S AN EXTRAORDINARILY GOOD IDEA!
HUH? WHAT IS?
I AM GROOT.
OF COURSE, OF COURSE! AND THUS INITIATING A FORM OF RELATIVISTIC FEEDBACK!
I AM GROOT!
OH, SIRE! QUANTUM INHIBITORS TOO? THAT LAST TOUCH IS NOTHING SHORT OF GENIUS!

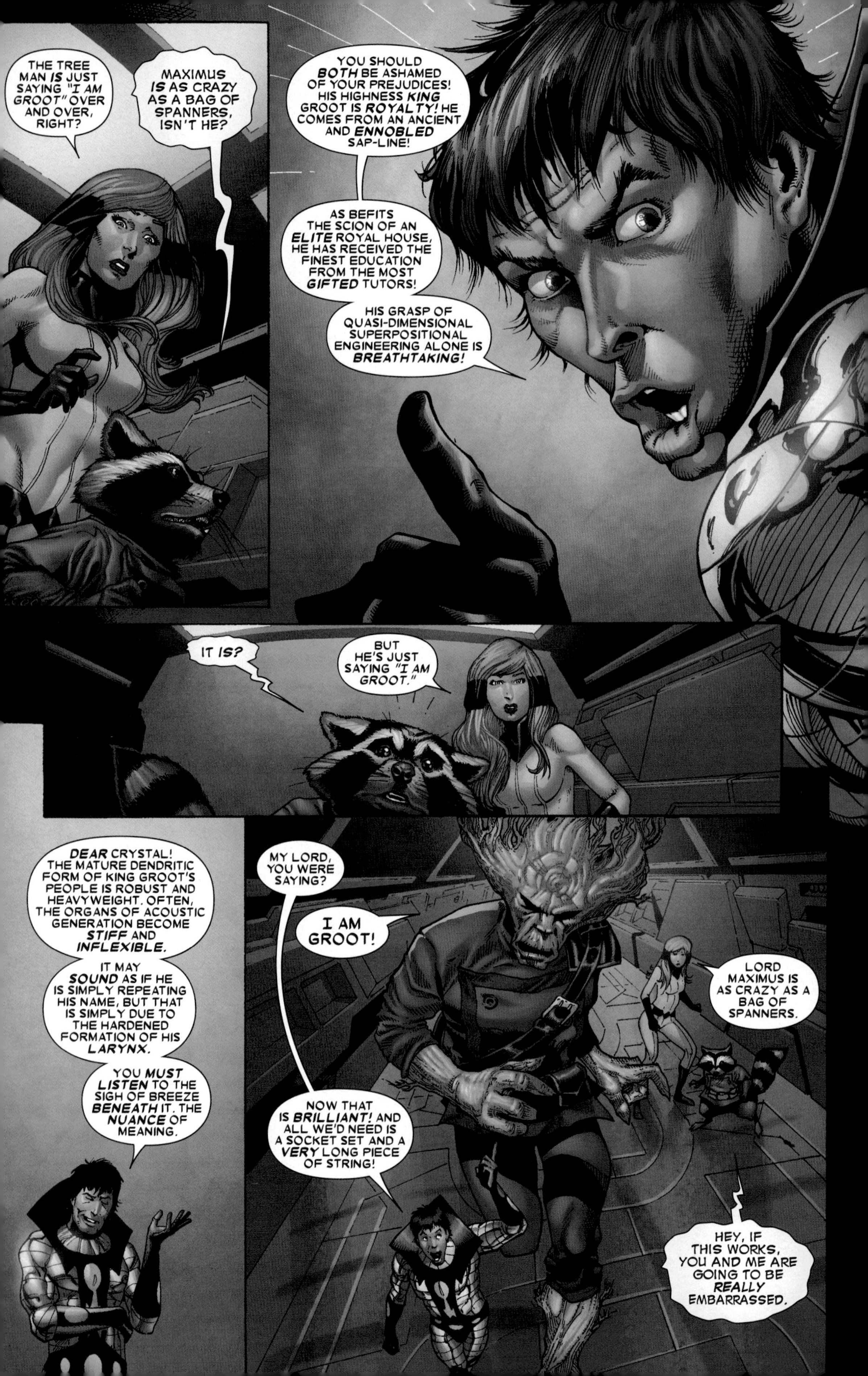
THE TREE MAN *IS* JUST SAYING "I AM GROOT" OVER AND OVER, RIGHT?
MAXIMUS *IS* AS CRAZY AS A BAG OF SPANNERS, ISN'T HE?
YOU SHOULD *BOTH* BE ASHAMED OF YOUR PREJUDICES! HIS HIGHNESS *KING* GROOT IS *ROYALTY!* HE COMES FROM AN ANCIENT AND *ENNOBLED* SAP-LINE!
AS BEFITS THE SCION OF AN *ELITE* ROYAL HOUSE, HE HAS RECEIVED THE FINEST EDUCATION FROM THE MOST *GIFTED* TUTORS!
HIS GRASP OF QUASI-DIMENSIONAL SUPERPOSITIONAL ENGINEERING ALONE IS *BREATHTAKING!*
IT *IS?*
BUT HE'S JUST SAYING "I AM GROOT."
DEAR CRYSTAL! THE MATURE DENDRITIC FORM OF KING GROOT'S PEOPLE IS ROBUST AND HEAVYWEIGHT. OFTEN, THE ORGANS OF ACOUSTIC GENERATION BECOME *STIFF* AND *INFLEXIBLE.*
IT MAY *SOUND* AS IF HE IS SIMPLY REPEATING HIS NAME, BUT THAT IS SIMPLY DUE TO THE HARDENED FORMATION OF HIS *LARYNX.*
YOU *MUST LISTEN* TO THE SIGH OF BREEZE *BENEATH* IT. THE *NUANCE* OF MEANING.
MY LORD, YOU WERE SAYING?
I AM GROOT!
NOW THAT IS *BRILLIANT!* AND ALL WE'D NEED IS A SOCKET SET AND A *VERY* LONG PIECE OF STRING!
LORD MAXIMUS IS AS CRAZY AS A BAG OF SPANNERS.
HEY, IF THIS WORKS, YOU AND ME ARE GOING TO BE *REALLY* EMBARRASSED.

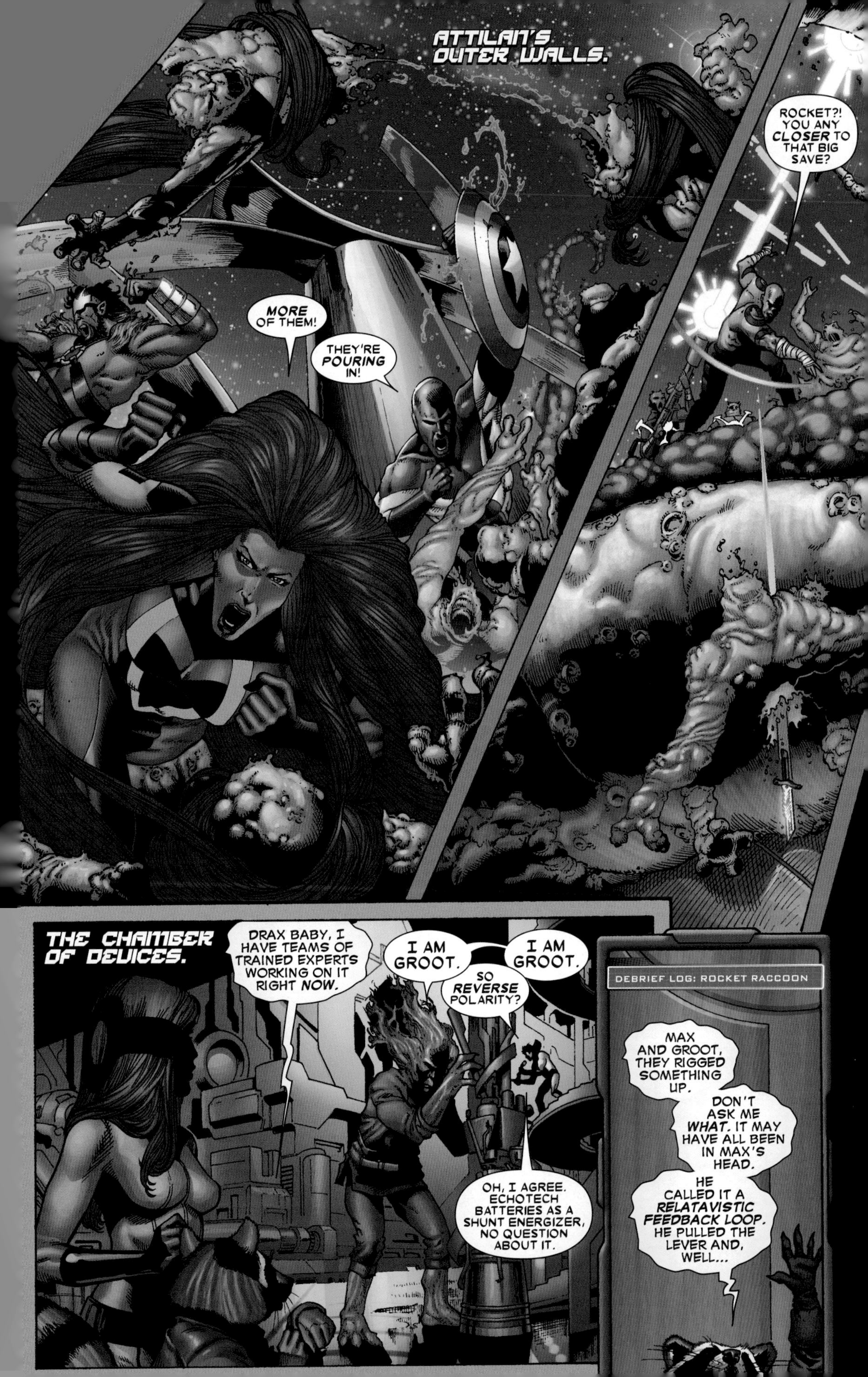
ATTILAN'S OUTER WALLS.
MORE OF THEM!
THEY'RE POURING IN!
ROCKET?! YOU ANY CLOSER TO THAT BIG SAVE?
THE CHAMBER OF DEVICES.
DRAX BABY, I HAVE TEAMS OF TRAINED EXPERTS WORKING ON IT RIGHT NOW.
I AM GROOT.
I AM GROOT.
SO REVERSE POLARITY?
OH, I AGREE. ECHOTECH BATTERIES AS A SHUNT ENERGIZER, NO QUESTION ABOUT IT.
DEBRIEF LOG: ROCKET RACCOON
MAX AND GROOT, THEY RIGGED SOMETHING UP.
DON'T ASK ME WHAT. IT MAY HAVE ALL BEEN IN MAX'S HEAD.
HE CALLED IT A RELATAVISTIC FEEDBACK LOOP. HE PULLED THE LEVER AND, WELL...

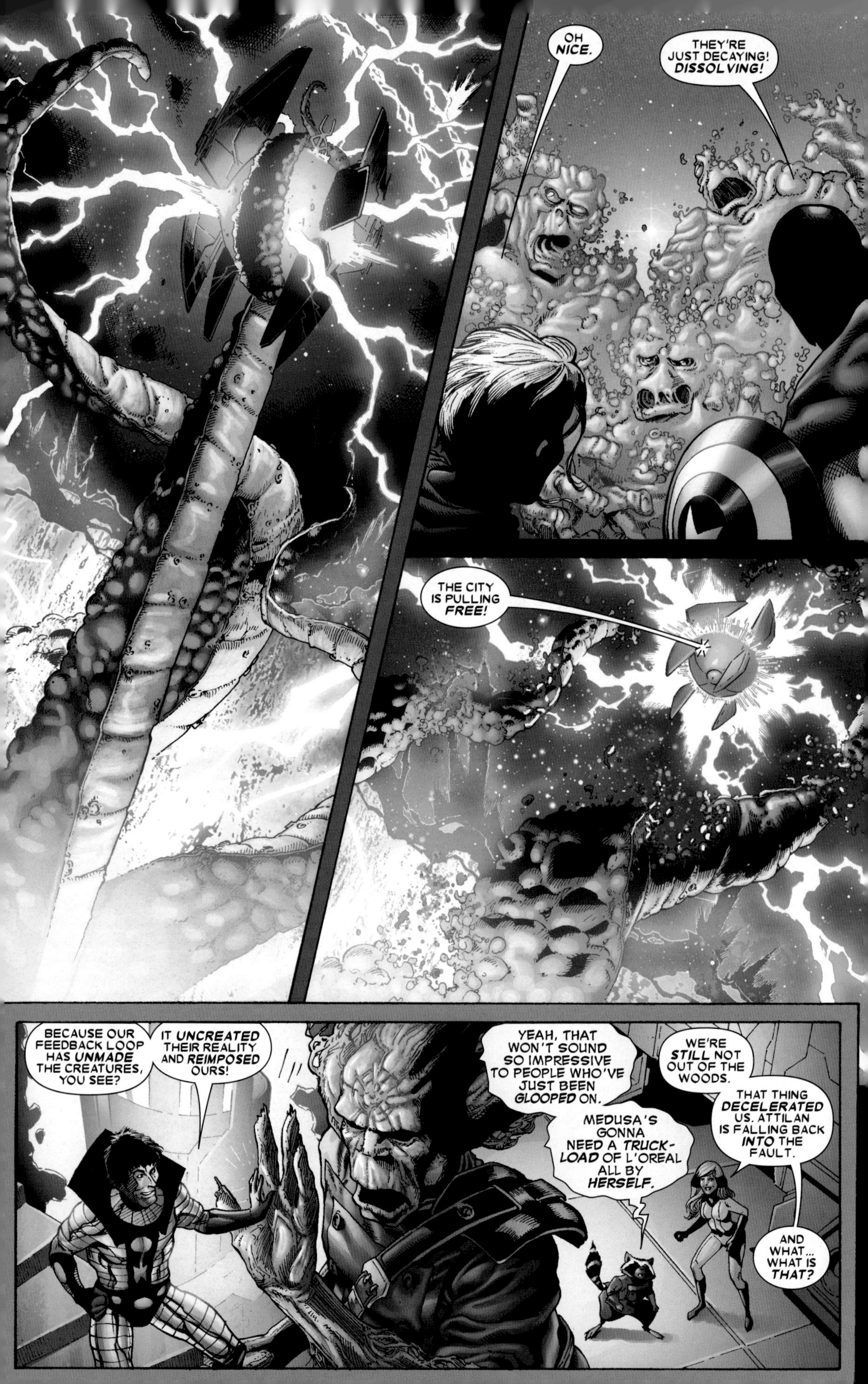
OH NICE.
THEY'RE JUST DECAYING! DISSOLVING!
THE CITY IS PULLING FREE!
BECAUSE OUR FEEDBACK LOOP HAS UNMADE THE CREATURES, YOU SEE?
IT UNCREATED THEIR REALITY AND REIMPOSED OURS!
YEAH, THAT WON'T SOUND SO IMPRESSIVE TO PEOPLE WHO'VE JUST BEEN GLOOPED ON.
MEDUSA'S GONNA NEED A TRUCK-LOAD OF L'OREAL ALL BY HERSELF.
WE'RE STILL NOT OUT OF THE WOODS.
THAT THING DECELERATED US. ATTILAN IS FALLING BACK INTO THE FAULT.
AND WHAT... WHAT IS THAT?

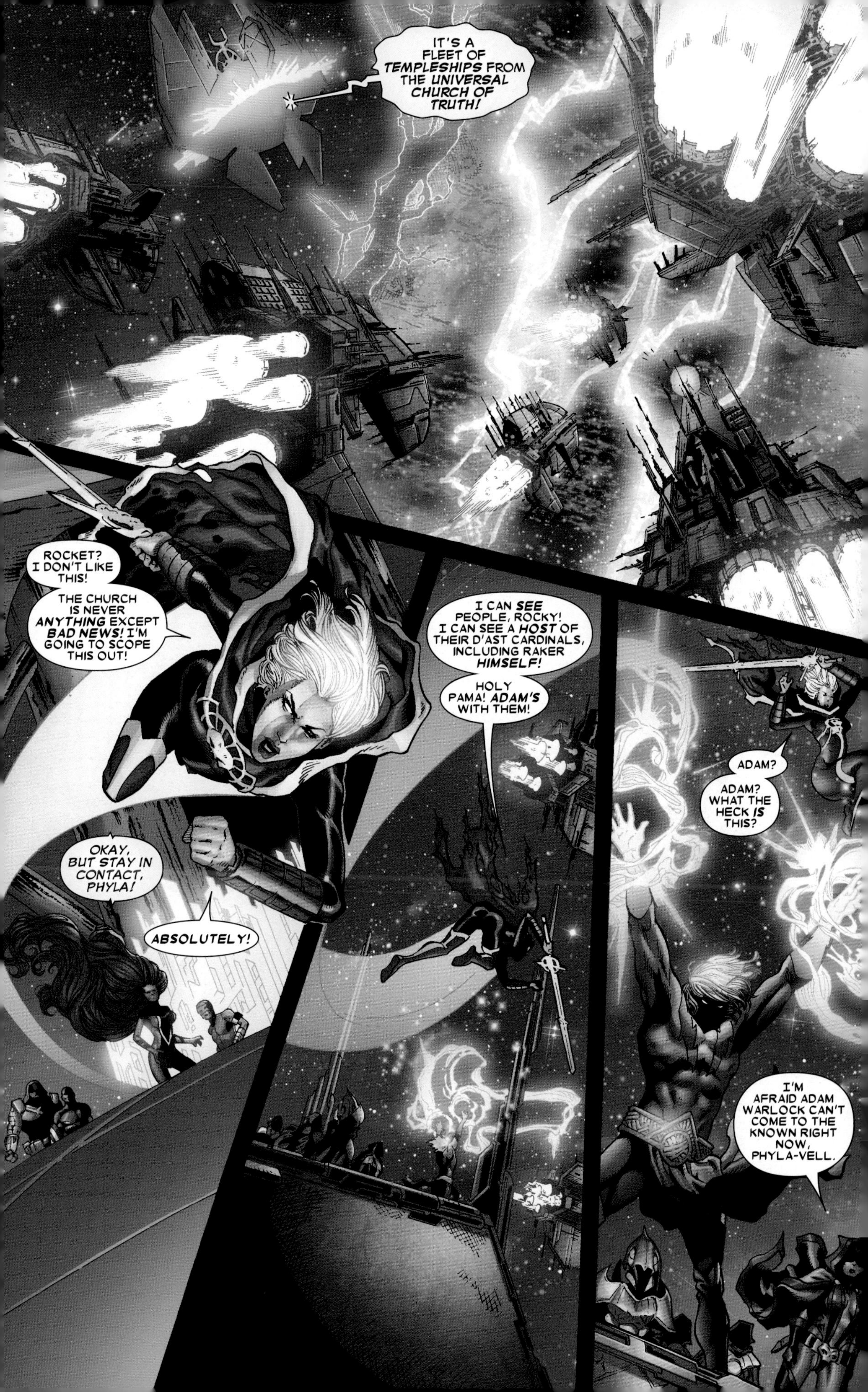
IT'S A FLEET OF TEMPLESHIPS FROM THE UNIVERSAL CHURCH OF TRUTH!
ROCKET? I DON'T LIKE THIS!
THE CHURCH IS NEVER ANYTHING EXCEPT BAD NEWS! I'M GOING TO SCOPE THIS OUT!
OKAY, BUT STAY IN CONTACT, PHYLA!
ABSOLUTELY!
I CAN SEE PEOPLE, ROCKY! I CAN SEE A HOST OF THEIR D'AST CARDINALS, INCLUDING RAKER HIMSELF!
HOLY PAMA! ADAM'S WITH THEM!
ADAM?
ADAM? WHAT THE HECK IS THIS?
I'M AFRAID ADAM WARLOCK CAN'T COME TO THE KNOWN RIGHT NOW, PHYLA-VELL.

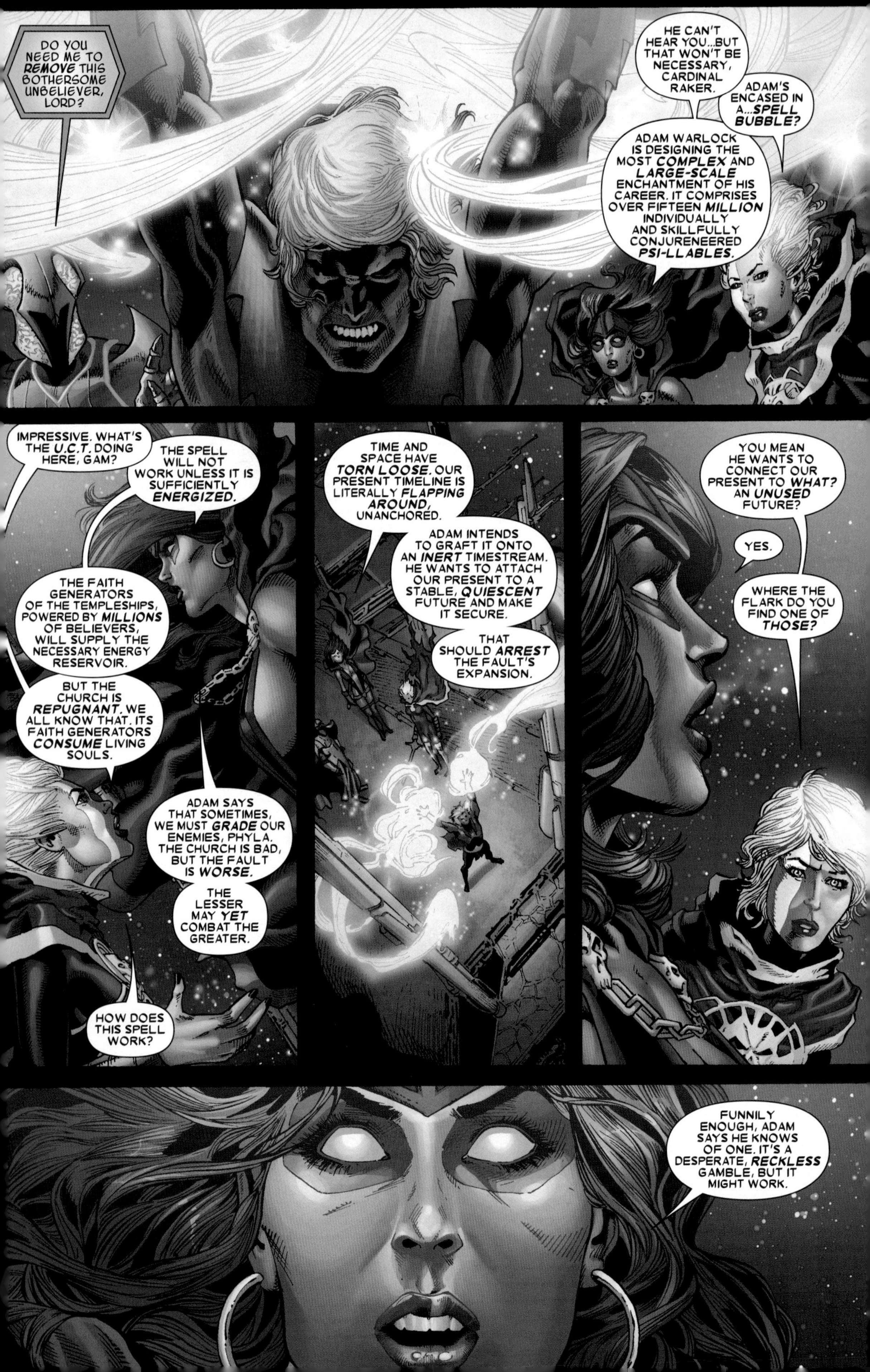
DO YOU NEED ME TO REMOVE THIS BOTHERSOME UNBELIEVER, LORD?
HE CAN'T HEAR YOU...BUT THAT WON'T BE NECESSARY, CARDINAL RAKER.
ADAM'S ENCASED IN A...SPELL BUBBLE?
ADAM WARLOCK IS DESIGNING THE MOST COMPLEX AND LARGE-SCALE ENCHANTMENT OF HIS CAREER. IT COMPRISES OVER FIFTEEN MILLION INDIVIDUALLY AND SKILLFULLY CONJURENEERED PSI-LLABLES.
IMPRESSIVE. WHAT'S THE U.C.T. DOING HERE, GAM?
THE SPELL WILL NOT WORK UNLESS IT IS SUFFICIENTLY ENERGIZED.
THE FAITH GENERATORS OF THE TEMPLESHIPS, POWERED BY MILLIONS OF BELIEVERS, WILL SUPPLY THE NECESSARY ENERGY RESERVOIR.
BUT THE CHURCH IS REPUGNANT. WE ALL KNOW THAT. ITS FAITH GENERATORS CONSUME LIVING SOULS.
ADAM SAYS THAT SOMETIMES, WE MUST GRADE OUR ENEMIES, PHYLA. THE CHURCH IS BAD, BUT THE FAULT IS WORSE.
THE LESSER MAY YET COMBAT THE GREATER.
HOW DOES THIS SPELL WORK?
TIME AND SPACE HAVE TORN LOOSE. OUR PRESENT TIMELINE IS LITERALLY FLAPPING AROUND, UNANCHORED.
ADAM INTENDS TO GRAFT IT ONTO AN INERT TIMESTREAM. HE WANTS TO ATTACH OUR PRESENT TO A STABLE, QUIESCENT FUTURE AND MAKE IT SECURE.
THAT SHOULD ARREST THE FAULT'S EXPANSION.
YOU MEAN HE WANTS TO CONNECT OUR PRESENT TO WHAT? AN UNUSED FUTURE?
YES.
WHERE THE FLARK DO YOU FIND ONE OF THOSE?
FUNNILY ENOUGH, ADAM SAYS HE KNOWS OF ONE. IT'S A DESPERATE, RECKLESS GAMBLE, BUT IT MIGHT WORK.

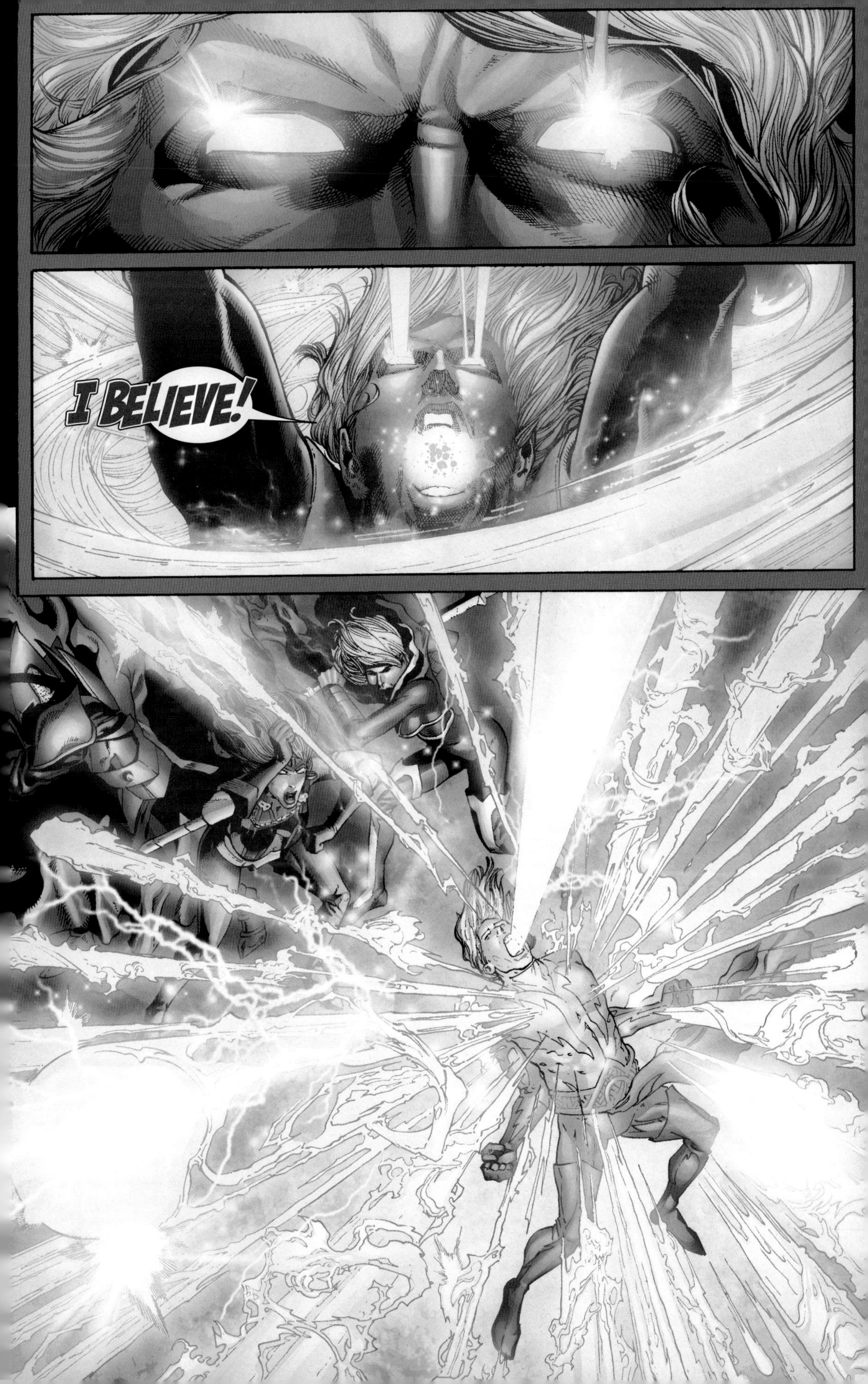
I BELIEVE!

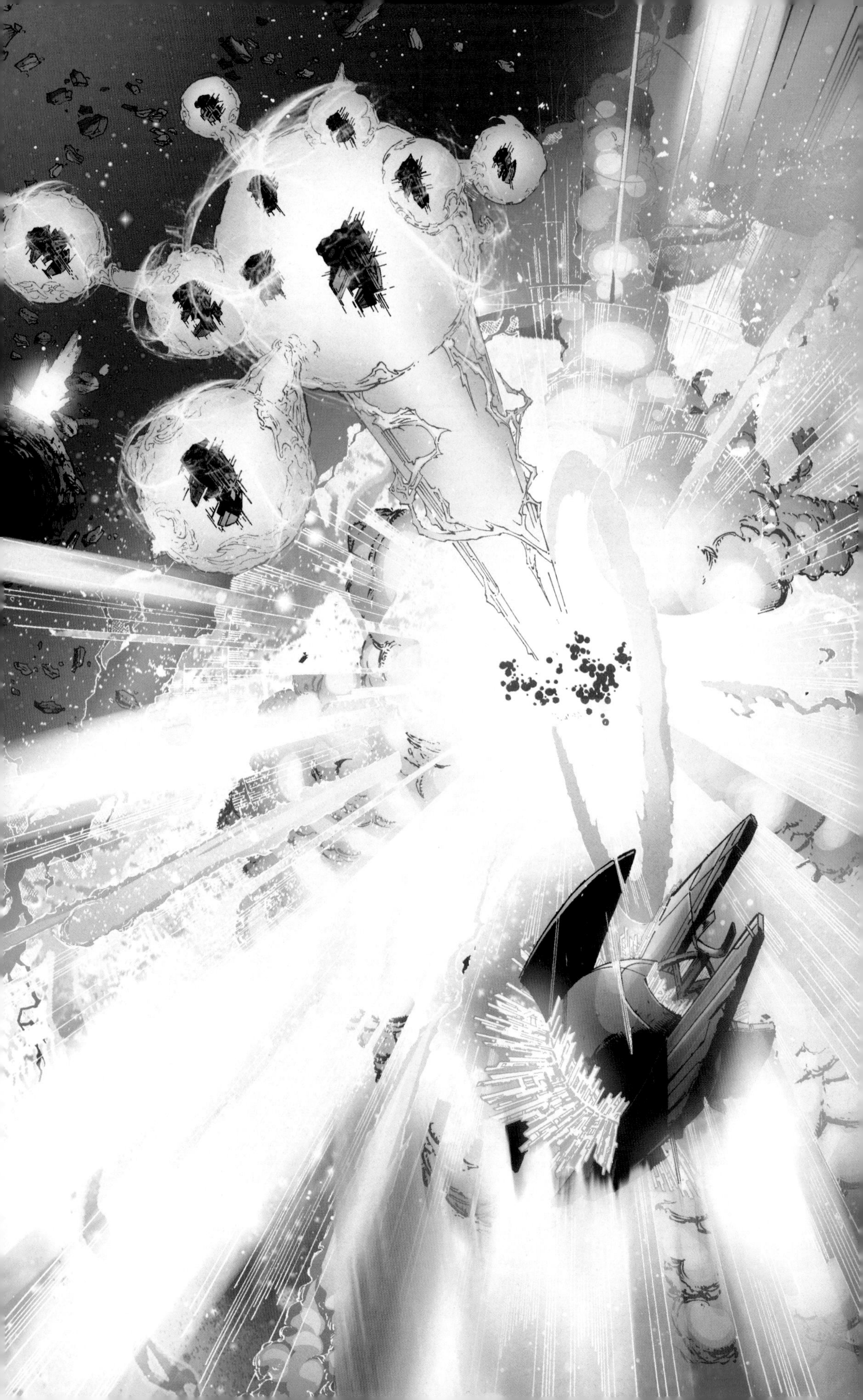

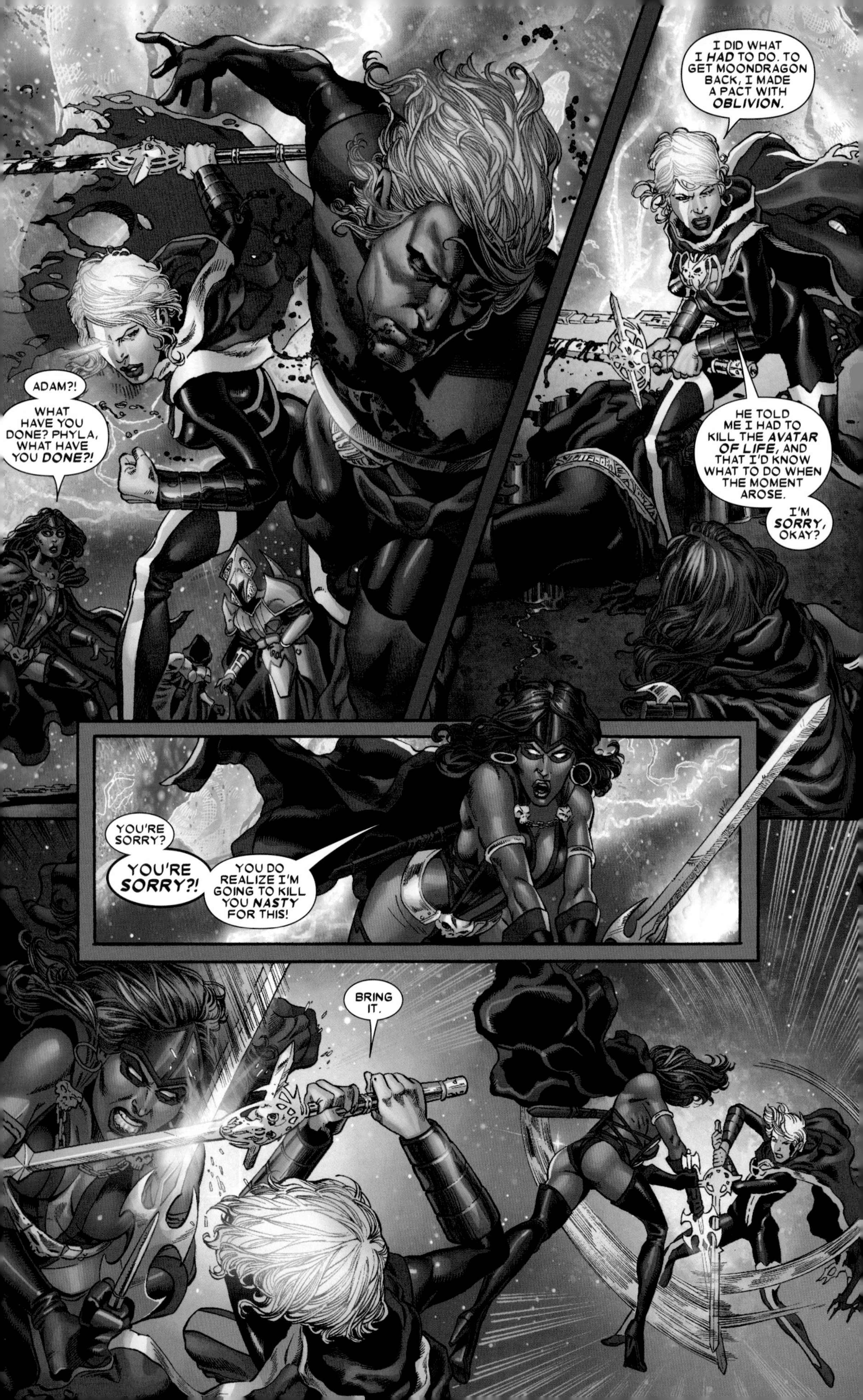
ADAM?!
WHAT HAVE YOU DONE? PHYLA, WHAT HAVE YOU DONE?!
I DID WHAT I HAD TO DO. TO GET MOONDRAGON BACK, I MADE A PACT WITH OBLIVION.
HE TOLD ME I HAD TO KILL THE AVATAR OF LIFE, AND THAT I'D KNOW WHAT TO DO WHEN THE MOMENT AROSE.
I'M SORRY, OKAY?
YOU'RE SORRY?
YOU'RE SORRY?!
YOU DO REALIZE I'M GOING TO KILL YOU NASTY FOR THIS!
BRING IT.

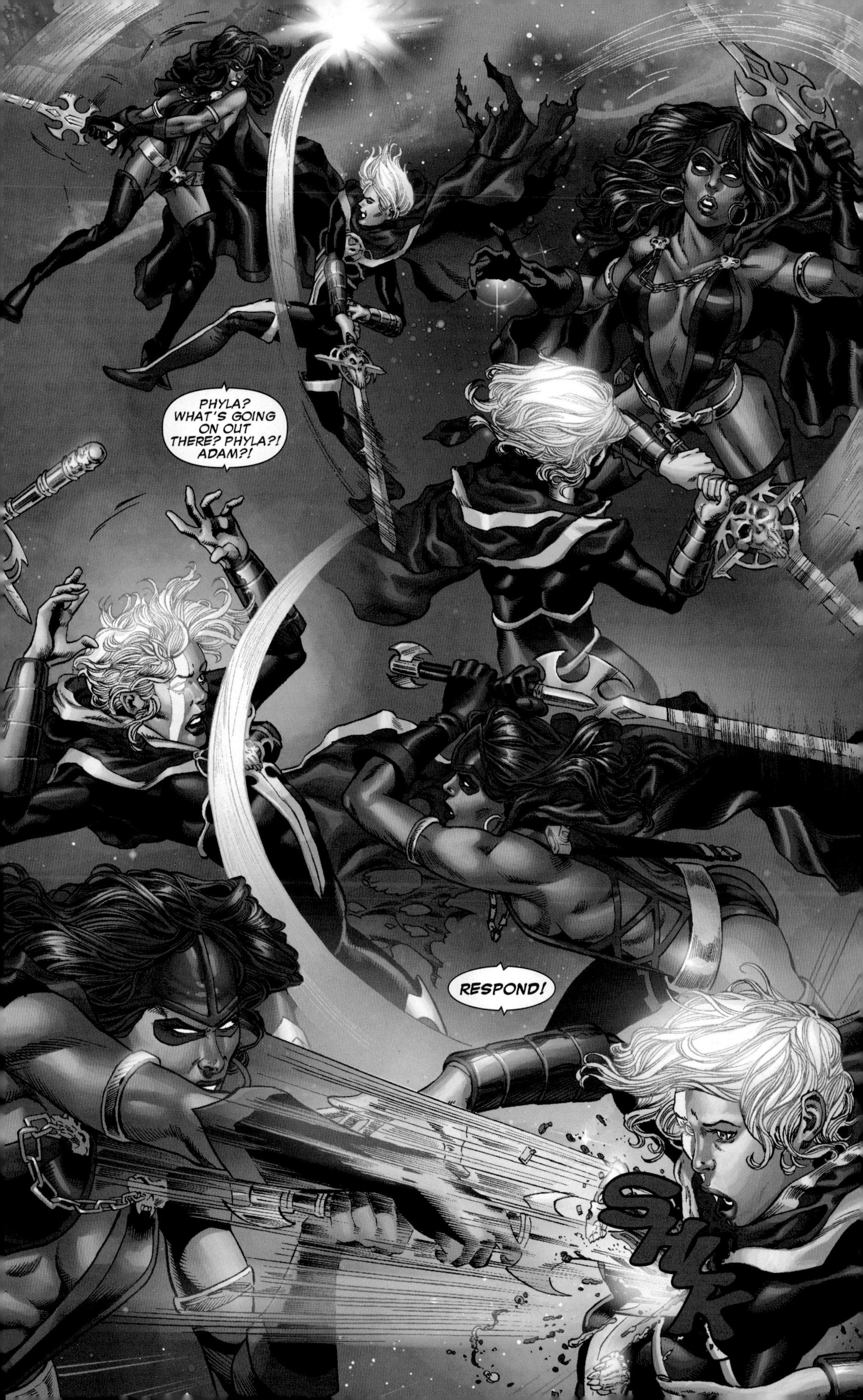
PHYLA? WHAT'S GOING ON OUT THERE? PHYLA?! ADAM?!
RESPOND!
SHK

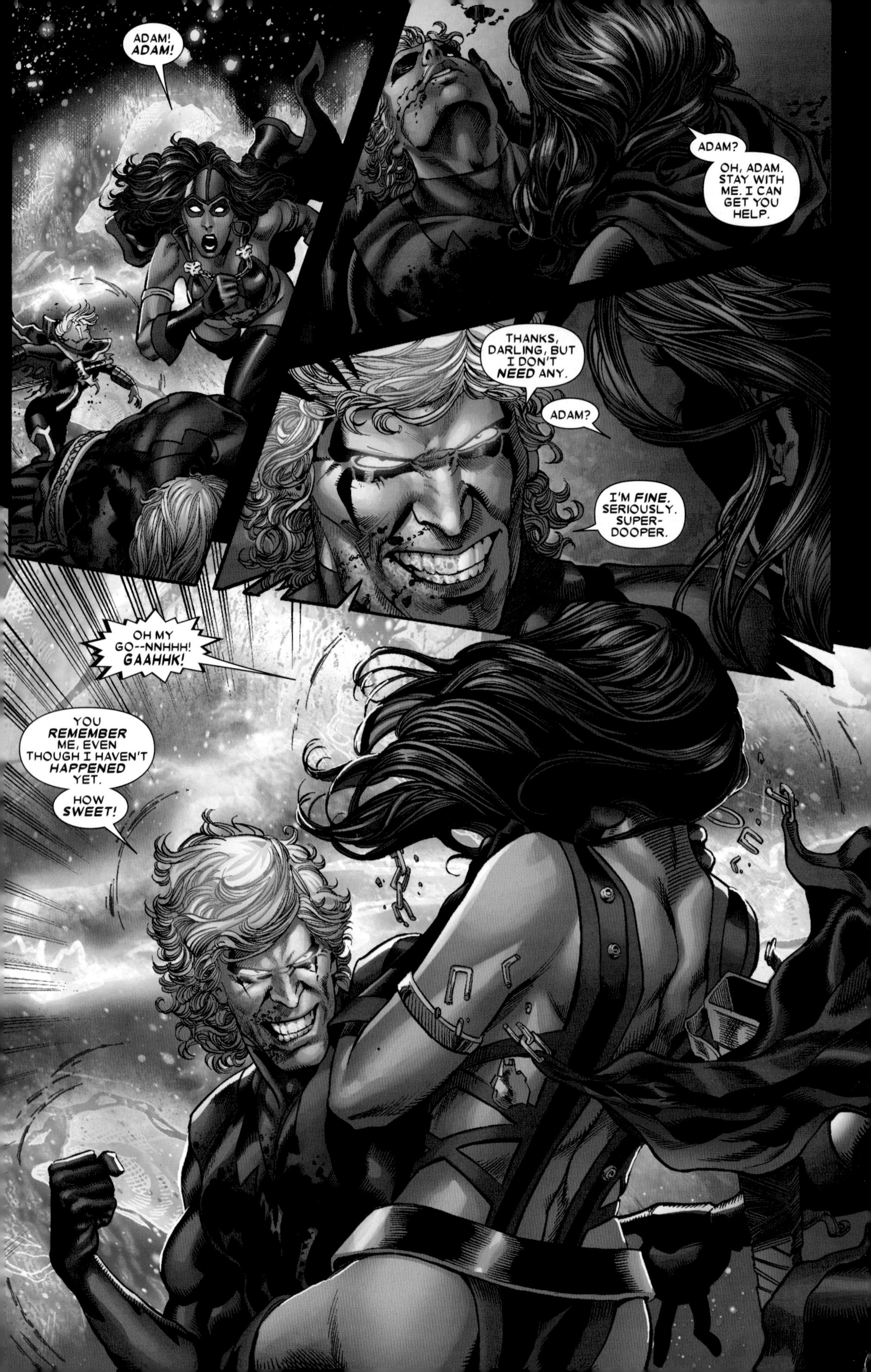
ADAM! ADAM!
ADAM?
OH, ADAM. STAY WITH ME. I CAN GET YOU HELP.
THANKS, DARLING, BUT I DON'T NEED ANY.
ADAM?
I'M FINE. SERIOUSLY. SUPER-DOOPER.
OH MY GO--NNHHH! GAAHHK!
YOU REMEMBER ME, EVEN THOUGH I HAVEN'T HAPPENED YET.
HOW SWEET!

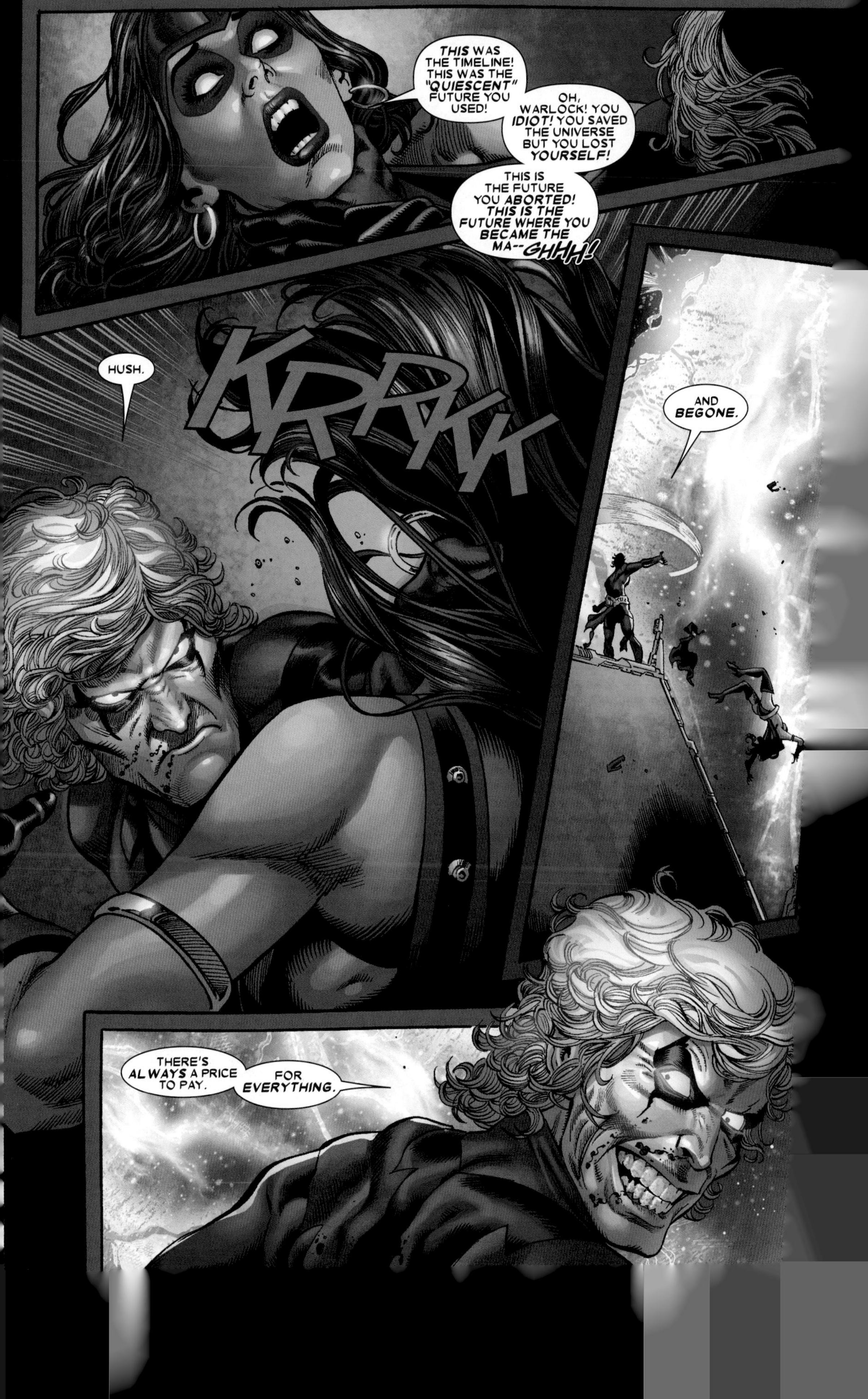

THIS WAS THE TIMELINE! THIS WAS THE "QUIESCENT" FUTURE YOU USED!
OH, WARLOCK! YOU IDIOT! YOU SAVED THE UNIVERSE BUT YOU LOST YOURSELF!
THIS IS THE FUTURE YOU ABORTED! THIS IS THE FUTURE WHERE YOU BECAME THE MA--GHHH!
HUSH.
KRRKK
AND BEGONE.
THERE'S ALWAYS A PRICE TO PAY.
FOR EVERYTHING.

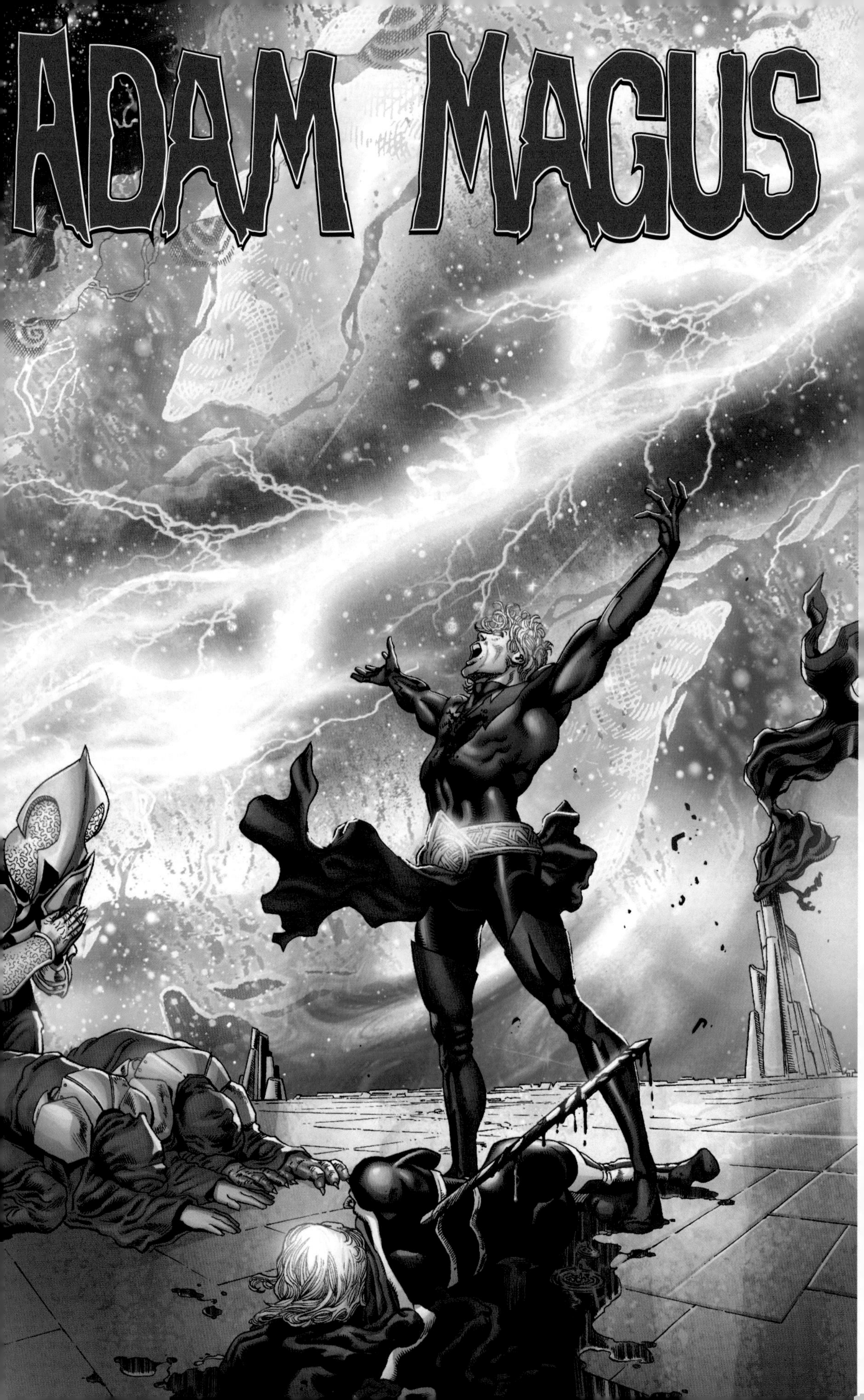
ADAM MAGUS

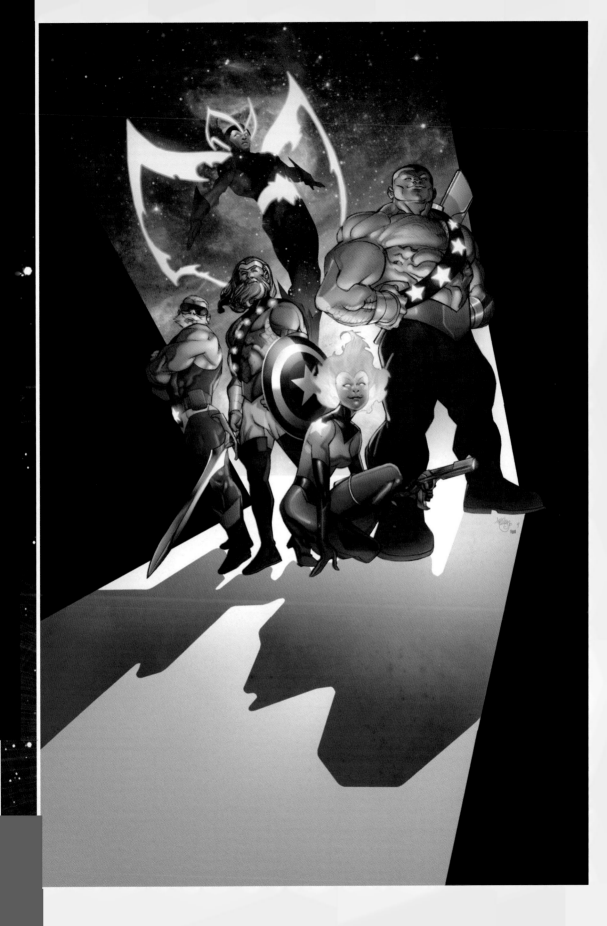

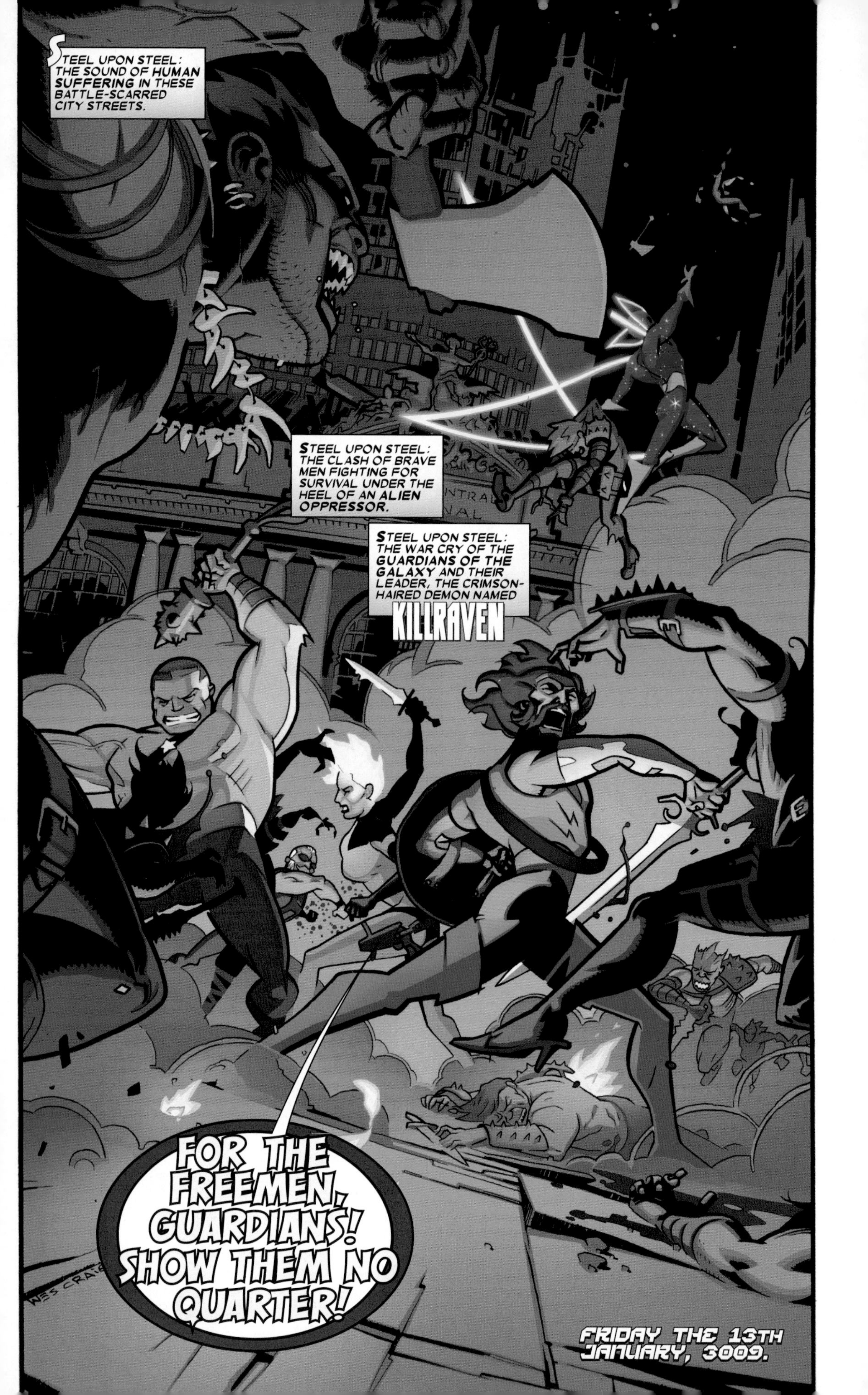
STEEL UPON STEEL: THE SOUND OF HUMAN SUFFERING IN THESE BATTLE-SCARRED CITY STREETS.
STEEL UPON STEEL: THE CLASH OF BRAVE MEN FIGHTING FOR SURVIVAL UNDER THE HEEL OF AN ALIEN OPPRESSOR.
STEEL UPON STEEL: THE WAR CRY OF THE GUARDIANS OF THE GALAXY AND THEIR LEADER, THE CRIMSON-HAIRED DEMON NAMED
KILLRAVEN
FOR THE FREEMEN, GUARDIANS! SHOW THEM NO QUARTER!
FRIDAY THE 13TH JANUARY, 3009.
WES CRAIG

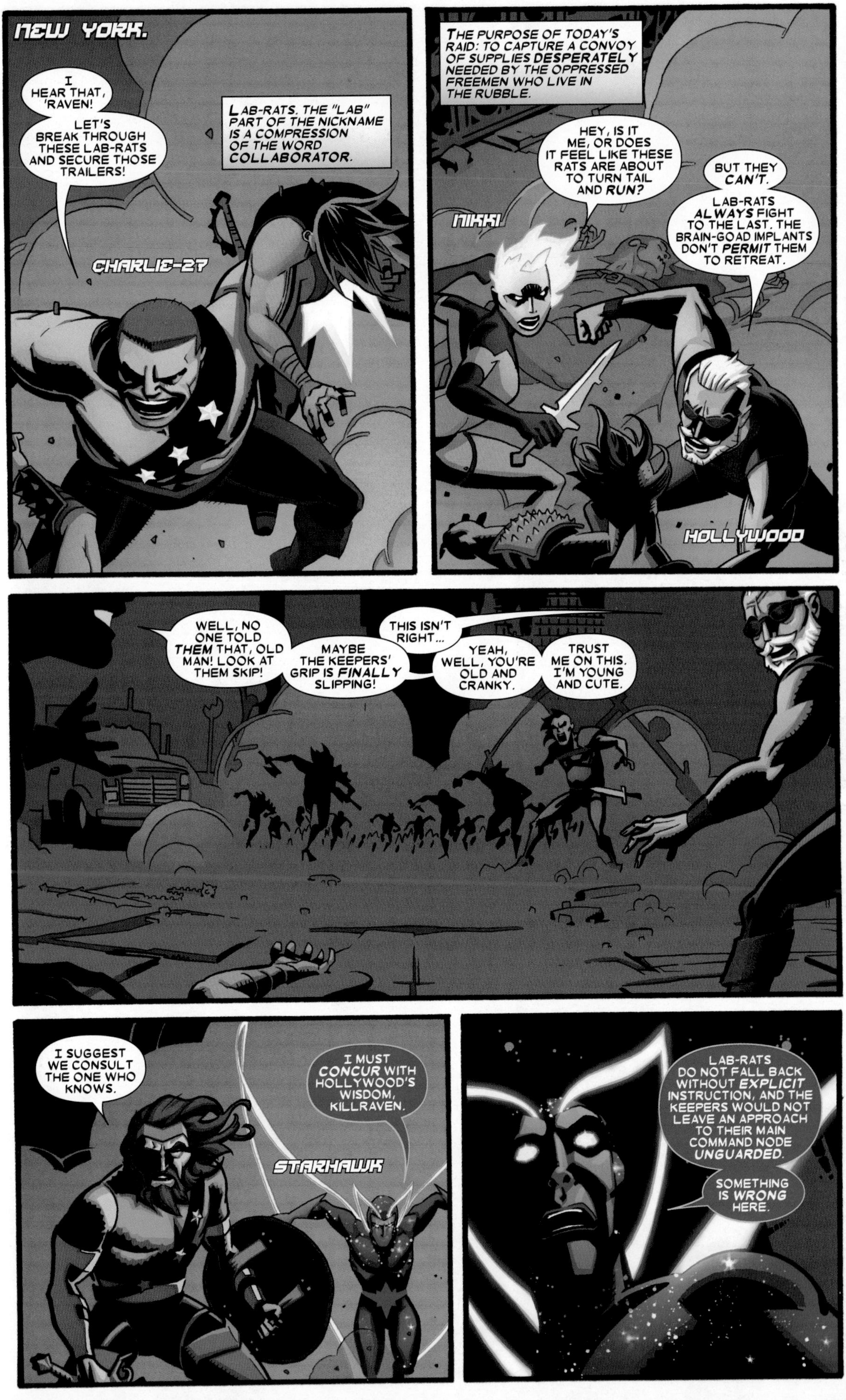
NEW YORK.
I HEAR THAT, 'RAVEN! LET'S BREAK THROUGH THESE LAB-RATS AND SECURE THOSE TRAILERS!
LAB-RATS. THE "LAB" PART OF THE NICKNAME IS A COMPRESSION OF THE WORD COLLABORATOR.
CHARLIE-27
THE PURPOSE OF TODAY'S RAID: TO CAPTURE A CONVOY OF SUPPLIES DESPERATELY NEEDED BY THE OPPRESSED FREEMEN WHO LIVE IN THE RUBBLE.
HEY, IS IT ME, OR DOES IT FEEL LIKE THESE RATS ARE ABOUT TO TURN TAIL AND RUN?
NIKKI
BUT THEY CAN'T.
LAB-RATS ALWAYS FIGHT TO THE LAST. THE BRAIN-GOAD IMPLANTS DON'T PERMIT THEM TO RETREAT.
HOLLYWOOD
WELL, NO ONE TOLD THEM THAT, OLD MAN! LOOK AT THEM SKIP!
MAYBE THE KEEPERS' GRIP IS FINALLY SLIPPING!
THIS ISN'T RIGHT...
YEAH, WELL, YOU'RE OLD AND CRANKY.
TRUST ME ON THIS. I'M YOUNG AND CUTE.
I SUGGEST WE CONSULT THE ONE WHO KNOWS.
I MUST CONCUR WITH HOLLYWOOD'S WISDOM, KILLRAVEN.
STARHAWK
LAB-RATS DO NOT FALL BACK WITHOUT EXPLICIT INSTRUCTION, AND THE KEEPERS WOULD NOT LEAVE AN APPROACH TO THEIR MAIN COMMAND NODE UNGUARDED.
SOMETHING IS WRONG HERE.

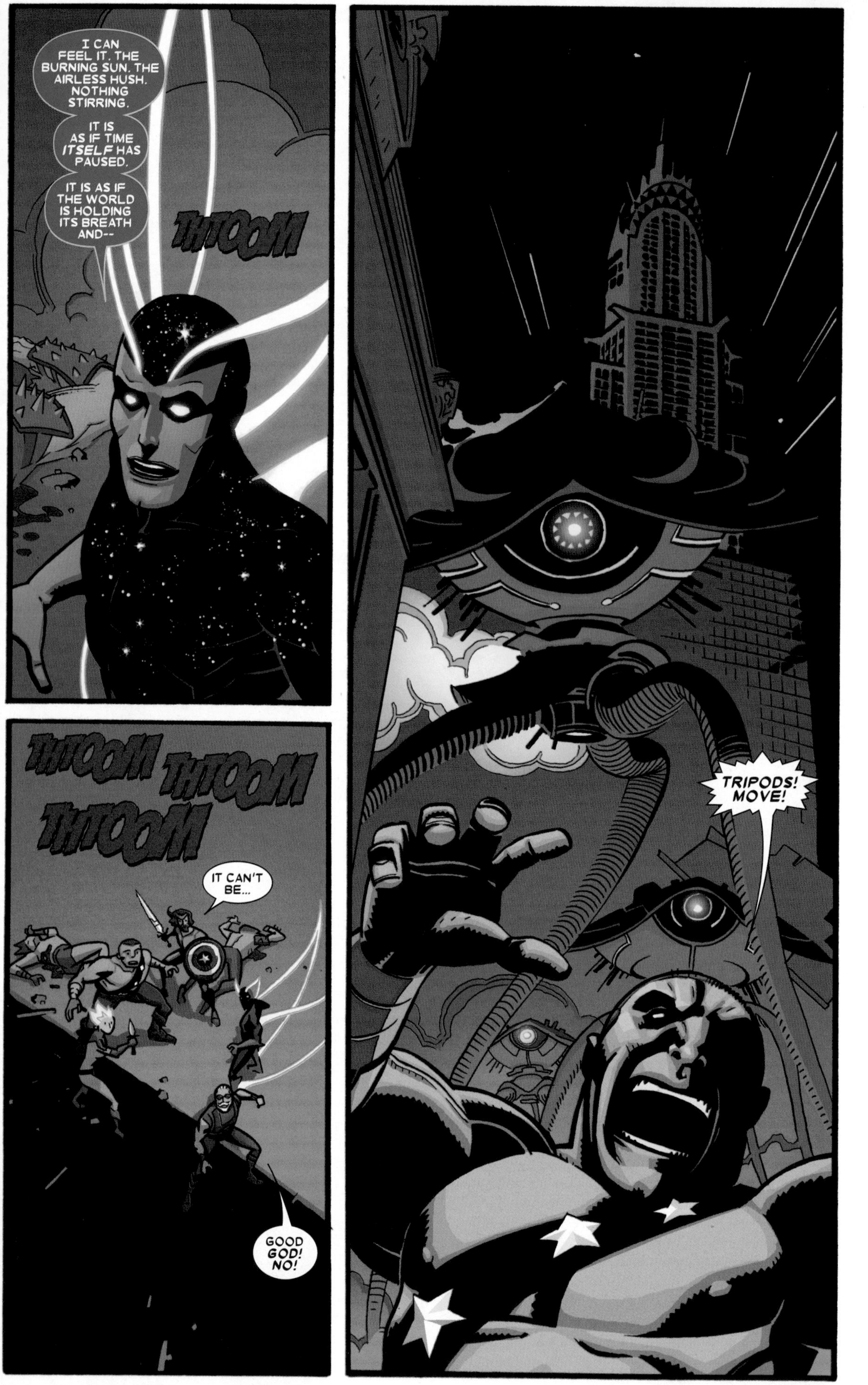

I CAN FEEL IT. THE BURNING SUN. THE AIRLESS HUSH. NOTHING STIRRING.
IT IS AS IF TIME ITSELF HAS PAUSED.
IT IS AS IF THE WORLD IS HOLDING ITS BREATH AND--
THTOOM
THTOOM THTOOM THTOOM
IT CAN'T BE...
GOOD GOD! NO!
TRIPODS! MOVE!

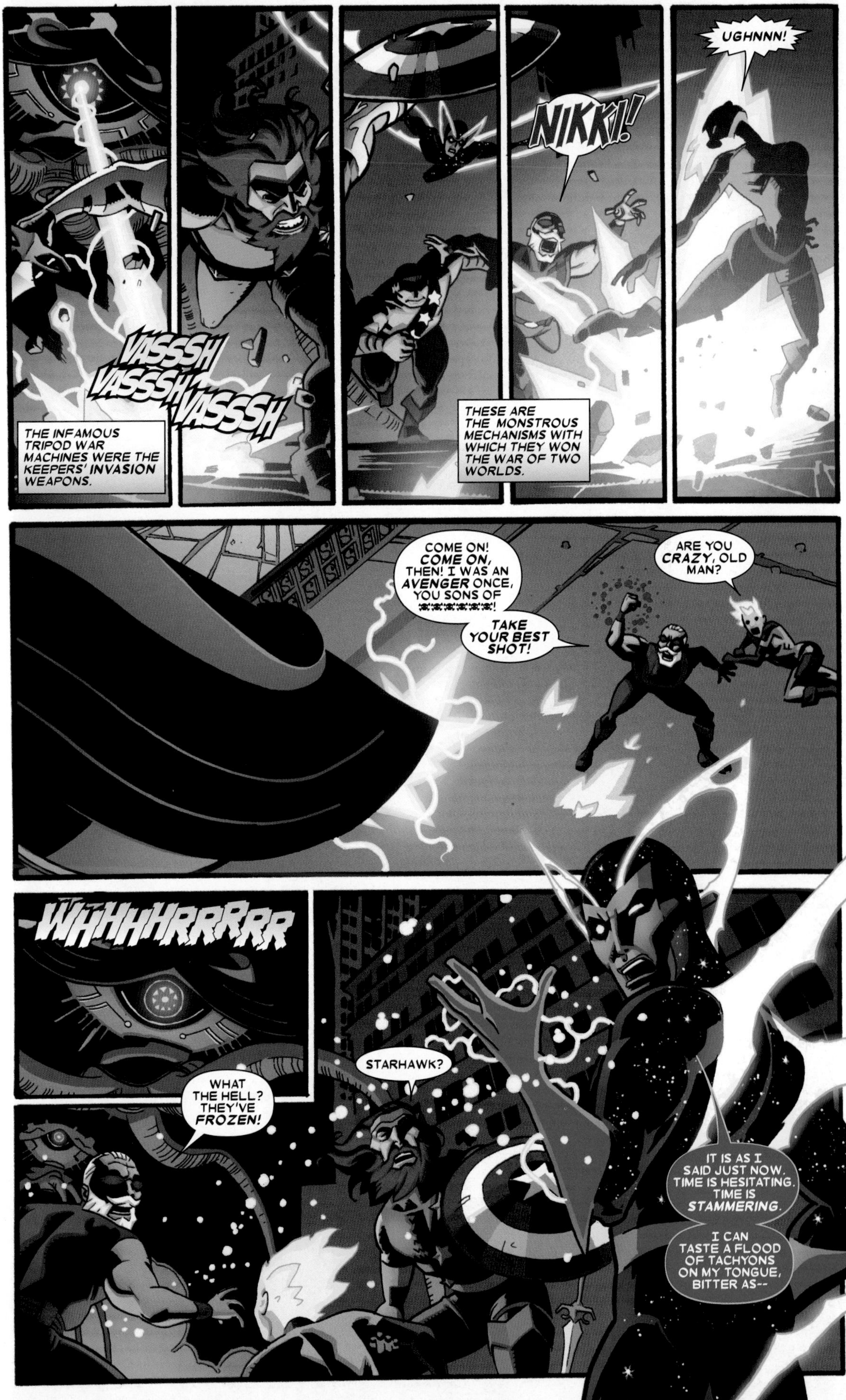
VASSSH VASSSH VASSSH
THE INFAMOUS TRIPOD WAR MACHINES WERE THE KEEPERS' INVASION WEAPONS.
THESE ARE THE MONSTROUS MECHANISMS WITH WHICH THEY WON THE WAR OF TWO WORLDS.
NIKKI!
UGHNNN!
COME ON! COME ON, THEN! I WAS AN AVENGER ONCE, YOU SONS OF
TAKE YOUR BEST SHOT!
ARE YOU CRAZY, OLD MAN?
WHHHHRRRRR
WHAT THE HELL? THEY'VE FROZEN!
STARHAWK?
IT IS AS I SAID JUST NOW. TIME IS HESITATING. TIME IS STAMMERING.
I CAN TASTE A FLOOD OF TACHYONS ON MY TONGUE, BITTER AS--

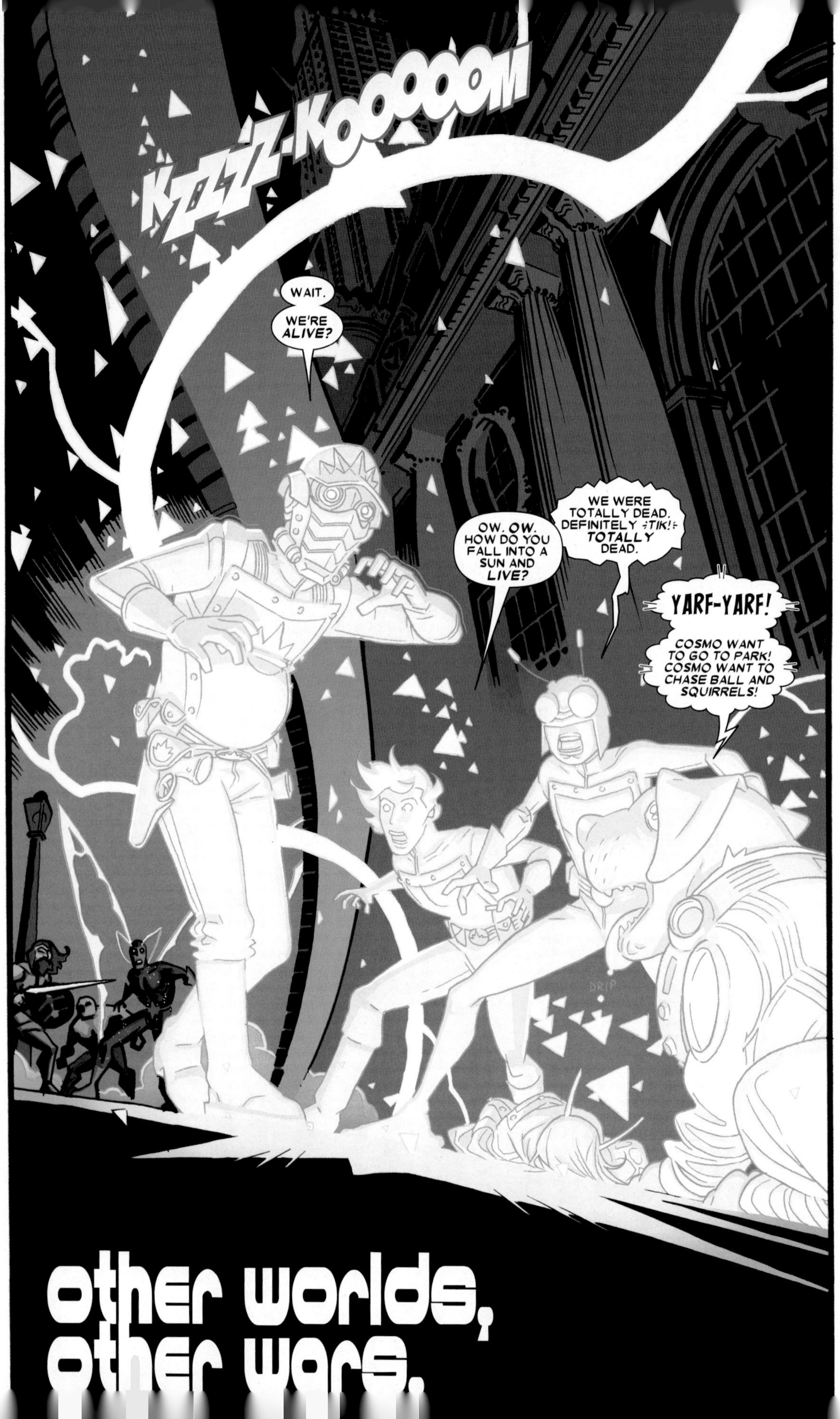
KZZZZ-KOOOOOM
WAIT.
WE'RE ALIVE?
OW. OW. HOW DO YOU FALL INTO A SUN AND LIVE?
WE WERE TOTALLY DEAD. DEFINITELY ≑TIK!≑ TOTALLY DEAD.
YARF-YARF!
COSMO WANT TO GO TO PARK! COSMO WANT TO CHASE BALL AND SQUIRRELS!
DRIP
other worlds, other wars.

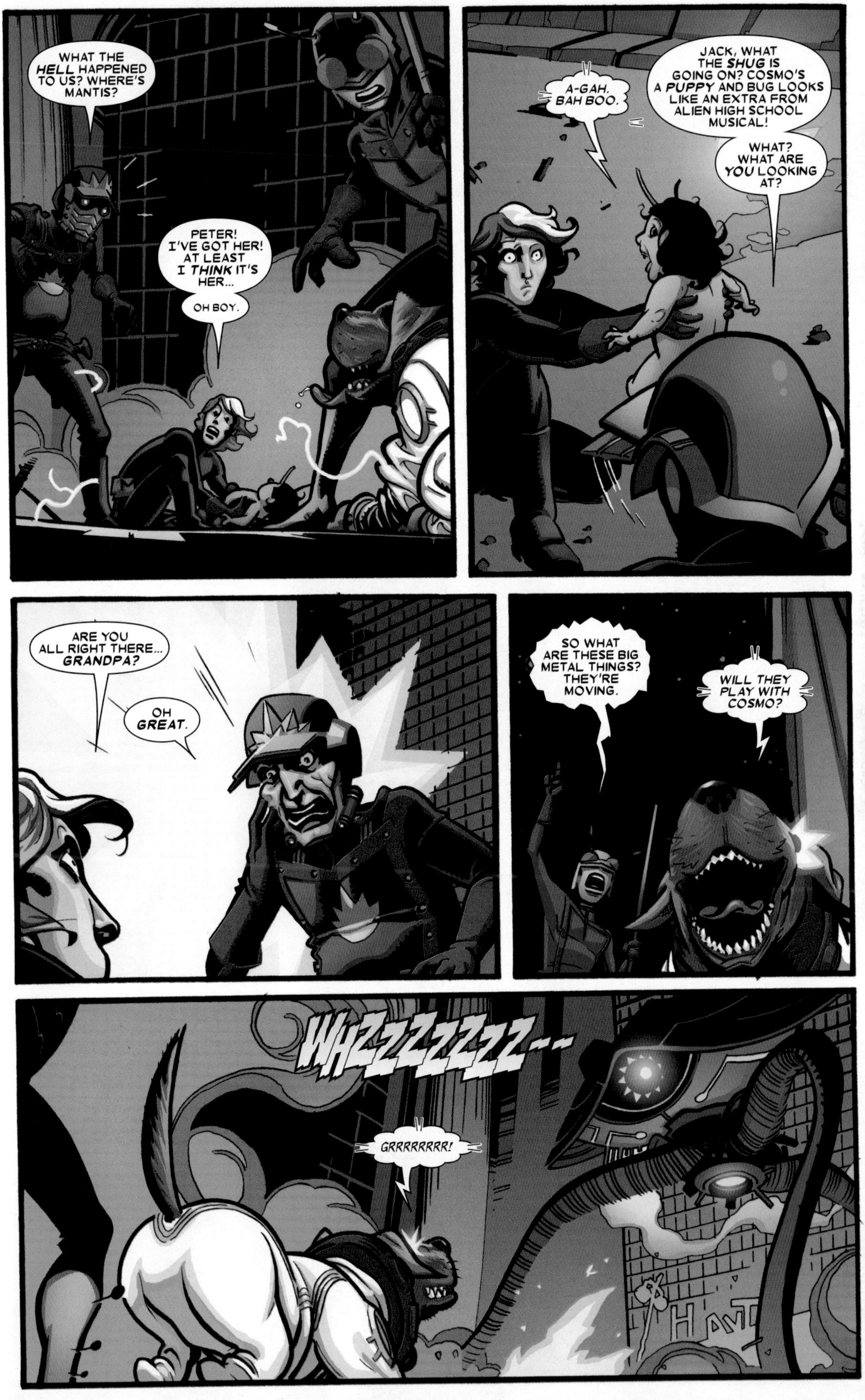
WHAT THE HELL HAPPENED TO US? WHERE'S MANTIS?
PETER! I'VE GOT HER! AT LEAST I THINK IT'S HER...
OH BOY.
A-GAH. BAH BOO.
JACK, WHAT THE SHUG IS GOING ON? COSMO'S A PUPPY AND BUG LOOKS LIKE AN EXTRA FROM ALIEN HIGH SCHOOL MUSICAL!
WHAT? WHAT ARE YOU LOOKING AT?
ARE YOU ALL RIGHT THERE... GRANDPA?
OH GREAT.
SO WHAT ARE THESE BIG METAL THINGS? THEY'RE MOVING.
WILL THEY PLAY WITH COSMO?
WHZZZZZZZ--
GRRRRRRRR!

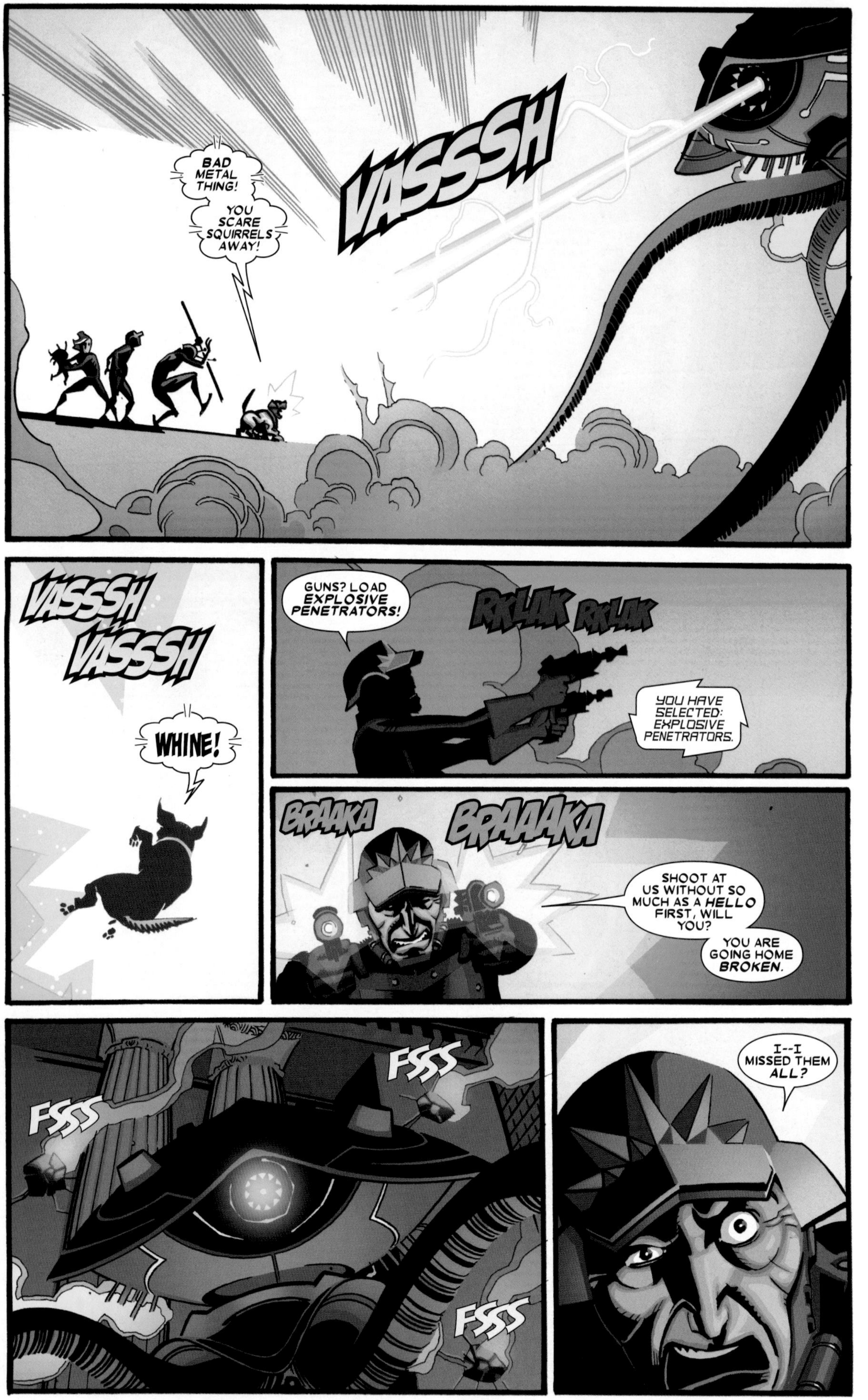
BAD METAL THING!
YOU SCARE SQUIRRELS AWAY!
VASSSH
VASSSH
VASSSH
WHINE!
GUNS? LOAD EXPLOSIVE PENETRATORS!
RKLAK RKLAK
YOU HAVE SELECTED: EXPLOSIVE PENETRATORS.
BRAAKA
BRAAAKA
SHOOT AT US WITHOUT SO MUCH AS A HELLO FIRST, WILL YOU?
YOU ARE GOING HOME BROKEN.
FSSS
FSSS
FSSS
I--I MISSED THEM ALL?

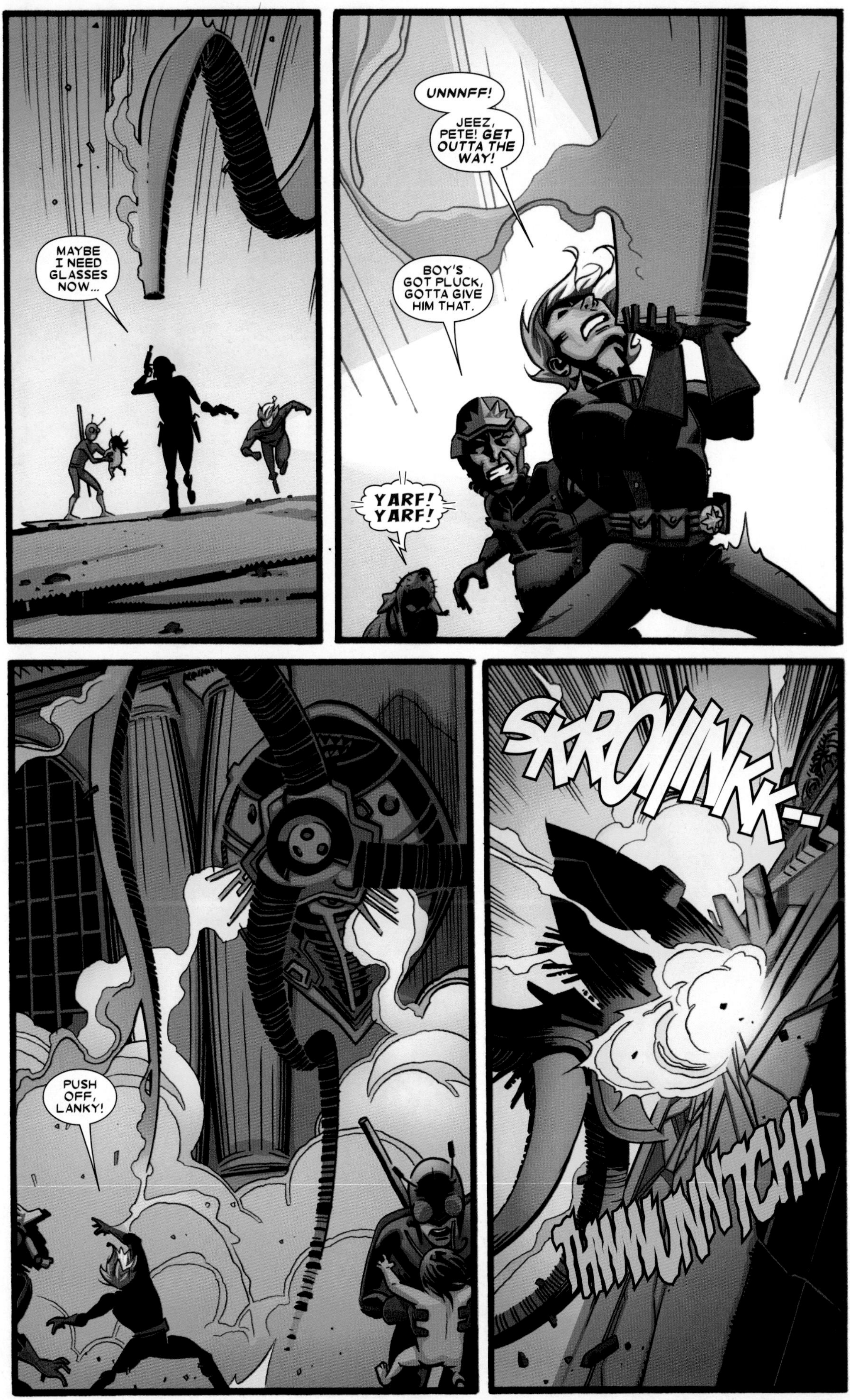
MAYBE I NEED GLASSES NOW...
UNNNFF!
JEEZ, PETE! GET OUTTA THE WAY!
BOY'S GOT PLUCK, GOTTA GIVE HIM THAT.
YARF! YARF!
PUSH OFF, LANKY!
SKROIIINKK--
THWUNNTCHH

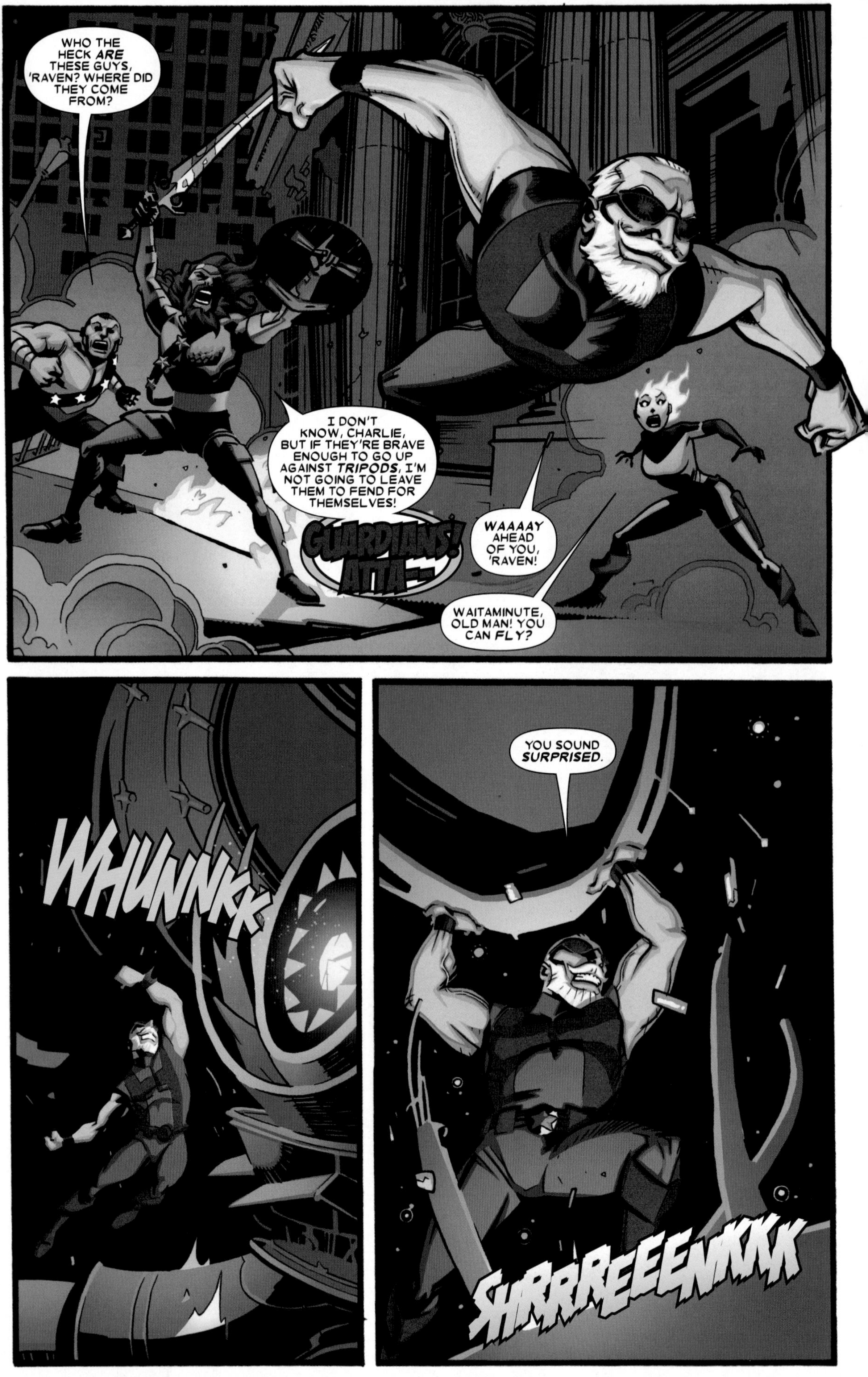
WHO THE HECK *ARE* THESE GUYS, 'RAVEN? WHERE DID THEY COME FROM?
I DON'T KNOW, CHARLIE, BUT IF THEY'RE BRAVE ENOUGH TO GO UP AGAINST *TRIPODS*, I'M NOT GOING TO LEAVE THEM TO FEND FOR THEMSELVES!
GUARDIANS! ATTA--
WAAAAY AHEAD OF YOU, 'RAVEN!
WAITAMINUTE, OLD MAN! YOU CAN *FLY*?
WHUNNKK
YOU SOUND *SURPRISED*.
SHRRREEENKKK

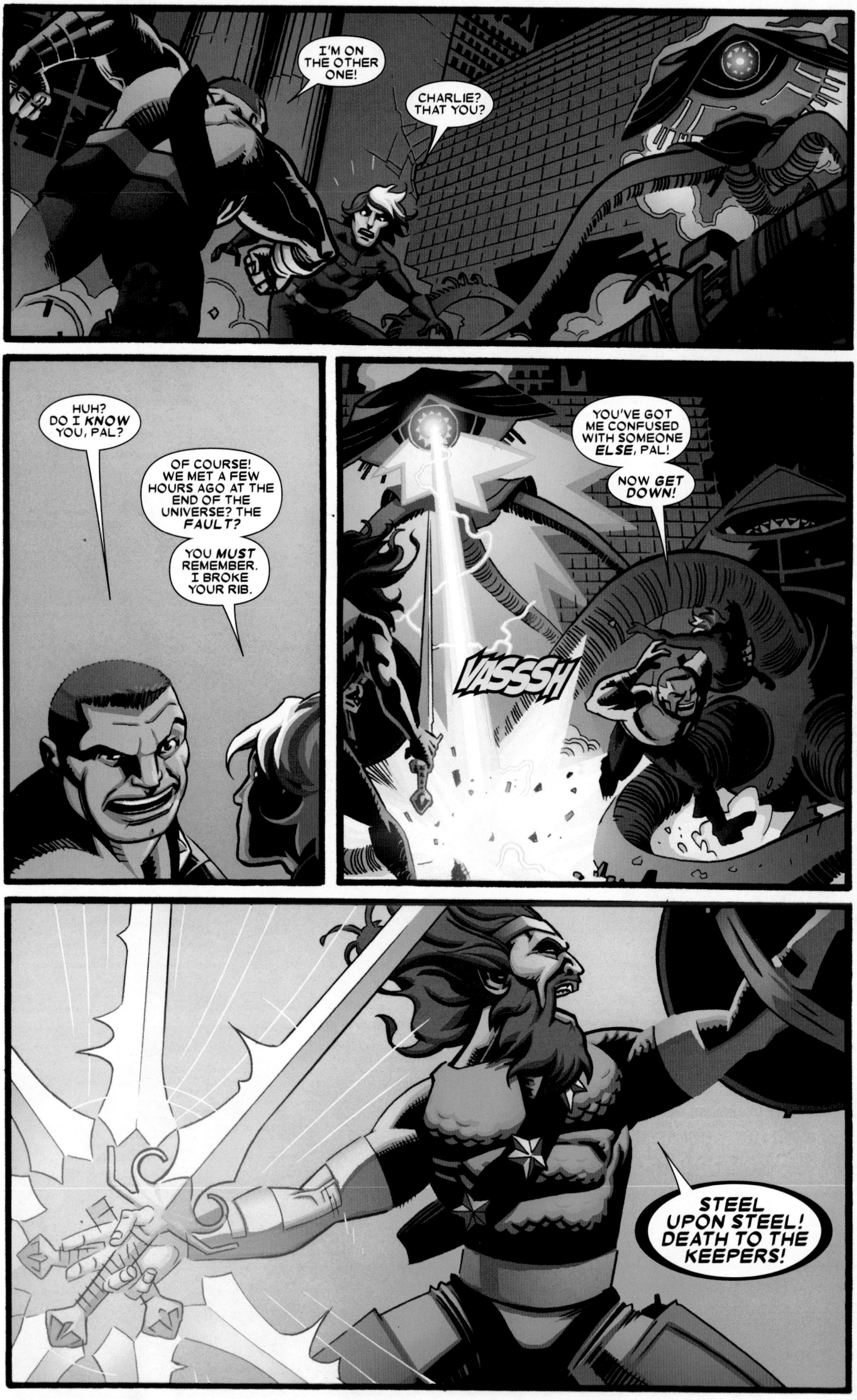

I'M ON THE OTHER ONE!
CHARLIE? THAT YOU?
HUH? DO I KNOW YOU, PAL?
OF COURSE! WE MET A FEW HOURS AGO AT THE END OF THE UNIVERSE? THE FAULT?
YOU MUST REMEMBER. I BROKE YOUR RIB.
YOU'VE GOT ME CONFUSED WITH SOMEONE ELSE, PAL!
NOW GET DOWN!
VASSSH
STEEL UPON STEEL! DEATH TO THE KEEPERS!

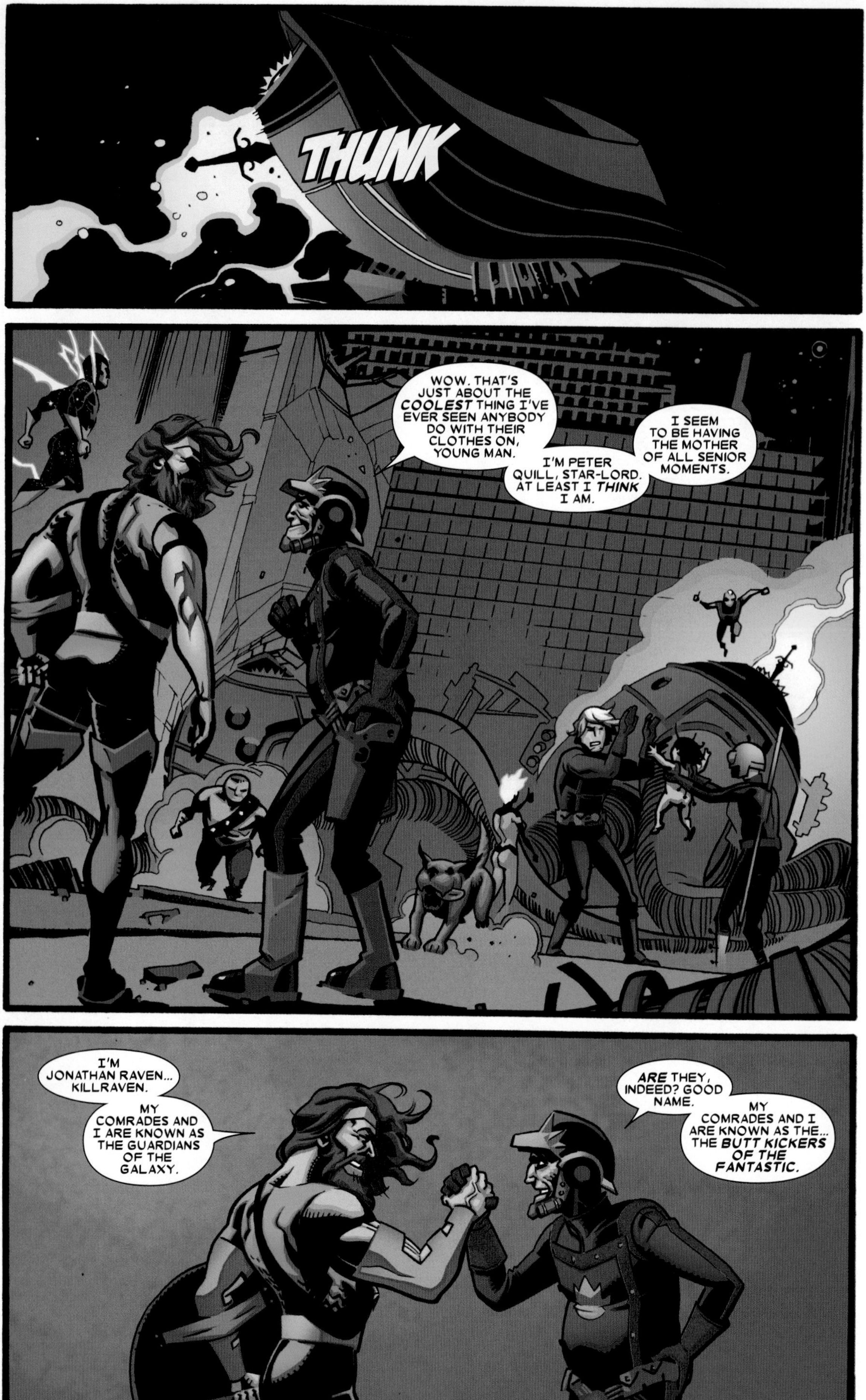
THUNK
WOW. THAT'S JUST ABOUT THE COOLEST THING I'VE EVER SEEN ANYBODY DO WITH THEIR CLOTHES ON, YOUNG MAN.
I SEEM TO BE HAVING THE MOTHER OF ALL SENIOR MOMENTS.
I'M PETER QUILL, STAR-LORD. AT LEAST I THINK I AM.
I'M JONATHAN RAVEN... KILLRAVEN.
MY COMRADES AND I ARE KNOWN AS THE GUARDIANS OF THE GALAXY.
ARE THEY, INDEED? GOOD NAME.
MY COMRADES AND I ARE KNOWN AS THE... THE BUTT KICKERS OF THE FANTASTIC.

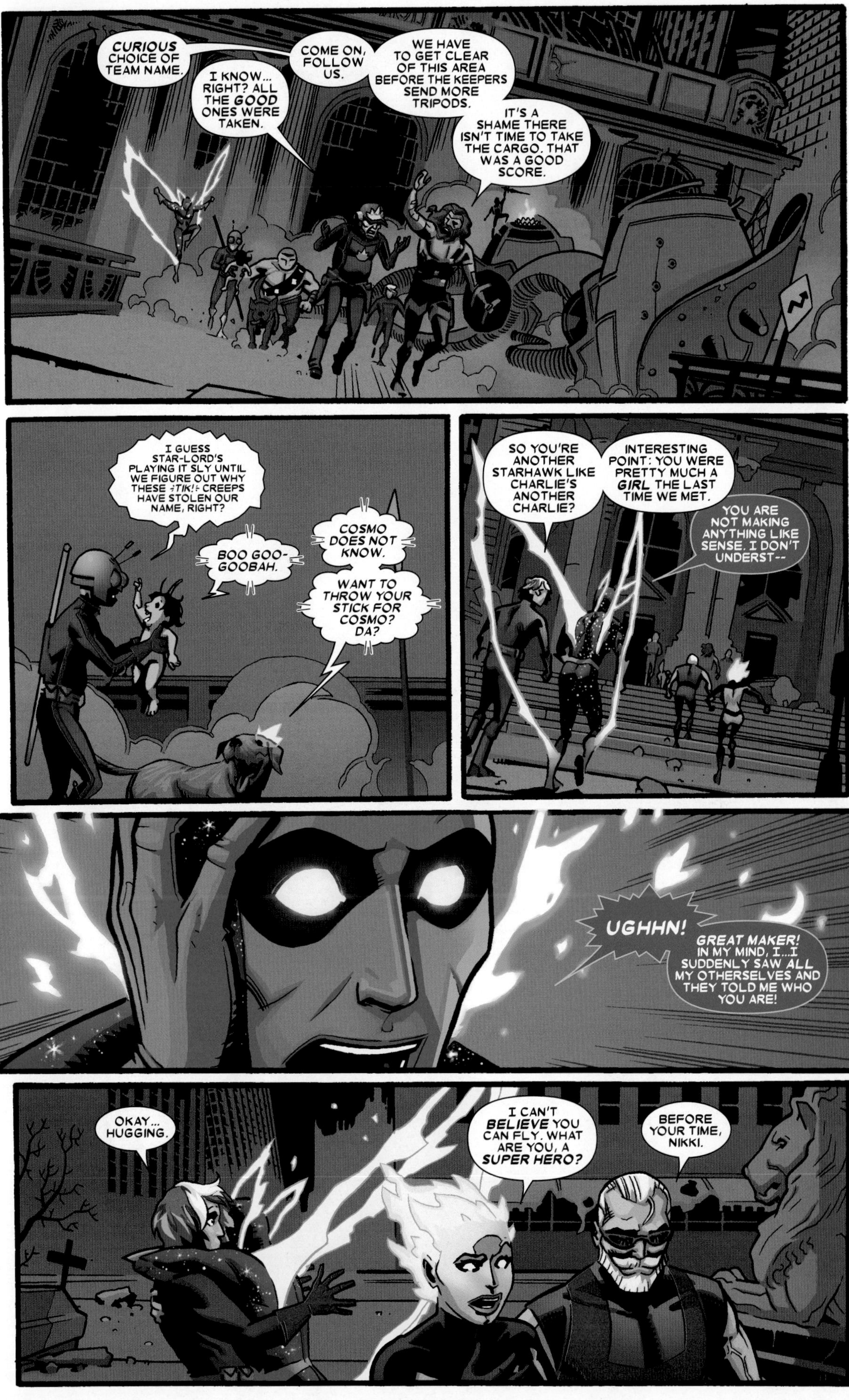
CURIOUS CHOICE OF TEAM NAME.
I KNOW... RIGHT? ALL THE GOOD ONES WERE TAKEN.
COME ON, FOLLOW US.
WE HAVE TO GET CLEAR OF THIS AREA BEFORE THE KEEPERS SEND MORE TRIPODS.
IT'S A SHAME THERE ISN'T TIME TO TAKE THE CARGO. THAT WAS A GOOD SCORE.
I GUESS STAR-LORD'S PLAYING IT SLY UNTIL WE FIGURE OUT WHY THESE ÷TIK!÷ CREEPS HAVE STOLEN OUR NAME, RIGHT?
BOO GOO-GOOBAH.
COSMO DOES NOT KNOW.
WANT TO THROW YOUR STICK FOR COSMO? DA?
SO YOU'RE ANOTHER STARHAWK LIKE CHARLIE'S ANOTHER CHARLIE?
INTERESTING POINT: YOU WERE PRETTY MUCH A GIRL THE LAST TIME WE MET.
YOU ARE NOT MAKING ANYTHING LIKE SENSE. I DON'T UNDERST--
UGHHN!
GREAT MAKER! IN MY MIND, I...I SUDDENLY SAW ALL MY OTHERSELVES AND THEY TOLD ME WHO YOU ARE!
OKAY... HUGGING.
I CAN'T BELIEVE YOU CAN FLY. WHAT ARE YOU, A SUPER HERO?
BEFORE YOUR TIME, NIKKI.

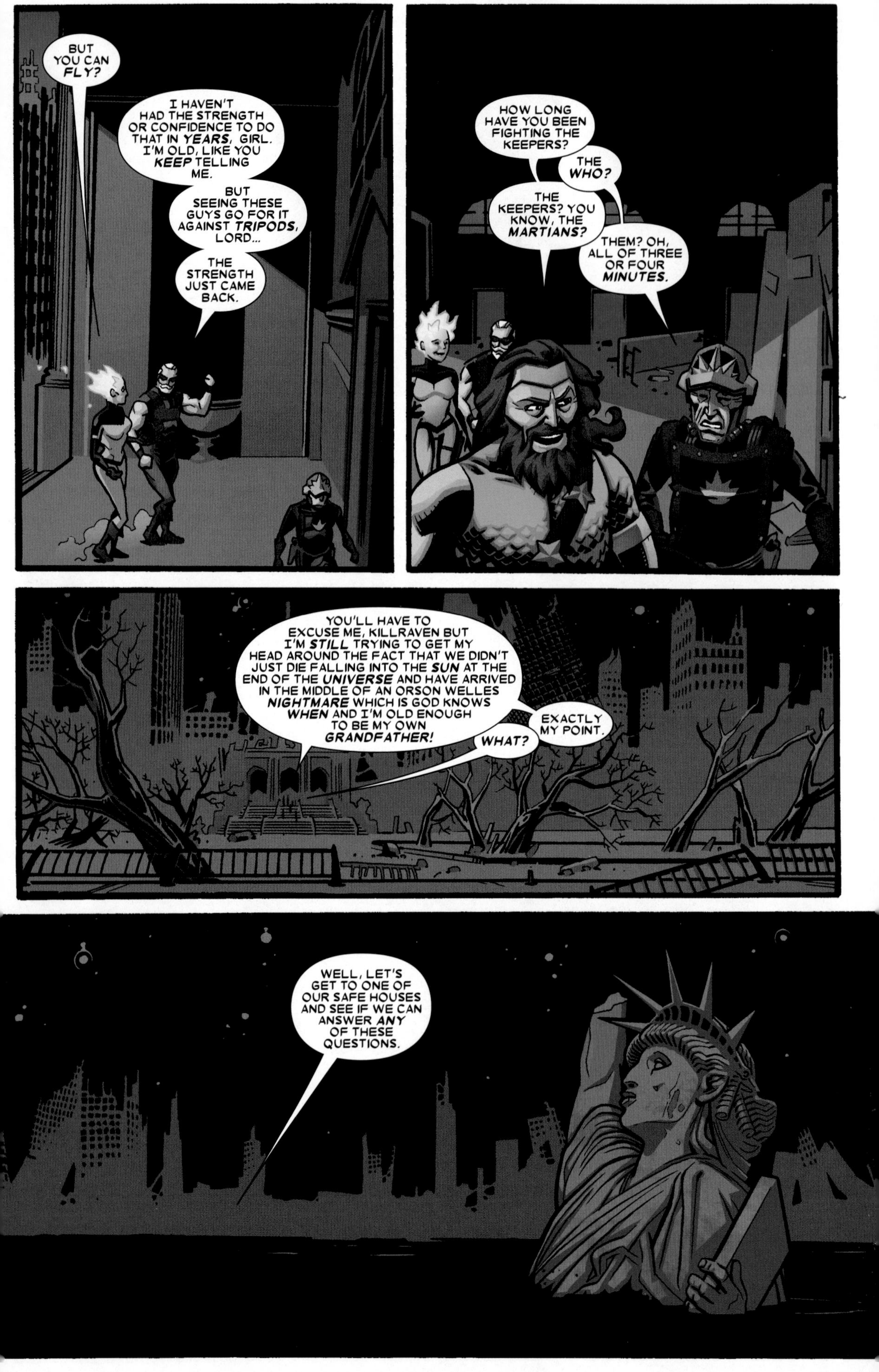
BUT YOU CAN FLY?
I HAVEN'T HAD THE STRENGTH OR CONFIDENCE TO DO THAT IN YEARS, GIRL. I'M OLD, LIKE YOU KEEP TELLING ME.
BUT SEEING THESE GUYS GO FOR IT AGAINST TRIPODS, LORD...
THE STRENGTH JUST CAME BACK.
HOW LONG HAVE YOU BEEN FIGHTING THE KEEPERS?
THE WHO?
THE KEEPERS? YOU KNOW, THE MARTIANS?
THEM? OH, ALL OF THREE OR FOUR MINUTES.
YOU'LL HAVE TO EXCUSE ME, KILLRAVEN BUT I'M STILL TRYING TO GET MY HEAD AROUND THE FACT THAT WE DIDN'T JUST DIE FALLING INTO THE SUN AT THE END OF THE UNIVERSE AND HAVE ARRIVED IN THE MIDDLE OF AN ORSON WELLES NIGHTMARE WHICH IS GOD KNOWS WHEN AND I'M OLD ENOUGH TO BE MY OWN GRANDFATHER!
EXACTLY MY POINT.
WHAT?
WELL, LET'S GET TO ONE OF OUR SAFE HOUSES AND SEE IF WE CAN ANSWER ANY OF THESE QUESTIONS.

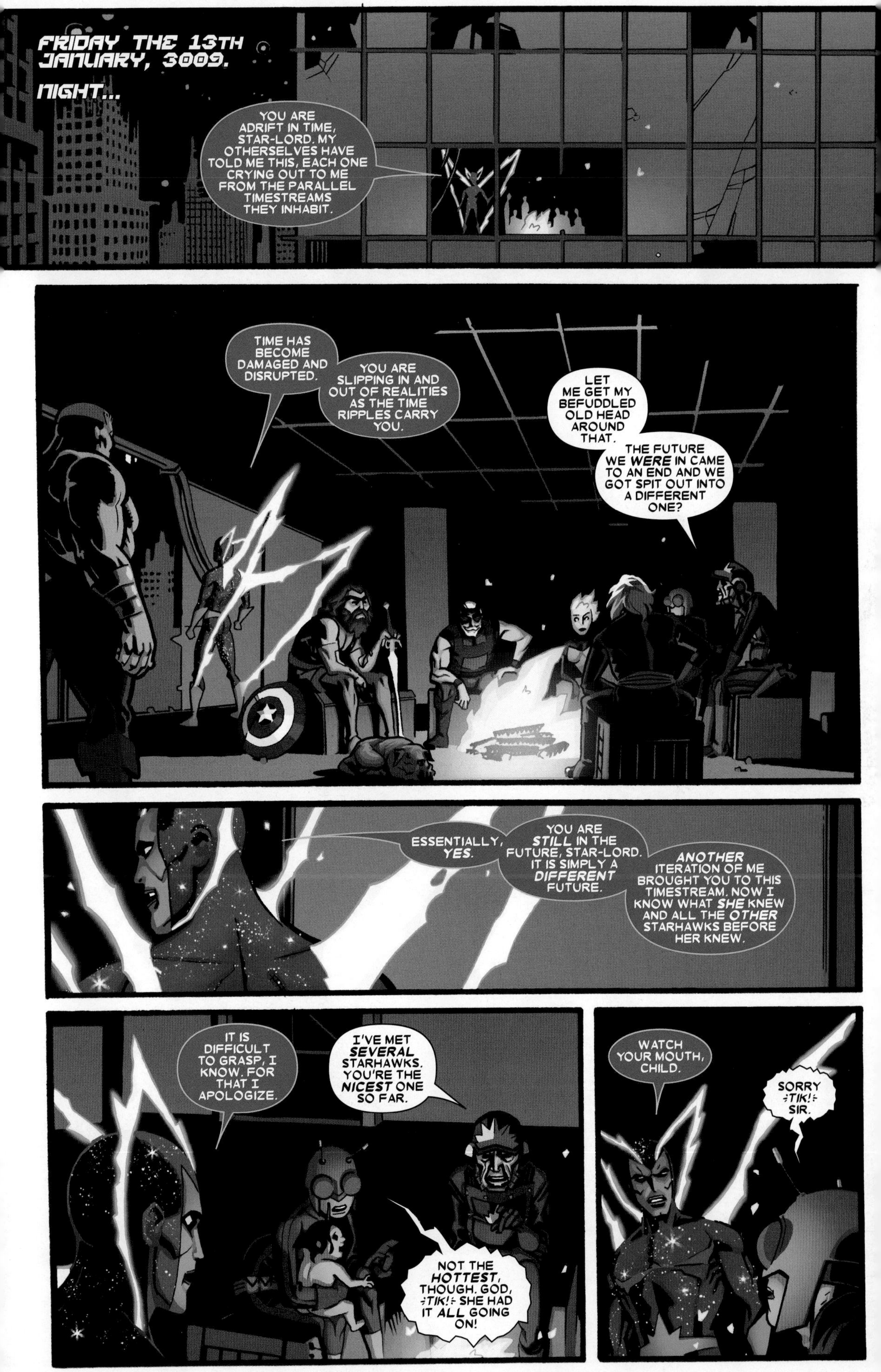
FRIDAY THE 13TH JANUARY, 3009.
NIGHT...
YOU ARE ADRIFT IN TIME, STAR-LORD. MY OTHERSELVES HAVE TOLD ME THIS, EACH ONE CRYING OUT TO ME FROM THE PARALLEL TIMESTREAMS THEY INHABIT.
TIME HAS BECOME DAMAGED AND DISRUPTED.
YOU ARE SLIPPING IN AND OUT OF REALITIES AS THE TIME RIPPLES CARRY YOU.
LET ME GET MY BEFUDDLED OLD HEAD AROUND THAT.
THE FUTURE WE WERE IN CAME TO AN END AND WE GOT SPIT OUT INTO A DIFFERENT ONE?
ESSENTIALLY, YES.
YOU ARE STILL IN THE FUTURE, STAR-LORD. IT IS SIMPLY A DIFFERENT FUTURE.
ANOTHER ITERATION OF ME BROUGHT YOU TO THIS TIMESTREAM. NOW I KNOW WHAT SHE KNEW AND ALL THE OTHER STARHAWKS BEFORE HER KNEW.
IT IS DIFFICULT TO GRASP, I KNOW. FOR THAT I APOLOGIZE.
I'VE MET SEVERAL STARHAWKS. YOU'RE THE NICEST ONE SO FAR.
NOT THE HOTTEST, THOUGH. GOD, -TIK!- SHE HAD IT ALL GOING ON!
WATCH YOUR MOUTH, CHILD.
SORRY -TIK!- SIR.

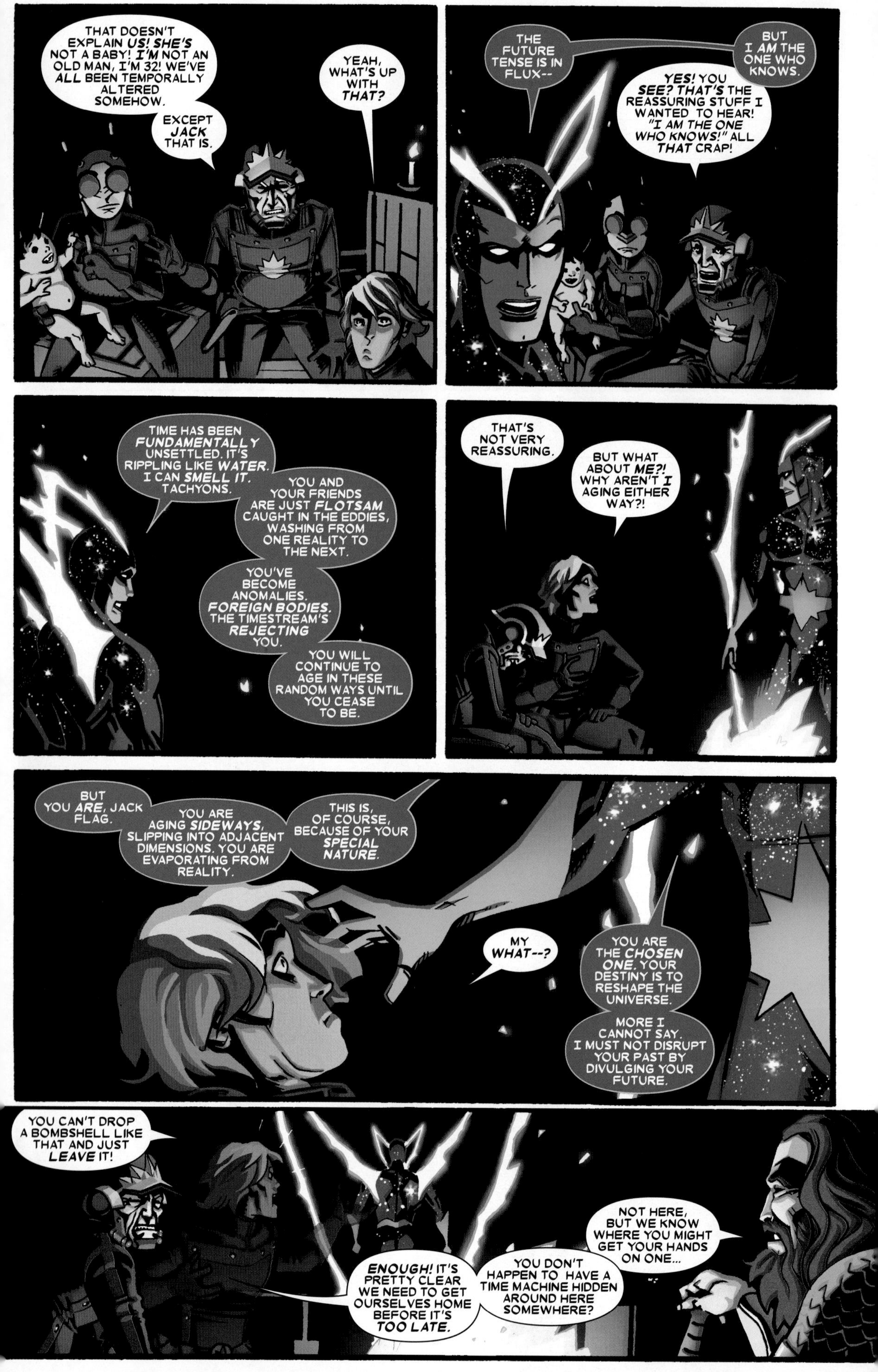

THAT DOESN'T EXPLAIN US! SHE'S NOT A BABY! I'M NOT AN OLD MAN, I'M 32! WE'VE ALL BEEN TEMPORALLY ALTERED SOMEHOW.
EXCEPT JACK THAT IS.
YEAH, WHAT'S UP WITH THAT?
THE FUTURE TENSE IS IN FLUX--
BUT I AM THE ONE WHO KNOWS.
YES! YOU SEE? THAT'S THE REASSURING STUFF I WANTED TO HEAR! "I AM THE ONE WHO KNOWS!" ALL THAT CRAP!
TIME HAS BEEN FUNDAMENTALLY UNSETTLED. IT'S RIPPLING LIKE WATER. I CAN SMELL IT. TACHYONS.
YOU AND YOUR FRIENDS ARE JUST FLOTSAM CAUGHT IN THE EDDIES, WASHING FROM ONE REALITY TO THE NEXT.
YOU'VE BECOME ANOMALIES. FOREIGN BODIES. THE TIMESTREAM'S REJECTING YOU.
YOU WILL CONTINUE TO AGE IN THESE RANDOM WAYS UNTIL YOU CEASE TO BE.
THAT'S NOT VERY REASSURING.
BUT WHAT ABOUT ME?! WHY AREN'T I AGING EITHER WAY?!
BUT YOU ARE, JACK FLAG.
YOU ARE AGING SIDEWAYS, SLIPPING INTO ADJACENT DIMENSIONS. YOU ARE EVAPORATING FROM REALITY.
THIS IS, OF COURSE, BECAUSE OF YOUR SPECIAL NATURE.
MY WHAT--?
YOU ARE THE CHOSEN ONE. YOUR DESTINY IS TO RESHAPE THE UNIVERSE.
MORE I CANNOT SAY. I MUST NOT DISRUPT YOUR PAST BY DIVULGING YOUR FUTURE.
YOU CAN'T DROP A BOMBSHELL LIKE THAT AND JUST LEAVE IT!
ENOUGH! IT'S PRETTY CLEAR WE NEED TO GET OURSELVES HOME BEFORE IT'S TOO LATE.
YOU DON'T HAPPEN TO HAVE A TIME MACHINE HIDDEN AROUND HERE SOMEWHERE?
NOT HERE, BUT WE KNOW WHERE YOU MIGHT GET YOUR HANDS ON ONE...

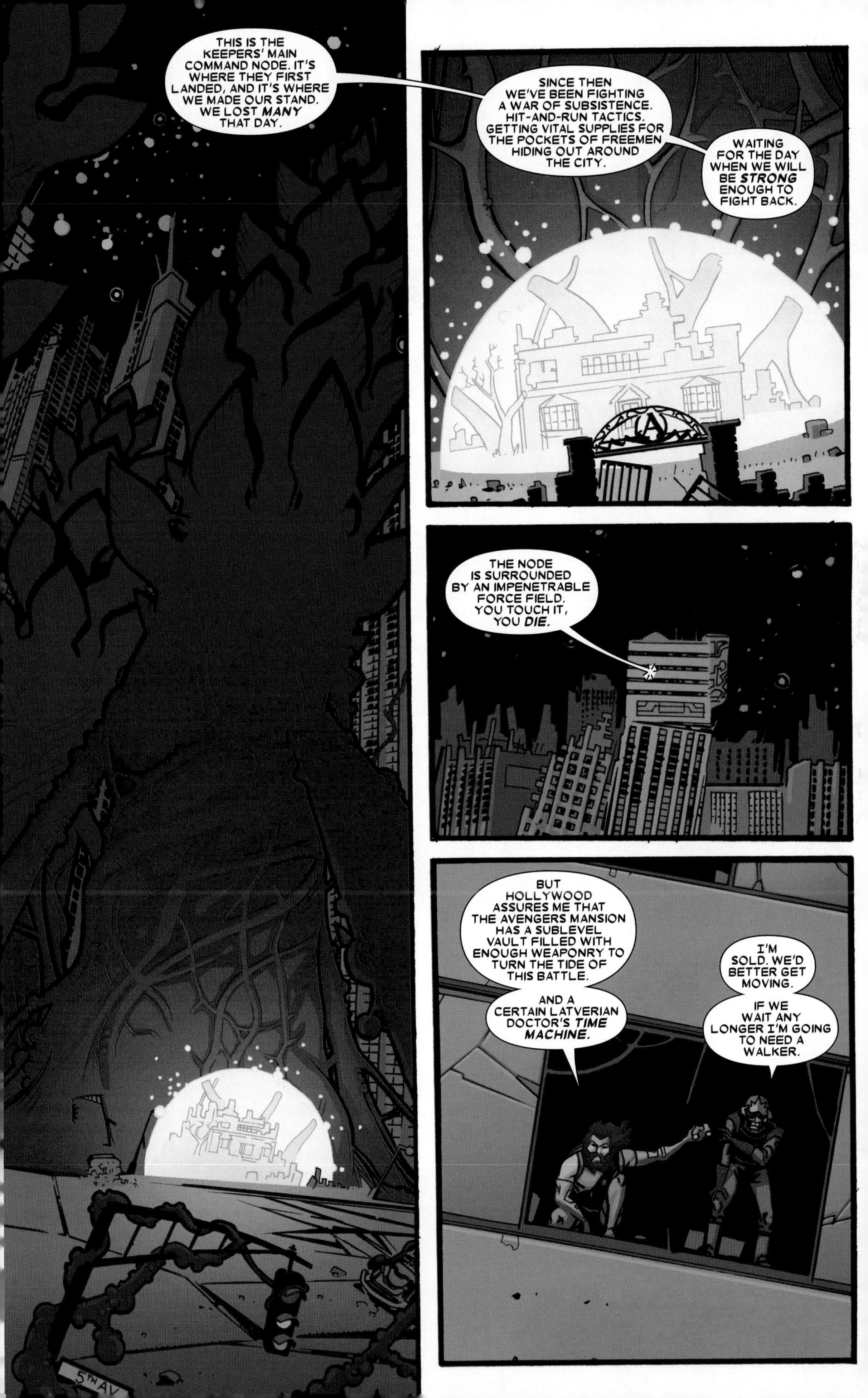
THIS IS THE KEEPERS' MAIN COMMAND NODE. IT'S WHERE THEY FIRST LANDED, AND IT'S WHERE WE MADE OUR STAND. WE LOST *MANY* THAT DAY.
SINCE THEN WE'VE BEEN FIGHTING A WAR OF SUBSISTENCE. HIT-AND-RUN TACTICS. GETTING VITAL SUPPLIES FOR THE POCKETS OF FREEMEN HIDING OUT AROUND THE CITY.
WAITING FOR THE DAY WHEN WE WILL BE *STRONG* ENOUGH TO FIGHT BACK.
THE NODE IS SURROUNDED BY AN IMPENETRABLE FORCE FIELD. YOU TOUCH IT, YOU *DIE.*
BUT HOLLYWOOD ASSURES ME THAT THE AVENGERS MANSION HAS A SUBLEVEL VAULT FILLED WITH ENOUGH WEAPONRY TO TURN THE TIDE OF THIS BATTLE.
AND A CERTAIN LATVERIAN DOCTOR'S *TIME MACHINE.*
I'M SOLD. WE'D BETTER GET MOVING.
IF WE WAIT ANY LONGER I'M GOING TO NEED A WALKER.
5TH AV

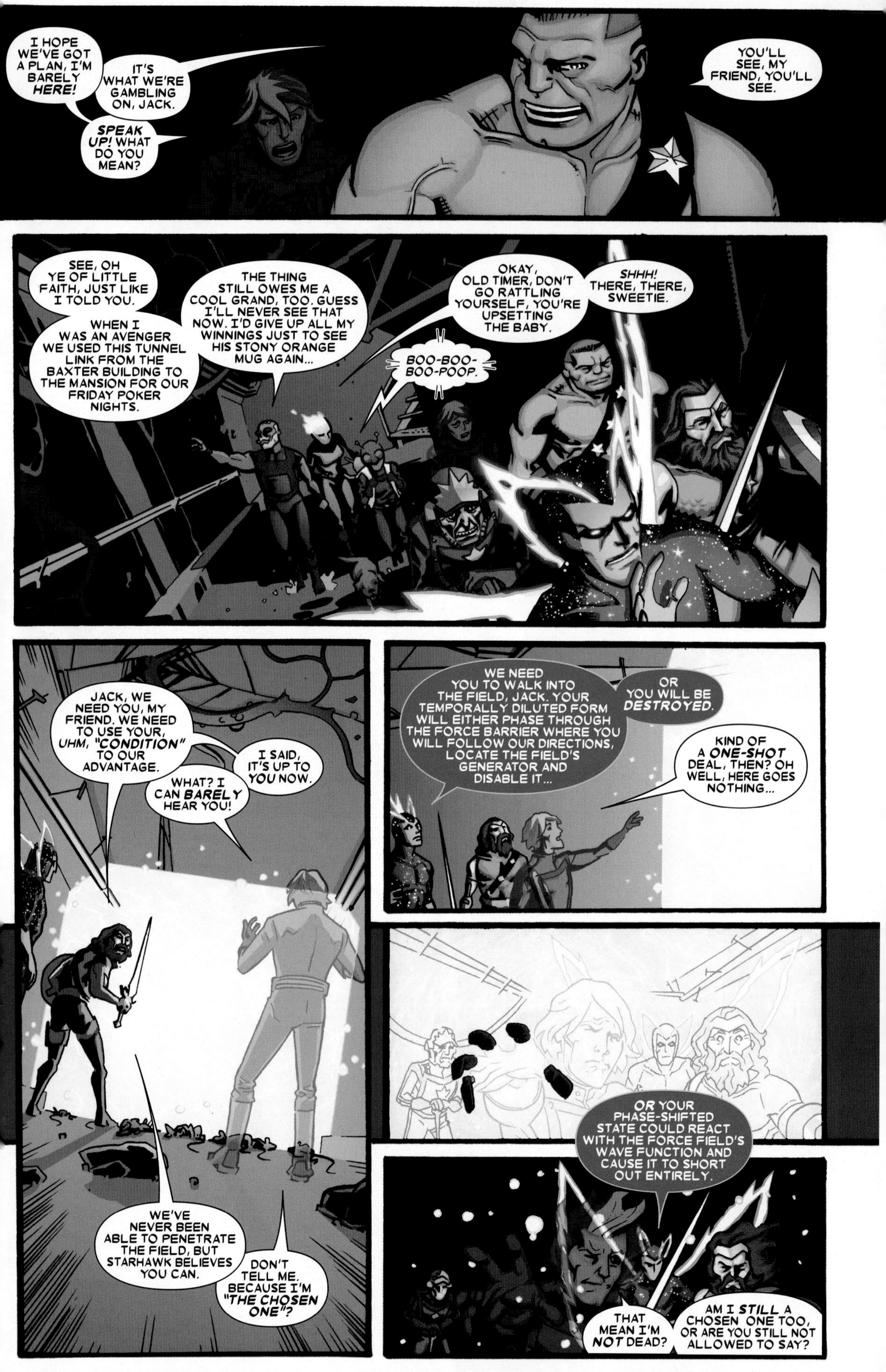
I HOPE WE'VE GOT A PLAN, I'M BARELY HERE!
IT'S WHAT WE'RE GAMBLING ON, JACK.
SPEAK UP! WHAT DO YOU MEAN?
YOU'LL SEE, MY FRIEND, YOU'LL SEE.
SEE, OH YE OF LITTLE FAITH, JUST LIKE I TOLD YOU.
WHEN I WAS AN AVENGER WE USED THIS TUNNEL LINK FROM THE BAXTER BUILDING TO THE MANSION FOR OUR FRIDAY POKER NIGHTS.
THE THING STILL OWES ME A COOL GRAND, TOO. GUESS I'LL NEVER SEE THAT NOW. I'D GIVE UP ALL MY WINNINGS JUST TO SEE HIS STONY ORANGE MUG AGAIN...
BOO-BOO-BOO-POOP.
OKAY, OLD TIMER, DON'T GO RATTLING YOURSELF, YOU'RE UPSETTING THE BABY.
SHHH! THERE, THERE, SWEETIE.
JACK, WE NEED YOU, MY FRIEND. WE NEED TO USE YOUR, UHM, "CONDITION" TO OUR ADVANTAGE.
I SAID, IT'S UP TO YOU NOW.
WHAT? I CAN BARELY HEAR YOU!
WE'VE NEVER BEEN ABLE TO PENETRATE THE FIELD, BUT STARHAWK BELIEVES YOU CAN.
DON'T TELL ME. BECAUSE I'M "THE CHOSEN ONE"?
WE NEED YOU TO WALK INTO THE FIELD, JACK. YOUR TEMPORALLY DILUTED FORM WILL EITHER PHASE THROUGH THE FORCE BARRIER WHERE YOU WILL FOLLOW OUR DIRECTIONS, LOCATE THE FIELD'S GENERATOR AND DISABLE IT...
OR YOU WILL BE DESTROYED.
KIND OF A ONE-SHOT DEAL, THEN? OH WELL, HERE GOES NOTHING...
OR YOUR PHASE-SHIFTED STATE COULD REACT WITH THE FORCE FIELD'S WAVE FUNCTION AND CAUSE IT TO SHORT OUT ENTIRELY.
THAT MEAN I'M NOT DEAD?
AM I STILL A CHOSEN ONE TOO, OR ARE YOU STILL NOT ALLOWED TO SAY?

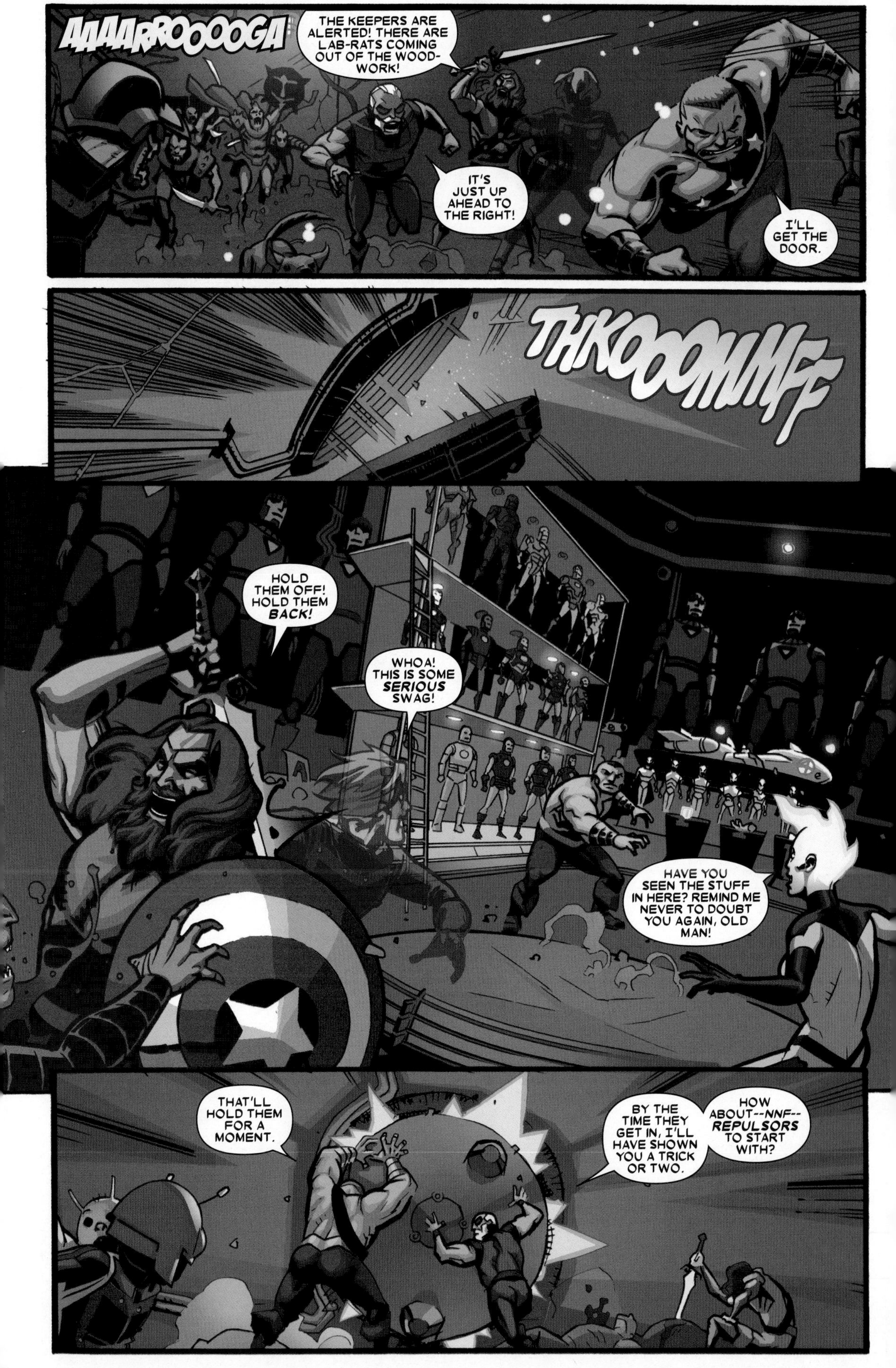
AAAARROOOOGA
THE KEEPERS ARE ALERTED! THERE ARE LAB-RATS COMING OUT OF THE WOOD-WORK!
IT'S JUST UP AHEAD TO THE RIGHT!
I'LL GET THE DOOR.
THKOOOMMFF
HOLD THEM OFF! HOLD THEM BACK!
WHOA! THIS IS SOME SERIOUS SWAG!
HAVE YOU SEEN THE STUFF IN HERE? REMIND ME NEVER TO DOUBT YOU AGAIN, OLD MAN!
THAT'LL HOLD THEM FOR A MOMENT.
BY THE TIME THEY GET IN, I'LL HAVE SHOWN YOU A TRICK OR TWO.
HOW ABOUT--NNF--REPULSORS TO START WITH?

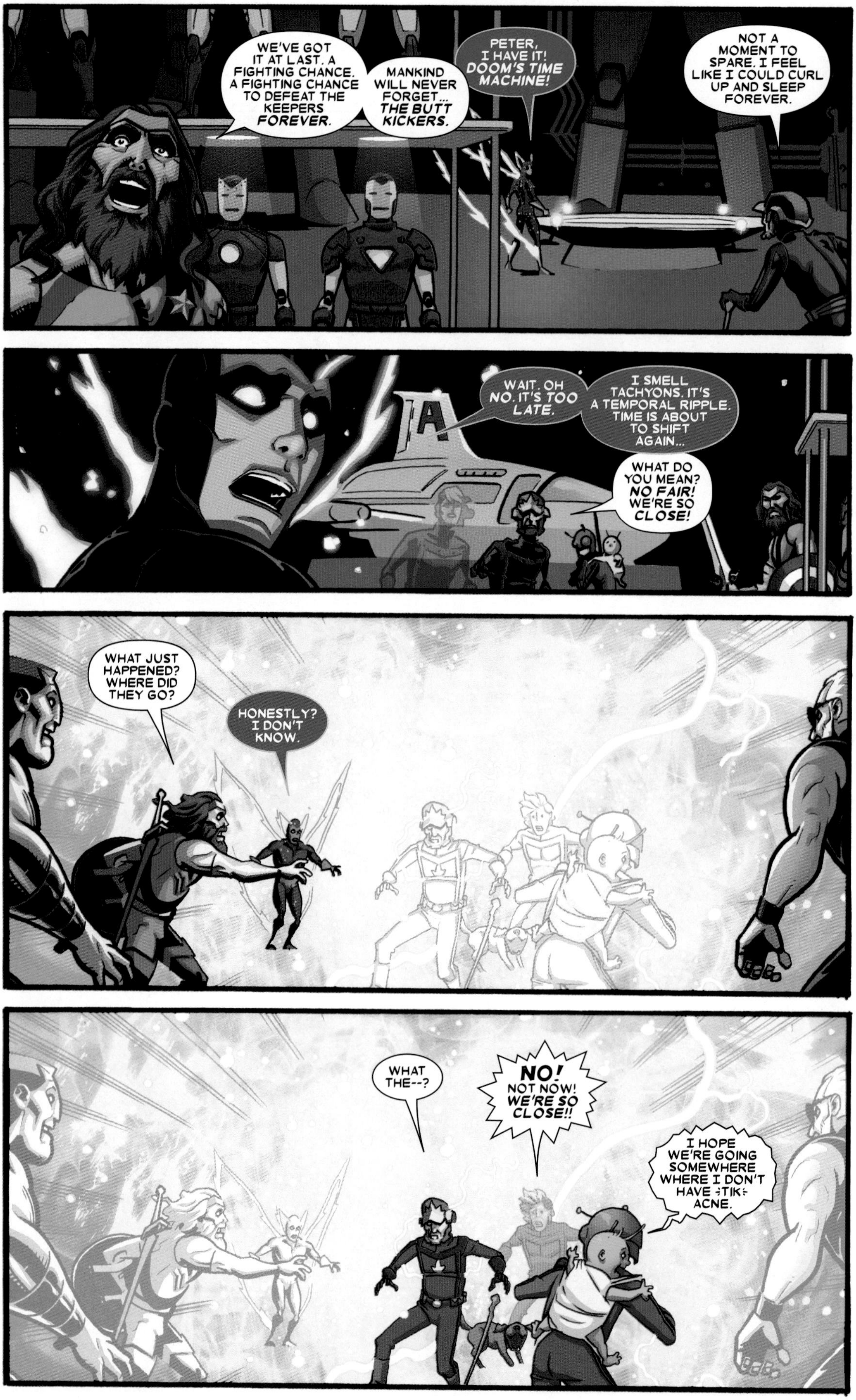
WE'VE GOT IT AT LAST. A FIGHTING CHANCE. A FIGHTING CHANCE TO DEFEAT THE KEEPERS FOREVER.
MANKIND WILL NEVER FORGET... THE BUTT KICKERS.
PETER, I HAVE IT! DOOM'S TIME MACHINE!
NOT A MOMENT TO SPARE. I FEEL LIKE I COULD CURL UP AND SLEEP FOREVER.
WAIT. OH NO. IT'S TOO LATE.
I SMELL TACHYONS. IT'S A TEMPORAL RIPPLE. TIME IS ABOUT TO SHIFT AGAIN...
WHAT DO YOU MEAN? NO FAIR! WE'RE SO CLOSE!
WHAT JUST HAPPENED? WHERE DID THEY GO?
HONESTLY? I DON'T KNOW.
WHAT THE--?
NO! NOT NOW! WE'RE SO CLOSE!!
I HOPE WE'RE GOING SOMEWHERE WHERE I DON'T HAVE ÷TIK÷ ACNE.

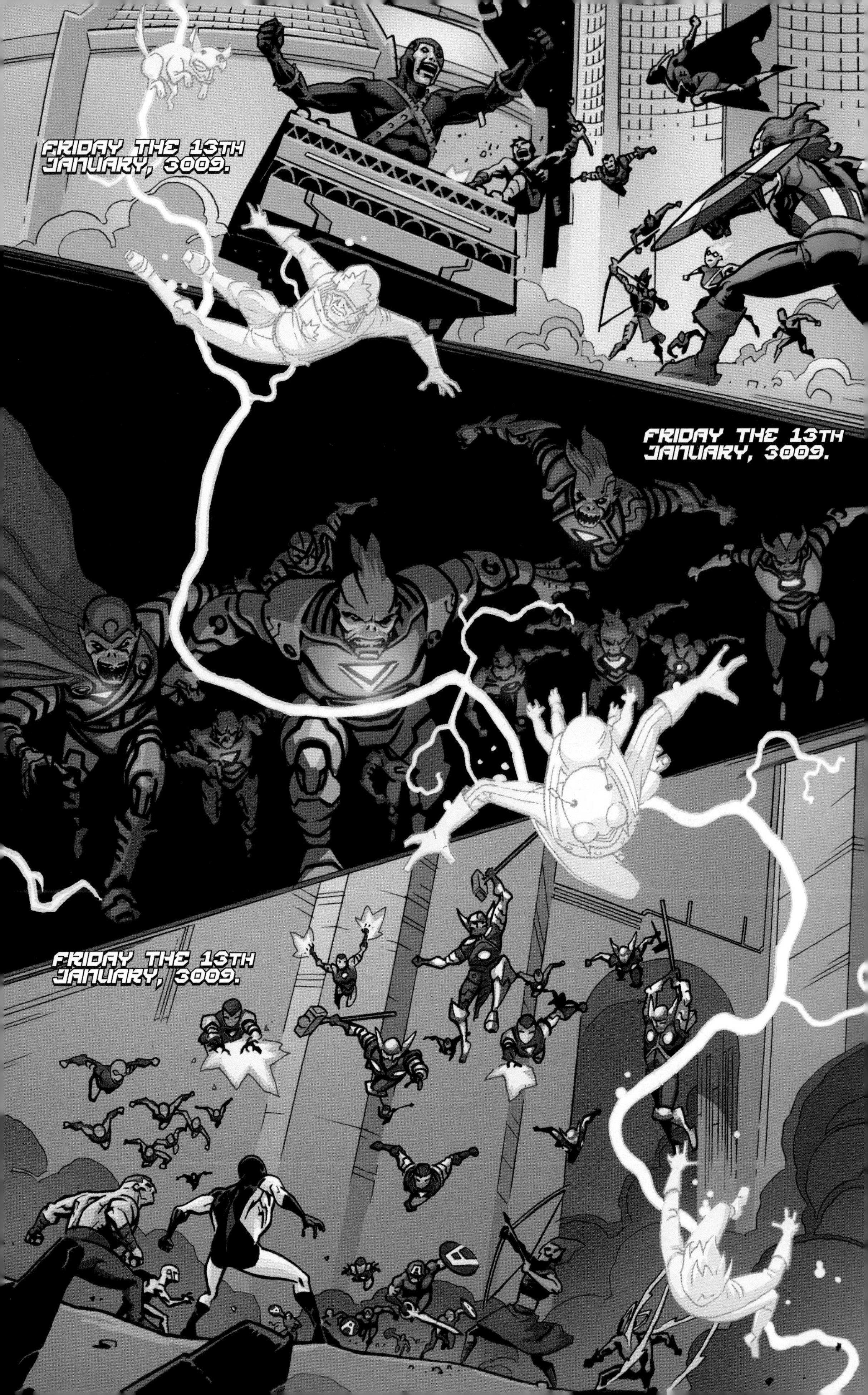
FRIDAY THE 13TH JANUARY, 3009.
FRIDAY THE 13TH JANUARY, 3009.
FRIDAY THE 13TH JANUARY, 3009.

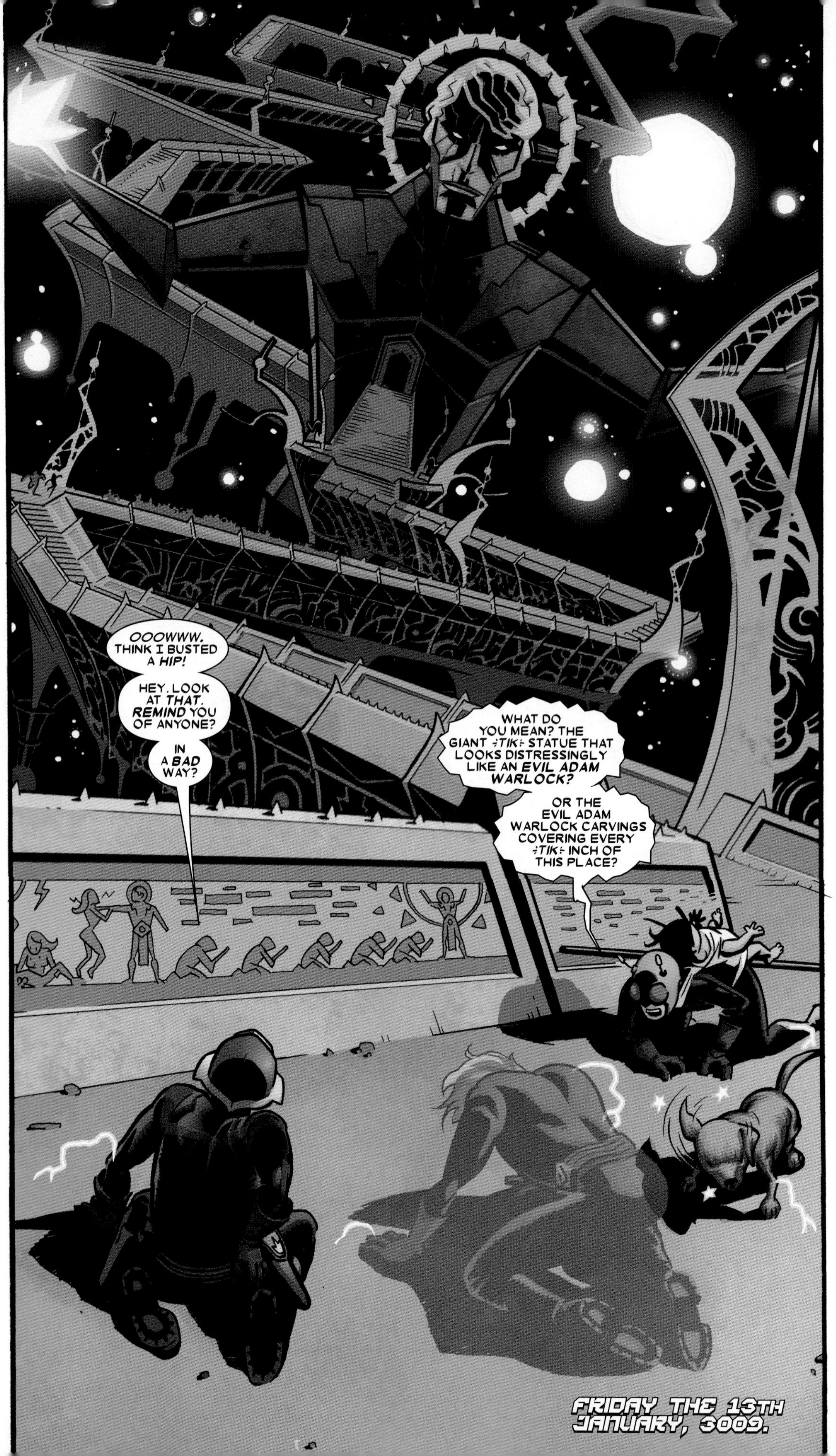
OOOWWW. THINK I BUSTED A HIP!
HEY. LOOK AT THAT. REMIND YOU OF ANYONE?
IN A BAD WAY?
WHAT DO YOU MEAN? THE GIANT ≑TIK≑ STATUE THAT LOOKS DISTRESSINGLY LIKE AN EVIL ADAM WARLOCK?
OR THE EVIL ADAM WARLOCK CARVINGS COVERING EVERY ≑TIK≑ INCH OF THIS PLACE?
FRIDAY THE 13TH JANUARY, 3009.

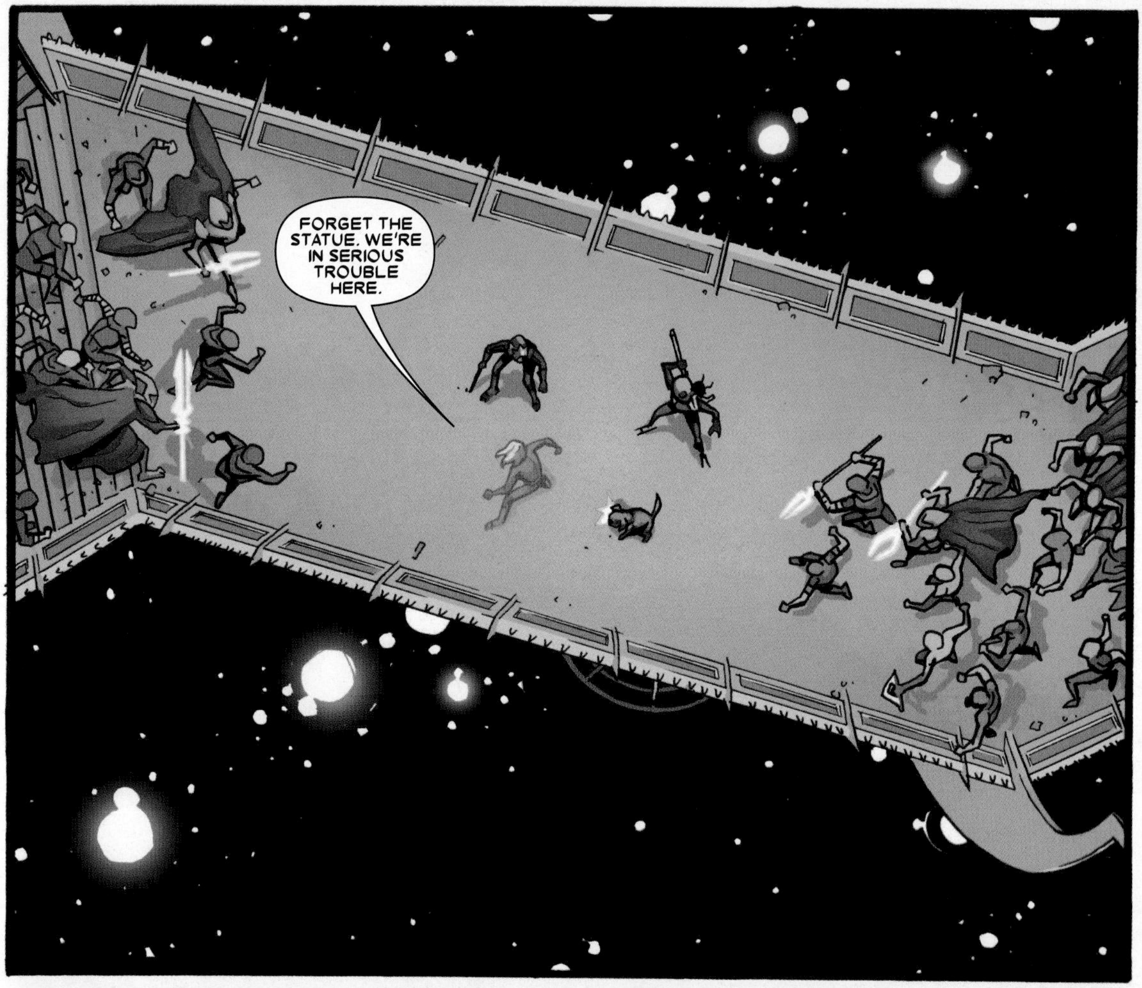
FORGET THE STATUE. WE'RE IN SERIOUS TROUBLE HERE.

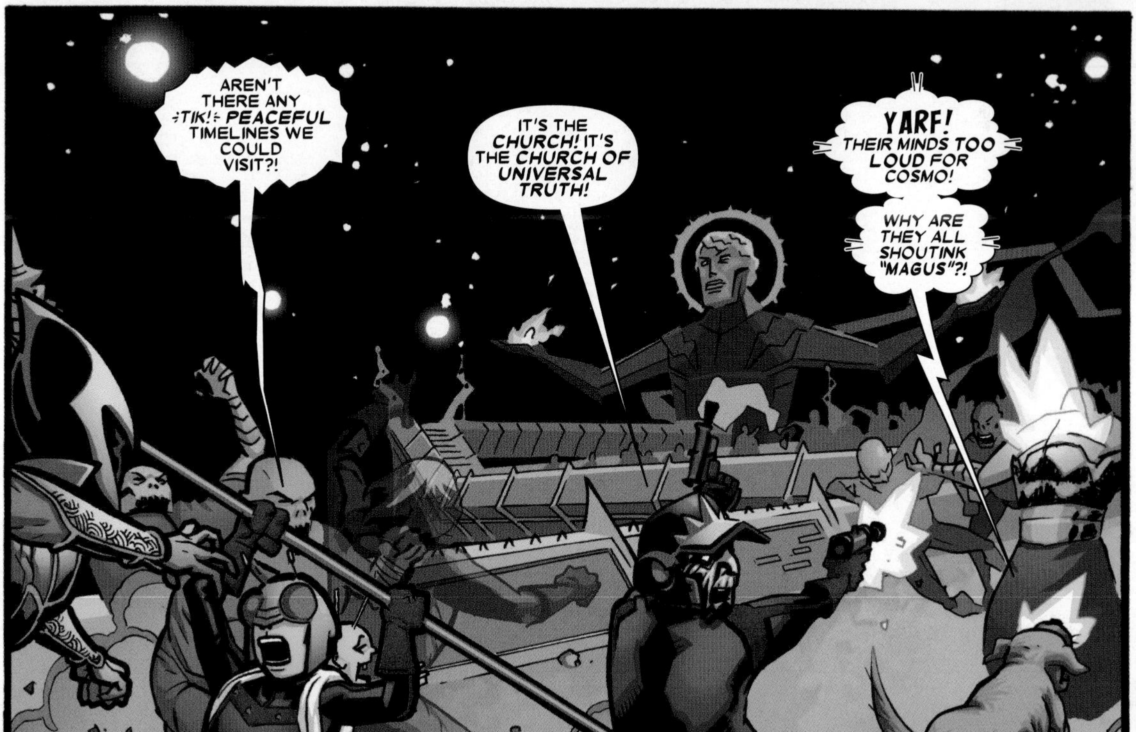
AREN'T THERE ANY ≠TIK!≠ PEACEFUL TIMELINES WE COULD VISIT?!
IT'S THE CHURCH! IT'S THE CHURCH OF UNIVERSAL TRUTH!
YARF! THEIR MINDS TOO LOUD FOR COSMO!
WHY ARE THEY ALL SHOUTINK "MAGUS"?!

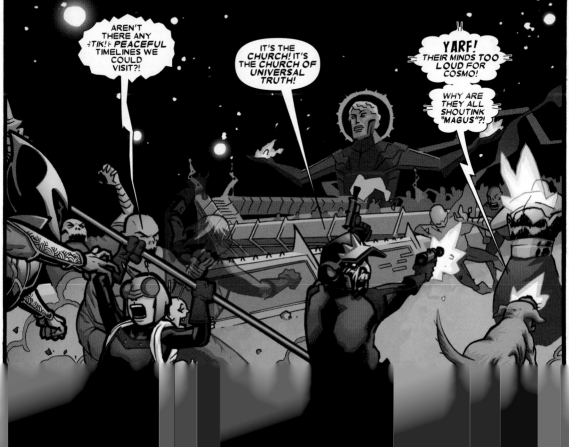

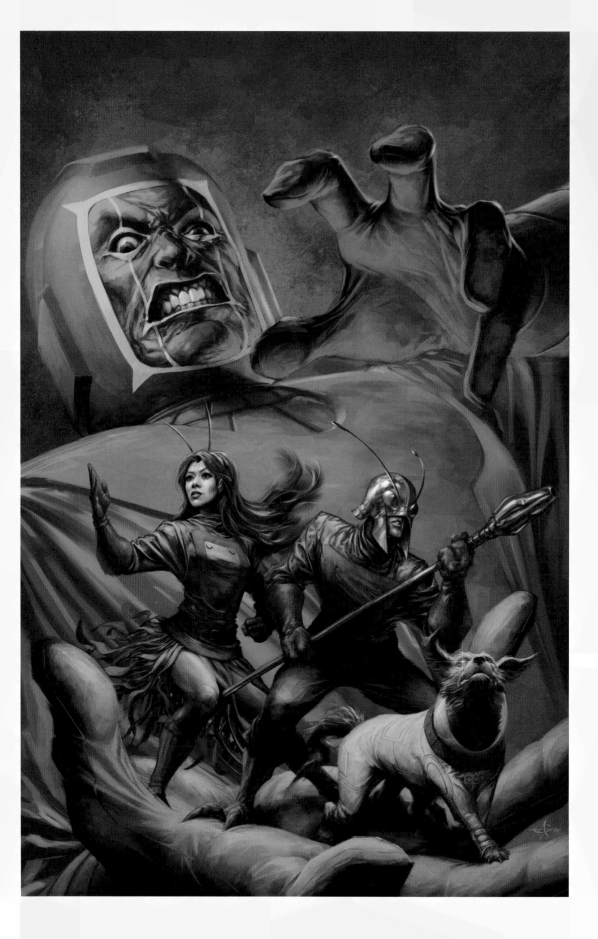

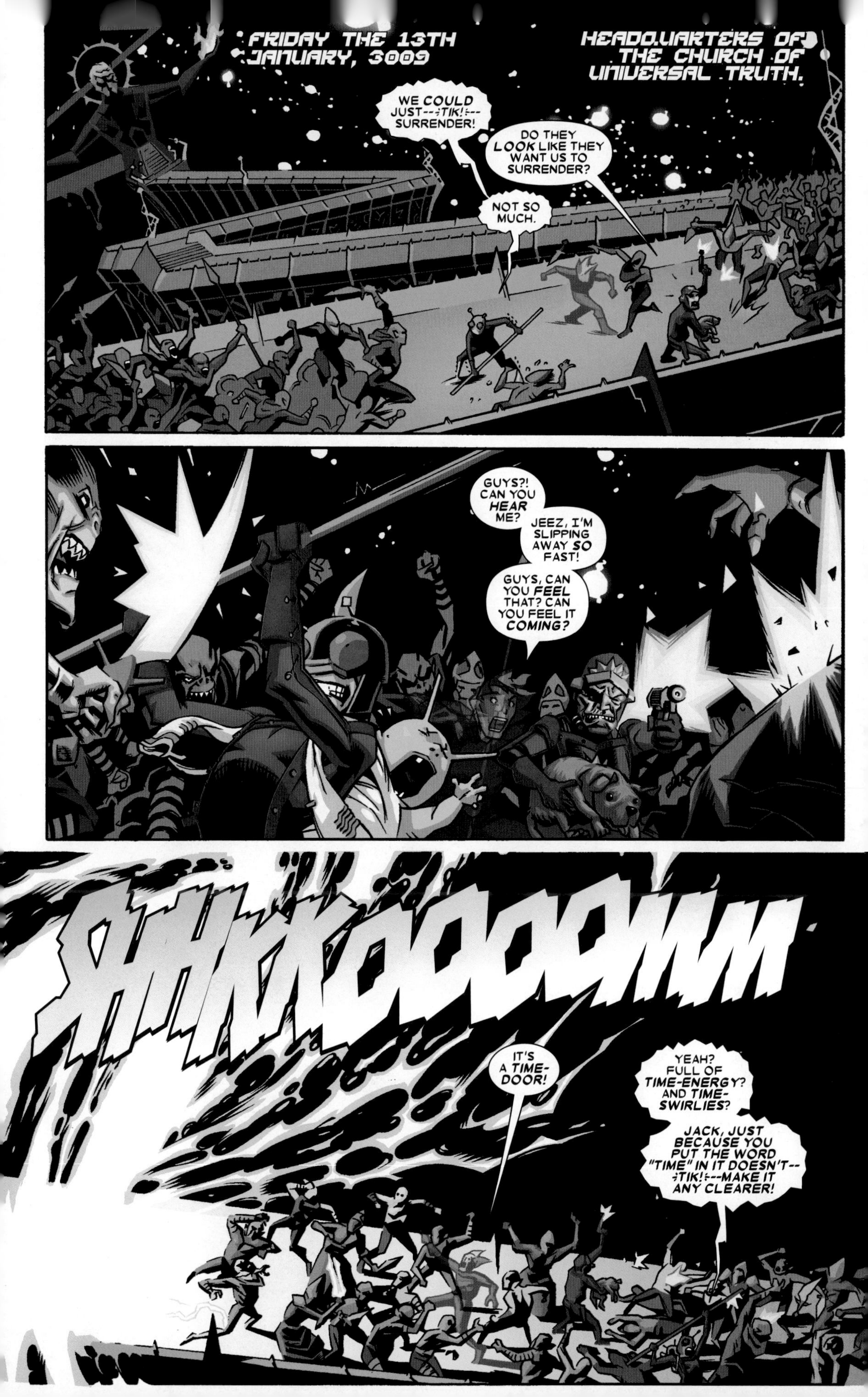
FRIDAY THE 13TH JANUARY, 3009
HEADQUARTERS OF THE CHURCH OF UNIVERSAL TRUTH.
WE COULD JUST--╡TIK!╞--SURRENDER!
DO THEY LOOK LIKE THEY WANT US TO SURRENDER?
NOT SO MUCH.
GUYS?! CAN YOU HEAR ME?
JEEZ, I'M SLIPPING AWAY SO FAST!
GUYS, CAN YOU FEEL THAT? CAN YOU FEEL IT COMING?
SHKOOOOOM
IT'S A TIME-DOOR!
YEAH? FULL OF TIME-ENERGY? AND TIME-SWIRLIES?
JACK, JUST BECAUSE YOU PUT THE WORD "TIME" IN IT DOESN'T--╡TIK!╞--MAKE IT ANY CLEARER!

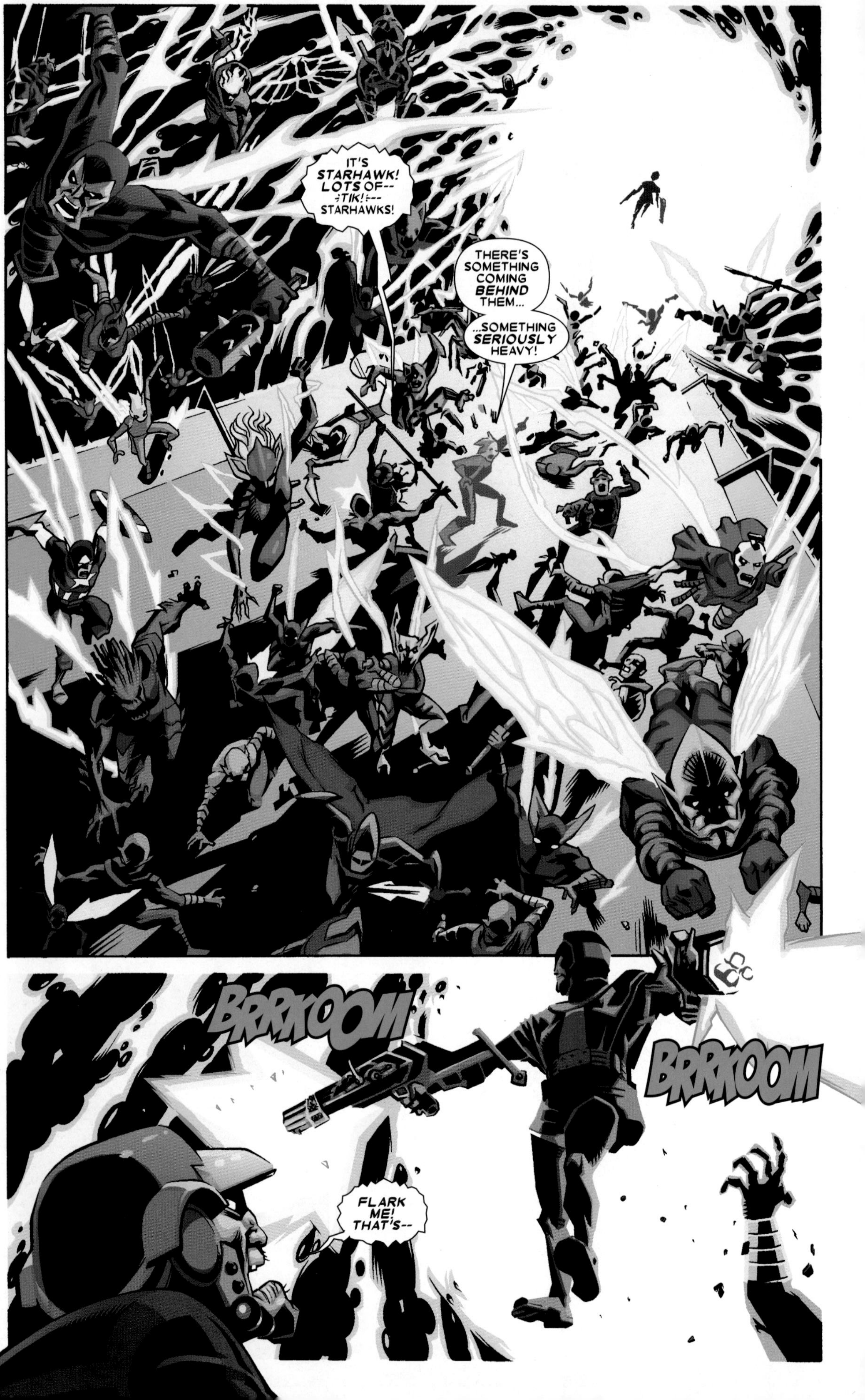
IT'S STARHAWK! LOTS OF-- ╡TIK!╞-- STARHAWKS!
THERE'S SOMETHING COMING BEHIND THEM...
...SOMETHING SERIOUSLY HEAVY!
BRRKOOM
BRRKOOM
FLARK ME! THAT'S--

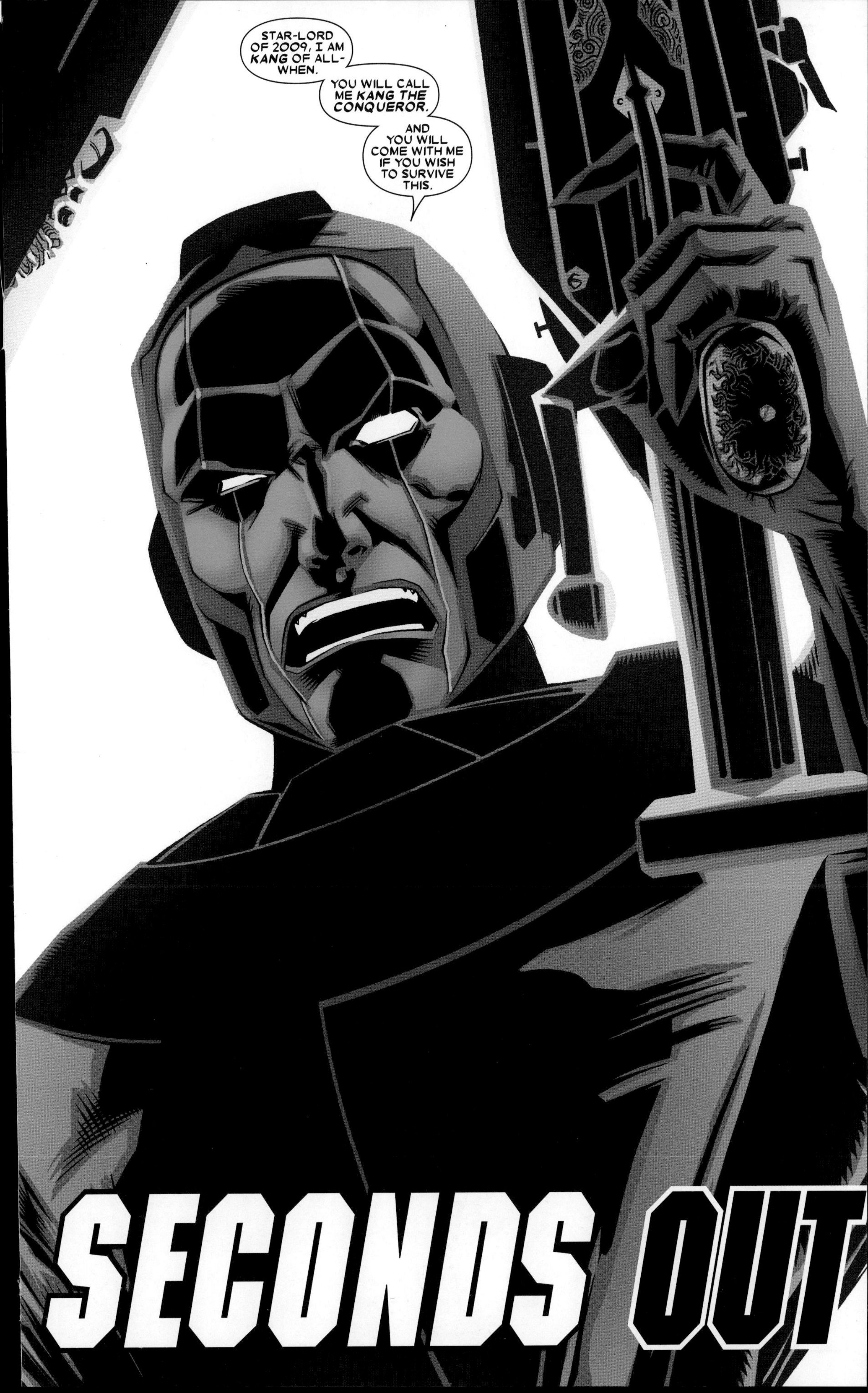
STAR-LORD OF 2009, I AM KANG OF ALL-WHEN.
YOU WILL CALL ME KANG THE CONQUEROR.
AND YOU WILL COME WITH ME IF YOU WISH TO SURVIVE THIS.
SECONDS OUT

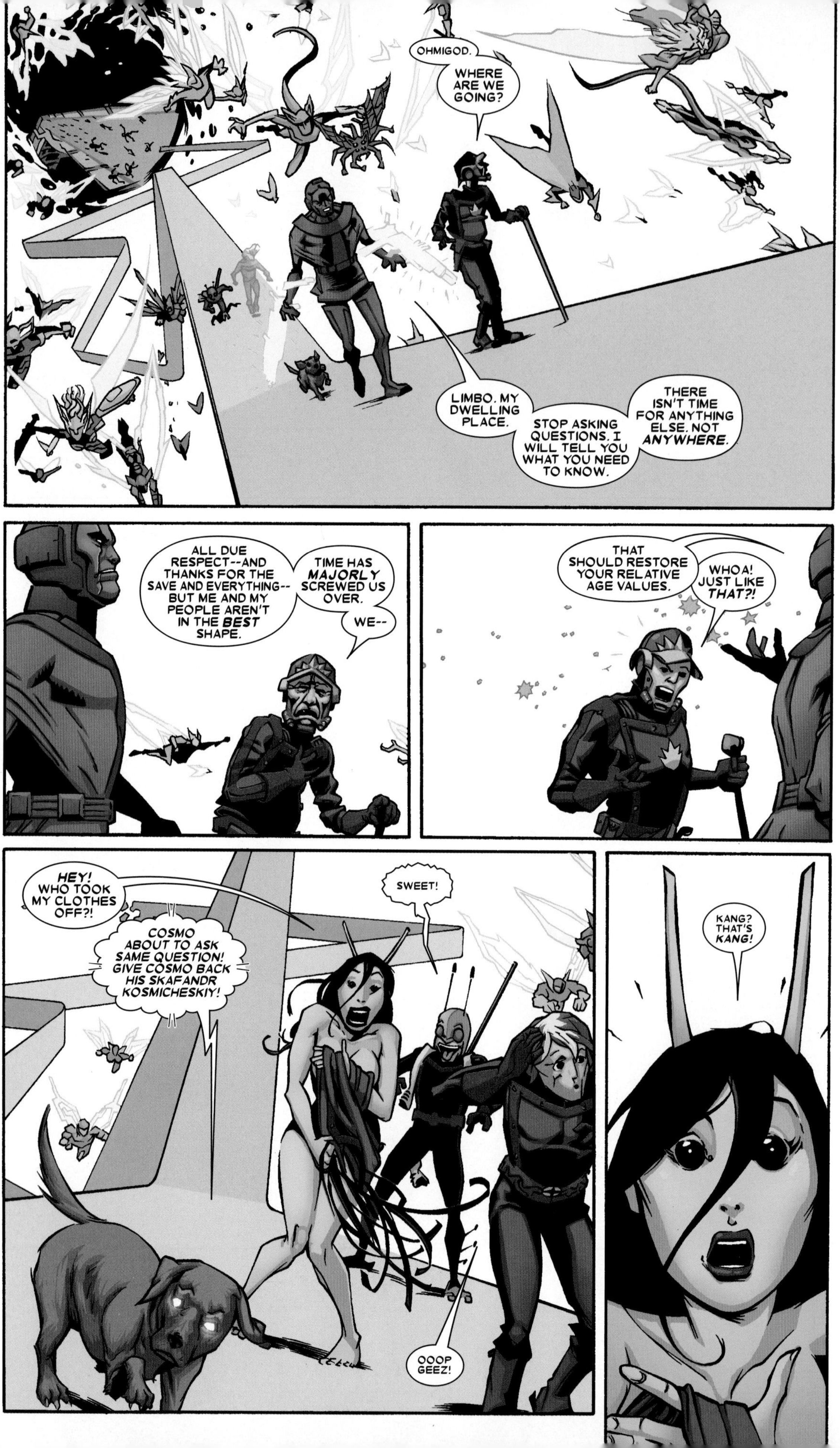
OHMIGOD.
WHERE ARE WE GOING?
LIMBO. MY DWELLING PLACE.
STOP ASKING QUESTIONS. I WILL TELL YOU WHAT YOU NEED TO KNOW.
THERE ISN'T TIME FOR ANYTHING ELSE. NOT ANYWHERE.
ALL DUE RESPECT--AND THANKS FOR THE SAVE AND EVERYTHING--BUT ME AND MY PEOPLE AREN'T IN THE BEST SHAPE.
TIME HAS MAJORLY SCREWED US OVER.
WE--
THAT SHOULD RESTORE YOUR RELATIVE AGE VALUES.
WHOA! JUST LIKE THAT?!
HEY! WHO TOOK MY CLOTHES OFF?!
COSMO ABOUT TO ASK SAME QUESTION! GIVE COSMO BACK HIS SKAFANDR KOSMICHESKIY!
SWEET!
OOOP GEEZ!
KANG? THAT'S KANG!

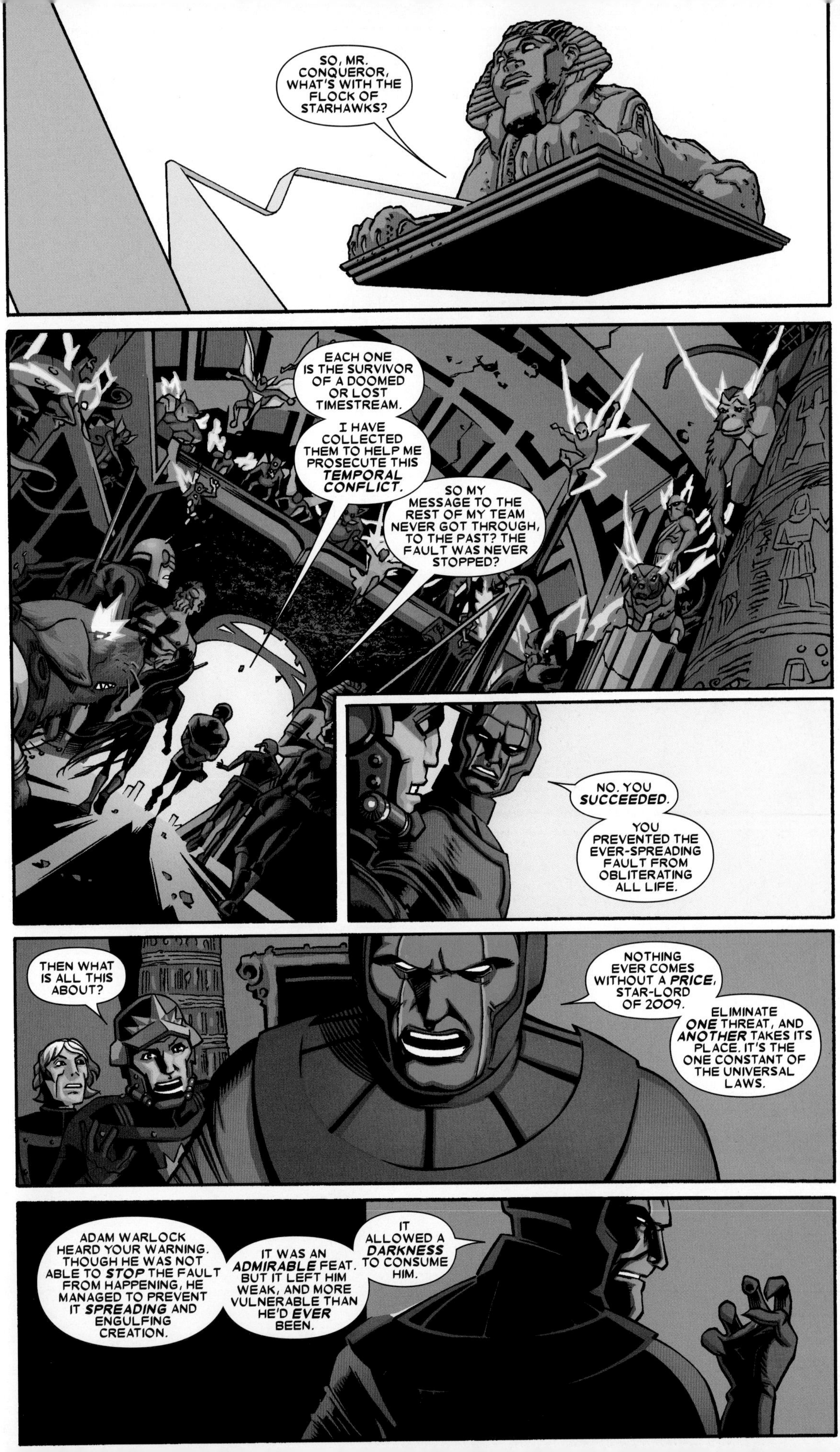
SO, MR. CONQUEROR, WHAT'S WITH THE FLOCK OF STARHAWKS?
EACH ONE IS THE SURVIVOR OF A DOOMED OR LOST TIMESTREAM.
I HAVE COLLECTED THEM TO HELP ME PROSECUTE THIS *TEMPORAL CONFLICT*.
SO MY MESSAGE TO THE REST OF MY TEAM NEVER GOT THROUGH, TO THE PAST? THE FAULT WAS NEVER STOPPED?
NO. YOU *SUCCEEDED*.
YOU PREVENTED THE EVER-SPREADING FAULT FROM OBLITERATING ALL LIFE.
THEN WHAT IS ALL THIS ABOUT?
NOTHING EVER COMES WITHOUT A *PRICE*, STAR-LORD OF 2009.
ELIMINATE *ONE* THREAT, AND *ANOTHER* TAKES ITS PLACE. IT'S THE ONE CONSTANT OF THE UNIVERSAL LAWS.
ADAM WARLOCK HEARD YOUR WARNING. THOUGH HE WAS NOT ABLE TO *STOP* THE FAULT FROM HAPPENING, HE MANAGED TO PREVENT IT *SPREADING* AND ENGULFING CREATION.
IT WAS AN *ADMIRABLE* FEAT. BUT IT LEFT HIM WEAK, AND MORE VULNERABLE THAN HE'D *EVER* BEEN.
IT ALLOWED A *DARKNESS* TO CONSUME HIM.

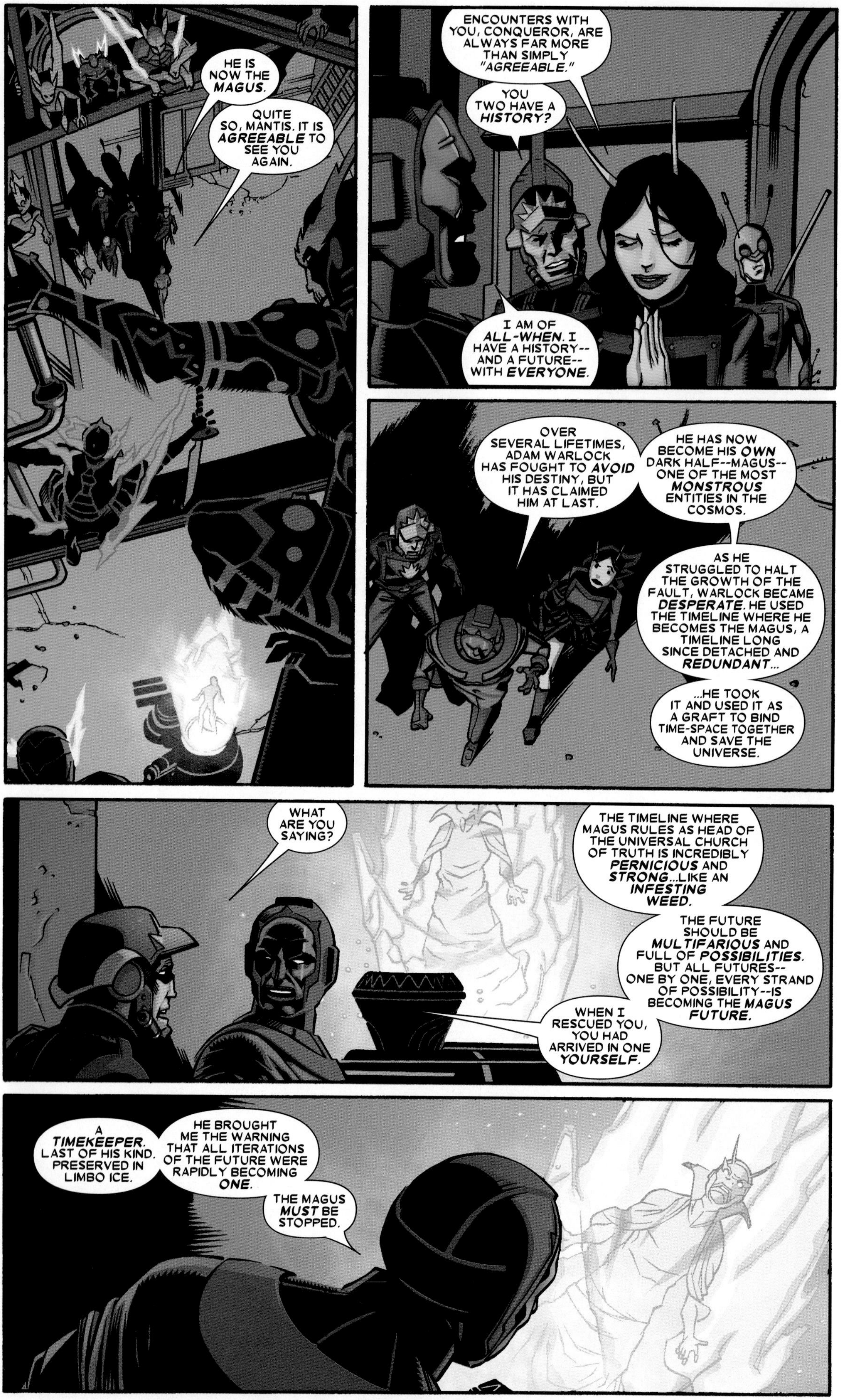
HE IS NOW THE *MAGUS*.
QUITE SO, MANTIS. IT IS *AGREEABLE* TO SEE YOU AGAIN.
ENCOUNTERS WITH YOU, CONQUEROR, ARE ALWAYS FAR MORE THAN SIMPLY *"AGREEABLE."*
YOU TWO HAVE A *HISTORY?*
I AM OF *ALL-WHEN*. I HAVE A HISTORY-- AND A FUTURE-- WITH *EVERYONE*.
OVER SEVERAL LIFETIMES, ADAM WARLOCK HAS FOUGHT TO *AVOID* HIS DESTINY, BUT IT HAS CLAIMED HIM AT LAST.
HE HAS NOW BECOME HIS *OWN* DARK HALF--MAGUS-- ONE OF THE MOST *MONSTROUS* ENTITIES IN THE COSMOS.
AS HE STRUGGLED TO HALT THE GROWTH OF THE FAULT, WARLOCK BECAME *DESPERATE*. HE USED THE TIMELINE WHERE HE BECOMES THE MAGUS, A TIMELINE LONG SINCE DETACHED AND *REDUNDANT*...
...HE TOOK IT AND USED IT AS A GRAFT TO BIND TIME-SPACE TOGETHER AND SAVE THE UNIVERSE.
WHAT ARE YOU SAYING?
THE TIMELINE WHERE MAGUS RULES AS HEAD OF THE UNIVERSAL CHURCH OF TRUTH IS INCREDIBLY *PERNICIOUS* AND *STRONG*...LIKE AN *INFESTING WEED.*
THE FUTURE SHOULD BE *MULTIFARIOUS* AND FULL OF *POSSIBILITIES*. BUT ALL FUTURES-- ONE BY ONE, EVERY STRAND OF POSSIBILITY--IS BECOMING THE *MAGUS FUTURE.*
WHEN I RESCUED YOU, YOU HAD ARRIVED IN ONE *YOURSELF*.
A *TIMEKEEPER*. LAST OF HIS KIND. PRESERVED IN LIMBO ICE.
HE BROUGHT ME THE WARNING THAT ALL ITERATIONS OF THE FUTURE WERE RAPIDLY BECOMING *ONE*.
THE MAGUS *MUST* BE STOPPED.

MAGUS CONTROLS SO *MUCH* OF THE TIME-STREAM THAT IF I MOVE *DIRECTLY* AGAINST HIM, HE WILL SEE ME COMING.

BUT YOU ARE *ANOMALIES,* UNTETHERED IN TIME. I INTEND TO SEND YOU BACK, *THROUGH* HIS DEFENSES, TO THE POINT OF HIS CREATION.

TO DO *WHAT?*

STOP HIM WITH *THIS.*

A *COSMIC CUBE!*

THE *LAST* ONE. I'VE CALIBRATED IT TO ASSIST YOU.

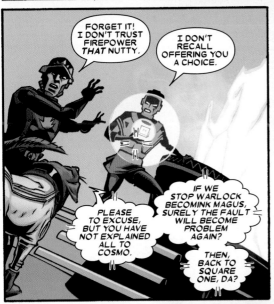

FORGET IT! I DON'T TRUST FIREPOWER *THAT* NUTTY.

I DON'T RECALL OFFERING YOU A CHOICE.

PLEASE TO EXCUSE, BUT YOU HAVE NOT EXPLAINED ALL TO COSMO.

IF WE STOP WARLOCK BECOMINK MAGUS, SURELY THE FAULT WILL BECOME PROBLEM AGAIN?

THEN, BACK TO SQUARE ONE, DA?

I HAVE CALCULATED THAT THERE IS A VERY SMALL WINDOW OF OPPORTUNITY...JUST A MATTER OF *SECONDS.*

WARLOCK SEALS THE FAULT. LESS THAN A MINUTE LATER, HE *BECOMES* THE MAGUS.

THAT IS WHEN YOU STRIKE.

AND DO WHAT? LIKE PETER ASK, WHAT ARE YOU *SUGGESTINK* WE DO?

WHATEVER IT TAKES TO SAVE THE UNIVERSE.

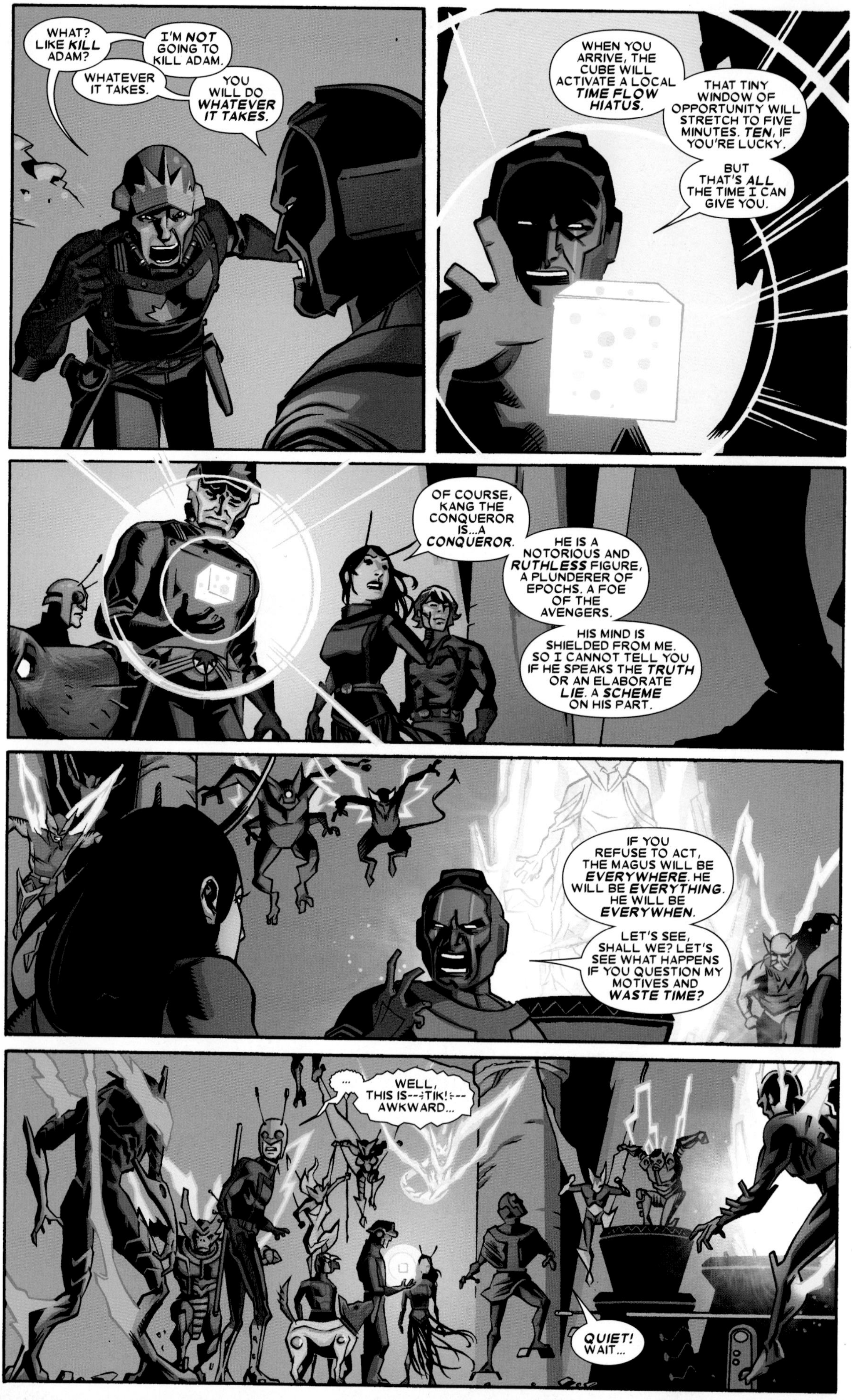
WHAT? LIKE KILL ADAM?
I'M NOT GOING TO KILL ADAM.
WHATEVER IT TAKES.
YOU WILL DO WHATEVER IT TAKES.
WHEN YOU ARRIVE, THE CUBE WILL ACTIVATE A LOCAL TIME FLOW HIATUS.
THAT TINY WINDOW OF OPPORTUNITY WILL STRETCH TO FIVE MINUTES. TEN, IF YOU'RE LUCKY.
BUT THAT'S ALL THE TIME I CAN GIVE YOU.
OF COURSE, KANG THE CONQUEROR IS...A CONQUEROR.
HE IS A NOTORIOUS AND RUTHLESS FIGURE, A PLUNDERER OF EPOCHS. A FOE OF THE AVENGERS.
HIS MIND IS SHIELDED FROM ME. SO I CANNOT TELL YOU IF HE SPEAKS THE TRUTH OR AN ELABORATE LIE. A SCHEME ON HIS PART.
IF YOU REFUSE TO ACT, THE MAGUS WILL BE EVERYWHERE. HE WILL BE EVERYTHING. HE WILL BE EVERYWHEN.
LET'S SEE, SHALL WE? LET'S SEE WHAT HAPPENS IF YOU QUESTION MY MOTIVES AND WASTE TIME?
...
WELL, THIS IS--TIK!--AWKWARD...
QUIET! WAIT...

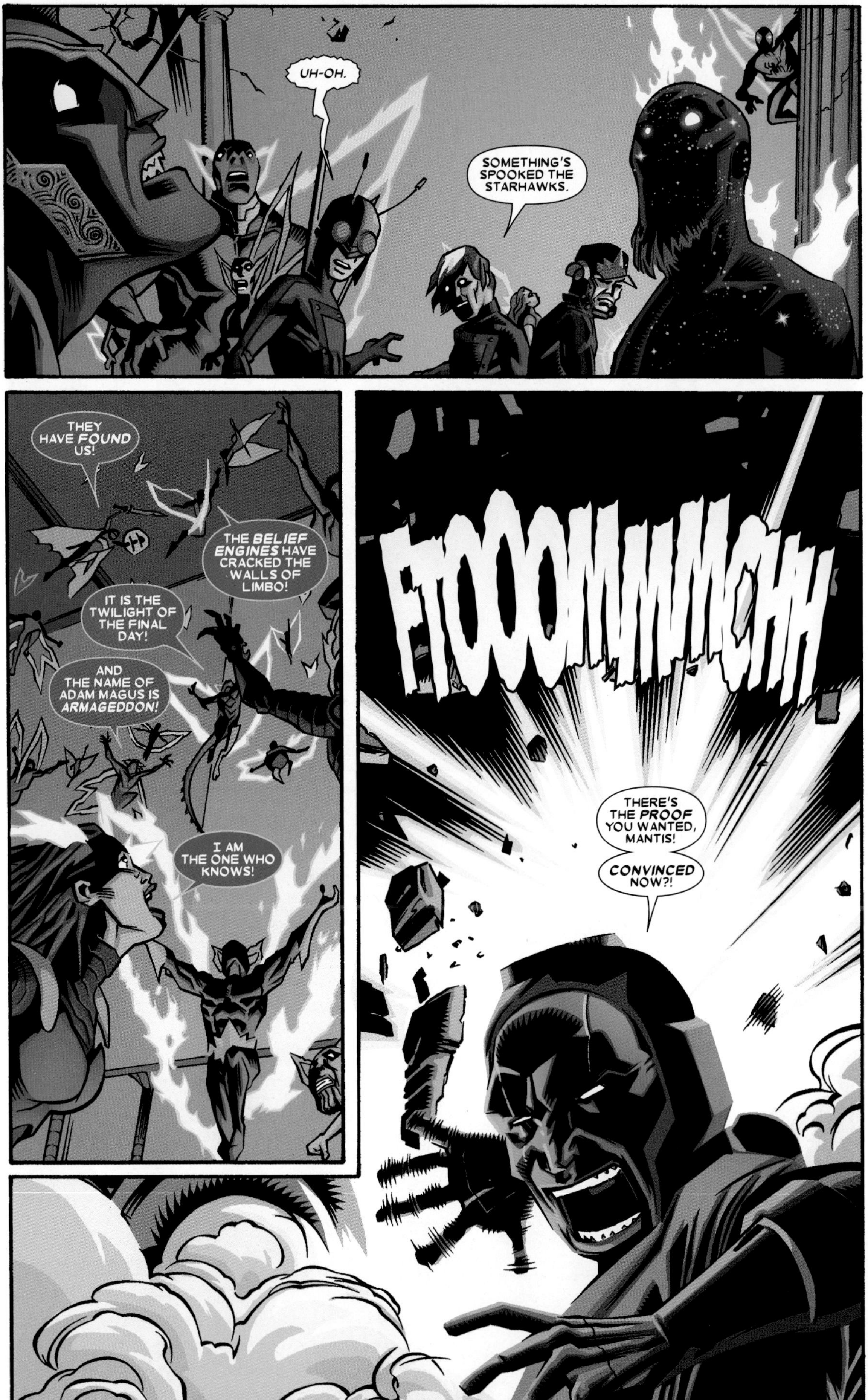
UH-OH.
SOMETHING'S SPOOKED THE STARHAWKS.
THEY HAVE *FOUND* US!
THE *BELIEF ENGINES* HAVE CRACKED THE WALLS OF LIMBO!
IT IS THE TWILIGHT OF THE FINAL DAY!
AND THE NAME OF ADAM MAGUS IS *ARMAGEDDON!*
I AM THE ONE WHO KNOWS!
FTOOOMMMCHH
THERE'S THE *PROOF* YOU WANTED, MANTIS!
CONVINCED NOW?!

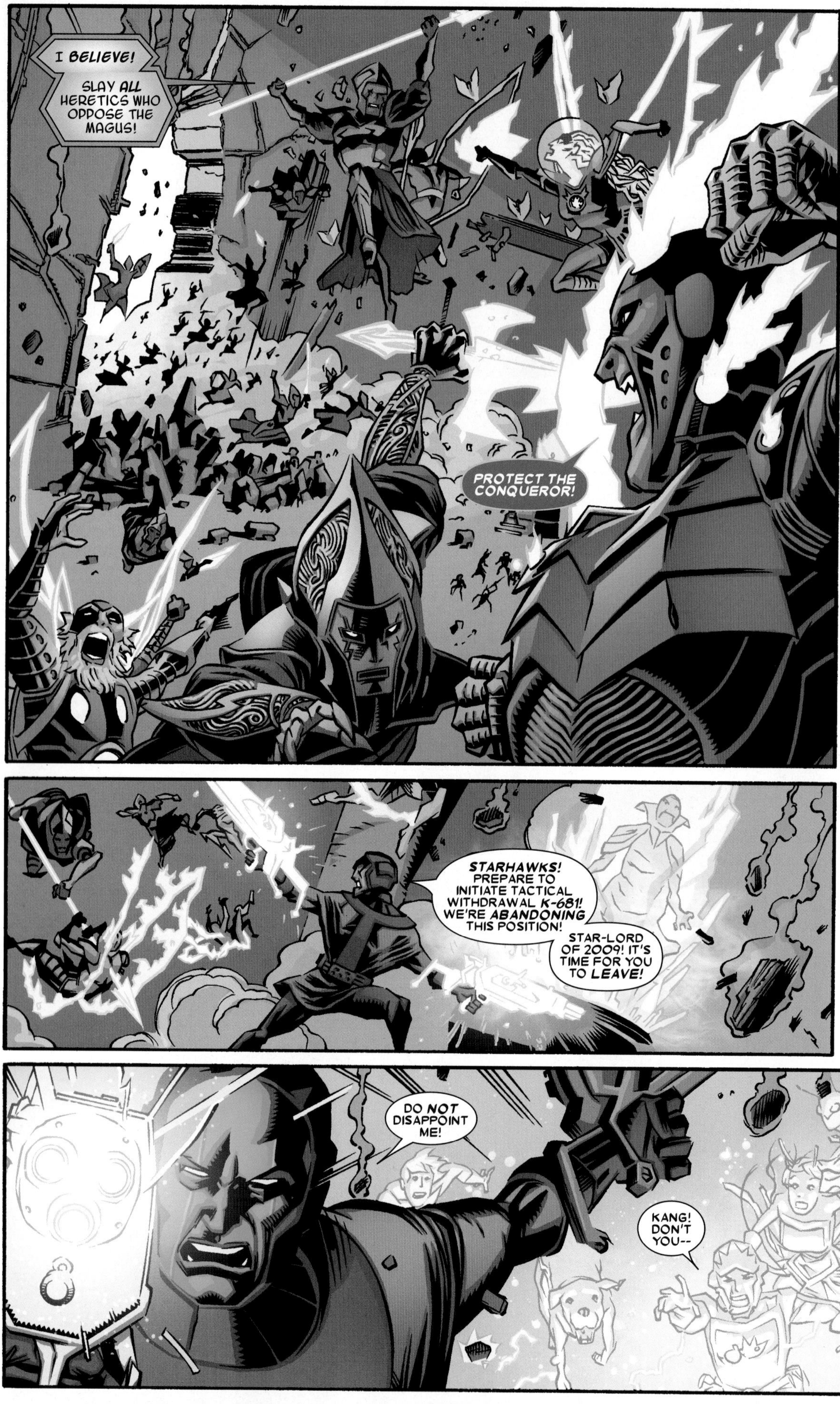
I BELIEVE!
SLAY ALL HERETICS WHO OPPOSE THE MAGUS!
PROTECT THE CONQUEROR!
STARHAWKS! PREPARE TO INITIATE TACTICAL WITHDRAWAL K-681! WE'RE ABANDONING THIS POSITION!
STAR-LORD OF 2009! IT'S TIME FOR YOU TO LEAVE!
DO NOT DISAPPOINT ME!
KANG! DON'T YOU--

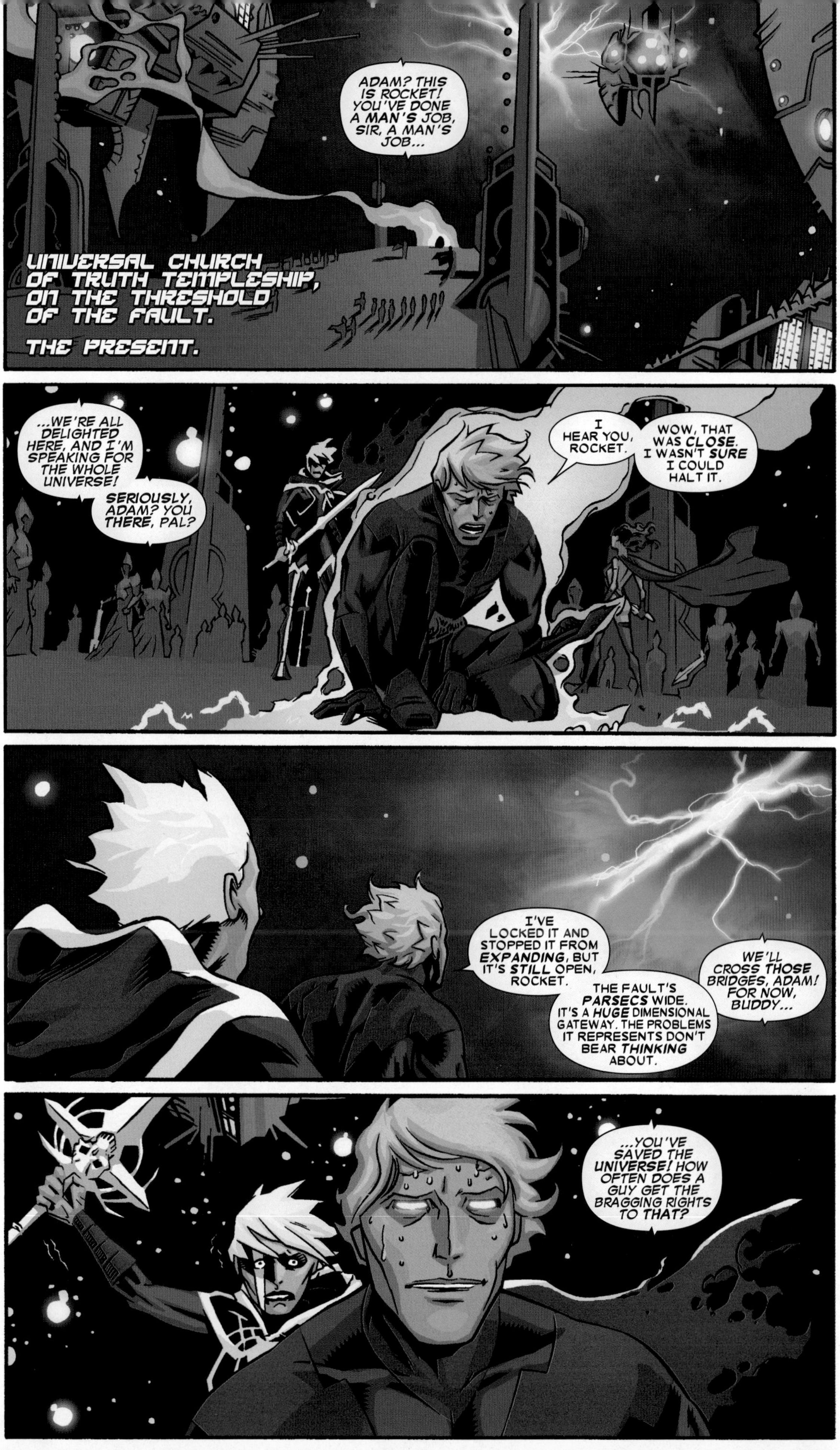
ADAM? THIS IS ROCKET! YOU'VE DONE A MAN'S JOB, SIR, A MAN'S JOB...
UNIVERSAL CHURCH OF TRUTH TEMPLESHIP, ON THE THRESHOLD OF THE FAULT.
THE PRESENT.
...WE'RE ALL DELIGHTED HERE, AND I'M SPEAKING FOR THE WHOLE UNIVERSE!
SERIOUSLY, ADAM? YOU THERE, PAL?
I HEAR YOU, ROCKET.
WOW, THAT WAS CLOSE. I WASN'T SURE I COULD HALT IT.
I'VE LOCKED IT AND STOPPED IT FROM EXPANDING, BUT IT'S STILL OPEN, ROCKET.
THE FAULT'S PARSECS WIDE. IT'S A HUGE DIMENSIONAL GATEWAY. THE PROBLEMS IT REPRESENTS DON'T BEAR THINKING ABOUT.
WE'LL CROSS THOSE BRIDGES, ADAM! FOR NOW, BUDDY...
...YOU'VE SAVED THE UNIVERSE! HOW OFTEN DOES A GUY GET THE BRAGGING RIGHTS TO THAT?

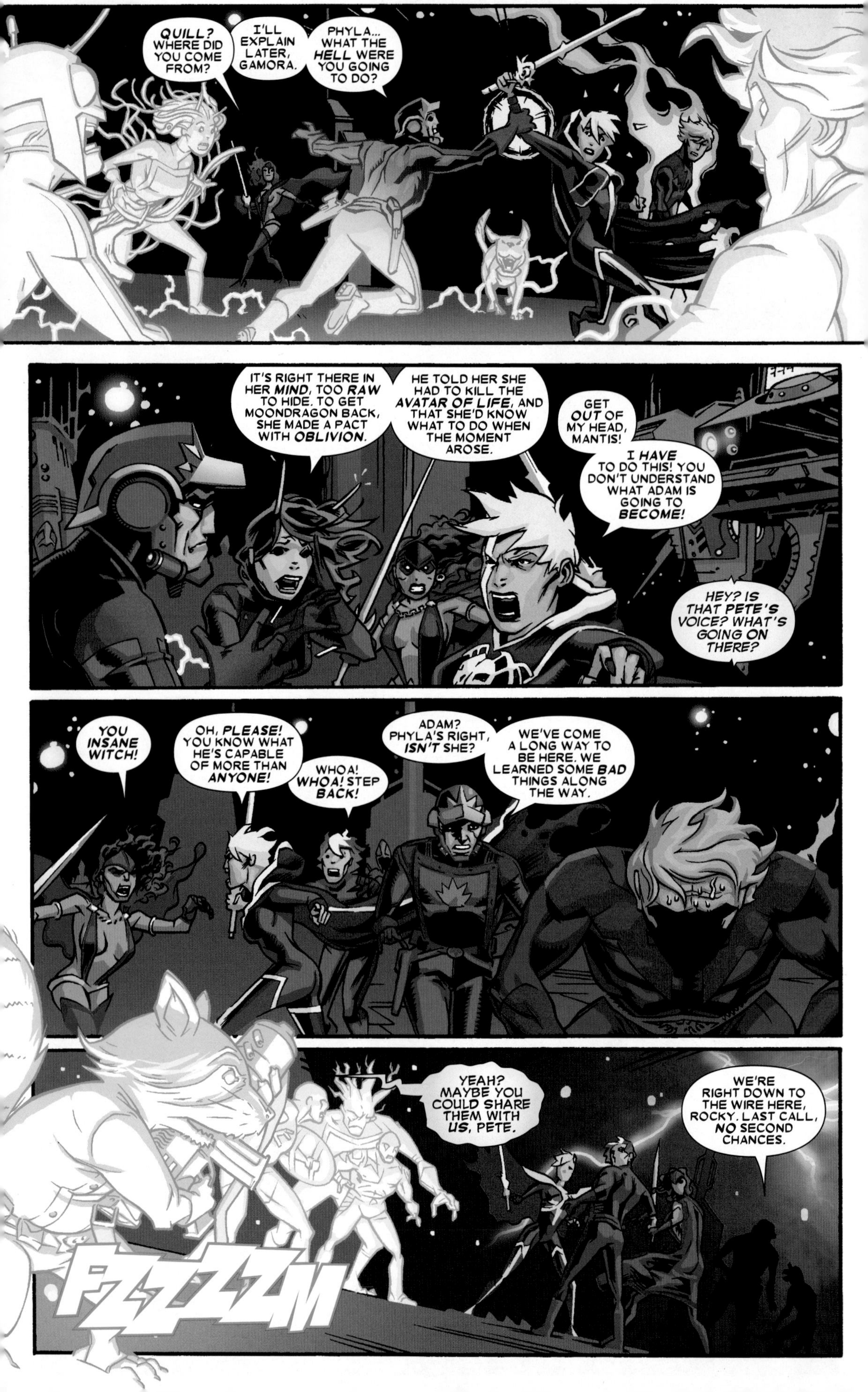
QUILL? WHERE DID YOU COME FROM?
I'LL EXPLAIN LATER, GAMORA.
PHYLA... WHAT THE HELL WERE YOU GOING TO DO?
IT'S RIGHT THERE IN HER MIND, TOO RAW TO HIDE. TO GET MOONDRAGON BACK, SHE MADE A PACT WITH OBLIVION.
HE TOLD HER SHE HAD TO KILL THE AVATAR OF LIFE, AND THAT SHE'D KNOW WHAT TO DO WHEN THE MOMENT AROSE.
GET OUT OF MY HEAD, MANTIS!
I HAVE TO DO THIS! YOU DON'T UNDERSTAND WHAT ADAM IS GOING TO BECOME!
HEY? IS THAT PETE'S VOICE? WHAT'S GOING ON THERE?
YOU INSANE WITCH!
OH, PLEASE! YOU KNOW WHAT HE'S CAPABLE OF MORE THAN ANYONE!
WHOA! WHOA! STEP BACK!
ADAM? PHYLA'S RIGHT, ISN'T SHE?
WE'VE COME A LONG WAY TO BE HERE. WE LEARNED SOME BAD THINGS ALONG THE WAY.
YEAH? MAYBE YOU COULD SHARE THEM WITH US, PETE.
WE'RE RIGHT DOWN TO THE WIRE HERE, ROCKY. LAST CALL, NO SECOND CHANCES.
FZZZZM

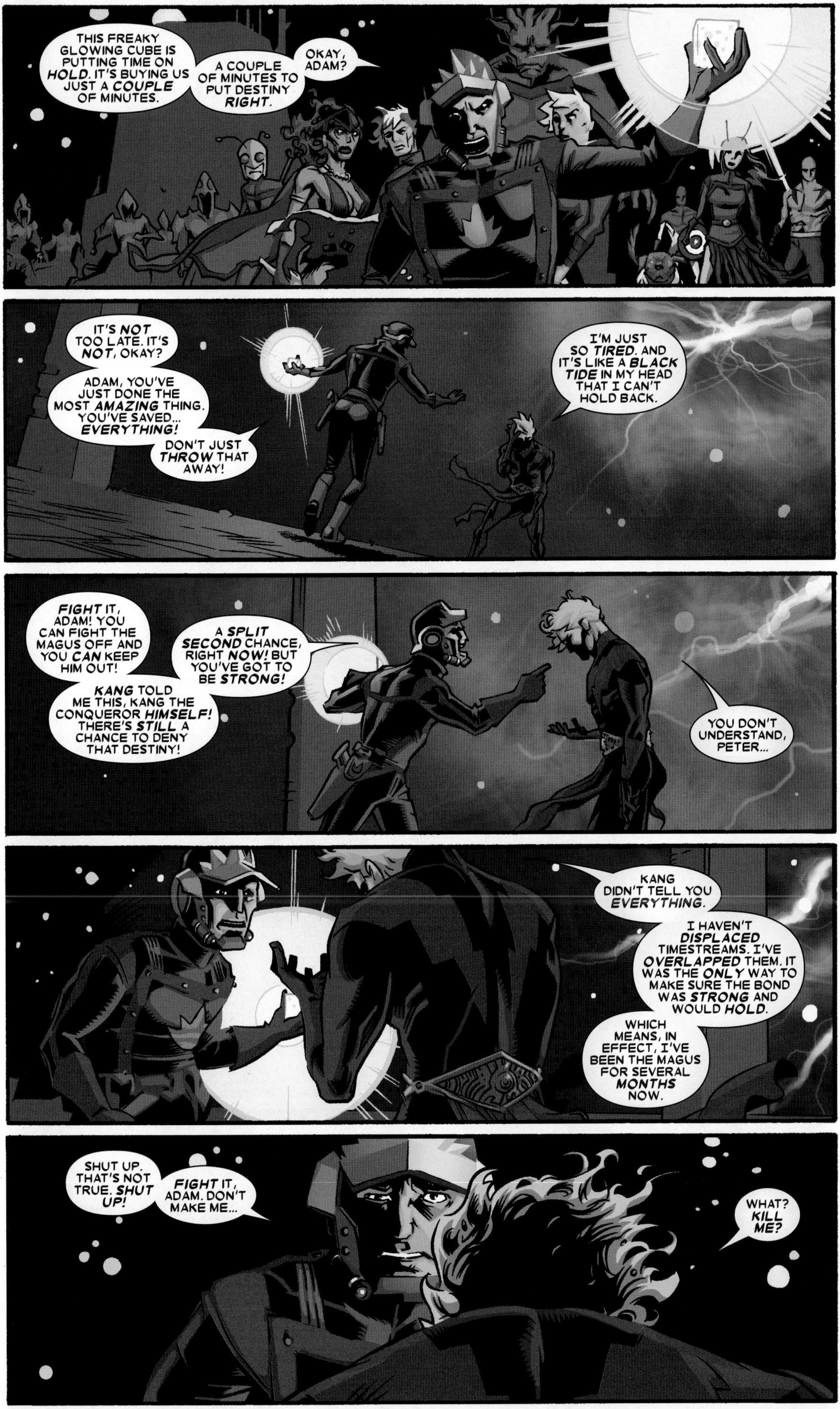
THIS FREAKY GLOWING CUBE IS PUTTING TIME ON HOLD. IT'S BUYING US JUST A COUPLE OF MINUTES.
A COUPLE OF MINUTES TO PUT DESTINY RIGHT.
OKAY, ADAM?
IT'S NOT TOO LATE. IT'S NOT, OKAY?
ADAM, YOU'VE JUST DONE THE MOST AMAZING THING. YOU'VE SAVED... EVERYTHING!
DON'T JUST THROW THAT AWAY!
I'M JUST SO TIRED. AND IT'S LIKE A BLACK TIDE IN MY HEAD THAT I CAN'T HOLD BACK.
FIGHT IT, ADAM! YOU CAN FIGHT THE MAGUS OFF AND YOU CAN KEEP HIM OUT!
A SPLIT SECOND CHANCE, RIGHT NOW! BUT YOU'VE GOT TO BE STRONG!
KANG TOLD ME THIS, KANG THE CONQUEROR HIMSELF! THERE'S STILL A CHANCE TO DENY THAT DESTINY!
YOU DON'T UNDERSTAND, PETER...
KANG DIDN'T TELL YOU EVERYTHING.
I HAVEN'T DISPLACED TIMESTREAMS. I'VE OVERLAPPED THEM. IT WAS THE ONLY WAY TO MAKE SURE THE BOND WAS STRONG AND WOULD HOLD.
WHICH MEANS, IN EFFECT, I'VE BEEN THE MAGUS FOR SEVERAL MONTHS NOW.
SHUT UP. THAT'S NOT TRUE. SHUT UP!
FIGHT IT, ADAM. DON'T MAKE ME...
WHAT? KILL ME?

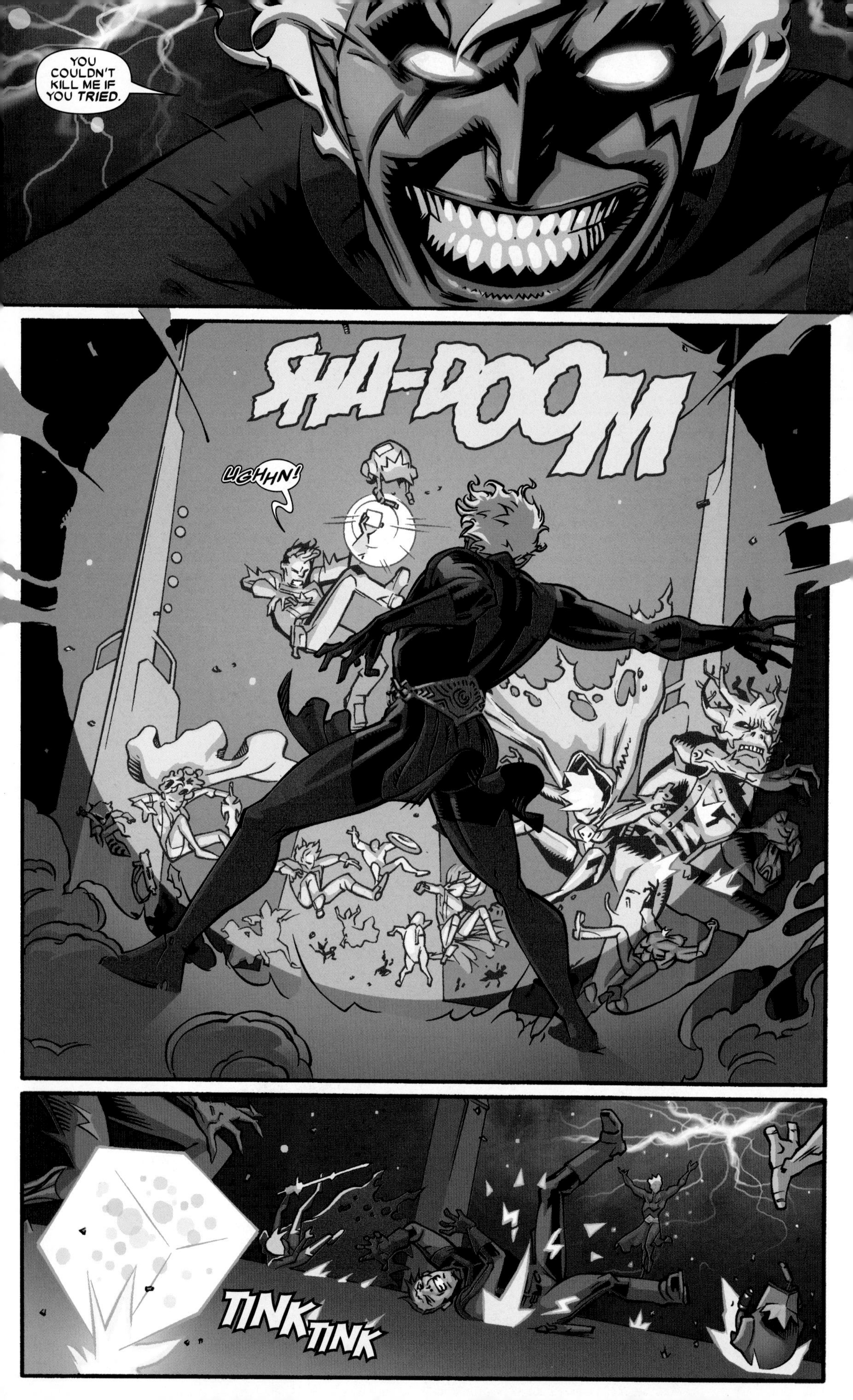
YOU COULDN'T KILL ME IF YOU TRIED.
SHA-DOOM
UGHHN!
TINK TINK

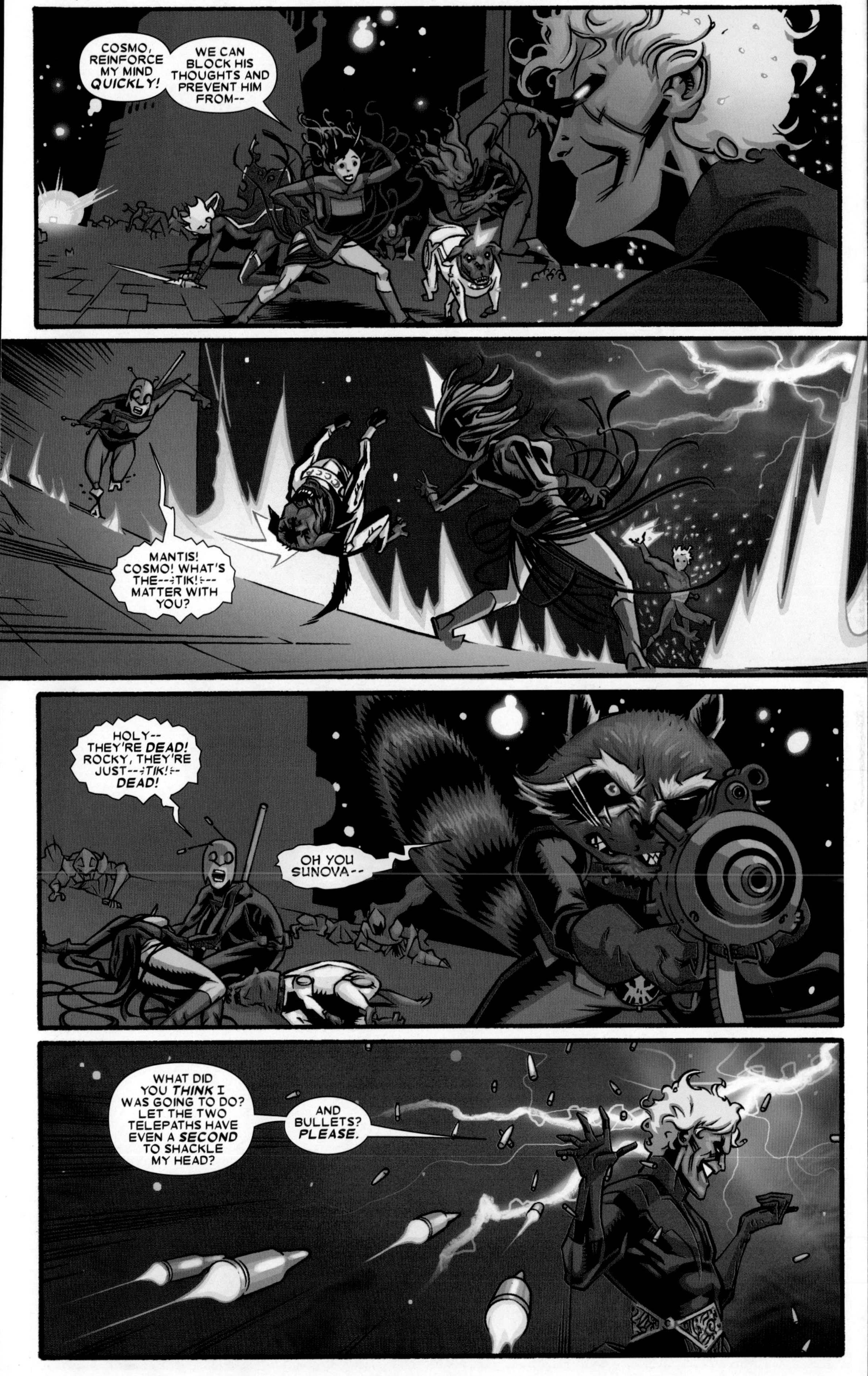
COSMO, REINFORCE MY MIND QUICKLY!
WE CAN BLOCK HIS THOUGHTS AND PREVENT HIM FROM--
MANTIS! COSMO! WHAT'S THE--*TIK!*--MATTER WITH YOU?
HOLY--THEY'RE DEAD! ROCKY, THEY'RE JUST--*TIK!*--DEAD!
OH YOU SUNOVA--
WHAT DID YOU THINK I WAS GOING TO DO? LET THE TWO TELEPATHS HAVE EVEN A SECOND TO SHACKLE MY HEAD?
AND BULLETS? PLEASE.

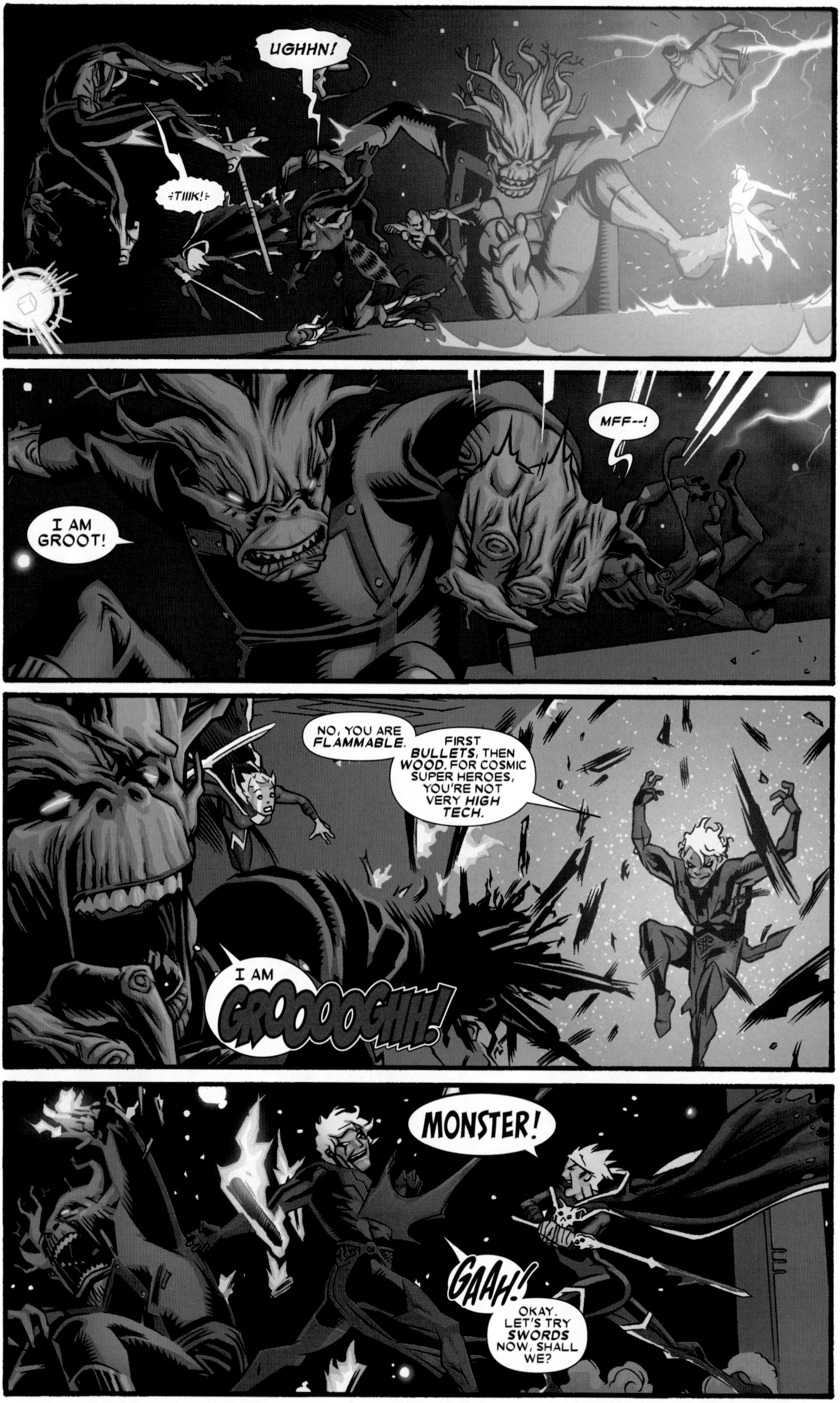

UGHHN!
TIIIK!
I AM GROOT!
MFF--!
NO, YOU ARE FLAMMABLE.
FIRST BULLETS, THEN WOOD. FOR COSMIC SUPER HEROES, YOU'RE NOT VERY HIGH TECH.
I AM GROOOOGHH!
MONSTER!
GAAH!
OKAY. LET'S TRY SWORDS NOW, SHALL WE?

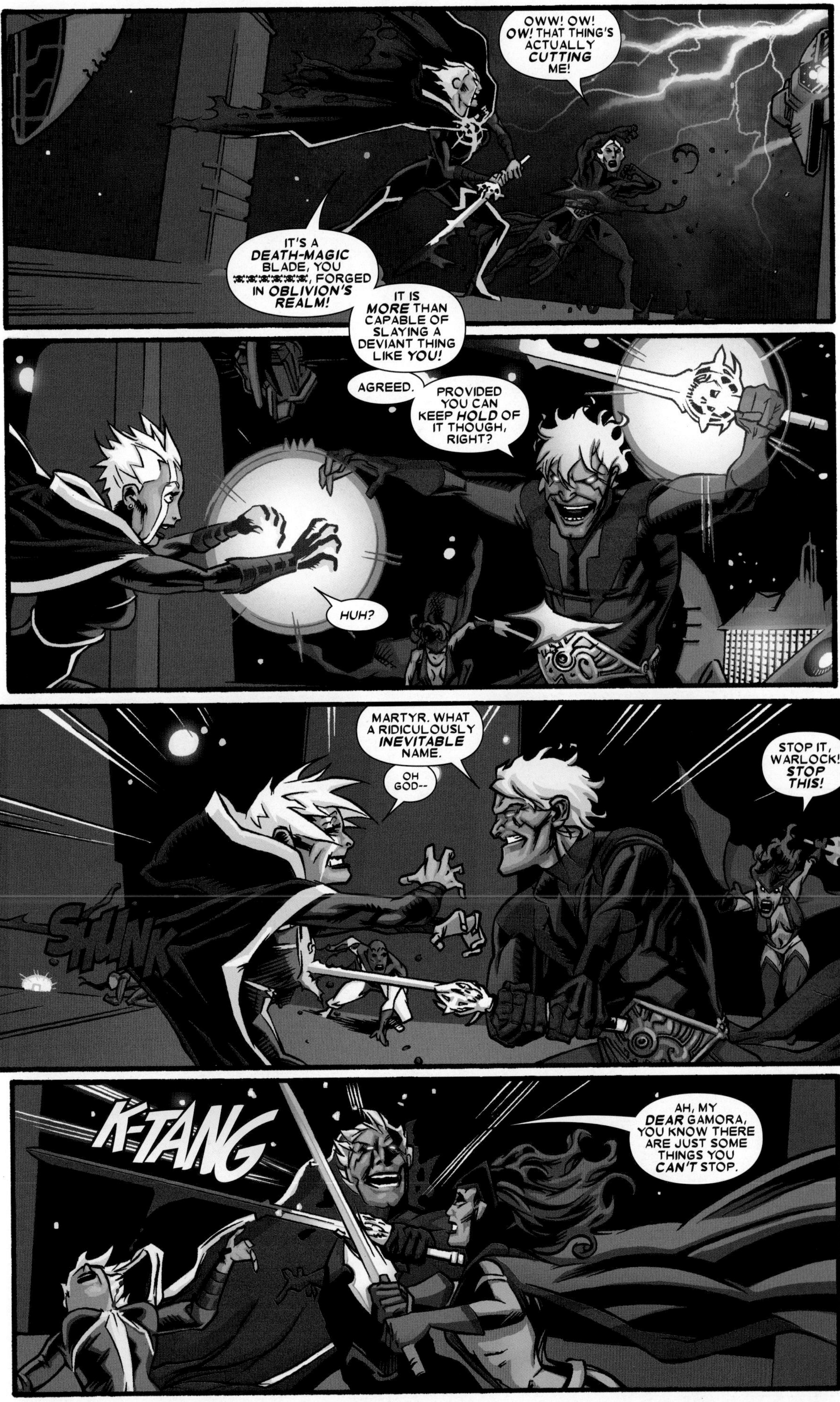
OWW! OW! OW! THAT THING'S ACTUALLY CUTTING ME!
IT'S A DEATH-MAGIC BLADE, YOU ☠☠☠☠☠☠, FORGED IN OBLIVION'S REALM!
IT IS MORE THAN CAPABLE OF SLAYING A DEVIANT THING LIKE YOU!
AGREED.
PROVIDED YOU CAN KEEP HOLD OF IT THOUGH, RIGHT?
HUH?
MARTYR. WHAT A RIDICULOUSLY INEVITABLE NAME.
OH GOD--
STOP IT, WARLOCK! STOP THIS!
SHUNK
K-TANG
AH, MY DEAR GAMORA, YOU KNOW THERE ARE JUST SOME THINGS YOU CAN'T STOP.

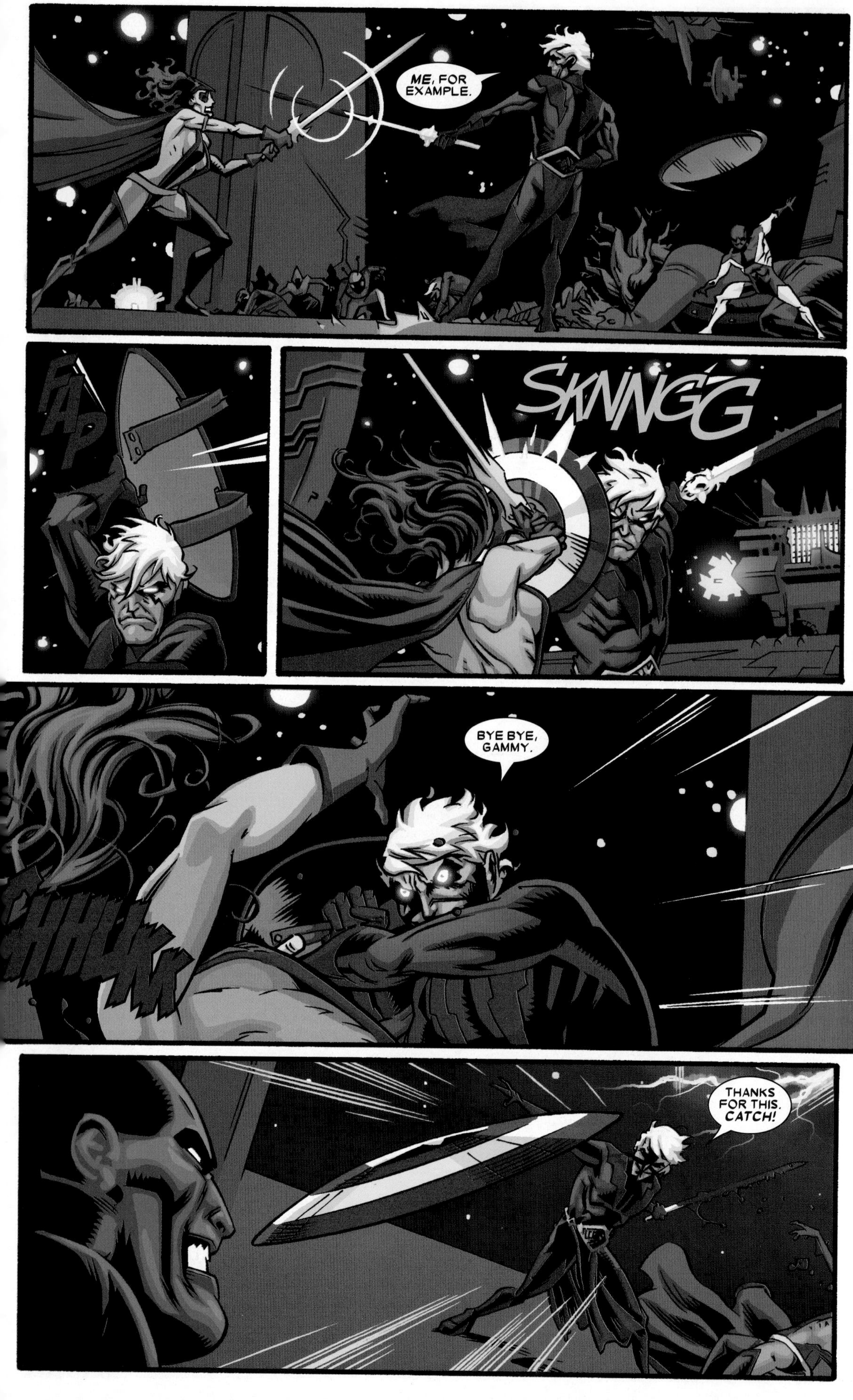
ME, FOR EXAMPLE.
FAP
SKNNGG
BYE BYE, GAMMY.
THANKS FOR THIS. CATCH!

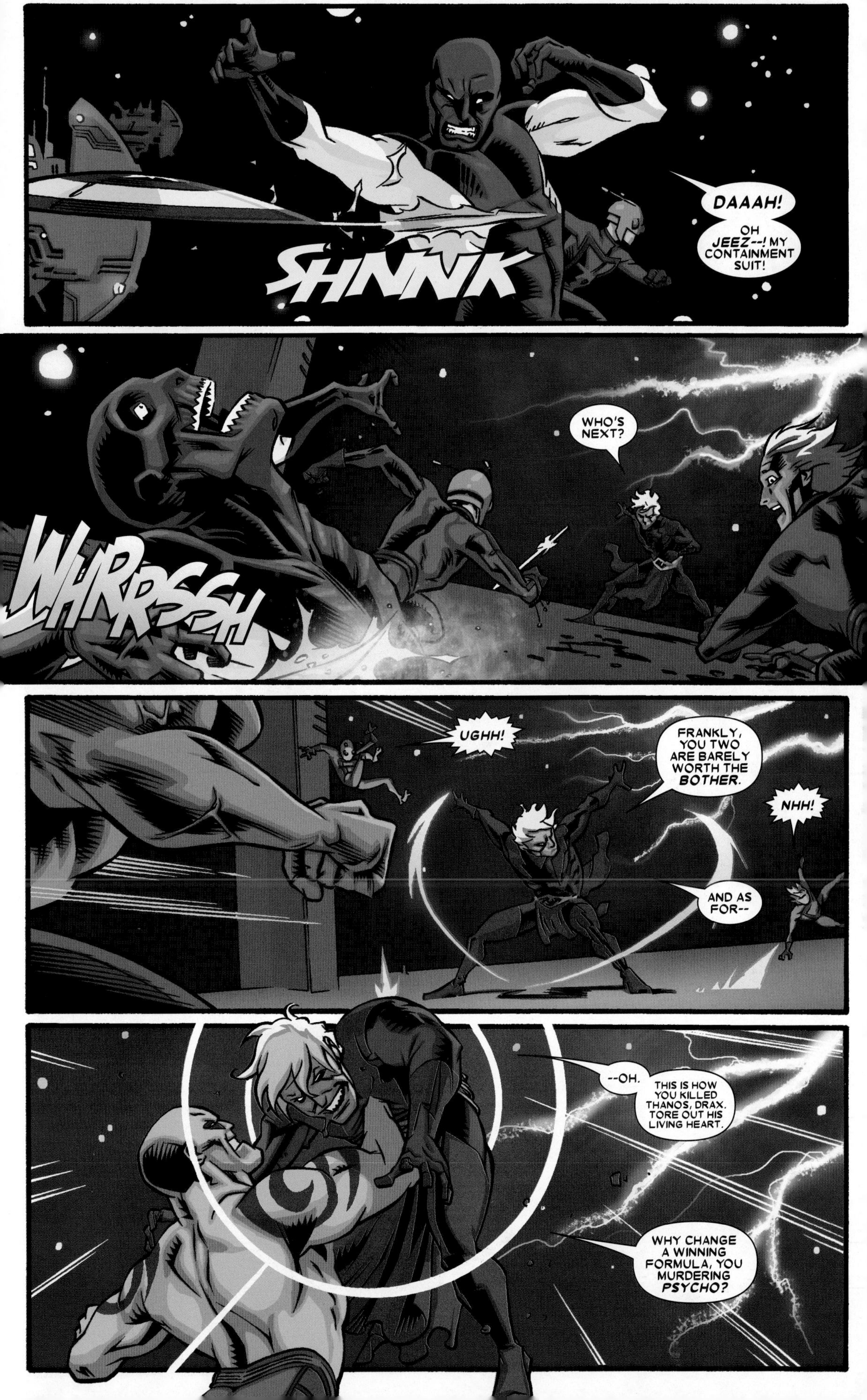
DAAAH!
OH JEEZ--! MY CONTAINMENT SUIT!
SHNNK
WHO'S NEXT?
WHRRSSH
UGHH!
FRANKLY, YOU TWO ARE BARELY WORTH THE BOTHER.
NHH!
AND AS FOR--
--OH.
THIS IS HOW YOU KILLED THANOS, DRAX. TORE OUT HIS LIVING HEART.
WHY CHANGE A WINNING FORMULA, YOU MURDERING PSYCHO?

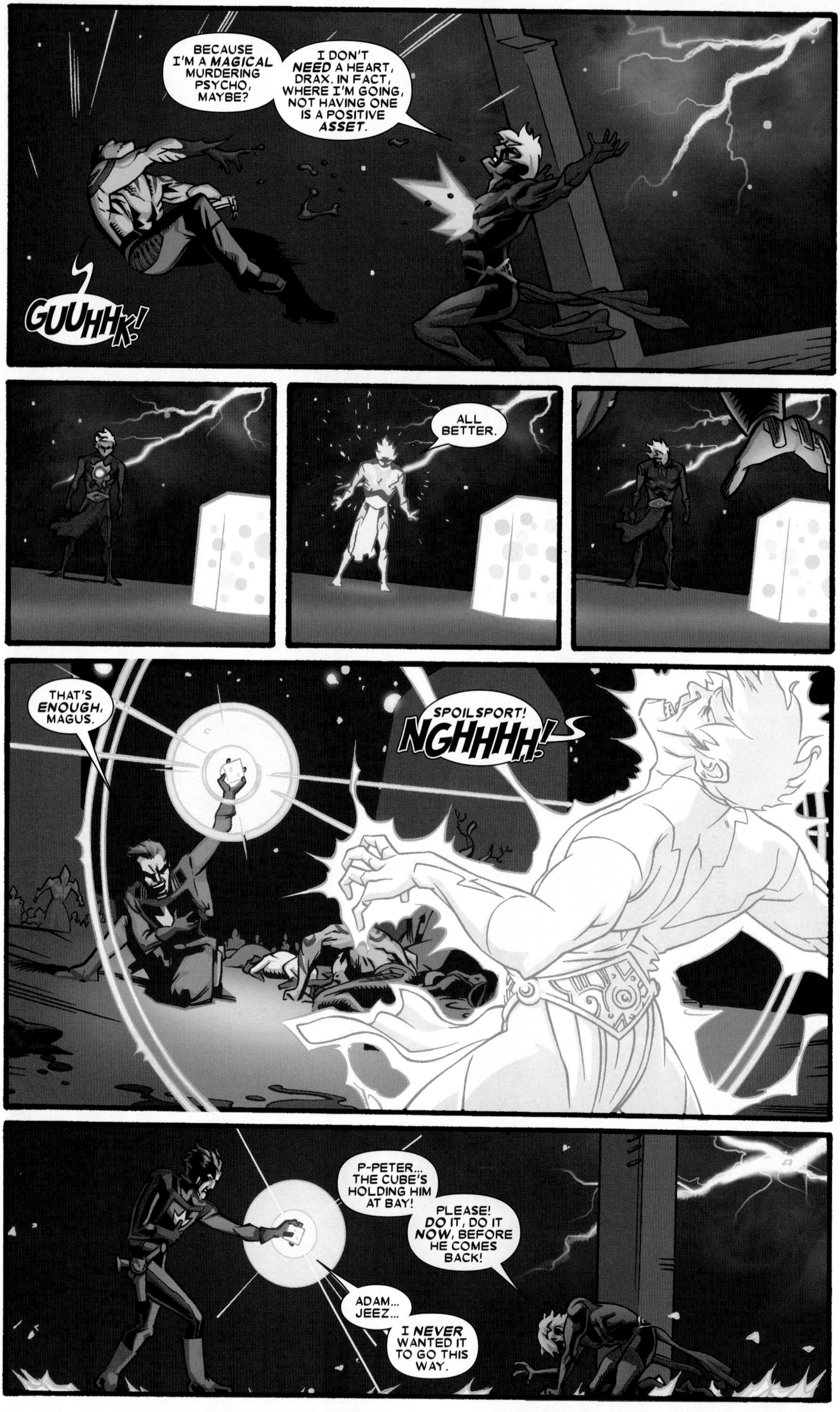
BECAUSE I'M A MAGICAL MURDERING PSYCHO, MAYBE?
I DON'T NEED A HEART, DRAX. IN FACT, WHERE I'M GOING, NOT HAVING ONE IS A POSITIVE ASSET.
GUUHHK!
ALL BETTER.
THAT'S ENOUGH, MAGUS.
SPOILSPORT!
NGHHHH!
P-PETER... THE CUBE'S HOLDING HIM AT BAY!
PLEASE! DO IT, DO IT NOW, BEFORE HE COMES BACK!
ADAM... JEEZ...
I NEVER WANTED IT TO GO THIS WAY.

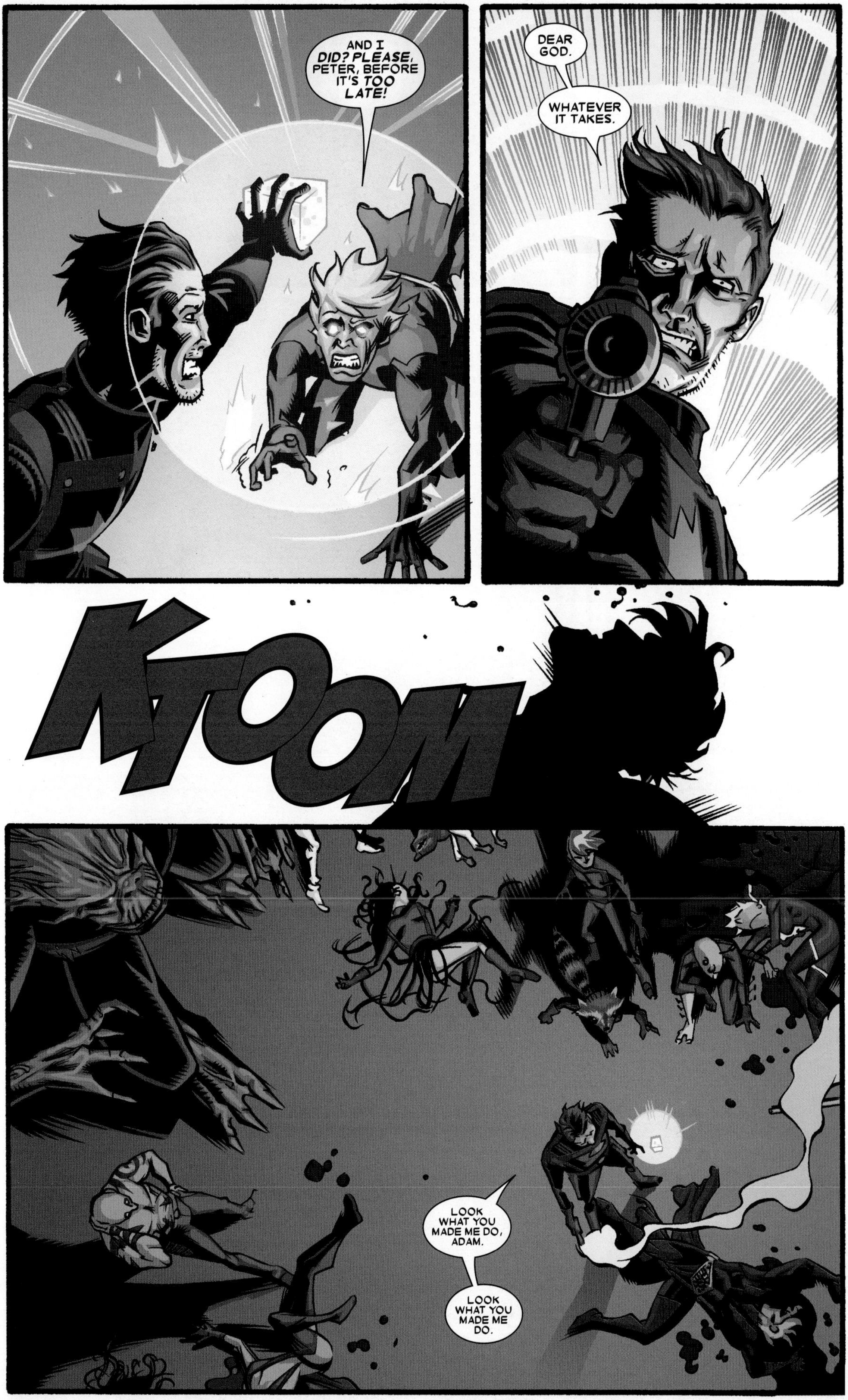
AND I DID? PLEASE, PETER, BEFORE IT'S TOO LATE!
DEAR GOD.
WHATEVER IT TAKES.
KTOOM
LOOK WHAT YOU MADE ME DO, ADAM.
LOOK WHAT YOU MADE ME DO.

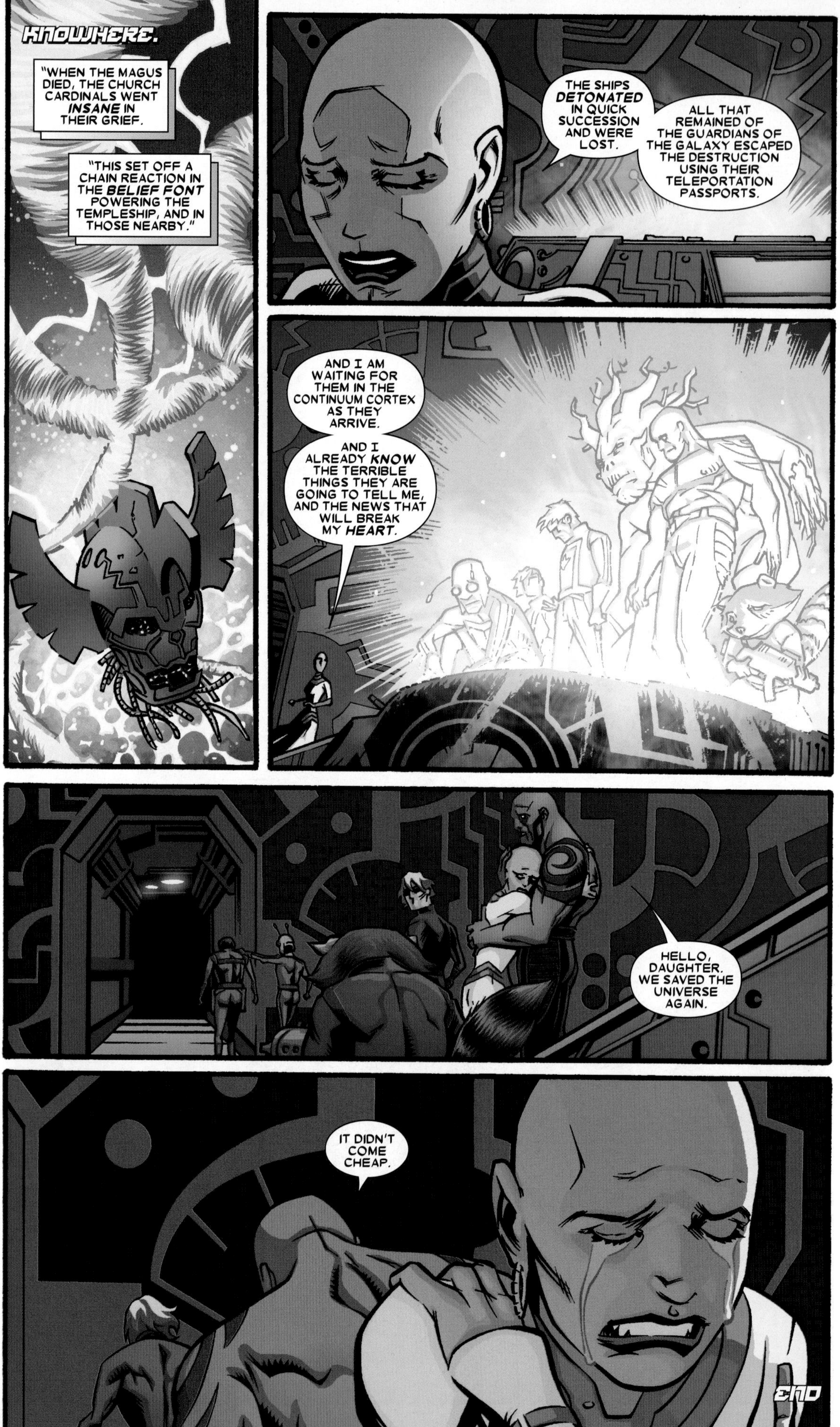
KNOWHERE.
"WHEN THE MAGUS DIED, THE CHURCH CARDINALS WENT *INSANE* IN THEIR GRIEF.
"THIS SET OFF A CHAIN REACTION IN THE *BELIEF FONT* POWERING THE TEMPLESHIP, AND IN THOSE NEARBY."
THE SHIPS *DETONATED* IN QUICK SUCCESSION AND WERE LOST.
ALL THAT REMAINED OF THE GUARDIANS OF THE GALAXY ESCAPED THE DESTRUCTION USING THEIR TELEPORTATION PASSPORTS.
AND I AM WAITING FOR THEM IN THE CONTINUUM CORTEX AS THEY ARRIVE.
AND I ALREADY *KNOW* THE TERRIBLE THINGS THEY ARE GOING TO TELL ME, AND THE NEWS THAT WILL BREAK MY *HEART*.
HELLO, DAUGHTER. WE SAVED THE UNIVERSE AGAIN.
IT DIDN'T COME CHEAP.
END

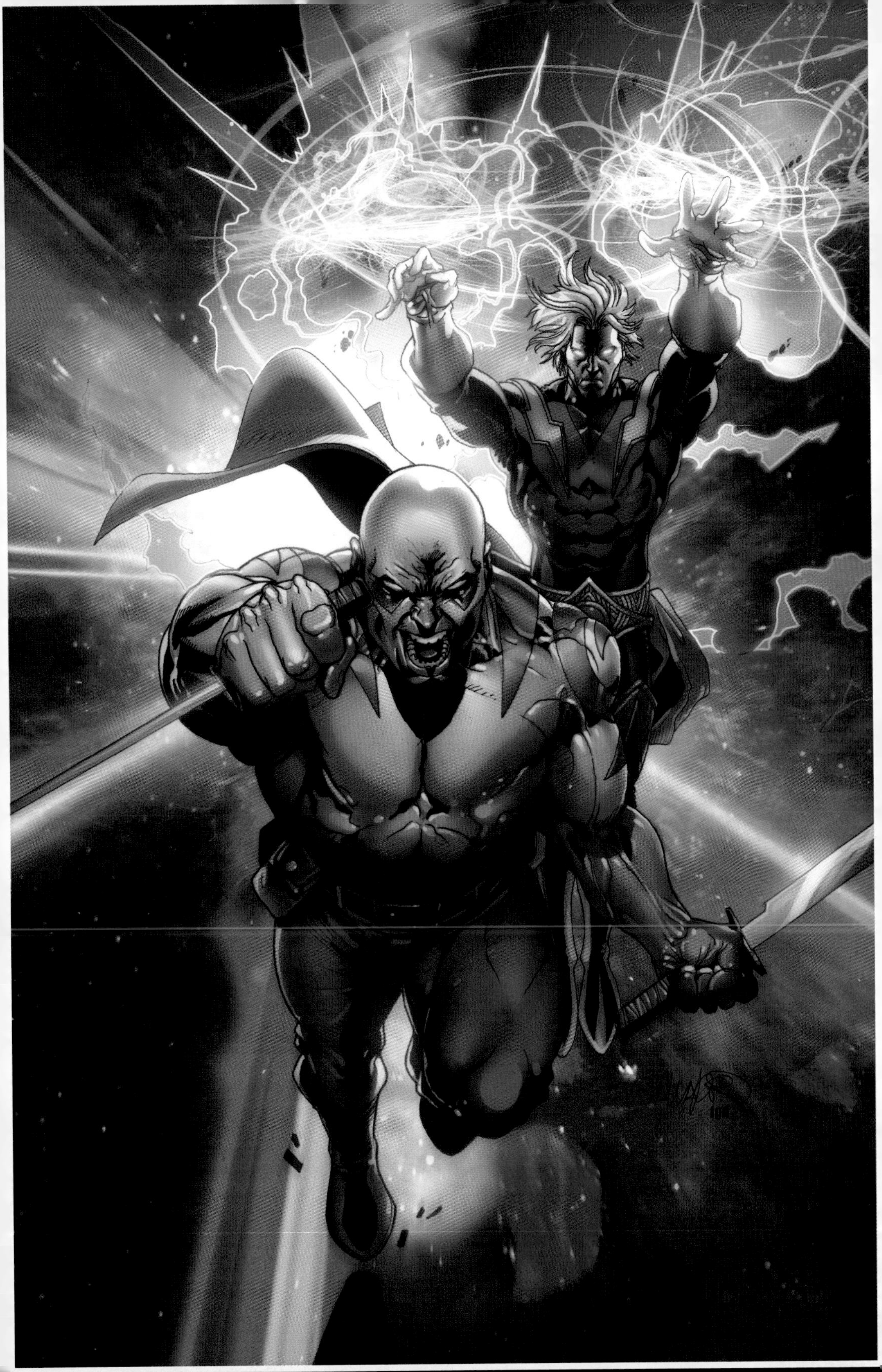

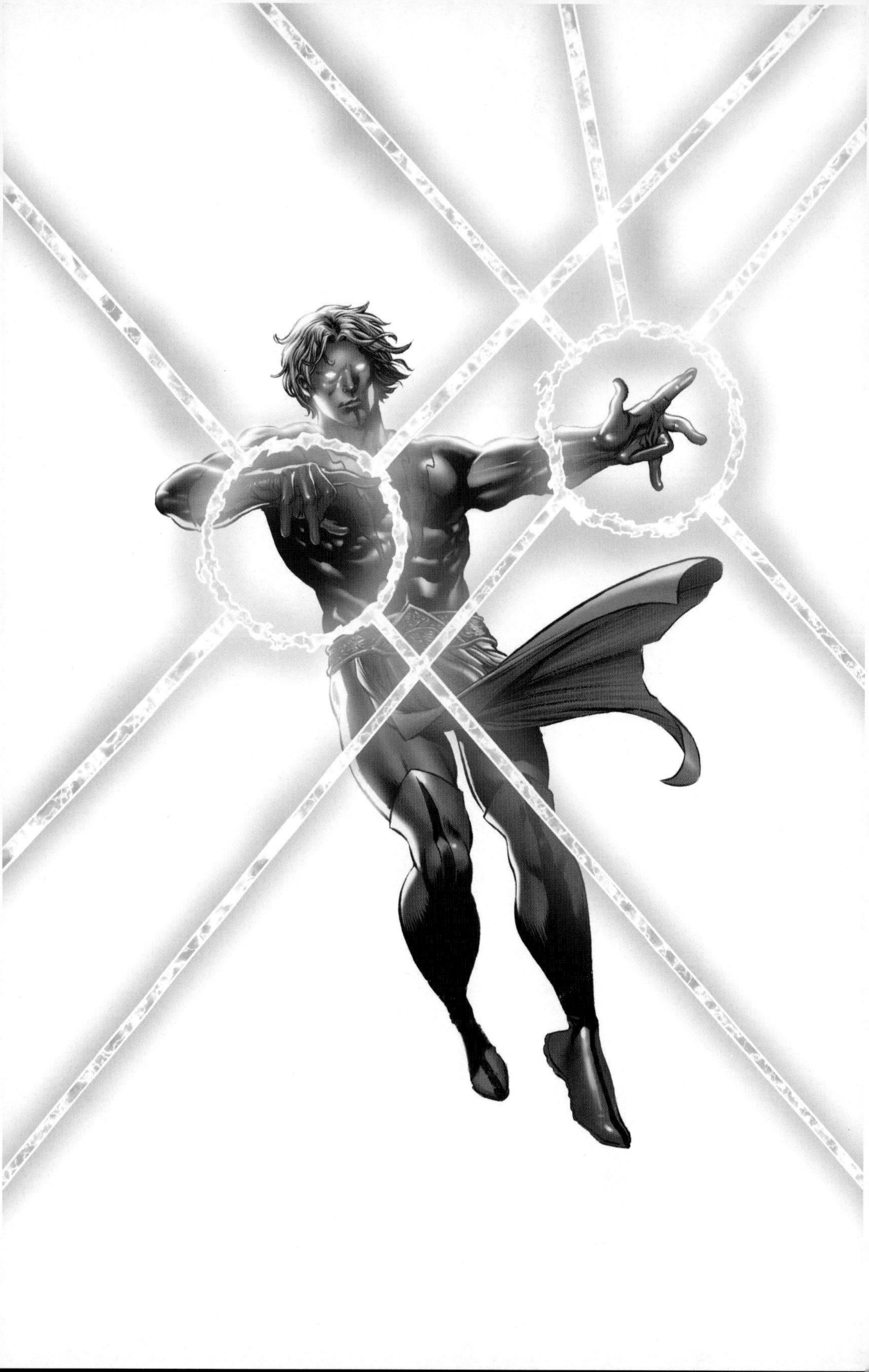

17 ***70th Anniversary Frame Variant*** by Mike Perkins

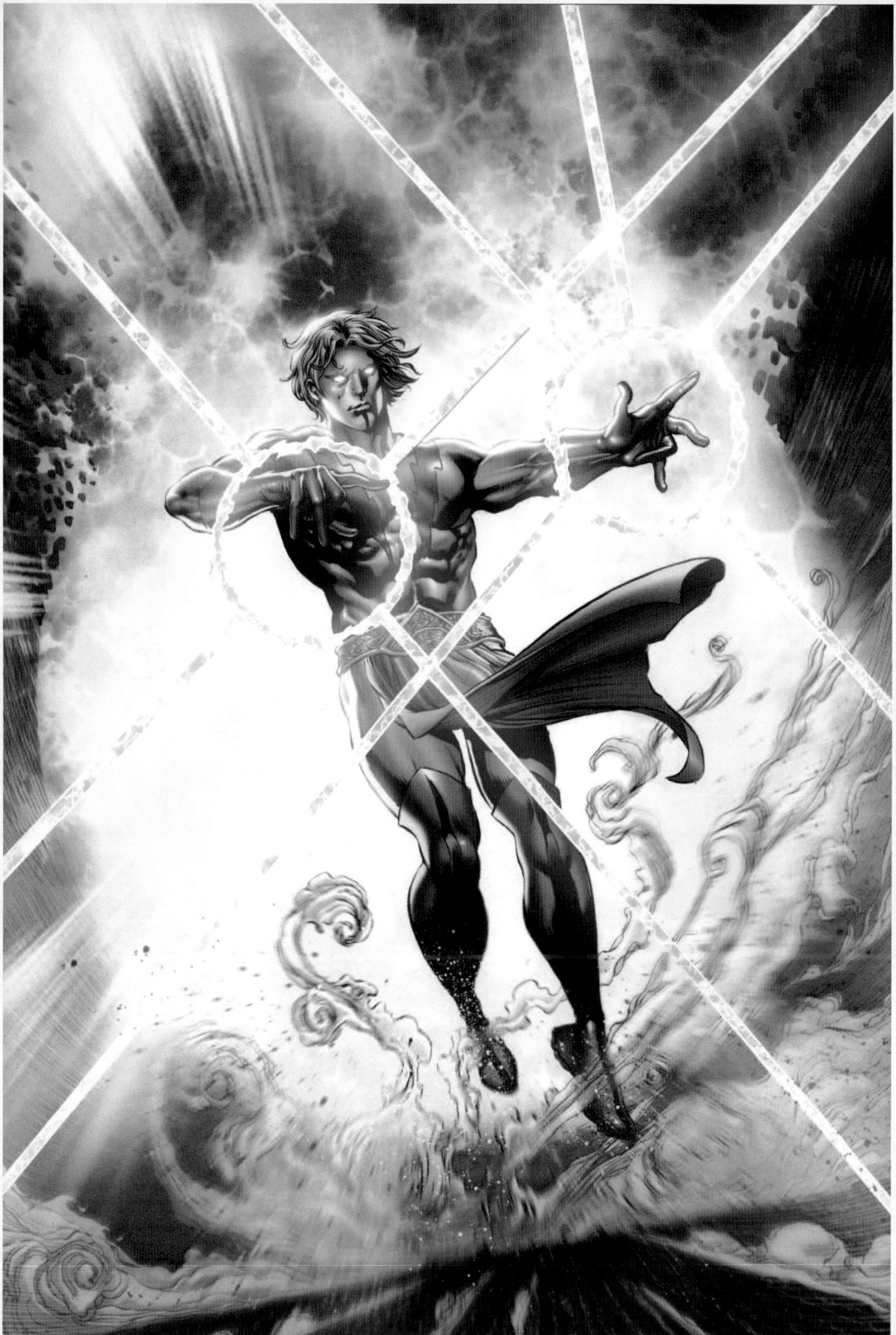

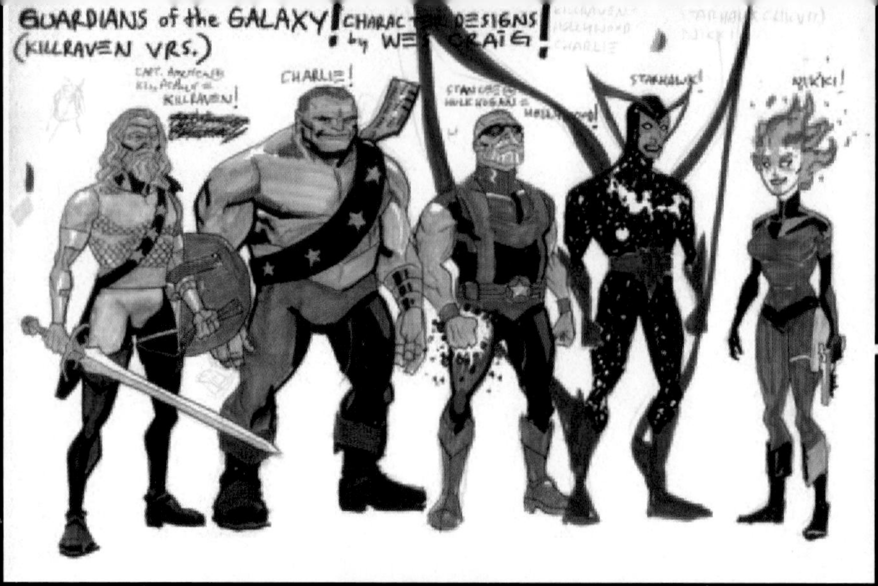
GUARDIANS of the GALAXY!
(KILLRAVEN VRS.)
CHARLIE!
STARHAWK!
NIKKI!

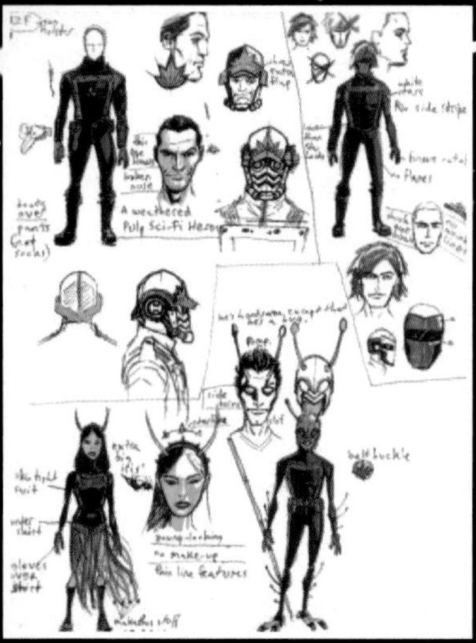
broken nose
A weathered Pulp Sci-Fi Hero
belt buckle

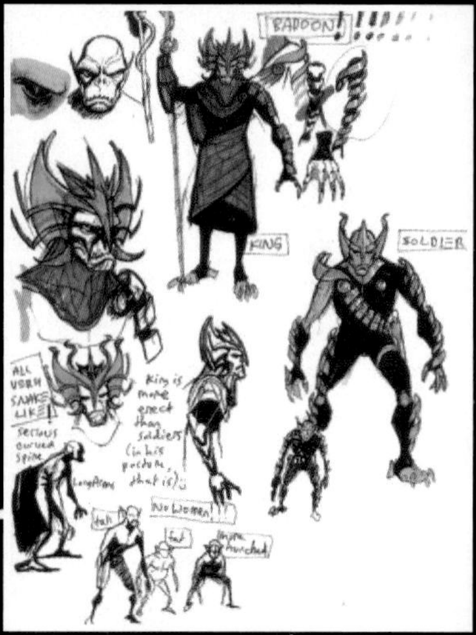
BADOON!
KING
SOLDIER
King is more erect than soldiers (in his posture, that is)
No Women!

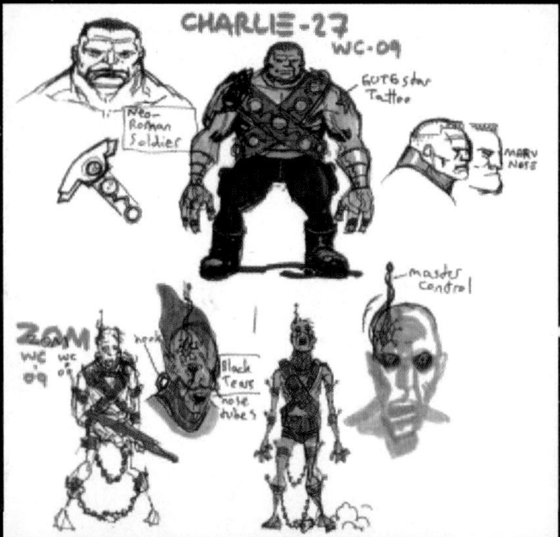
CHARLIE-27
WC-09
GOTG star Tattoo
Neo-Roman Soldier
master control
Black Tears
nose tubes

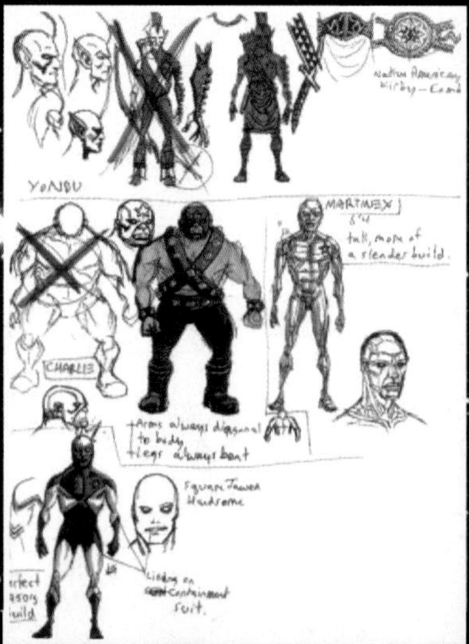
YONDU
MARTINEX
tall, more of a slender build.
CHARLIE
Square Jawed Handsome

Character Designs by Wesley Craig